NONPROLIFERATION NORMS

STUDIES IN SECURITY AND INTERNATIONAL AFFAIRS

NONPROLIFERATION NORMS

Why States Choose Nuclear Restraint

MARIA ROST RUBLEE

The University of Georgia Press
Athens & London

© 2009 by the University of Georgia Press

Athens, Georgia 30602

www.ugapress.org

All rights reserved

Designed by Walton Harris

Set in 10/14 Electra by Graphic Composition, Inc.

Printed and bound by Thomson-Shore

The paper in this book meets the guidelines for
permanence and durability of the Committee on
Production Guidelines for Book Longevity of the
Council on Library Resources.

Printed in the United States of America

13   12   11   10   09   C   5   4   3   2   1

13   12   11   10   09   P   5   4   3   2   1

Library of Congress Cataloging-in-Publication Data

Rublee, Maria Rost, 1971–

   Nonproliferation norms : why states choose nuclear
restraint / Maria Rost Rublee.

       p. cm. — (Studies in security and international
affairs)

   Includes bibliographical references and index.

   ISBN-13: 978-0-8203-3003-7 (hardcover : alk. paper)

   ISBN-10: 0-8203-3003-5 (hardcover : alk. paper)

   ISBN-13: 978-0-8203-3235-2 (pbk. : alk. paper)

   ISBN-10: 0-8203-3235-6 (pbk. : alk. paper)

  1. Nuclear nonproliferation. I. Title.

   JZ5675.R83 2009

   327.1'747 — dc22

                    2008024197

British Library Cataloging-in-Publication Data available

To my husband Greg

CONTENTS

List of Abbreviations and Acronyms   *xi*

Preface   *xiii*

CHAPTER ONE. Exploring Nuclear Restraint   *1*

CHAPTER TWO. Understanding the International
Social Environment   *34*

CHAPTER THREE. Japanese Nuclear Decision-Making   *53*

CHAPTER FOUR. Egyptian Nuclear Decision-Making   *99*

CHAPTER FIVE. Nuclear Decision-Making in Libya,
Sweden, and Germany   *150*

CHAPTER SIX. Reflections on Theory and Policy   *201*

Notes   *225*

Bibliography   *263*

Index   *285*

ABBREVIATIONS AND ACRONYMS

3NNP	Three Non-Nuclear Principles (Japan)
AEE	Atomic Energy Establishment (Egypt)
ACRS	Working Group on Arms Control & Regional Security (Middle East)
CTBT	Comprehensive Test Ban Treaty
DPJ	Democratic Party of Japan
ENDC	United Nations' Eighteen Nation Committee on Disarmament
EU	European Union
IAEA	International Atomic Energy Agency
ICBM	Intercontinental ballistic missile
INF	Intermediate-range nuclear forces
IO	International organization
IR	International relations
JCG	Japanese Coast Guard
JCP	Japanese Communist Party
JDA	Japan Defense Agency
JSP	Japanese Socialist Party
KEDO	Korean Peninsular Energy Development Organization
LDP	Liberal Democratic Party (Japan)
MIRV	Multiple independent re-entry vehicles

MLF	Multilateral nuclear force
MOFA	Ministry of Foreign Affairs (Japan)
NAC	New Agenda Coalition
NGO	Nongovernmental organization
NNWS	Non-nuclear weapons state
NPT	Nuclear Nonproliferation Treaty
NWFZ	Nuclear-weapon-free zone
PTBT	Partial Test Ban Treaty
SDF	Self Defense Forces (Japan)
SPD	Social Democratic Party (Germany)
TCA	Trade and Cooperation Agreements
UAR	United Arab Republic
UN	United Nations
UNSCOM	United Nations Special Committee
WMD	Weapons of mass destruction
WMDFZ	Weapons of mass destruction free zone

PREFACE

This project began during my one-year tenure in the U.S. intelligence community, where I analyzed countries with nuclear weapons programs. We focused a great deal of time and effort on these states: what activities they were engaged in, and more important, how we could stop them. However, a few months into the job, a series of questions struck me: What about the 95 percent of states that are not trying to develop nuclear weapons? Why aren't they? What can we learn from them? In our intelligence work, we were selecting on the dependent variable: examining only the states that wanted nuclear weapons. If we studied states that could develop a nuclear option but chose not to, what could we learn? Could we unearth insights to assist us in dealing with countries that did seek nuclear weapons? Given that almost all states have exercised nuclear restraint, was there a systemic variable at work — one that for some reason lacked influence in our rogue states?

That set of questions fueled the research that led to my dissertation and this book. I began by examining traditional approaches to proliferation and quickly found them wanting. Achieving better understanding of nuclear proliferation and its prevention required two dramatic changes. First, instead of focusing primarily on cases of proliferation, we also need to examine nonproliferation — the states that have considered the nuclear option and exercised restraint. Second, instead of focusing solely on a state's security environment, we also need to examine the social environment — the norms and ideas shaping how state elites conceptualize "security" and "success." The common refrain that state decisions about nuclear weapons are motivated by "security" is meaningless. The question is, what do states consider to help or hurt their security? Why do most states believe their security does not require nuclear weapons, while a few believe the opposite? How is it that a state such as Egypt — having lost in conflict against a nuclear-armed adversary and with regional competitors known to be working on nuclear weapons — does not require nuclear weapons for security, whereas South Africa — a state facing few external security threats — did want them?

By addressing these two issues, we open our analysis to a wider set of variables that influence state decision-making on nuclear weapons. *If we want to control nuclear proliferation, we must start by honestly addressing how states conceptualize the value of nuclear weapons.* This project proposes a framework, based on a combination of social psychology and constructivism, for identifying and measuring this wider set of variables. In addition, it offers insights into the psychological mechanisms whereby these variables shape choices on nuclear weapons. To test the utility of this framework in the real world, it is applied to five countries that have opted out of the nuclear arms race: Japan, Egypt, Germany, Sweden, and Libya. The results offer a much better understanding of how states make decisions about nuclear weapons and, as important, provide ideas about how to shape policy to promote nonproliferation and stop the spread of nuclear weapons around the globe.

Most authors owe both intellectual and practical debts to numerous people. I had no sense of how overwhelmingly true this was until embarking on my own manuscript, which benefited tremendously from the advice and scrutiny of my dissertation committee: Martha Finnemore, Deborah Avant, and Dalia Dassa Kaye. They provided guidance and suggestions over the course of several years, and this project would not have come to fruition without their assistance. I also owe thanks to readers Susan Sell and Nancy Gallagher, whose input helped sharpen the focus and clarify the needed revisions for a book. I am grateful to Mike Mochizuki for his close reading of the Japan chapter and his helpful suggestions. I began my graduate career as an East Asia specialist, and while the book is not East Asia–specific, it reflects many lessons learned about East Asia and comparative politics from my professors at George Washington University, in particular Bruce Dickson. In addition, it benefited greatly from the detailed comments of two anonymous reviewers, who offered excellent suggestions on both theory and case studies. The guidance of Peter Lavoy was instrumental in more theoretically sophisticated interpretation of case study data; I am indebted to him for his generous assistance. I also would like to thank the series editors, Gary Bertsch and Howard Wiarda, for their encouragement and advice.

Earlier versions of this work were presented at the annual meetings of the International Studies Association and the American Political Science Association, where I benefited from feedback. Presenting research at various government conferences on proliferation brought me helpful counsel from analysts

in the field. I presented my work on social psychology's insights into nonproliferation at the Japan Foundation–sponsored conference in Tampa, East Asian
Security: Challenges and Opportunities. I am grateful to participants for their
insights and to the Japan Foundation's Center for Global Partnership for funding the symposium. I shared my research at the Center for Nonproliferation
Studies, Monterey Institute for International Studies, and benefited a great
deal from the recommendations of William Potter and others at the center.
My students at the University of Tampa have provided excellent feedback on my
work as well. In particular, I would like to thank the honors students from my
Norms & Ideas seminar for their thoughtful critiques. Finally, I have discussed
my work informally with many academics and experts in the nonproliferation
community, including at the long-running Education in Weapons of Mass
Destruction summer conference, sponsored in part by the U.S. Institute of
Peace. These conversations helped shape the research.

Fieldwork in Japan and Egypt would have been impossible without the
backing of dozens of kind and supportive individuals. Mike Mochizuki introduced to me to many senior-level contacts in Japan. I am thankful for the assistance of Mitsuru Kurosawa, who generously facilitated interviews with numerous diplomats, particularly about the impact of peace groups on nuclear policy.
I am also grateful to Nobumasa Akiyama for his kind assistance in arranging
interviews in Hiroshima. Research in Egypt was helped tremendously by Ambassador Nabil Fahmy, who not only shared his thoughts on Egypt's nuclear
progress but also introduced me to numerous senior-level experts in Cairo. My
interviews on the nonproliferation regime in general were assisted by Ambassador Thomas Graham, who helped me make contact with several key experts.
Rose Gottemoeller and James Clay Moltz likewise generously provided aid in
interview contacts. I would also like to thank the Center for Nonproliferation
Studies at the Monterey Institute for International Studies for hosting me as
a Visiting Scholar. William Potter and his staff kindly allowed me to mine
the CNS library for hundreds of documents relating to nonproliferation and,
in particular, proliferation in lesser-known cases. Because of human subjects
rules, I am not permitted to name interviewees. But I would be remiss in not
thanking the dozens of diplomats, military personnel, scientists, policymakers,
analysts, and academics who gave of their time and their knowledge.

This project was materially supported by a number of different grants. A
dissertation grant from the Institute for the Study of World Politics funded my
research on social psychology's lessons for political science. Initial fieldwork

for Japan was supported by a Numata Field Research Grant from the Sigur Center for Asian Studies at the George Washington University. Follow-up research in Japan, as well as archival research on lesser-known case studies, was generously supported by travel and research grants from the University of Tampa. An article drawing upon my fieldwork in Egypt was published in the *Nonproliferation Review* 13, no. 3 (November 2006). An earlier version of my examination of Japanese nuclear decision-making was published in the *International Studies Review* 10, no. 3 (September 2008).

On a personal level, I want to thank my parents, who filled my childhood with books and political debate. They inspired in me intellectual curiosity and a love of reading, both of which have served me well in this project. I also owe thanks to my husband, Greg, who tirelessly supported my research, fieldwork, writing, and rewriting. His enthusiasm for constructivism and nuclear nonproliferation — as well as his tolerance for piles of paper and all-night writing sessions — went above and beyond the call of duty. My debt to him is immeasurable.

NONPROLIFERATION NORMS

CHAPTER ONE

Exploring Nuclear Restraint

The nuclear nonproliferation regime's list of high-profile and brazen failures is both long and discouraging. Consider that states that have not signed the Nuclear Nonproliferation Treaty (NPT) flaunt their nuclear programs; witness the 1998 nuclear tit-for-tat between India and Pakistan; and NPT signatories evade or ignore their own commitment not to pursue nuclear weapons acquisition, even after discovery, as in Iran and North Korea. Forcing compliance with NPT requirements takes prolonged international debate, drastic unilateral efforts, concerted multilateral pressure (Iran), or war (Iraq). Generous agreements designed to keep states from pursuing the nuclear option are exploited and then brazenly broken (North Korea). Even the regime's most powerful supporter will not ratify components important to its success (the U.S. failure to ratify the Comprehensive Test Ban Treaty). So glaring are the specific failures of the nuclear nonproliferation regime that it is easy to overlook the larger picture of success. When looked at from a bird's-eye view, the nuclear nonproliferation regime might even be called an overwhelming success: for more than three decades, almost all states in the international system chose to forgo nuclear weapons and, in some cases, even gave them up. Numerous reports in the 1960s warned that the number of new nuclear states could reach as high as twenty in a few decades.[1] Instead, the count by 2007 is only four.[2]

What explains the record of nuclear nonproliferation? Why have so many states abstained from nuclear weapons, while a few continue to pursue them against all odds? For the most part, these questions have not only gone unanswered but also *unasked*. The policy and academic literatures are filled with examinations of states that have acquired nuclear weapons, or continue to try to — such as Iraq, Iran, North Korea, India, and Pakistan. Of all of the states in today's world, the fact that only four have "gone nuclear" since the introduction of the NPT is a fact pregnant with potential for both theoretical and policy insights. If we can understand what influenced these states—those with the motive, means, and opportunity to develop nuclear weapons but that instead abstained—we will be much better prepared to handle today's potential proliferators. This is especially important given the growing numbers of "latent nuclear states," those with the "necessary industrial infrastructure and scientific expertise to build nuclear weapons on a crash basis if they chose to do so."[3] In 2004 the International Atomic Energy Agency estimated that more than forty countries were "nuclear latent states."[4] Insights on what propelled these states' behavior regarding nuclear weapons could inform our larger security and diplomatic policies on encouraging peace and containing conflict. In addition, such insights could help us should any of these nuclear potential states decide to seek a nuclear weapons program, as has been hinted at by states such as Brazil and Japan.[5] If we understand what kept the elites in these states from developing full-fledged nuclear weapons programs to begin with, it may help us in encouraging them to recommit to that decision.

To ask a new question, I advance a new analytical framework. Neither realists focusing largely on threat nor liberals focusing on economic incentives can explain why these forty states chose not to acquire nuclear weapons. Even more nuanced recent analyses looking at domestic conditions or regional environment are poor at predicting the variation in outcomes. Furthermore, the logic of their explanations does not capture the process of decision-making on the ground. To explain better both the range of outcomes and the processes by which they are reached, I turn to the social psychology literature to examine whether, why, and how social-normative influences affected policy decisions. Indeed, because this project uses social psychology to comprehend nuclear decision-making better, it is focused on state elites and policymakers, as opposed to approaching the state as a monolithic entity.[6] This examination helps us understand to what extent nuclear forbearance represents persuasion (behavior resulting from genuine transformation of preferences), social conformity (behavior resulting from the desire to maximize social benefits and/or minimize social costs, without a change in underlying preferences), or identification (behavior resulting from the desire or habit of following the actions of an important other). By examining that which has largely been ignored— cases of nonproliferation instead of proliferation, and states' social environment in addition to security environment—new understanding about nuclear decision-making can inform both theoretical and policy work.

THEORETICAL SIGNIFICANCE

For decades, realism dominated international relations, with proponents arguing that in a "self-help" world, states valued security above all else and made decisions by utilitarian cost-benefit calculations. Illustrated by Kenneth Waltz and Joseph Grieco, realism posits that since regimes have little independent power, states waste resources by funneling inherently ineffectual efforts through them.[7] An adaptation of the neorealist argument — termed neoliberal institutionalism — was made by theorists such as Robert Keohane and Lisa Martin, who argued that since multilateral organizations can reduce transaction costs, monitor compliance, and increase transparency, their use may change states' cost-benefit calculations to discourage "going nuclear" but *cannot* change states' essential desire to have nuclear weapons.

Only in the last decade have we seen a significant challenge to this rationalist domination, offered by constructivism, which focuses on nonmaterial incentives for states in a socially constructed international environment. Typified by Alexander Wendt and Martha Finnemore, constructivism indicates that multilateral institutions can socialize states and transform their basic preferences so that nuclear weapons are no longer a necessary or acceptable part of national defense. Proponents of the constructivist framework reject the assumption of stable preferences and "black-boxing" of preference formation, arguing instead that the creation and shaping of interests are among the most important questions in international relations. Now that the constructivist research agenda — showing that state preferences can be changed — has enjoyed success, an even more daunting task lies ahead: specifying *how* they change. How do norms and ideas (the building blocks of this "socially constructed" world) work, and through what processes and under what conditions? Why do some norms gain acceptance while others do not? The policy value to such specification is enormous. Charting out the major mechanisms through which norms exert influence, specifying the conditions under which the mechanisms are most likely to work, and identifying possible intervening and mediating variables would take us further in this quest.[8] By using insights from social psychology — in which one of the most significant themes is attitude change — this project contributes to addressing these issues. While not all the cause-effect relationships offered by social psychology translate smoothly for use in international relations, they do offer a rigorous, methodologically sound starting point.

POLICY SIGNIFICANCE

By understanding the policy choices of states that could have acquired nuclear weapons but did not, we sharpen our knowledge about different ways in which we transmit norms, how we can "assist" the processing of those norms, and what different types of influence outcomes we can expect. As a result, we can gain a better understanding of how to influence states that may not be wholly committed to nuclear forbearance as well as states that may in the future want to rethink their nuclear decisions. By breaking down the possible outcomes of the international social environment—into persuasion, conformity, and identification—we may be able to see if states that first complied because of conformity or identification later became "persuaded" because of repetition and internalization. If so, diplomatic "influence" tactics (such as backpatting or shaming) could be seen as tools not only for short-term reduction of nuclear proliferation but also for long-term change in state preferences. If states adhered to the NPT because of identification with the United States, how might changes in American behavior affect their actions?

Moreover, the theoretical implications of this project have policy consequences that extend beyond the nuclear realm. If realist expectations best predict reality, then using multilateralism to contain proliferation of any type is a fool's errand. However, if constructivist expectations are borne out, then U.S. policymakers may have several tools by which to continue to influence proliferation. To the extent that the effects of the international social environment on global security issues can be systematically studied, this project can contribute to a powerful theoretical framework to inform a spectrum of policy issues. Many policymakers agree that nonmaterial factors influence states' decisions, but without an underlying theoretical analysis of how and under what conditions, their beliefs are less likely to be accepted as a foundation for policy. This in turn means that very real tools to help encourage peace and reduce conflict—tools that use nonmaterial factors—may be more likely to gain credibility if their theoretical framework is better specified.

The project also gives insight into current concerns in nuclear nonproliferation. Iran promises to be the most challenging case for the regime in the next decade, as Iranian leadership continues to pursue uranium enrichment (under the guise of civilian technology) and periodically threatens to withdraw from the NPT Additional Protocol or even the NPT itself. An Iranian nuclear bomb would likely trigger responses across the Arab world, for a number of

Arab states believe that Iran may attempt to use a nuclear weapon to garner political and diplomatic leverage so as to exert hegemony over the Gulf region. In recent years, policymakers have created a mix of social and material inducements to move Iran slowly away from its nuclear weapons program. Creating a balanced mix of incentives is difficult, because too much social pressure or too little backpatting for progress could backfire and force the moderates to reject the regime, while too little in the way of material inducements could weaken the moderates vis-à-vis Iranian hard-liners. If policymakers conclude that Iranian elites have rejected social influence on the nuclear issue, then efforts at backpatting and shaming can be dispensed with, since they are unlikely to be effective, and more concrete and serious measures could be taken. This leads to another potential policy implication: if some state elites simply reject the social pressure applied through the nuclear nonproliferation regime, then the body that performs verification for the NPT, the International Atomic Energy Agency (IAEA), will need more resources to catch instances of cheating, and the regime will need more "teeth" to handle such "rogue" states properly.

With some asking whether the nuclear nonproliferation regime can handle the proliferation challenges of the future, discussions about the effect of social influence — and its limits — can give insight about the best ways to strengthen the regime's effectiveness. As already discussed, recognizing that some segments within a state may be more susceptible to social influence than others can help policymakers realize that inducements need to be offered with this in mind. While social influence may pull a more moderate coalition toward the regime, that very same social influence could push hard-liners against it. Thus the social influence would have to be delivered with material inducements, to ensure that moderate segments can defend their actions against hardliner attacks. In addition, the analysis of persuasion, identification, and social influence is likely applicable to other forms of weapons of mass destruction (WMD), potentially giving policymakers insight into strengthening both the chemical and biological weapons regimes.

CURRENT EXPLANATIONS

Before investigating how constructivism can help us achieve these theoretical and policy contributions, a review of the current literature is in order. What explanations have been offered for nuclear forbearance, and what explanations could be or have been offered by major theories in international relations (IR)?

Realism

While nuclear proliferation and nonproliferation have been addressed almost exclusively through the prism of realism for decades, this theoretical framework has come under increasing criticism due to its overprediction of proliferation.[9] The basic tenets of realism — anarchy and self-help — lead one to the prediction that once the splitting of the atom had been achieved, any state with the scientific and economic means to obtain this ultimate tool of deterrence would do so.[10] As leading realist theorist John Mearsheimer argues, anarchy and self-help combine to create powerful incentives for states to achieve the maximum military capability possible: "The greater the military advantage one state has over other states, the more secure it is. Every state would like to be the most formidable military power in the system because this is the best way to guarantee survival in a world that can be very dangerous. The aim is to acquire more military power at the expense of potential rivals."[11] If the international system makes cooperation unlikely and self-reliance imperative, then acquiring nuclear weapons is the most reasonable response by a rational state. As Sujeet Samaddar notes, "States, acting as rational and unitary actors, conduct foreign policy to maximize their own power through 'self-help' in order to survive and progress in an anarchical world. Realism provides a convincing justification for the acquisition of nuclear weapons, since it believes that the possession of a potent nuclear arsenal is the guarantee of absolute security, whereas conventional forces may only provide relative security."[12]

In addition, the realist argument that nuclear weapons discourage war would lead one to conclude that states should seek nuclear weapons. As argued by Kenneth Waltz, states with a second-strike nuclear capability are unlikely to be attacked by other states, since the cost of such a war would far outweigh the benefits.[13] Thus the value of nuclear weapons is even greater for states seeking security under conditions of anarchy, because it protects against not only nuclear war but conventional war as well.

However, the powerful structural arguments of realism do not match up with political reality: in almost four decades, only four states have developed and kept an indigenous nuclear deterrent. As T. V. Paul notes, "hard" realism does not explain the lack of nuclear proliferation very well:

> To begin with, hard realists, based on their assumption of anarchy, argue that cooperation is difficult if not impossible in the security area. The empirical

evidence — i.e., the cooperation thus far developed in non-proliferation — challenges this basic argument. Many states, both capable and not so capable of producing nuclear weapons, have adhered to the regime, which takes away part of their sovereignty in this matter. It seems that the number of countries that acquired nuclear weapons from the original five is so small that these cases seem more like an anomaly than the norm.[14]

Realists have developed a number of theoretical responses to the lack of nuclear proliferation. Benjamin Frankel posits that bipolarity artificially reduced proliferation because the role of superpowers "reduces the influence of systemic characteristics such as the security dilemma and reliance on self-help."[15] Multipolarity increases uncertainty, which makes states less likely to depend on alliances and security guarantees. As Frankel says, "In a multipolar world, it is not always clear who is siding with whom and for how long."[16] Thus Frankel predicted that with the end of bipolarity, we would see a new wave of nuclear proliferation. Mearsheimer predicted just such a spread of nuclear weapons in Europe after the end of Cold War, arguing that a nuclear status quo (in which no new states acquire nuclear weapons) would be unlikely because of the "substantial incentives" for non-nuclear states to acquire a nuclear deterrent.[17] Not only would small states seek nuclear weapons to avoid blackmail by Russia, Mearsheimer predicted, but Germany would feel insecure without its own nuclear force. Mearsheimer also argued that after the collapse of bipolarity, U.S. displays of unmatched military might (in the Gulf War, Afghanistan, Iraq, etc.) would teach countries that nuclear weapons are their only method of leveling the playing field — and thus we should see many states seeking to acquire nuclear weapons.[18] Again, however, realism is not well supported by the historical record. One could argue that of the four states that have developed nuclear weapons after the NPT entered into force, two (Pakistan and North Korea) did so after the end of the Cold War.[19] But several states gave up nuclear weapons or highly developed nuclear weapons programs after the end of Cold War, including South Africa, Ukraine, Belarus, Kazakhstan, Argentina, Brazil, and Libya. On balance, the end of the bipolarity has led to more nonproliferation than proliferation.

Another realist explanation of nuclear nonproliferation is that nuclear weapons can actually undermine a state's security. If a state perceived nuclear weapons as a threat to state survival (since they potentially make the state a target), then realists would predict that a state would not acquire them. Unless a nuclear state has a robust second-strike capability (which is more difficult and expensive to acquire than simple nuclear capability), then perhaps it is safer without any nuclear capability at all. However, it is hard to reconcile this cautiousness with the core assumptions of realism. At present, no state has actually been targeted due solely or largely due to its nuclear status.[20] If states can trust no one but themselves to secure their survival, why would they trade concrete nuclear deterrence against a theoretical, unproven risk of being targeted? As opposed to this theoretical risk of being targeted, a number of cases exist that could lead one to argue that nuclear weapons do provide a valuable deterrent against conventional and nuclear forces. Examples are the lack of war between the United States and the Soviet Union, the Israeli belief that their undeclared nuclear weapons have deterred Arab invasion, and recent North Korean statements that their nuclear weapons program serves as a deterrent against U.S. invasion.

Another realist explanation for nuclear forbearance deals with states' perceptions of security threats. States that perceive a serious threat to their security are more likely to develop nuclear weapons than those that do not. And the actions of some states that developed but then gave up their nuclear programs can be explained by a heightened security posture that later receded. However, by blending psychological factors with material factors, this argument dilutes some of the core assumptions of realism. The structural nature of the international system, according to the most basic premise of realism, has not changed and will not. While there may be lesser and greater degrees of security threats, according to realism, the state perception should always be of an anarchical world in which no one can secure a state's survival but itself.[21] As Jeffrey Legro and Andrew Moravcsik note:

Realism's central analytical leverage, parsimony, and distinctiveness derive from its ability to explain social life simply through variation in the distribution of objective material power capabilities, rather than preferences, perceptions, or norms. Yet while contemporary realists continue to speak of international 'power,' their midrange explanations of state behavior have subtly shifted the core emphasis from variation in objective power to variation in beliefs and perceptions of power. This poses a fundamental problem. *If the perceptions and beliefs about effective means-ends calculations of states, given adequate information, consistently fail to correspond to material power relationships, then power is at best one of a number of important fac-*

tors and perhaps a secondary one. The parsimony and coherence of realist theory is eroded. When recent realists theorize this relationship explicitly, moreover, they are forced to borrow propositions more fully elaborated in existing epistemic theories, which theorize the influence of societal beliefs that structure means-ends calculations and affect perceptions of the environment.[22] (Emphasis added.)

The difficult question that the record of nonproliferation poses to realists is this: under what conditions in an anarchical, self-help world would states feel so secure that they would pass up the ultimate weapon of deterrence that is accessible by rivals and can be developed largely in secret? If survival is the most important goal of states, nuclear weapons should be desirable, because if one waits until others develop nuclear weapons to match them, an unacceptable period of vulnerability will place the state's survival at risk. Additionally, why would a state with nuclear weapons give them up, especially if the program was secret (and thus would not risk the threat of being targeted)?

The most persuasive realist argument about the lack of proliferation is security guarantees. While strong states may be able to balance against threats by developing their own nuclear capability, weaker states may instead seek to balance by aligning with a powerful, nuclear-armed ally. Clearly, credible security guarantees have been an important component of nuclear decision-making in states such as Japan and Germany. Indeed, the U.S. nuclear umbrella may be a better explanation for nuclear forbearance during the Cold War than simple bipolarity. However, the argument still faces some challenges. At what point did Japan and Germany move from "weak" to "strong," and why did their nuclear decision-making not change at that point? Why have almost all states with the capability of building nuclear weapons refrained from doing so? Are they weak by definition only because they made the choice for nuclear forbearance? Why have some weak states managed, against all odds, to create their own nuclear deterrent? Jacques Hymans points out two additional difficulties with the security guarantee argument. First, to what extent can a security guarantee truly be credible to a survival-conscious state? He says: "It is hard to see why, from a realist perspective, anything less than an indigenous nuclear arsenal would be sufficient to deter outside threats. Realists spent the entire Cold War bemoaning the lack of credibility of extended deterrence: Could anyone really expect us to trade New York for Berlin?"[23] The second issue Hymans raises is whether even a nuclear guarantee that is credible today could resolve a state's long-term security concerns. He argues: "This is because at the very core of realism lies the notion that friends today may become enemies tomorrow — and a nuclear war would be over in the blink of an eye, while nuclear weapons take a long time to develop and deploy. Thus, the dominant strategy of states is to go for the bomb themselves and thus avoid any unpleasant surprises."[24] Mearsheimer echoes the idea of the fleeting nature of alliances, arguing that while self-help does not rule them out, "alliances are only temporary marriages of convenience, where today's alliance partner might be tomorrow's enemy, and today's enemy might be tomorrow's alliance partner."[25]

Realism offers a parsimonious and clear-cut explanation of the drivers of proliferation. However, as many authors note, realism tends to overpredict proliferation and has difficulty explaining why so few states have actually developed nuclear weapons.

Neoliberal Institutionalism

Neoliberal institutionalism offers a different perspective on the puzzle of nuclear forbearance. This theory predicts that states cooperate with regimes because of lowered transaction costs, greater transparency, and greater compliance monitoring — not because their essential desire for nuclear weapons has been changed.[26] Institutions are still rooted in power and interest that motivate realist theory, argue Keohane and Martin, but "institutions can provide information, reduce transaction costs, make commitments more credible, establish focal points for coordination, and in general facilitate the operation of reciprocity."[27] Thus neoliberal institutionalists might argue that states complied with the nonproliferation regime because the benefits (technology transfer and assistance with nuclear energy programs) outweighed perceived benefits of a costly nuclear weapons program.

However, neoliberal institutionalism might also predict that states would no longer comply with the regime once the material payoffs are transferred. In a self-help, anarchic world, reaping the benefits of the nuclear nonproliferation regime and then turning one's back on it to secure nuclear weapons might make a lot of sense, especially if it can be done without significant likelihood of detection. While some states do fit this description — North Korea and Iran, for example — most states that have joined the nonproliferation regime do not. Why not? Neoliberal institutionalism might also predict that states sought to escape the security dilemma by seeking cooperation through institutions. If so, why did states in similar material situations perceive their security needs differently (e.g., Egypt vs. India)? With the end of the Cold War, has this perception changed? These questions are critical to understanding why states cooperated with the nonproliferation regime, but neoliberalism cannot answer them due to its black-boxing of preference formation and preference change. Interests are assumed, not explored. Neoliberalism may not offer predictions contradictory to the facts, but it provides less than satisfactory assistance in explaining the puzzle of non-nuclear states in the nuclear age.

One prominent work on nuclear nonproliferation illustrates the difficulty neoliberalism has in answering the fundamental questions at stake. Etel Solingen's research into the domestic causes of nuclear nonproliferation does provide great insight into how internal workings within a state can influence its choices on nuclearization — or at least the timing of its choices. Certainly it could be argued that international forces strongly shape states' policy on nuclear forbearance — a description of how domestic politics shaped a state's nuclear policy does not necessarily "prove" that domestic issues caused the state's policy. Rather, it could be that international forces gave strength to particular coalitions and crusades within a domestic society. The ability of domestic politics to shape a state's nuclear policy is not at issue here, however. That is because Solingen's argument is, at heart, a neoliberal one:

> Domestic political coalitions pursuing economic liberalization seem more likely to embrace cooperative nuclear arrangements than their inward-looking, nationalist, and fundamentalist counterparts. The former, relying on an open economic system, are not only more susceptible to international inducements to join a regime but also favor denuclearization for its domestic political effects as well. . . . The historical record across regions suggests that where liberalizing coalitions had the upper hand, nuclear policy shifted toward more cooperative nuclear postures. Nationalist-confessional coalitions, in contrast, shied away from any commitments for effective denuclearization.[28]

In essence, Solingen argues that economic benefits of complying with the nonproliferation regime spurred domestic coalitions into supporting a non-nuclear policy, and in states where these coalitions had strength, they indeed moved toward this policy. To gain the benefits of foreign investment and better integration into the international economy, states gave up their nuclear ambiguity. This argumentation fits in with classic neoliberal institutionalism, which declares that states calculate costs and benefits to pursue stable, defined interests. As the democratic regimes took hold, they brought with them a different set of interests than the military regimes — specifically, a focus on economic growth as opposed to military might.

The evidence does point toward the interpretation that as states moved from authoritarian to democratic regimes, they also moved from being nuclear "fence-sitters" to becoming adherents to the nonproliferation regime. What is less clear is *why*. Solingen assumes that the policy changes toward the West were motivated solely by economic interests — domestic coalitions wanted economic liberalization. What she does not consider, but to which her evidence also points, is that these newly democratizing regimes wanted something larger than just access to foreign capital and markets, something that can be described as membership in the Western "club." That is, they saw the importance of becoming a part of the Western web of relationships, not just for economic reasons but also for status and social reasons. Being a legitimate member of the international community was certainly a goal for these domestic coalitions, and to do that, certain roles had to be played. One of those was to democratize, another was to liberalize the economy, and another was to join the nonproliferation regime.

For example, Solingen argues that domestic coalitions opposed to joining the nonproliferation regime were motivated by both economics and ideology, but those in favor of it were motivated only by the economic logic. Nationalist coalitions were strongly influenced by "radical or fundamentalist ideologies."[29] And such coalitions "thrive on popular resentment over adjustment policies they regard as externally imposed, reliance on foreign investment, and the 'Western' principles and norms embodied in most international regimes."[30] She notes that nationalist coalitions also have a material basis in the form of powerful import-substituting and state-based industrial interests. In some cases, she gives priority to the ideological components of the nationalist coalitions, arguing that they are the driving force.[31] Yet Solingen does not acknowledge any normative component to the liberalizing coalitions; she keeps her theoretical argument sanitized of any norm- or idea-based variables, despite the fact that some of her evidence points toward these. In part, she likely does this because she does not want to fall prey to the same criticism she (rightfully) levies against realists, who often have to "explain variation away through brief references to domestic considerations or to a rough-and-tumble bureaucratic-politics account."[32] Indeed, if she acknowledges an important normative component to the domestic coalitions supporting liberalization and the nonproliferation regime, she would then need some sort of systematic framework by which to analyze and explain it — something that neoliberal institutionalism is incapable of providing.

In what way does Solingen's argument suggest a normative component to the liberalizing coalition's support for the nonproliferation regime? She states: "By delivering a policy of nuclear disarmament, these [liberalizing] coalitions can enhance their bargaining power vis-à-vis international institutions and powerful states, who connect these coalitions to the promise of development, rationalization, and demilitarization."[33] In other words, the promise that lures these coalitions is not just one of economic benefits but rather a "package deal" of Western principles and concepts bringing status and prestige.

Solingen follows up this argument with reference to the South African case, noting that the state wanted to normalize relations with the international community and also gain access to the IAEA club. The newspaper article she cites includes even more normative reasoning for South Africa's decision to join the NPT: "[South Africa's] president characterized his government's decisions as a part of South Africa's broader efforts to normalize relations with the outside world and to 'take its rightful place in the international community.'"[34] Solingen is correct on two counts: to understand variation in nuclear decisions, we need to go beyond the structural level to look at policymaking and coalitions; and second, liberalizing coalitions are likely a force in getting fence-sitters to come down. However, the question of what motivates the liberalizing coalitions arises; pure economic analysis does not match with the facts. For this reason, we need a better understanding of the normative pull of becoming part of the club.

Idea-Centered Analysis

Much current nonproliferation analysis tends to equate "norms" or "ideas" with the nonproliferation regime, specifically the NPT. Then, because an immediate direct link between state decisions for nonproliferation and the NPT is not evident, both the effect of the regime and "norms" in general are dismissed. T. V. Paul provides a good example of this: "The case studies show that the regime is more of a facilitator than a determinant in this respect. In most of the cases studied in this book, states had chosen to give up their nuclear options prior to joining the Nuclear Non-Proliferation Treaty. Adherence to the treaty, however, formalized their choices."[35] He goes on to explain how in each case, the regime and the norms it embodies played little or no causal role in states' decisions on nuclear politics. While Paul says that the nonproliferation regime has little to do with nuclear forbearance, his reasoning demonstrates otherwise: middle and small states "may believe that their acquisition of nuclear weapons would hurt the international norms and laws that give them legitimacy and power. General adherence to regime principles and norms and observance of the NPT appear to restrain other states in the region."[36] In other words, because of the norms created and sustained by the international nonproliferation regime, states can run cost-benefit calculations and have their security increased by nonacquisition. Without the regime and the norms promoted by it, such a cost-benefit calculation would not create such a result.

A few researchers have emphasized ideational arguments. For example, Jacques Hymans uses a constructivist lens to understand why Australia initially pursued a nuclear weapons capability but later discontinued that quest.[37] He argues that a specific type of threat perception, combined with a specific type of national identity, creates a high probability for nuclear ambition. According to Hymans, the perception of an existential threat combined with nationalism leads policymakers to seek nuclear capability. In the case of Australia, he argues that an analysis of the leading statesmen in Australia supports his theory: when those in power had both the perception of a serious security threat and a high level of nationalism, Australia moved toward nuclear acquisition; but when those in power had only one or neither of these, Australia moved away from it. Hymans clearly sheds light on at least part of the puzzle of nuclear nonproliferation. However, his argument is somewhat hampered because it rests on one key assumption:

> Nuclear weapons are essentially only useful to deter a nuclear or other equally total attack. If few states have desired nuclear weapons, it is because few have faced or have considered themselves to be facing a clear and present nuclear (or other existential) threat. Moreover, they have understood that to "go nuclear" could dramatically weaken their security by making them targets for nuclear attack. I would thus argue that in the absence of an extraordinary threat, a sense that one's very existence is at stake, states do not seek to acquire sovereign control of nuclear weapons.[38]

If states sought nuclear weapons for reasons other than the perception of a grave nuclear threat, then Hymans's thesis does not hold, given that this perception is one of the two elements that combine to create nuclear ambition. In a sense, Hymans offers a more sophisticated version of the realist hypothesis: he clarifies why a state's assessment of security threat (elite perceptions) might change and then adds the factor of national identity. By doing so, he turns the argument into a constructivist one, positing that threats are socially constructed and that identity helps filter how elites believe they should respond to those threats.[39] His argument is correct but less than complete because its key assumption conflicts with the factual record: states have developed nuclear weapons in the absence of a direct and grave nuclear threat. While his "threat perception + nationalism = nuclear ambition" equation is most likely true, it is by no means the only avenue to nuclear ambition.

Another idea-centered examination of nuclear acquisition is William Long and Suzette Grillot's "Ideas, Beliefs, and Nuclear Policies: The Cases of South Africa and Ukraine."[40] They posit that neither realist nor domestic-politics arguments about nuclear rollback incorporate a necessary element: the influence of ideas and beliefs on policymakers. Specifically, they argue that ideas and beliefs can affect decision-making at two key points: as basic interests are transformed into policy preferences, and as preferences and the environment combine to create policy strategy.

> Thus, the decision-making chain begins with an actor's basic interests. In pursuit of these interests, the actor forms preferences. Given these preferences, the actor searches for the best available strategies to achieve them. We argue that strategy selection — like preference formation — includes an ideational component. Actors choose strategies based on beliefs about expected returns under environmental constraints. As the environment changes, it may induce a change in beliefs about the efficacy of a strategy in achieving long-standing preferences. A change in beliefs can thus lead to a change in state/actor strategy.[41]

Long and Grillot present a strong case for both Ukraine's and South Africa's elites being driven by their beliefs and identity. However, as is often the case with ideational argumentation, one cannot help but wonder why some beliefs were incorporated into policymakers' cost-benefit calculations as opposed to others. A description of competing ideas, and more thorough explanation of how and why specific beliefs "won out," would have enriched the discussion. In addition, to examine the larger field of nuclear nonproliferation, one has to wonder if all causality goes back to individual policymakers' preformed ideas.

If we see a large-scale pattern in behavior (as in nuclear nonproliferation), to what extent is that caused by structural factors such as the international social environment? To answer that, we need to answer how individual policymakers' beliefs are formed and influenced and transformed—which is not addressed by the static model proposed in this article.

While the realist and neoliberal-institutionalism arguments about nonproliferation offer useful insights, they are incomplete and in some cases clash with the factual record. Arguments incorporating ideas and identity provide greater insights for resolving the puzzle of nonproliferation, but what is needed is a more comprehensive and thorough model of how norms affect nuclear decision-making. To contribute to this, I offer constructivist explanations about nuclear forbearance and about the processes and mechanisms guiding states to that outcome. This chapter is focused on the contributions of social psychology to help us understand how social factors shape nuclear decision-making and nuclear forbearance. Some might assume that for constructivists, nuclear forbearance automatically means the state has been persuaded of the inherent value in forgoing nuclear weapons. However, research from social psychology helps us understand how social factors can lead to other outcomes that result in nuclear forbearance without such "persuasion." In the next chapter, I examine in more depth the international social environment that influences state decision-makers with regard to nuclear issues, and the specific processes and methods by which this happens.

POTENTIAL CONTRIBUTIONS OF SOCIAL PSYCHOLOGY

Specifying the effect of norms is a daunting task indeed.[42] To crack the code of norms—how they matter, under what conditions, why some and not others—we need a rigorous methodology. I propose using that offered by social psychology, where persuasion and influence have been systematically studied for decades. Defined as "the scientific study of how individuals think and feel about, interact with, and influence one another, individually and in groups," social psychology offers a rich bed of hypotheses and research on attitude and behavior creation and change.[43] Social psychology literature is especially relevant for nuclear decision-making since such policy is normally made by small, selective groups of political elites, even in democracies. All lessons from social psychology probably do not apply. However, this field offers us the best starting point for understanding the powerful phenomenon of normative influence.

Applying social psychology to political science, and to international relations in particular, is not new.[44] But no one has yet combined social psychology's lessons on attitude change and group dynamics with constructivism, with the exception of Alastair Iain Johnston, whose work is discussed in depth later. To start, we must first examine how attitudes and behavior are linked, especially how similar behaviors can be produced by different attitudes.

Behavior is ultimately what concerns international relations scholars. Attitudes are important because they are linked to behavior. If attitude had no correlation to behavior, or attitude change to behavior change, we would be much less interested in studying it. How can social psychology help us assess behavioral changes in international relations? Behavior change can be traced back to one of two main mechanisms. The first might be articulated as a *cost-benefit calculation leading to change in behavior* (I), with no change in underlying preferences. It has two subsets: material costs and benefits (I.A.), and social costs and benefits (I.B.). The second mechanism is *change in preferences that leads to change in behavior* (II). Constructivists have typically been concerned with the second type of change, preference-driven changes. In fact, constructivists have been admonished not to be concerned with any other type of change. Rodger Payne argues that "constructivists should be relatively uninterested in outcomes determined by such distortions [coercion and advertising] and instead should seek to explain norms grounded in bona fide persuasion and shared understandings."[45] According to Payne, social costs and benefits (I.B.) should be off-limits to constructivists. However, explaining behavioral change in international relations is the important point, even if it is not preference-driven change. One of the greatest contributions of constructivism is the notion that international relations are socially constructed. If some of those social constructions lead to behavior that is not preference-driven, it is still worth examining and understanding.

Iain Johnston has taken the field considerably forward by his identification of two methods of behavior change: persuasion and social influence. Johnston argues that in addition to this transformation of state interests (what he terms *persuasion*), multilateral institutions can also exert, or provide a forum through which members exert, *social influence* — essentially, a social version of material carrot-stick factors that states include in cost-benefit calculations. Persuasion can be characterized roughly as "I now see that X is better than Y," and social influence can be characterized as "I think Y is correct (or I like Y better), but since everyone else says X, I will do X so I don't rock the boat."[46] Social rewards for conformance with institutional norms include backpatting; for nonconformance, shaming. Social influence, then, is a cost-benefit calculation made with social factors (I.B.). Persuasion is preference change (II). Distinguishing between full-fledged persuasion and social conformity is critical to nuclear policymaking. As Ariel Levite argues, some states that have adhered to the NPT may actually be engaged in "nuclear hedging" — that is, not actively engaging in nuclear weapons development but maintaining capacity to develop them quickly if desired. On the surface, what looks like NPT compliance and what seems to indicate persuasion may better be described as social conformity.[47]

I contend that our model of persuasion and influence needs to be more detailed to provide a robust guide in our exploration. First, instead of using social influence, I propose the use of *social conformity* to signal outward acceptance with private rejection, because in social psychology literature, this is the terminology most often used.[48] Beyond this terminology issue, in addition to persuasion and social conformity, we must also include *identification* as a method of behavioral change.[49] Identification takes place when an actor wants to be like another and changes actions to mimic the entity admired. It can take place when a friend agrees with another friend not because of a change of mind but because it is important to a significant other. Herbert Kelman, the first scholar to document identification through research and experiments, defines identification in this way:

> Identification can be said to occur when an individual accepts influence because he wants to establish or maintain a satisfying self-defining relationship to another person or group. This relationship may take the form of classical identification, in which the individual takes over the role of the other, or it may take the form of a reciprocal role relationship. The individual actually believes in the responses which he adopts through identification, but their specific content is more or less irrelevant. He adopts the induced behavior because it is associated with the desired relationship.[50]

Identification falls between outright persuasion (where preferences have changed) and social conformity (where preferences have not changed).[51] In fact, while identification can be an influence outcome between individuals, it is a common result of group membership, known as "in-group identification." M. B. Brewer and R. J. Brown note that "when a collection of individuals believe that they share a common in-group membership, they are more likely to act in the interest of collective welfare than are individuals in the same situation who do not have a sense of group identity."[52] In contrast to social conformity (which is strategic and motivated by straightforward utility maximization), identification is based on an affective desire to create, maintain, or strengthen a relationship.[53]

With this new influence outcome of identification, we add another mechanism through which behavior can change. Previously, we identified two: The first was cost-benefit calculation leading to change in behavior (with no change in underlying preferences), which can include material costs and benefits (I.A.) or social costs and benefits (I.B.). The second was change in preferences that lead to changes in behavior (II). Identification would be the third: change in relationship(s) leads to change in preferences, which leads to change in behavior (III). As is shown in chapter 2, a fourth mechanism occurs through consistency/commitment effects (IV): change in behavior leads to change in beliefs or preferences to reduce cognitive dissonance.

Why is it important to include identification as a third method of behavioral change? After all, models are theoretical constructs that help us to understand reality, not to chart it out in full detail. However, mechanisms that produce original policy results *should be* included in models. That is, if the behavioral change mechanism of identification leads to different policy results than persuasion and social influence, then it should be included. A current example from the nonproliferation arena illustrates the point. Over the past decade, the United States has backed away from some of its obligations in the nonproliferation regime: failure to ratify the CTBT; failure to make any serious movement toward disarmament as required by the NPT (as was highlighted during the NPT extension conference in 2005); public declaration of the decision to continue designing and computer-testing new nuclear weapons; and most recently, the announced decision to employ a limited ballistic missile defense system. If an ally of the United States (Ally X) had initially followed the U.S. lead on nuclear nonproliferation due to persuasion, Ally X would remain persuaded, and thus would likely express disappointment as well as encourage the United States to get back on course. If, however, another ally's behavior was based on identification with the United States (Ally Y), then would Ally Y identify with the United States of action or the United States of rhetoric?[54]

In addition, because states in reality are not unitary actors, the distinctions between persuasion, conformity, and identification likely play out in domestic politics. In fact, it is likely that each of the influence outcomes could be represented by some segment of society interested in nuclear policy. Examples would be that NGOs and activists are "persuaded" that nuclear weapons are detrimental to state prestige and identity, while policy wonks in the diplomatic corps "identify" with their Western allies, and members of the military bow to "social conformity."[55] In each case, the behavior is the same: nuclear forbearance. The reasons behind the actions are different, however, and material or social changes could lead to behavioral changes. A short narrative of how different domestic factions might play out in Ally X and Ally Y illustrates this; my intent is not to describe any two countries but simply to highlight what differently influenced groups might look like with regard to nuclear policy and how they might react to U.S. behavior.

Allies X and Y both confront changing U.S. behavior with regard to the nuclear nonproliferation regime. Ally X's nuclear policy could be supported by a coalition of civil servants in a bureaucracy that has supported the NPT for many years, political appointees who believe in nonproliferation, and antinuclear activists with embedded ties to the policymaking apparatus — all of whom are persuaded. The current U.S. actions probably would inspire disappointment, resentment, disgust — but a change of heart is not likely because these actors are genuinely persuaded of the merits of nonproliferation. However, other elements in that government and state — those who support nonproliferation because of identification or social conformity — will likely have a different reaction. Those who believe their state should forgo nuclear weapons due to the negative diplomatic effects of any other position might rethink their position in light of the U.S. stance as well as of mild world reactions after the Indian and Pakistani tests in May 1998, the U.S. proposed nuclear deal with India, and the lack of dramatic response to the North Korea nuclear tests in 2006. In the short run, it is not likely that the state's behavior would change, but in the long run, those persuaded may change their minds or may lose ground to growing ranks of those who disagree. In the case of Ally Y, where nuclear policy is guided by identification with the United States, confusion is likely to result, based on the gap between U.S. rhetoric and actions. How do you behave when the entity after which you have patterned yourself starts to do something different from what it has said all along? Depending on the strength of the persuaded and conforming segments, and the result of any internal struggle between them, the state could move more definitively against nuclear acquisition or could move toward exploring the nuclear option.[56]

So far we have outlined the puzzle of nuclear forbearance, explained why current explanations do not satisfy, and explored how constructivism allows us to understand why nuclear forbearance actually represents three different outcomes. The next step is to detail how constructivism sheds light on nuclear forbearance, alongside the findings of realism and neoliberal institutionalism.

METHODOLOGY

The central endeavor of this project is to investigate the *why* and *how* of state decisions not to pursue the nuclear option. *Why* tests the constructivism-informed model of social-normative influence as well as alternate explanations offered by neorealism and neoliberal institutionalism. *How* explores what mechanisms lead states to their decisions not to go nuclear. To investigate these questions, I review five anomalous states — states that had both motive and means to develop nuclear weapons but that instead abstained — and use the case study method to examine why their decision-makers did not pursue a nuclear weapons program. Specifically, the exercise generates expectations against which to compare observations, both for the social-normative model of influence and for the two traditional frameworks of realism and neoliberal institutionalism. Then evidence can be compared with expectations to assess to what extent each of the three approaches is supported, and how.

Once case studies are identified and initial evidential expectations for the theories are explicitly spelled out, matching evidence against the expectations illustrates which theories are supported. In addition, the processes of persuasion, conformity, and identification are spelled out in detail in chapter 2. These are used to assist in process tracing: to what extent do we see the types of actions that theory predicted?

EXPECTATIONS

What might realism, neoliberal institutionalism, and constructivism expect to see happening in the many states that could have acquired nuclear weapons but did not? For each, I offer the major cause-effect relationships proposed, and then expected actions and discussions we should see if each cause-effect relationship is accurate.[57] Expected discussion in the course of decision-making gives insight into how policymakers framed the debate and the things they considered important (and unimportant). The discussions in question are those taking place among people trying to influence the issue. In many states this interchange is limited to the policymakers involved, since nuclear politics often remains secretive and restricted to those directly involved. But in some states (notably those with democratic governments), I expect an engaged public or citizens' groups to attempt to exert influence on the process.

Expectations from Realism

States value security above all else and make decisions by utilitarian cost-benefit calculations. As illustrated by Kenneth Waltz and Joseph Grieco, neorealism posits that since regimes have little independent power, states waste resources by funneling inherently ineffectual efforts through them. In a self-help world, alliances and agreements cannot form the basis of state security. Nuclear weapons are the ultimate tool of offense and defense and should be a prized part of national security. Why might states forgo nuclear weapons? Neorealism offers a number of possibilities, outlined in the sections that follow.

LACK OF THREAT

EXPECTATION 1:   States seek to acquire nuclear weapons to balance threats posed by potential adversaries. Therefore, states without threats from potential adversaries will not seek to acquire nuclear weapons.

To operationalize threat, I follow Stephen Meyer and James Walsh by using these three conditions: having a nuclear-armed adversary, an adversary with a latent nuclear weapons capability, or an adversary with overwhelming conventional military threat.[58] What types of evidence would confirm Expectation 1?

Expected Actions I expect that states without threats from potential adversaries will not seek to acquire nuclear weapons, and states with threats from potential adversaries will seek to acquire nuclear weapons.

Expected Discussion I would expect discussion to center around the material capabilities of potential adversaries. I would expect only limited debate to focus on the relationship of the state to the potential adversary (such as to what extent that relationship may mitigate the need to see another state as a threat). In fact, in the cases of states with which relations are friendly, I would expect some suspicion as to whether these states' good intentions can really be trusted. For states without potential adversaries, I expect a discussion of lack of threat and therefore no sense of need for a nuclear weapons program.

LACK OF REGIONAL THREAT

EXPECTATION 2:   States seek nuclear weapons to balance threats from potential regional adversaries. Therefore, states without potential regional adversaries will not seek nuclear weapons.

As suggested by T. V. Paul, regional adversaries are especially likely to prompt a state to seek nuclear weapons.

Expected Actions I expect that states without threats from potential regional or global adversaries will not seek to acquire nuclear weapons. States without threats from potential regional adversaries, but with threats from global adversaries, are less likely to seek nuclear weapons. States with threats from potential regional adversaries are expected to seek nuclear weapons.

Expected Discussion For states with potential regional adversaries, I expect discussion to center around the need to balance that threat. For states without potential regional adversaries but with potential adversaries located outside their region, I expect discussion of the lack of regional threat, with focus on the stability of regional politics, and dismissal of the "global" threat.

SECURITY GUARANTEES

EXPECTATION 3:   Because states seek nuclear weapons to balance threats from potential adversaries, security guarantees can mitigate the need for nuclear weapons.

Security guarantees are operationalized by the presence of a formal commitment to protect a state in case of outside attack. Because they are normally official, public documents, they are easy to verify.

Expected Actions I expect that states with security guarantees are not likely to seek nuclear weapons, and states without security guarantees are more likely to seek nuclear weapons.

Expected Discussion I expect that states with security guarantees will discuss the reliability of the guarantee. In times when the reliability may be questioned (such as when there are troop withdrawals by the patron state), I expect debate about the reliability of the security guarantee and the possible need for the state to develop an indigenous nuclear weapons capability.

NUCLEAR WEAPONS WEAKEN SECURITY

EXPECTATION 4: Because states value security above all else, if they perceive that nuclear weapon acquisition will harm their security, they will not seek nuclear weapons.

The most common argument along these lines states that nuclear acquisition can actually make a state a target for other nuclear weapons states. By opting out of the nuclear field, states can reduce the potential for hostile attention from other states.

Expected Actions I expect that states with concerns of becoming a target due to nuclear acquisition are less likely to seek nuclear weapons. Conversely, states that are not concerned about becoming a target are more likely to seek nuclear weapons.

Expected Discussion If a state forgoes nuclear weapons due to concerns that these could make it a target, I expect this would be evident in policy discussions. Discussions would likely weigh the benefits of the security provided by a nuclear deterrent against the costs such a nuclear program could bring by making the state a target.

ALTERNATIVE MEANS OF DETERRENCE

EXPECTATION 5: Deterrence against nuclear weapons can be obtained through acquisition of chemical or biological weapons.

The argument has been made that states can achieve parity with nuclear weapons states through less expensive weapons of mass destruction: chemical or biological weapons. If this were the case, it would explain why some states have not acquired nuclear weapons. What type of evidence would confirm this argument?

Expected Actions I expect that states with stocks of chemical or biological weapons will not seek nuclear weapons. Additionally, I expect that non-nuclear weapons states will likely seek some type of weapons of mass destruction, whether nuclear, chemical or biological.

Expected Discussion I expect that policy discussions would weigh whether chemical or biological weapons would provide acceptable deterrence against nuclear blackmail, with the answer in the affirmative. In addition, I expect that these discussions would be made public, along with some sort of public disclosure of the state's acquisition of chemical or biological weapons — for if the deterrence is to have any effectiveness, the potential adversaries must know about it.

Expectations from Neoliberal Institutionalism

An adaptation of the neorealist argument — termed neoliberal institutionalism — was made by theorists such as Robert Keohane and Lisa Martin, who argued that since multilateral organizations can reduce transaction costs, monitor compliance, and increase transparency, their use may change states' cost-benefit calculations to discourage going nuclear but *cannot* change states' essential desire to have nuclear weapons. Explanations for non-nuclear states in a nuclear world would likely center around utility calculations. Neoliberalism keeps the core assumptions of neorealism, so it would predict that states would highly prize nuclear weapon acquisition. However, mitigating factors involving material cost-benefit calculations may influence a state's decision-making.

NPT'S MATERIAL BENEFITS

EXPECTATION 6:   The material benefits offered by the NPT (technology transfer, foreign assistance, etc.) will lead states to choose nuclear forbearance.

This argument focuses on the inducements offered by the NPT, which gave assistance to members in the development of nuclear energy.

Expected Actions I expect that states without independent sources of energy are likely to value nuclear energy and are thus more likely to sign onto the NPT and forgo nuclear weapons. However, states with independent sources of energy are less likely to value nuclear energy programs and are thus less likely to sign onto the NPT and forgo nuclear weapons. States that desire nuclear energy and that have independent sources of fuel for nuclear reactors are likely to leave the NPT once the bulk of the material benefits are received. States that desire nuclear energy and do not have independent sources of fuel for nuclear reactors will attempt to acquire an independent capacity to do so but will remain in the NPT until they have done so.

Expected Discussions I expect discussions to revolve around the benefits of joining the NPT and acquiring the capability for nuclear energy or, for energy-rich states, on the lack of need to join the NPT for assistance in building a nuclear energy program.

ESCAPING THE SECURITY DILEMMA

EXPECTATION 7:   States that wish to escape the security dilemma will join the NPT, which increases transparency and provides for compliance monitoring.

The classic neoliberal argument is that international regimes can mitigate anarchy by providing independent means of compliance verification, decreasing transaction costs, and increasing transparency. Though some realists, such as Kenneth Waltz, argue that stability is enhanced by greater numbers of nuclear weapons states, others argue that having nuclear-armed neighbors does not increase security. If the latter view is correct, what type of evidence would we expect?

Expected Actions I expect that states joining the NPT to escape the security dilemma will either propose or strongly support measures that increase transparency or strengthen monitoring of compliance. In addition, states that join the NPT to escape the security dilemma will also join other WMD treaties and refrain from pursuing other WMD. If the NPT's ability to monitor compliance is weakened, I expect states to be more likely to leave it.

Expected Discussion I expect states that join the NPT to escape the security dilemma will signal this during policy discussions. Because the state's security rests on the reliability of compliance monitoring, I expect that states will discuss the reliability and be satisfied with it. I expect that after times in which the NPT's ability to monitor compliance is tested, discussion about reliability will resume.

Expectations from Constructivism

Rather than defining state actions by an overwhelming quest for security or a set of cost-benefit calculations, constructivism looks to the international social environment and the roles states play in it. Using the influence outcomes explained earlier, I propose three sets of expectations.

PERSUASION

EXPECTATION 8:   Changes in how states think about security lead them to forgo nuclear weapons.

Expected Actions I expect "persuaded" states to lead the nuclear nonprolifera-tion and disarmament movements. States that choose nuclear forbearance due to internalized convictions can be expected to act on those convictions — that is, to put effort into having their beliefs realized. This would include both policy commitments that are carried out and financial resources being com-mitted and spent. One would not expect someone persuaded on a topic to hem and haw on its implementation but rather to be at the forefront.

Expected Discussion I expect dialogue to include reference to a redefined no-tion of security, one that encompasses diplomatic, economic, and "human" se-curity, all of which are less than compatible with a nuclear weapons program. I also expect discussion regarding the incompatibility of nuclear weapons with the identity or interests of the state, the moral implications of nuclear policy, and the need for others to adopt the regime's position; I would expect lack of discussion regarding limitations the regime places on the state's sovereignty.

SOCIAL CONFORMITY

EXPECTATION 9:   The fear of social costs and the desire for social rewards can motivate states to exercise nuclear forbearance.

States that forgo nuclear weapons due to social conformity do so not because they believe it is the best choice for their security but rather because of cost-benefit calculations of the social costs and rewards involved. What type of behavior would we expect if this were the case?

Expected Action I expect that states forgoing nuclear weapons due to social conformity will do only what is required by the NPT and related treaties, nothing more, and are more likely to engage in stalling tactics. Additionally, states that forgo nuclear weapons due to social conformity will look for and, where feasible, exploit loopholes in NPT and other related treaties.

Expected Discussion I expect discussion of nonmaterial factors, such as status and international acceptance, as part of a cost-benefit calculation, and discussion of the need for compliance with the international regime if the state is to become a full partner in international society. Discussion likely will also include talk about the inevitability of the need for compliance.

IDENTIFICATION

EXPECTATION 10: States that highly value a potential or current relationship with a high-status NPT proponent or alliance will be more likely to forgo nuclear weapons.

Expected Action I expect states forgoing nuclear weapons due to identification will follow closely to the lead of the valued state or alliance, neither surpassing its efforts nor lagging far behind. I also expect the state to avoid behavior that would strain the relationship with the valued state or alliance.

Expected Discussion I expect discussion regarding the need to align with high-status partners that favored the NPT (such as the United States), a focus on the importance of supporting allied efforts, or a general lack of debate because of the presumption that the state would likely go along with the United States.

Case Study Selection, or Who Wants Nukes Anyway?

What cases can help us test the predictions generated by these theories? Since the predictions relate to why states would forgo a nuclear weapons program, the obvious first criterion is that selected states should not have developed or acquired nuclear weapons. The next logical step would be to narrow the field of acceptable case studies to those states that do have both the security motivation for and the capability to create a nuclear weapons capacity. It is at this point that the criteria become less objective and less clear. For some realists, all states should have the desire for nuclear weapons; for others who also call themselves realists, few states should want nuclear weapons. Capability is likewise open to question: while some states struggled to develop nuclear weapons and eventually gave up the quest (such as Egypt), other states with lower levels of economic development managed to achieve a nuclear weapons program (Pakistan, India, North Korea).

To circumscribe reasonably the universe of nuclear potential states, first I propose that a state have both security motivation and capability. Then I offer definitions of each and list the states that meet these definitions. This allows us to see which states meet both definitions and gives us a rough idea of potential nuclear states. I define states with a security motivation for nuclear weapons acquisition as those states with one or more nuclear-armed neighbors.[59] States that fall into this category are listed in table 1. I define states with nuclear capacity as those states with nuclear facilities.[60] These are listed in table 2. States that meet both definitions — thus, states that are potential nuclear states — are listed in table 3.

Framing nuclear potential states in this way has both benefits and drawbacks. It does circumscribe the universe of potential nuclear states more tightly than other methods might. For example, taking states' GNP (proxy for economic development) and percentage of GNP devoted to military expenditures (proxy for perception of a security threat) and comparing these to India's as a baseline, we end up with more than sixty states that exceed both India's economic development and its perception of a security threat — which could indicate nuclear potential states. For example, one state that exceeds India on both counts but that does not appear in table 3 is Saudi Arabia. Nonetheless, I perceive this more tightly drawn definition as a benefit, for I believe it is better to select cases from the most obvious suite as opposed to those that may be perceived as outliers.[61]

A number of these countries would make interesting case studies. The two selected for close examination, Japan and Egypt, both face nuclear-armed adversaries. While Israel is not a declared nuclear state, its nuclear status has been understood for decades.[62] Israel is not just a potential adversary for Egypt; Egypt was in fact humbled by Israel in military conflict.[63] In addition, Egypt has publicly acknowledged that it has considered a nuclear weapons program

Table 1 Non-Nuclear Weapons States with One or More Nuclear-Armed
Neighbors (63 total)

Afghanistan	Finland	Lithuania	Spain
Armenia	Georgia	Malaysia	Sri Lanka
Austria	Germany	Mexico	Sudan
Azerbaijan	Hungary	Moldova	Sweden
Bahrain	Indonesia	Mongolia	Switzerland
Bangladesh	Iran	Nepal	Syria
Belarus	Iraq	Netherlands	Taiwan
Belgium	Italy	Norway	Tajikistan
Bhutan	Japan	Oman	Thailand
Burma	Jordan	Philippines	Turkey
Cambodia	Kazakhstan	Poland	Ukraine
Canada	Korea, South	Portugal	United Arab
Czech Republic	Kyrgyzstan	Romania	Emirates
Denmark	Latvia	Saudi Arabia	Uzbekistan
Egypt	Lebanon	Slovak Republic	Vietnam
Estonia	Libya	Slovenia	Yemen

Table 2 Non-Nuclear Weapons States Engaging in Nuclear Activities
(56 total)[1]

Algeria	Egypt	Libya	Slovakia
Argentina	Finland	Lithuania	Slovenia
Armenia	Gabon	Malaysia	South Africa
Australia	Germany	Mexico	Spain
Austria	Greece	Morocco	Sweden
Bangladesh	Hungary	Namibia	Switzerland
Belgium	Indonesia	Netherlands	Syria
Bulgaria	Iran	Niger	Taiwan
Canada	Italy	Norway	Thailand
Central African	Jamaica	Peru	Turkey
Republic	Japan	Philippines	Ukraine
Colombia	Kazakhstan	Poland	Venezuela
Czech Republic	Korea, South	Portugal	Vietnam
Denmark	Latvia	Romania	Zaire

1. "Nuclear activities" indicates nuclear power reactor, nuclear research reactor, and/or nuclear
materials exporter. "Nuclear Activities," *Arms Control Today* (March 1995): 33–36.

Table 3 Nuclear Potential States (40 total)

Armenia	Germany	Lithuania	Slovenia
Australia	Hungary	Malaysia	Spain
Austria	Indonesia	Mexico	Sweden
Bangladesh	Iran	Netherlands	Switzerland
Belgium	Italy	Norway	Syria
Canada	Japan	Philippines	Taiwan
Czech Republic	Kazakhstan	Poland	Thailand
Denmark	Korea, South	Portugal	Turkey
Egypt	Latvia	Romania	Ukraine
Finland	Libya	Slovak Republic	Vietnam

to balance its neighbor. Japan faces not one but three nuclear-armed neighbors, all of which it has engaged in military conflict in the past hundred years: China, Russia, and North Korea. Some might argue that Japan is unlikely to seek nuclear weapons because it is the only state to have had nuclear weapons dropped on its soil. However, for precisely that reason, it could be forcefully argued that the only way for Japan to ensure that such a tragedy never happens again is to acquire not only nuclear weapons but also a robust second-strike capability. In terms of capacity, an argument could be made that Egypt's economy makes it unlikely the state could fund a nuclear weapons development program. However, in 1980, 1990, and 2000, Egypt's GNP exceeded that of India — a state that was able to marshal the necessary resources. (Egypt also spent a higher percentage of its GNP on defense than India for all three years.) Japan's capacity for nuclear weapons development is unquestioned; it is publicly acknowledged that given its advanced scientific and technical resources and well-developed nuclear infrastructure, Japan could develop nuclear weapons within months.

Japan and Egypt both present robust puzzles: why have they not developed nuclear weapons? They also offer two interesting comparisons: regime type and security guarantees. How does regime type — authoritarian state versus democratic system — interplay with nuclear decision-making? Are social-normative influences filtered differently? Another oft-cited factor in states' nuclear calculations is the presence of security guarantees from other states. While Japan is under the U.S. nuclear umbrella, Egypt is not and has not been. How does this make a difference for two states that have both opted out of the nuclear arms race? In addition, both states offer interesting case studies for the potential of norms. Given the strong antinuclear sentiment in Japan due to the country's historical experience, one would expect that norms would be more likely to influence policy here than in any other state. Thus, if norms have little impact in Japan, perhaps there is less hope for normative explanations for other states. In Egypt's case, the public has not expressed antinuclear norms; rather, the diplomatic elite has taken on the cause of nonproliferation globally, exerting some of the strongest leadership in this arena worldwide. How is it that this strong normative influence grew out of a state that once sought nuclear weapons and lost several wars with a nuclear-armed neighbor?

Finally, both Japan and Egypt are important cases because of their currency. After the North Korean nuclear tests in October 2006, many analysts predicted that Japan would soon go nuclear in response. This has not been the case, but concerns over a potential Japanese nuclear option remain. Should Japan leave the NPT, the international regime could come apart at the seams. Likewise, Egypt has responded to the Iranian nuclear program with promises of a large-scale nuclear power infrastructure, raising concerns that the country may be interested in a possible nuclear option as well. Given Egypt's leadership in the nuclear nonproliferation regime, an Egyptian withdrawal from the NPT would also severely stress the institution.

After in-depth examination of Japanese and Egyptian nuclear decision-making, three additional cases are analyzed to see if the lessons learned from Japan and Egypt apply to other countries: Libya, Sweden, and Germany. Libya is important because it is the only known case in which the same person made the decision to start and end a nuclear weapons program. In addition, the Libyan case offers hope in a decidedly bleak nonproliferation environment. If the lessons of Japan and Egypt apply to Libya, then we know that these tools are still relevant today. Sweden is a critical case because the country originally intended to acquire a nuclear deterrent. As the emerging nuclear nonproliferation regime took shape, however, Sweden had to struggle with what nuclear weapons meant for their security and identity. Thus, the Swedish case gives us a clear picture of how the regime helped to transform thinking about the value of nuclear weapons. Germany's importance springs from the fact that early on, the country was the critical case for the nonproliferation regime. In the formative days of the nonproliferation regime, a number of other countries (including Sweden) indicated that they were not willing to give up a nuclear option unless Germany did. Success of the nonproliferation norm in Germany can therefore be seen as success for the norm worldwide. In addition to historical significance, Germany is one of only a few countries today that could develop nuclear weapons in a very short period of time. Thus, assessing Germany's commitment to the regime is important for policy's sake.

Before beginning case study examinations, I turn first to a closer examination of the international social environment, describing what it is, what its components are, and what effects we might expect it to have on elite decision-making.

CHAPTER TWO

Understanding the International Social Environment

The international social environment influences elite decision-making regarding nuclear weapons acquisition, and chapter 1 outlines three major outcomes from that influence: persuasion, conformity, and identification.[1] Questions remain, however: what comprises this international social environment, and how does it influence elite decision-making? This chapter provides the theoretical tools that can answer these questions. I draw on social psychology research to examine the processes of persuasion: the different ways norms are transmitted, the different ways actors process those norms, and the different conditions that affect the influence of norms. This discussion is not intended as a comprehensive review of literature on persuasion and influence but rather as an examination of the concepts most likely to shed light on how a social environment can influence policy outcomes. Before discussing how the nuclear nonproliferation regime shapes normative expectations, I first review the larger normative context surrounding nuclear weapons and then discuss the specific aspects of the nonproliferation regime that contribute to this context.

NORMS AND THE NUCLEAR ISSUE

The international normative context surrounding nuclear weapons arose before the first atomic bomb was ever created. In 1914 H. G. Wells published his novel *The World Set Free*, describing a catastrophic war fought with "atomic bombs" that led survivors to create a world government. The book made such an impact on physicist Leo Szilard, a peer of Albert Einstein's, that in the late 1930s he lobbied scientists from around the world to keep all research on nuclear fission secret.[2] Although his campaign was not successful, he was the first in the line of many scientists who would warn against potential evils of nuclear weapons. However, popular sentiment against nuclear weapons did not strengthen until after the United States dropped atomic bombs on Hiroshima and Nagasaki in June 1945. Before the bombings, the U.S. leadership did not consider the atomic bombs to be a different class of weapons.[3] After learning of the tremendous destruction the bombs caused, however, U.S. president Harry Truman was loath to use them again. "His administration spent considerable energy pursuing the Baruch Plan for international control of atomic weapons at the UN, and Truman established the precedent of civilian control over nuclear weapons, thus signaling their special status."[4] Truman's change of heart was also due in part to the immediate negative reaction to the bombings from around the world. "From the outset, U.S. government leaders were shaken by the enormous destructiveness of the Hiroshima bombing and by the sharp criticism that it generated."[5] Both the Vatican and the Federal Council of Churches condemned the atomic bombings, and citizens' movements against the bomb sprang up worldwide.[6] The first resolution issued by the UN General Assembly in 1946 called for "the elimination from national armaments of atomic weapons."[7] In the United States the public strongly supported Truman's decision to drop the atomic bombs, but as the devastating results of the weapons became clear, unease with and fear of nuclear weapons became widespread. Nina Tannenwald documents how international opinion against nuclear weapons had hardened so much that, by 1953, U.S. policymakers acknowledged that "in the present state of world opinion, we could not use an A-bomb."[8]

In 1954 nuclear testing generated even greater antinuclear sentiment. Paul Boyer notes:

> The 1954 test series spread radioactive ash over seven thousand square miles of the Pacific Ocean and brought illness and death to Japanese fishermen working 85 miles from the test sites [known as the Lucky Dragon incident]. Soviet hydrogen bomb tests, begun in 1954 and continued through the decade, further contaminated the atmosphere. In 1955, radioactive rain fell on Chicago. In 1959, deadly strontium-90 began to show up in wheat and milk. A two-part *Saturday Evening Post* feature that year was entitled, "Fallout: The Silent Killer." Linus Pauling, Barry Commoner, and other scientists warned of leukemia, bone cancer, and long-term genetic damage triggered by nuclear testing. A full-blown fallout scare pervaded the nation.[9]

Not only did the nuclear tests create persistent fear in the public; they also generated severe criticism internationally. India's Prime Minister Jawaharlal

Nehru called for an immediate ban on nuclear testing.[10] By August 1955 the world's first conference protesting nuclear weapons was held in Hiroshima.[11] The next year the U.S. Democratic presidential candidate, Adlai Stevenson, proposed an end to aboveground nuclear tests.[12] While Eisenhower dismissed the proposal when he was reelected, "considerable pressure by powerful popular movements" prodded him to begin expert talks with the Soviets on the possibility of an enforceable test ban.[13] These grassroots movements—composed of diverse elements such as intellectuals, scientists, students, religious organizations, pacifists, and housewives—led Eisenhower to remark in August 1958, "The new thermonuclear weapons are tremendously powerful; however, they are not . . . as powerful as is world opinion today in obliging the United States to follow certain lines of policy."[14]

By 1962 the negotiations were formalized in the United Nations' Eighteen-Nation Disarmament Committee (ENDC). Within a year the Partial Test Ban Treaty had been concluded. As early as 1959, Ireland began calling for the negotiation of a nuclear nonproliferation treaty in the UN General Assembly, which found better traction after the 1962 Cuban missile crisis made elites believe the potential for nuclear war was real. The French nuclear tests of February 1960 also generated support for a global nonproliferation treaty: "For the first time in history, a country had developed its own bomb independently and against the will of the superpowers. This raised fears regarding which other countries would follow suit."[15] By 1965 both the Americans and the Soviets proposed draft treaties to the ENDC. While the United States and Soviet Union were able to negotiate privately to come to an agreement on treaty differences, the non-nuclear weapons states demanded changes through their voice on the ENDC. One U.S. expert noted: "The very first drafts of the NPT submitted by both the Soviets and the U.S. did not contain articles 4, 5 or 6. Those articles were negotiated in by the non-nuclear weapons states."[16] (Articles 4 and 5 deal with states' rights to nuclear energy and technological assistance from nuclear weapons states, while Article 6 calls on the nuclear weapons states to work toward disarmament.) In particular, the non-aligned countries on the ENDC successfully insisted on a link between nonproliferation and disarmament. "The U.S. took the criticism to heart to a certain extent. In their draft of January 18, 1968, an article was included in which the nuclear weapons states promised to negotiate in good faith on effective measures relating to the cessation of the nuclear arms race at an early date."[17] In July 1968 the Nuclear

Nonproliferation Treaty (NPT) was opened for signature; the treaty entered into force in 1970.

With the creation of international treaties to manage the terror of nuclear weapons, popular political participation in the antinuclear cause declined. The public tended to believe that through current treaties and ongoing arms control negotiations, the risk of nuclear holocaust had diminished; pacifist groups turned their focus to Vietnam War protests.[18] But by the late 1970s and the close of the Vietnam War, antinuclear activists began to regroup, driven in part by fear of contamination from nuclear power plants and in part by the fact that despite treaties and arms control negotiations, the nuclear arms race had not slowed. The first special session of the UN General Assembly on Disarmament, held in 1978, served as a focal point for the groups.[19] By the early 1980s the "most extensive citizens' campaign on nuclear arms issues" in the United States was under way, known as the nuclear freeze movement, with the goal of pressuring the superpowers to halve immediately "all testing, production, and deployment of nuclear weapons."[20] In the 1995 NPT Review Conference, antinuclear nongovernmental organizations (NGOs) took especially active roles, holding seminars through the NPT preparation process, organizing a fast for the abolition of nuclear weapons, and presenting a statement from the NGO Nuclear Abolition Caucus, signed by more than two hundred NGOs representing more than ten million people.[21]

Though it has taken a variety of forms, the rough normative trajectory within the international social environment has been to delegitimize nuclear weapons. Tannenwald notes: "Whereas in the 1950s, U.S. leaders argued that nuclear weapons should be viewed as conventional, just like any other weapon, no one makes this argument today. This stigmatization of nuclear technology is probably the peace movement's most important contribution to world history."[22] Nonetheless, the spread of the norm has been uneven and, in some cases, continues to face substantial resistance. For example, nuclear tests by India and Pakistan in 1998, and by North Korea in 2006, show that policymakers in some countries do consider nuclear weapons valuable additions to their security posture. Indeed, the U.S. Nuclear Posture Review in 2001 indicated that Washington might consider using nuclear weapons against non-nuclear weapons states. Thus, while nuclear weapons are no longer seen as simply conventional weapons and the nonproliferation norm has spread widely, the global normative context is by no means uniform or unchanging.[23]

Understanding the full context of this international social environment is important to understanding how state policymakers came to decisions on nuclear forbearance. However, this project focuses on the international social environment through the lens of the NPT and associated nuclear nonproliferation frameworks. Doing so provides a useful research window, particularly because nuclear decision-making in the case studies often occurred as a result of the need to make a public decision regarding the nuclear nonproliferation regime (e.g., whether to sign the NPT, whether to ratify the NPT, whether to support the NPT's indefinite extension, etc.). Furthermore, using international institutions to understand social environments is currently a rich field of inquiry.[24] In addition, with the creation of the NPT, antinuclear NGOs often used the official conferences and preparatory sessions of the regime as focal points for lobbying and protests. Thus, using the NPT as a research window allows capture of the influence of these groups in their attempts to shape the normative discourse on nuclear weapons. The next section therefore describes the particulars of the nuclear nonproliferation regime. The rest of the chapter is devoted to examining how the regime contributes to the influence of international social environment on policymakers' nuclear decision-making.

THE NUCLEAR NONPROLIFERATION REGIME

As noted, for nuclear nonproliferation, the social environment — the network of formal and informal structures and relationships that send messages about what is and is not officially and unofficially acceptable — is shaped in no small measure by the NPT and related treaties and agreements. The NPT, opened for signature in 1968 and entered into force in 1970, is now the most universal disarmament treaty, with 187 member states and only four states outside it (India, Pakistan, Israel, and North Korea).[25] The original duration of the NPT was twenty-five years, with review conferences held every five years. In 1995 states agreed to extend the NPT indefinitely, an accomplishment made possible "because many developing nations have come to recognize that nuclear proliferation threatens international peace and security."[26] However, the nuclear nonproliferation regime is more than just the NPT; it is an interlocking network of multilateral and bilateral agreements, structures, and relationships, all supported by the NPT. Other important components include the International Atomic Energy Agency (IAEA), which conducts audits and inspections, known collectively as "safeguards," to verify compliance with the NPT; the Comprehensive Test Ban Treaty (CTBT), adopted by the UN General Assembly in 1996; supplier control mechanisms (two informal, voluntary coalitions, the Zangger Coalition and the Nuclear Suppliers Group) that control the export of equipment and materials potentially useful in a nuclear weapons program; and six Nuclear-Weapon-Free Zones, in which states agree to keep their region free of nuclear weapons.[27]

In the past decade other actors have sought to go beyond the NPT framework to uphold the nuclear nonproliferation norm and strengthen it further. This indicates the strength of that norm, showing that it is not merely the regime that spurs states to act; the norm spurs states and others to act even outside the regime. For example, the European Union recently tied Trade and Cooperation Agreements (TCA) to states' WMD nonproliferation status: in December 2003, "the EU adopted a nonproliferation strategy that reinforced the recently adopted principles and made clear that WMD would now become a fundamental condition in all future EU agreements."[28] Even as states seek to enforce the nuclear nonproliferation norm outside the NPT, the main message of this collection of treaties, agreements, and enforcement mechanisms is that nuclear weapons are not acceptable weapons of war, that no new states should be allowed to obtain them, and that states with nuclear weapons should work to reduce and eventually eliminate them.

The NPT and associated agreements comprise a great trade-off: states without nuclear weapons will not seek them because over time, nuclear weapons states will reduce their inventories and eventually disarm. In turn, nuclear weapons states will not have nuclear competitors, but they must eventually move toward disarmament. Underlying the trade-off was the mutually agreed-upon assumption that the world is better off without nuclear weapons than with them. For the first time, the NPT codified the sentiment that states should not seek to acquire nuclear weapons. To the extent that all states adhered to the NPT mandate, the social environment prohibiting nuclear weapons acquisition has been strengthened. However, as states (both nuclear weapons states and non-nuclear weapons states) depart from the mandate, the social environment is weakened.

NORMS AND THE INTERNATIONAL SOCIAL ENVIRONMENT

A framework deriving from social psychology literature on persuasion and influence permits exploration of this international social environment in greater depth. Besides enabling us talk about the international social environment, it also helps us see what causal mechanisms might be in place through which influence can occur. In other words, if we are looking to see how state elites have or have not been persuaded, what things might we see? The next section explains the concepts and then describes how they relate to the social expectations created and maintained by the nuclear nonproliferation regime. These expectations are not meant to be statements of fact about how I expect norms to influence policymakers. Rather, they are simply possible relationships generated by research in social psychology. They are raised to see if they are indeed useful in understanding how norms may influence elite decision-making.

How Are Norms Transmitted?

Commonly defined in international relations as "a standard of appropriate behavior for actors with a given identity," norms are *shared* belief systems.[29] As a result, when we study norms, we must look at both the actor's norm processing and the social environment in which the actor is embedded. Norms are generally thought of in terms of rhetoric, declarations, and other pronouncements, but they include a much broader spectrum of activity. Social psychology pinpoints three major types of norms, classified by how they are transmitted: descriptive norms, injunctive norms, and subjective norms.[30]

DESCRIPTIVE NORMS. These are simply an elaborate way of saying people notice what you do at least as much as what you say. Observing others helps people understand what is "correct" or "normal" in a novel, ambiguous, or uncertain situation. The greater the number of actors behaving in a certain way, the more we believe that behavior is correct. The concept of descriptive norms tells us that watching what others do does more than just give us information — it shapes our perception of social reality and our understanding of the proper response. "A wide variety of research shows that the behavior of others in our social environment shapes our own interpretation of and response to a situation, even without overt indoctrination."[31]

INJUNCTIVE NORMS. Most of us are familiar with these: "Clean your plate," "Don't lie or cheat," "Don't seek weapons of mass destruction." Injunctive norms can prescribe proper behavior or proscribe improper behavior. Such norms usually bring social rewards for those who comply, or social sanctions for those who do not, whether stated or not. While the reframing effect of descriptive norms is subtle, injunctive norms clearly set out to change perspectives and interpretations.[32]

SUBJECTIVE NORMS. These are our perceptions of others' views of norms. This third type of norm is defined as "the person's perception that most people who are important to him think he should or should not perform the behavior in question."[33] Study of subjective norms came about when researchers found that strength of attitude combined with subjective norms predicted behavior much better than did strength of attitude alone. In the international arena, what other actors believe we should do is not always clear: Does North Korea think China is for or against its nuclear program? And is China for or against a *hidden* nuclear program? Subjective norms are developed by an actor's interpretation of descriptive and injunctive norms as well as by absorption of messages from international organizations, NGOs, media, and more.[34]

Norm transmission sounds sterile and not particularly earth shattering. And yet it encompasses some of the messiest and most contentious activities internationally, and it is at the heart of how actors try to persuade others. A great number of actors transmit norms — from states to politicians, from international organizations and NGOs to norm entrepreneurs. From Greenpeace stalking a tuna ship to President Bush admonishing the "Axis of Evil," when injunctive norm transmission takes place, it is generally obvious. Injunctive messages are meant to be heard: *Do this!* or *That's wrong!* Usually, both transmitter and receiver are clear about the intended message.

However, descriptive norm transmission often occurs without the "transmitter" realizing it. This occurs whenever an actor or group of actors behaves in a regular fashion with regard to a normative issue (or what could be interpreted as a normative issue). For example, not returning the telephone calls of subordinates sends the message that those people and their calls are unimportant. The U.S. refusal to ratify the CTBT, and its withdrawal from the Anti-Ballistic Missile Treaty, certainly send a message. This becomes especially pertinent when the descriptive norms of an actor or group clash with the injunctive norms it transmits. For example, although the United States promotes itself as an unselfish "liberator," others note cynically that we tend to get involved militarily only when we have important interests at stake (Iraq, Kuwait, Haiti, as opposed to Rwanda and a very long delay in Bosnia). In addition, descriptive norm transmission can be "received" without the recipient being consciously aware of it: "The behavior of others in our social environment shapes our own interpretation and response to a situation, even without overt indoctrination."[35] For instance, when large numbers of actors behave in a certain way, this behavior can become automatic or unquestioned — simply what a civilized state does — whether referring to constructing science bureaucracies, signing the UN declaration on human rights, or signing the NPT.

Subjective norms technically are not transmitted; they are an actor's interpretation of what others believe about a norm.[36] However, all sorts of transmittals are critically important in the creation of subjective norms. Television coverage of protests, newspaper reports of statements by world leaders, even messages passed through back-door diplomatic channels all shape what an actor thinks important others view as the best course of action. Obviously, the clearer you can make your message, the more likely it is that subjective norms will match your injunctive norms, especially if the actor considers you an important other.[37]

Norm Transmission and the International Social Environment

The NPT's opening for signature in 1968 and entry into force in 1970 served and still serve as the main source of formal normative transmissions regarding nuclear nonproliferation. Before the negotiations leading to the creation of the NPT, there were no formally agreed-upon behavioral expectations regarding acquiring nuclear weapons. After the NPT, there were clear formal normative transmittals that designated nuclear weapons acquisition as unacceptable. The NPT's injunctive normative content was quickly reinforced by descriptive norms — that is, the very large number of states that signed and ratified the NPT. Within ten years of coming into force, the NPT had 111 member states.[38] After the dissolution of the Soviet Union, states saw that new countries gave up the nuclear weapons on their territory and joined the NPT.

Since the mid-1990s, however, descriptive norm transmissions regarding nuclear nonproliferation have been murkier. India and Pakistan both detonated nuclear weapons, with muted reaction from the international community. While the official U.S. justification for its invasion of Iraq was to keep that state from acquiring nuclear weapons, North Korea is basically permitted to flaunt a nuclear weapons program. The United States began a new drive to modernize its nuclear forces as well as began new nuclear weapons research into bunker busters and miniaturized nuclear weapons, for example. The head of Japan's Defense Agency threatened that Japan might be forced to start a nuclear weapons program if North Korea's efforts were not curtailed. While the large majority of states have adhered to their NPT commitments, the anomalies seem to dominate world news. At this point, it would be fair to say that when it comes to nuclear nonproliferation, injunctive and descriptive norms are in contention.

Additionally, subjective norms have not always supported the nonproliferation regime. The Canadians at times believed the United States wanted them to consider acquiring a nuclear capability, because American diplomats informally conveyed that message.[39] More recently, members of the U.S. Congress have encouraged Japan to consider having its own nuclear weapons capability, potentially leading members of the Japanese elite to wonder whether the United States would formally agree to such a move. Had the Canadian and Japanese leadership refrained from nuclear weapons development because of identification or social conformity, they might have followed the U.S. suggestion and acquired the bomb. In the case of identification, the elites would want to preserve the relationship and so would be more open to the lead of the United States. In the case of social conformity, elites would have refrained from nuclear weapons development only because of the social rewards for doing so and/or the social costs in acquiring a nuclear capacity. If the United States not only "gave permission" for these states to do so but actually encouraged it, then the calculation of social costs and rewards would have changed dramatically, perhaps enough to change decision-makers' minds on the value of nuclear forbearance. But if descriptive and/or subjective norms are in contention with an internalized injunctive norm, the internalized norm likely will win out — at least in the short term. Over the long term, decision-makers may change their minds, or they may be replaced with a different set of elites who are more open to the descriptive and/or injunctive messages.

This background on normative transmission allows me to cull out a number of expectations that predict how states might react to the variety of norms generated within the international social environment.

DESCRIPTIVE NORMS: The more states publicly commit to forgoing nuclear weapons, the more likely it is that outlying states will join in and forgo nuclear weapons. The more states that withdraw from or hedge on their commitment to the NPT, the more likely it is that other states will consider doing the same.

INJUNCTIVE NORMS: The more a state is publicly and privately admonished to commit to forgoing nuclear weapons (by individual states, international organizations, etc.), the more likely it is to commit to forgo nuclear weapons.

SUBJECTIVE NORMS: The more convinced policymakers are that "important others" (domestic or international) believe they should forgo nuclear weapons, the more likely they are to make decisions leading to rejection of a nuclear weapons program.

How Are Norms Processed?

International actors are bombarded with large numbers of normative messages, many of them conflicting, from both external and domestic sources. It may seem that using norms as an explanatory variable is impossible, since the numerous norms in circulation support just about any course of action. How do actors process and sort through normative transmissions, and how do we understand which norms matter and why? Based on social psychology research, three main mechanisms are proposed through which norms are processed, helping us begin to understand why some norms win out over others. In addition, norm transmitters may experience greater success in persuasion if they are able to frame their messages in ways amenable to these mechanisms.

LINKING. A classic example of linking is an advertisement by People for the Ethical Treatment of Animals, aimed toward environmentalists; it reads, "If you give a damn about the earth, become a vegetarian." Linking connects a norm to well-established values. In evaluating how to respond to a norm, actors often consider how it fits in with their current value system. For the nuclear nonproliferation regime, adherence to the norm has often been linked to international legitimacy. With near-universal membership, states face pariah status in remaining outside the NPT. South Africa's president acknowledged as much, saying that his decision to take apart his state's nuclear weapons program was fueled in part by his desire for South Africa "to take its rightful place in the international community."[40]

ACTIVATION. Even within social psychology, the use of norms as an explanatory tool has been criticized on the basis that a variety of norms apply to any given situation, some of which may be incompatible (for example, the norm of nuclear nonproliferation versus the norm of national pride). Further research uncovered that situational cues can activate one norm over another. As R. B. Cialdini and M. R. Trost observe, "There may be multiple, and even incompatible norms vying for attention in many situations, and our actions may depend to a large extent on the type of norm that is triggered by the context." In short, activation means "being made focal" or "having been highlighted." In some cases, injunctive norms and descriptive norms, or subjective norms and descriptive norms, were in direct competition with each other — the norm that had been emphasized tended to win out. Cialdini and Trost concluded: "This series of studies indicated that, at any given time, an individual's behavior is likely to flow with the norm that is currently focal, even when other types of norms might be relevant and even contrary in the situation."[41] In one study, subjects who were given paper trash and saw another person litter were far more likely to litter than subjects who were given paper trash but saw another person throw litter into a trash receptacle. In the real world, norm activation is much more complex, since decisions have far more import than littering, and a host of norms are activated by a number of different actors at any one time. However, it is important to note that people are more likely to adhere to a norm that has been emphasized, which means that the activity of emphasizing norms is not a useless one.[42]

What specifically does "activation" look like? Activities that highlight or make a norm a focal point qualify as activation. Holding a dramatic public relations event to convey a message would count. For example, when Greenpeace members chained themselves to the front door of the U.S. Environmental Protection Agency headquarters to protest what they considered a weak ruling on clean air issues, they received press coverage, and Greenpeace members were able to state their views on the issue. Agency officials had to respond to the criticisms. In effect, the norm of environmental protection was activated, with Greenpeace able to explain why their view of the norm was superior and agency officials being forced to defend their interpretation as well as to engage a group they would otherwise ignore. Another example of activation would be submitting a UN resolution to call attention to an issue. Egypt has made an art of activation of the nuclear nonproliferation norm in this manner. In 1974 Egypt sponsored an Iranian resolution calling for a nuclear-weapon-free zone (NWFZ) in the Middle East. Each year since then, Egypt has itself crafted and sponsored the resolution. By 1980 Israel no longer abstained, and the resolution has been adopted by consensus in the UN General Assembly. Other forms of activation could include devoting a speech to an issue, taking out a full-page advertisement in the *New York Times* to show a proposal's long list of important signatories, or coordinating a series of events around a specific topic to promote a particular interpretation of a norm.

CONSISTENCY. Social psychology has found that the best predictor of future behavior is past behavior. The need to appear and be consistent is a powerful motivator. This need is often engaged through making commitments; once they are made, people tend to behave in ways that are consistent with them. In particular, commitments that are active, effortful, public, and viewed as internally motivated are most likely to generate consistent future behavior.[43] In fact, small commitments, once met, make actors much more likely to commit to larger actions. Social psychologists theorize that this is the case "because performance of the initially requested action causes a self-perception change; that is, individuals come to see themselves as possessing certain behavior-related traits." Indeed, Cialdini describes this phenomenon as commitments "growing their own legs," so that once an initial request is completed, commitments lead to inner change.[44] People often generate additional reasons to justify their commitments—new reasons that have nothing to do with the initial request. Then external requests are no longer necessary to gain compliance, since it has become internally motivated.[45]

This brings up an interesting question for international relations scholars: do actors who comply based on identification or social conformity experience this internal change, leading ultimately to the influence outcome of persuasion?[46] Since leaders and policymakers come and go in states, especially in democratic states, does this internalization process have enough time to take place before new people take the reins? Are civil servants the mainstay of internalized commitment, since they tend to remain on the job for years? Another important question is whether the political elite, in democracies especially, would be sensitive to the need for consistent behavior; as Philip Tetlock and James Goldgeier argue, "this internalization process should be especially reliable in democracies, in which leaders must justify departures from widely held norms of fair play to a variety of constituencies."[47]

The processing mechanism of consistency also casts doubt on the claims that constructivists should not study distorted or warped persuasive appeals (the argument being that any persuasion occurring is not legitimate). Rodger Payne says:

> As Kratochwil (1989: 228), borrowing theoretically from the work of Jurgen Habermas, argued in regard to how bribes taint conversion, mechanisms that threaten or pander to selfish interests are not "distortion free." Scholars wanting to understand the way persuasion helps construct legitimate norms, with an emphasis on the resonant claims (or "better arguments") of advocates, should view coercion and advertising as fairly uninteresting communicative acts (Barry 1990: 2). As Crawford (1993: 52) observes, "norms established through coercion . . . lack legitimacy."[48]

Indeed, what Payne describes is not persuasion. It may, however, fit under conformity or identification. And given that internalization of norms can occur even when they are not advanced under the best of conditions, we should not dismiss this kind of internalization as uninteresting or illegitimate. Rather, we should acknowledge these norms for what they are and be open to studying if and how they transform.

Norm Processing and the International Social Environment

The international social environment fostered by the NPT has encouraged states to process and accept the norm of nuclear nonproliferation. The preamble of the NPT is a series of "links" that connect universally held values and previously made commitments to its own establishment, with the implication that just as states hold these values and honor these commitments, so should they commit to the NPT. In terms of activation, the negotiations leading up to and the actual creation of the NPT gave interested parties something to "activate." Before this, non-nuclear activists could not point to a formal document in which states agreed to refrain from nuclear acquisition. With the emergence, establishment, and strengthening of the NPT, an actor (whether a state, NGO, or individual) interested in influencing potential proliferators can activate — that is, bring to the forefront — the norm of nonproliferation. Suddenly, the potential proliferator must face this norm and risk defying it.

The mere activation of a norm does not mean it will prevail; in complex policymaking decisions, certainly a number of norms are being activated at the same time. But without the NPT, the nuclear nonproliferation norm had no official platform from which to be activated, and less credibility with which to be activated. The realm of competing norms was enlarged by the NPT, and with its continued success, the nuclear nonproliferation norm is not easily dismissed. Now that the nuclear nonproliferation norm has been established and maintained by the NPT framework, some states are activating the norm outside that framework. For example, the Big Three (Britain, France, and Germany) sought to engage Iran on its troublesome nuclear program, offering a mix of social and material inducements, so that the IAEA would not have to declare Iran in violation of its NPT agreements.[49]

Consistency is potentially a powerful force in keeping states in adherence to the nuclear nonproliferation norm for two reasons: public commitments and past behavior. First, once a state commits publicly to the treaty, even if policymakers do not intend to abide by it, any violations of the treaty may cause cognitive dissonance among state elite, potentially making such behavior less likely. Because individual elites commit a state to a treaty, however, this may make consistency less powerful. If a new set of elites comes to power, they may feel less commitment to a treaty ratified by their political opponents. Yet the value of public commitment to forgoing nuclear weapons can be seen in the establishment of nuclear-weapon-free zones, in which states' policymakers agreed to keep nuclear weapons out of the region. "Nuclear-weapon-free zones have sought to establish norms against the acquisition of nuclear weapons without even attempting to establish supporting sanctions or rewards."[50] Second, for the large group of states that have not only ratified the NPT but have also abided by it, their previous adherence creates momentum to continued adherence. Violating the NPT means violating a public commitment and reversing decades of compliance with and support for a widely held international norm.

This background on normative processing leads to a number of expectations about how political elites might process norms given the international social environment created by the NPT framework:

LINKING: The more links policymakers see between the nuclear nonproliferation norm and their current values, the more likely they are to commit to forgoing nuclear weapons.

ACTIVATION: The more the nuclear nonproliferation norm is activated, the more likely policymakers are to commit to forgoing nuclear weapons.

CONSISTENCY: The longer a state has been a member of the NPT, and the more support it has given the NPT, the more likely it is to continue to adhere to the nuclear nonproliferation norm.

What Conditions Might Affect the Influence of Norms?

Norm transmission takes place under a wide variety of conditions, some favorable to norm acceptance and some less favorable. Political science has something to say on this topic; for example, a rule of thumb in comparative politics is that cultural changes come more easily in times of crisis. Social psychology offers a broad perspective on the topic, helping us to see how different conditions affect the influence of norms. By understanding these conditions, norm entrepreneurs and others interested in winning adherents can attempt to create or avoid these conditions. The following three conditions may influence the potency of normative transmissions:

UNCERTAINTY. Without a doubt, uncertainty exerts the largest and most wide-ranging effect on influence outcomes. Decades of research have consistently shown that actors are more likely to accept group influence when dealing with a subjective task as opposed to an objective task — because the subjectivity creates uncertainty. In addition, uncertainty increases the likelihood of an actor internalizing group influence (persuasion) as opposed to simply conforming. Whether a task itself is unclear, or the results of a decision are hard to predict, actors are more open to outside influence. A cost-benefit equation in flux — when costs and/or benefits seem to be rising or falling — would meet this definition. Ambiguous costs and/or benefits, or those open to debate, would also meet it. For example, do nuclear weapons really provide the benefit of security, or do they undermine it by making a state a target? A clear but difficult task or decision also evokes uncertainty. People are more likely to accept outside input under these conditions, in part because of the perception of increased room for error.[51]

SIMILARITY. When a norm transmitter is similar to us, or is someone with whom we desire a good relationship, we are more open to normative influence from that source.[52] A number of studies confirm that "a similar source can trigger normative behavior more easily than a dissimilar source."[53] Why? Identification. When actors want to establish or maintain a relationship, they are more likely to defer to requests and to accept influence from one another. When members of a group believe they are valued by the group, or when they value the group, conformity increases.[54]

CONFLICT. Of the three main conditions that affect normative influence, conflict is the only one that decreases its potency. Any explicit intergroup division creates group polarization, but it is possible to overcome in-group/out-group divisions through contact. However, intergroup conflict immediately quashes efforts at cooperation and influence. During conflict, members automatically side with their own group and close themselves off from outside sources of influence, thus shutting down a potential transmission mechanism.

Norm Potency and the International Social Environment

The international social environment created by the nuclear nonproliferation framework has influenced the potency of the nuclear nonproliferation norm in a number of ways. First, the NPT and associated frameworks undermined to some extent the traditional notion that nuclear weapons enhance a state's security, and thus created uncertainty for policymakers, making them more likely to accept group norms. How did this happen? The NPT created social and material incentives for forgoing nuclear weapons as well as making it technically and practically difficult to develop a nuclear weapons program. In other words, the NPT dramatically changed the cost-benefit equation for nuclear weapons acquisition. Certainty about the value of nuclear weapons was replaced by uncertainty over whether these weapons were worth the new economic and social costs as well as uncertainty about whether the weapons were needed, given the commitment of nuclear weapons states not to use such weapons against non-nuclear weapons states. The continued strengthening of IAEA protocols (strengthened after the Gulf War and currently being strengthened through the signature of additional protocols) lets policymakers know that the cost-benefit equation continues to shift, as inspections become more intrusive and the costs of hiding noncompliance increase. Unilateral actions, such as Israel's bombing of the Iraqi Osirak nuclear reactor and the U.S.

invasion of Iraq in 2003, also continue to shift the cost-benefit equation. The likely effect of such uncertainty is to convince many policymakers to accept the group norm.

Understanding that actors are more likely to accept the influence of similar others gives us a more refined view of how persuasion occurs in the nuclear nonproliferation arena. Given that the strong normative message has been for nuclear forbearance, why do some states continue to violate the NPT? One potential explanation is that those outside the NPT are also outside the international community. Iraq, Iran, Libya, and North Korea could all be described as dissatisfied with the international status quo. When their political elites "receive" normative transmissions regarding nuclear nonproliferation, these may backfire because the states actively oppose the status quo that created the NPT. As John M. Levine and E. Tory Higgins argue, "Majorities produce public compliance but not private acceptance in minorities. . . . Social influence only occurs if the source and targets are members of the same group and the source's position represents (is prototypical of) the group norm."[55] Their group of "similar others" may actually be working on nuclear programs as well (for example, recent news of Pakistani scientist A. Q. Khan's unauthorized assistance for the secret Iranian nuclear program). The major outlier to this explanation is Israel. It can be considered a supporter of the international community, but one can also argue that Israel receives support for its nuclear program through U.S. refusal to act against Israel because of it.

Explicit intergroup conflict certainly decreases the likelihood of influence regarding nuclear nonproliferation. For example, the official reason that North Korea gave for its withdrawal from the NPT was its inclusion in President Bush's "Axis of Evil." While this no doubt is largely posturing, it is clear that being called part of the Axis of Evil did not make North Korea more receptive to U.S. influence regarding nuclear forbearance.

This background generates expectations about how conditions might affect how political elites process norms created by the NPT framework:

UNCERTAINTY: The greater the perception of uncertainty regarding potential costs and benefits of nuclear weapons, the more likely policymakers are to be open to considering a change in their nuclear stance.

SIMILARITY: The more policymakers consider that similar or admired others would like that state to commit to forgoing nuclear weapons, the more likely they are to join the NPT.

CONFLICT: The greater the perception of conflict between a state and those attempting to influence it, the less likely the state is to give in to that influence.

With this background on the substance of the international social environment created by the nuclear nonproliferation regime, and the potential effects of that social environment, we turn next to case studies to see how nuclear forbearance came about.

CHAPTER THREE

Japanese Nuclear Decision-Making

Japan's continued non-nuclear status seems rather puzzling. With high levels of economic, scientific, and technological development, and a sophisticated nuclear energy program, including a plutonium-based fuel cycle, Japan certainly has the means to develop a nuclear weapons program. And bordered by nuclear-armed neighbors with which it has had armed conflicts, Japan also has the motive to acquire nuclear weapons. "Japan lives in a dangerous neighborhood," as one senior U.S. Japan expert notes, especially in light of the continuing North Korean nuclear crisis.[1] As noted in chapter 1, although one can argue that not seeking nuclear weapons may result from having had such weapons dropped on its territory, one can also argue that acquiring nuclear weapons and second-strike capability is the way to avoid recurrence of that tragedy.

Japan's non-nuclear status is not due to a lack of debate about it. Since the 1950s, Japanese leadership has considered the nuclear question several times. But for almost forty years, Japanese decision-makers have continued to forgo nuclear weapons and affirm the Nuclear Nonproliferation Treaty. The question for policymakers is *why*. To answer that question, this chapter first examines the social and security environments that undergird Japan's nuclear stance. Next, the chapter explores the four major periods of nuclear decision-making in Japan, before turning to how the international social environment influenced Japanese nuclear forbearance. Finally, findings are compared to the theoretical expectations presented in chapter 1 to see which the evidence supports and in what ways. The case study evidence leads to a conclusion that early on, a mix of realist and constructivist expectations best explains Japanese nuclear forbearance. During that time, many political elites wanted their own nuclear deterrent but chose not to pursue that option for two reasons. First, domestic political opponents, motivated by normative commitments and strengthened in part by the international norm against proliferation, would have made such a choice very costly and perhaps impossible for pronuclear elites. Thus, the "persuaded" segment of Japanese society forced the pronuclear politicians into a policy of social conformity. This was likely possible due to the second reason, the U.S. guarantee of extended deterrence, without which the conservatives might not have accepted Japan's non-nuclear status. As time passed, more of the political elite grew to accept the international and domestic norm against nuclear acquisition, leading to a larger percentage being "persuaded." In conjunction with this, the Japanese elite underwent profound changes in perspective on security and the best means of achieving it. Thus, even though Japan's security and material environment has changed for the worse in the past several years, the country remains firmly committed to cooperation, diplomacy, and a non-nuclear policy.

JAPANESE SOCIAL AND SECURITY ENVIRONMENT

In Japanese nuclear decision-making, the social and security environments loom large.[2] In terms of social environment, while many issues shape the nuclear debate in Japan, the following discussion highlights the three most important: the Japanese Peace Constitution, domestic antimilitarism and antinuclear sentiment, and the Three Non-Nuclear Principles. In terms of security environment, this chapter addresses three main issues: the lack of discussion in Japan of all security issues, the U.S.-Japan Security Treaty, and Japanese concern over the Chinese military threat.

Japanese Peace Constitution

The Japanese constitution is often referred to as the Peace Constitution, and Japanese often refer to their state as a Peace Nation, due to Article 9 of their constitution, which states: "Aspiring sincerely to an international peace based on justice and order, the Japanese people forever renounce war as a sovereign right of the nation and the threat or use of force as a means of settling international disputes. In order to accomplish the aim of the preceding paragraph, land, sea and air forces, as well as other war potential, will never be maintained. The right of the belligerency of the state will not be recognized."[3]

Over the past fifty years, Article 9 has become an integral part of Japanese identity.[4] Tetsuya Kataoka notes, "Article 9 is to the Japanese constitution what the right to life, liberty, and the pursuit of happiness is to the American constitution: more than mere written words on a piece of document, it has become the very essence of the Japanese regime or polity."[5] Various attempts to amend or rewrite Article 9 have met with public outcry and failed.[6] The Japanese government has maintained since the late 1950s that Article 9 does not prohibit the development of a nuclear weapons program, so long as it is only for deterrence purposes.[7] However, many outside the government argue that because an offensive use is inherent in deterrence, nuclear weapons are not permissible under Article 9.[8] One defense expert estimated that approximately one-third of the Japanese public believes that nuclear weapons are forbidden by the Japanese constitution.[9]

Domestic Antimilitarism and Antinuclear Sentiment

Closely connected to the Japanese identity as a Peace Nation are Japanese antimilitarism and antinuclear sentiment. Antimilitarism in Japan was cultivated by the United States during Occupation and found fertile ground based on the Japanese feeling of victimization.[10] Thomas Berger notes:

> The Japanese felt doubly victimized. First they felt victimized by the West, which they felt had cynically refused to respect Japan's right to defend its legitimate interests in Manchuria, and had threatened it with a crippling oil embargo. At the same time, the majority of Japanese also felt victimized by their own military for having dragged them into a war that rationally could only end in tragedy, and for conducting that war without regard for the suffering that was inflicted on the Japanese people. Consequently, the military was seen as innately inclined to take matters into its own hands, and hostile towards human rights and democracy. The profound Japanese distrust of its own military has consistently been reflected in the Japanese debate over defense and national security throughout the postwar era.[11]

As John Dower notes, rejection of the "old" militarism and enthusiastic acceptance of the "new" pacifism could be seen in post–World War II Japanese art, music, publications, and other popular media. His analysis of the Japanese "embrace" of defeat shows the extent to which the militarism of the previous period was resoundingly discarded and a new identity was created. "The two most familiar slogans of the early postwar period — 'Construct a Nation of Peace' (*Heiwa Kokka Kensetsu*) and 'Construct a Nation of Culture' (*Bunka Kokka Kensetsu*) — resurrected two key themes of wartime propaganda, construction and culture, and turned them into rallying cries for the creation of a nation resting on democratic, antimilitaristic principles."[12]

While antimilitarism flourished after the war, antinuclear sentiment surprisingly took longer to spring forth. Most Japanese were not immediately aware of the devastating effects of the atomic bombs dropped on Hiroshima and Nagasaki.[13] As knowledge spread, many Japanese feared the radiation damage suffered by the *hibakusha* (atomic bomb survivors), who were shunned rather than supported. In March 1954 the Lucky Dragon incident changed that.[14] Twenty-three crew members of *Daigo Fukuryu-Maru* (Lucky Dragon), a tuna boat, were fishing off the coast of Japan when the United States tested the Bravo hydrogen bomb at Bikini Atoll, eighty-five miles away. Within hours, the crew was covered in white ash, and when they returned home that night, all twenty-three were hospitalized due to severe illness. One crew member eventually died from radiation complications, and the Japanese destroyed tons of seafood out of fear of contamination.[15] A passionate antinuclear movement was born, generating sympathy even in conservative circles. Only one month later, both houses of the Japanese Diet "unanimously passed resolutions that called for the prohibition of nuclear weapons and international control of nuclear energy."[16] Tokyo housewives organized a signature collection campaign, and within a few months, over half of Japan's registered voters signed petitions demanding immediate prohibition of nuclear tests.[17] By August 1955 the world's first conference protesting nuclear weapons was held in Hiroshima.[18]

The incident, which was closely covered by the press, shook the Japanese public. A signature campaign against atomic and hydrogen bombs began, and the movement spread like wildfire throughout the country. In cities, farming and fishing villages, offices and factories, declarations were adopted against nuclear testing or nuclear weapons. The movement spread across the political spectrum with such traditionally conservative groups as town councils, young men's associations, and women's associations running the signature campaign, while labor unions and political parties participated as well. The signature campaign introduced many Japanese citizens to the voices of the victims of Hiroshima and Nagasaki who had already been calling for the abolition of nuclear bombs. The fear of the "ashes of death" aroused by the Bikini disaster and the anti-war feelings inspired by a new awareness of the terrible reality of Hiroshima and Nagasaki combined to generate a powerful movement against A- and H-bombs.[19]

The antimilitary and antinuclear sentiments have weakened somewhat but remain potent even today. Some younger Japanese declare they have no "nuclear allergy."[20] But a recent poll reported that only 7 percent of the Japanese public supports a nuclear option.[21] This is in part due to what one Japanese defense expert called "reproduced memories of Hiroshima and Nagasaki." Cartoons, comic books, movies, radio programs, and television shows have exposed generations of Japanese to the atomic devastation Japan experienced.[22] Peace education is a mandatory component in schools, and even the Ministry of Foreign Affairs spends money on antinuclear education programs.[23] As a result, the Japanese dread of nuclear weapons is deep-seated and long lasting. One prominent defense official, who received training in the United States and other Western countries, observed: "As a graduate student in the United States, I felt very uneasy when I tried to discuss topics like nuclear strategy objectively, leaving those moral judgments aside. I somehow do not like nuclear weapons. More instinctively, I hate them."[24] A number of Japanese defense analysts argue that it is almost impossible for non-Japanese to understand their perspective on nuclear weapons. One academic asked, "Is there any other country in the world where the definition of nuclear weapons is a political issue that is thoroughly debated in the Diet? Why would we do that? Because we do not want them in our country. For example, the Diet debated whether a wireless transmission can 'be' a nuclear weapon — if a transmission point in Japan could be part of a nuclear strike order, then does Japan have nuclear weapons?"[25] Overall, the effect is that "the first entry point of any conversation on nuclear weapons is Hiroshima and Nagasaki — not the role of weapons in terms of security or strategy, but the atomic devastation Japan suffered."[26] Japanese politicians avoid the "political hot potato" of nuclear weapons; those who do not are either forced to retract their statements or, in some cases, resign from office.

Three Non-Nuclear Principles

While Japanese government officials may argue that their constitution does not prohibit them from acquiring nuclear weapons, they do have to contend with an official policy known as the Three Non-Nuclear Principles (3NNP). These principles are not enshrined in law, but do not need to be, because they are enshrined in the Japanese psyche. Formally expressed in the injunction that Japan "will not manufacture or possess nuclear weapons or allow their introduction into this country," the 3NNP were a pledge from Prime Minister Eisaku Sato to the Japanese Diet in December 1967.[27] Sato had previously expressed his desire for the Japanese people to overcome their nuclear allergy and consider a nuclear weapons option. But in late 1967, he faced public demand to guarantee that if Japan continued to allow the United States to use the Okinawan bases after Okinawa's reversion to Japan, nuclear weapons would not be brought onto Japanese soil. Under pressure in a question and answer session, he impulsively declared the 3NNP to the Diet.[28] The principles immediately resonated with the public, to Sato's dismay.[29]

When he realized the extent to which the 3NNP were embraced, and the resulting implications for Japanese security policy, Sato tried to blunt the impact of the 3NNP by announcing, only a month later, the "Four Pillars" of Japan's non-nuclear policy.[30] The Four Pillars included the 3NNP, reliance on the U.S.-Japan Security Treaty and U.S. extended deterrence, nuclear disarmament, and peaceful use of nuclear energy. In other words, the 3NNP were downgraded — they were no longer the central theme of Japan's nuclear policy but only one of four parts. In addition, Sato implied that the 3NNP were contingent on Japan's protection under the U.S. nuclear umbrella. However, Sato's pronouncement only agitated antinuclear groups, which began calling for the 3NNP to be made law. In 1971 the Diet passed a resolution affirming the 3NNP and promoting them to the status of *kokuze* (irrevocable policy), but it fell short of making them law.[31] When Sato was awarded the Nobel Peace Prize in 1974 for his nuclear nonproliferation activities — including his establishment of the 3NNP — it gave the principles further weight and prestige.

Today the 3NNP still exert an enormous effect on Japan's nuclear policy. In June 2002 Chief Cabinet Secretary Yasuo Fukuda hinted that they could be modified, saying, "The [three non-nuclear] principles are just like the Constitution. But in the face of calls to amend the Constitution, the amendment of the principles is also likely."[32] A public uproar ensued, with opposition leaders calling for Fukuda's resignation. Prime Minister Junichiro Koizumi denied that his government planned to revise the 3NNP, and Fukuda issued a retraction and delivered a formal apology to the Diet.[33] Even after the North Korean nuclear tests in October 2006, the public remains strongly antinuclear; a *Yomiuri Shimbun* poll conducted in November 2006 revealed that 80 percent of the populace supported upholding the 3NNP, while only 18 percent believed they should be revised.[34]

Lack of Discussion of Security Issues

Japan's social-normative environment shapes — or, some would argue, squashes — debate on security issues, which in turn influences nuclear decision-making. Early on, any discussion of military matters was taboo for politicians. From the beginning, the Japan Socialist Party (JSP) and Japan Communist Party (JCP) wielded strong political force, and both opposed military build-up as well as the security relationship with the United States. In the 1960s the JSP held approximately one-third of Diet seats, so the ruling Liberal Democratic Party (LDP) had to take a soft line on security issues to avoid losing support. The fate of Prime Minister Nobuske Kishi, who sought to strengthen the U.S.-Japan Security Treaty and see it ratified by the Diet, illustrates the cost of making military issues a priority. According to one report,

> During the Diet session on ratification of the U.S.-Japan Security Treaty in May 1960, ardent anti-treaty movements caused political turmoil. Protesting citizens surrounded the Diet building, and 500 policemen had to forcibly remove opposition party Diet members from the Lower House so that the LDP could force through the vote. In June, more than 5 million workers participated in a strike to demonstrate their objections to the agreement. On top of that, these domestic upheavals forced President Dwight Eisenhower to cancel his visit to Japan, which was scheduled to commemorate a new era of U.S.-Japanese security relations. Kishi himself paid his political price by resigning the top cabinet post in July, leaving heavy frustrations and an increasing anti-militarist trend in the public.[35]

The opposition to Japanese participation in military-related ventures continues today. In the summer of 2007 Prime Minister Shinzo Abe argued for an extension of the terrorism special-measures law, to allow Japanese Self Defense Forces (SDF) to continue their refueling mission in the Indian Ocean to assist U.S.-led antiterrorism operations in Afghanistan. Controversial to begin with, the law has become more unpopular; both the major opposition party, the Democratic Party of Japan (DPJ), and the public have opposed its extension. The DPJ has instead proposed that Japanese SDF participate only in UN-sponsored humanitarian missions.[36]

The result of Japan's aversion to military issues of all types has been large-scale avoidance of any public discussion of security issues. For example, no major Japanese university offered a security studies program until 2003. Should Japanese students try to cobble together security classes, they soon realize that their prospects for employment after graduation are dim, and so they switch majors, usually to finance.[37] Not surprisingly, little or no public debate has taken place on Japan's nuclear posture, which for the past fifty years has been a sea of platitudes regarding the immorality of nuclear weapons, punctuated every so often with a call for discussion of the nuclear option, followed by retraction, resignation, or reinterpretation by the politician imprudent enough to issue such a call.[38]

The climate has changed somewhat in recent years: academics have begun discussing the issue of nuclear weapons more openly, but it is still largely a taboo subject for anyone connected with the government. For example, after the 2006 North Korean nuclear tests, both LDP Policy Chief Shoichi Nakagawa and Foreign Minister Taro Aso argued that Japan should consider the nuclear option. However, after outcries from the opposition, the public, and the nuclear power industry, both men said they believed Japan should uphold the 3NNP and that their intention was only to promote public discussion — not to advocate for an indigenous nuclear capability.[39] While this type of "reinterpretation" is not the same as resignation or retraction, the fact that the officials believed it was needed — even after North Korea's nuclear tests — speaks to the continued, though somewhat weakened, taboo on discussion of nuclear weapons.

Japanese experts lament this taboo because they believe it makes the Japanese non-nuclear position less credible to the outside world, which may find it hard to believe that the deeply ingrained nuclear allergy is enough to keep Japan from pursuing the nuclear option.[40] Kazumi Mizumoto argues that discussing the nuclear option would be more convincing, although at present it would need to be done by nongovernmental agents, since the topic is too controversial for the government to explore:

> The idea of holding self-evident a non-nuclear policy based on having been a victim of the atomic bomb does not go over very well in the rest of the world. Rather, putting forth the idea that Japan has adopted its non-nuclear strategy, rejecting theories of nuclear armaments after thorough consideration of the military logic, technical feasibility, economic impact, and political risk of the nuclear option, would be a more convincing, more easily accepted, explanation. The idea of the Japanese Government, or at least

the Defense Agency, taking it upon itself to study the nuclear option would, however, be susceptible to generating domestic misunderstandings. For this reason, a more desirable approach would be for research institutes to make these studies and publish the results, or for scientists and professionals to debate them in Track II conferences or symposia, in such a way as to avoid them being connected with the Government.[41]

U.S.-Japan Security Treaty

Another major factor critical to understanding the social and security environment is Japan's security relationship with the United States. After returning control of the Japanese government to Tokyo, the United States pledged to protect Japan through the Japan-U.S. Security Treaty. After the Chinese nuclear detonation in 1964, Japan sought further assurance from the United States and received it in the form of Article 8 of the U.S.-Japan Joint Communiqué of January 1965: "[President Johnson] reaffirmed the United States' determination to abide by its commitment under the treaty to defend Japan against any armed attack from the outside."[42] The phrase "any armed attack" assured the Japanese that the United States would come to their defense in the case of either conventional or nuclear threat. In addition, in 1970, President Richard Nixon articulated the U.S. commitment to retaliate with nuclear weapons against any attack (conventional or otherwise) on Japan: "The nuclear capability of our strategic theatre nuclear forces serves as a deterrent to full-scale Soviet attack on NATO Europe or Chinese attack on our Asian allies."[43]

In essence, the United States brought Japan under its nuclear umbrella and protected it by extending U.S. deterrence. For almost fifty years the security relationship has survived and even flourished. Llewelyn Hughes notes, "*The Defense of Japan*, a report that is prepared annually by the Japan Defense Agency and represents the official record of Japan's defense posture and the agency's assessment of Japan's strategic environment, continues to note simply that Japan's alliance with the United States is crucial to the defense of Japan."[44] In times of insecurity, the Japanese seek—and the Americans provide—reaffirmation of the U.S. commitment to Japanese defense. For example, after the North Korea nuclear tests in October 2006, U.S. secretary of state Condoleezza Rice traveled to Japan to reaffirm the U.S. commitment to protect Japan with all means necessary.[45] The security treaty has continued to be the basis not only for the U.S.-Japanese diplomatic relationship but also for

Japan's entire national defense. Because of Article 9, Japan's defensive forces are extremely limited, and attempts to expand them create domestic turmoil. As a consequence, the Japanese are quite dependent on the United States.

Concern about China

The final factor critical to Japan's security environment is Japanese concern about the China threat. Japan's first formal inquiry into whether to develop an independent nuclear deterrent resulted largely from the Chinese nuclear tests in 1964.[46] During the late 1960s the Japanese were not especially concerned about a direct attack from the Chinese but were disturbed about the possibility of nuclear blackmail by Chinese leadership and about the potential for long-range competition between the two countries.[47] As the Cold War continued, Japanese anxiety about the Chinese threat continued as well, although in the context of long-range Chinese extension of influence over Asia. Since the end of the Cold War Tokyo has become increasingly concerned about a more direct threat from Beijing. Indeed, Japan's long-term concern is not North Korea; it is China. With China's aggressive, nontransparent military build-up, the Japanese are concerned about their ability to balance the potential super-power.[48] Having the United States on the side of Japan lessens the concern. However, should Washington make a strategic decision to align with China, Japanese concern will spike. As one defense expert noted bluntly, one of the best ways for the United States to keep Japan from going nuclear is: "Don't abandon us for China."[49]

JAPAN'S NUCLEAR WEAPON DECISION-MAKING

Given the social and security context, how and in what ways did the Japanese elite make the decision to remain non-nuclear? As a sovereign nation, Japan could have reversed its non-nuclear policy at any time and begun a nuclear weapons program. Instead, the nuclear option was seriously considered but rejected four times: in the mid-1960s, due to the 1964 Chinese nuclear test; the mid-1970s, when Japan debated whether to ratify the NPT; in the mid-1990s, when Japan debated indefinite extension of the NPT; and in the current time frame, due to the North Korean nuclear crisis. Each of these debates is examined to understand the factors the Japanese considered in deciding to forgo nuclear weapons.

Responding to China, Mid-1960s

After China detonated its first nuclear bomb in 1964, the Japanese government ordered a secret study to assess the costs and benefits of a Japanese nuclear weapons program.[50] Commissioned by Sato's Cabinet Information Research Office, the study was performed by a group of four nongovernmental academics with expertise in international security and nuclear science.[51] The group issued reports in 1968 and 1970. The first dealt with technical and economic aspects of Japanese nuclearization, while the second examined political and strategic issues. The reports remained secret until November 1994, when the influential daily newspaper *Asahi Shimbun* received a leaked copy and exposed it in a front-page story.[52] While it is not known to what extent policymakers relied on the reports in their decision-making, it is likely that the reports summarize the major costs and benefits most informed Japanese considered at the time. In addition, because the government could not conduct its own studies on nuclearization due to public sensitivities, the reports were likely the most thorough analysis of the issues available to decision-makers and thus likely influenced policy.

The technical and economic report concluded that although it would be costly to develop a nuclear weapons program, Japan had the requisite scientific expertise and materials.[53] The second report addressed political and strategic costs and benefits of doing so, concluding that it was not the best option for Japan.[54] One of the authors later told a reporter that "technically, there were no impediments but politically it would not be wise."[55] After the Chinese nuclear detonation, the Japanese sought — and received — strengthened security commitments from the United States. Therefore, the report weighed the threat posed by the Chinese nuclear program against the security guarantees promised by the United States.

A Japanese nuclear program would harm the U.S.-Japan relationship without providing much security against a Chinese nuclear threat, given how vulnerable densely populated Japan was to a nuclear strike. In addition, a Japanese nuclear program would lead to deterioration of the security environment in the region, as well as likely diplomatic isolation. The report did acknowledge that an indigenous nuclear program would allow Japan to forgo dependence on the United States, which had defeated Japan militarily (through the use of atomic weapons, no less) less than two decades before. Japan would not have to rely on U.S. extended deterrence, the credibility of which some Japanese questioned. In addition, Japan would regain national pride by joining the nuclear "club." The report addressed these "benefits" by analyzing the case of France, where leaders questioned whether the United States would sacrifice New York to save Paris. The report authors concluded that while the French may have felt more pride because of their indigenous nuclear program, in effect it provided only a smaller nuclear umbrella under the U.S. nuclear umbrella; France did not gain "great power" status from its nuclear program. For these reasons, the potential benefits of a Japanese nuclear weapons program were not sufficiently sure or weighty to overcome its significant political costs. The report included in its assessment the impact of Japanese public opinion on a possible nuclear program, but the authors said they considered only "rational" factors and that conclusions were based on analysis, not sentiment.[56] Yuri Kase summed up the findings: "The authors felt, in conclusion, that Japan's security would best be attained through a multi-dimensional approach including political and economic efforts, and not through a traditional militaristic, power-based approach."[57]

The report reflected the debates taking place in Japanese political circles at the time. Prime Minister Sato told U.S. president Lyndon Johnson that "if the Chi-Coms have nuclear weapons, the Japanese should also have them."[58] When China developed its intercontinental ballistic missile (ICBM) capability, with which it could strike the United States, the credibility of U.S. extended deterrence came into question. Some argued that the United States was unlikely to defend Japan against a Chinese nuclear attack if such defense might result in mass U.S. casualties. Some advocated the deployment of an antiballistic missile defense; others argued for the development of robust second-strike capability. Kase reports:

> A member of the Japanese Upper House at the time, Shintaro Ishihara . . . defined the U.S. nuclear umbrella as a "broken umbrella," which covered only the United States and Canada. He believed that Japan would consequently suffer from "nuclear rain," as the U.S. nuclear umbrella had a "hole" just above Japanese territory. He concluded, therefore, that Japan had to develop its own multiple independently targetable re-entry vehicle (MIRV) nuclear missiles and nuclear-capable submarines, in order to deter any external threat.[59]

Others asserted that Japan needed to forsake the U.S. nuclear umbrella because it increased the likelihood of conflict, rather than reducing it. This argument, known as *makikomare ron*, anticipated military confrontation between the United States and China. Should such conflict break out, China would likely strike the U.S. bases on Japanese territory. In particular, some Japanese experts feared that once China achieved second-strike capability, it would launch an aggressive campaign to retake Taiwan, embroiling the United States (and by extension, Japan) in a potential nuclear conflict. Abandoning the U.S. nuclear umbrella was the only logical way to protect Japan.[60]

In addition, the emerging nuclear nonproliferation norm likely influenced the Japanese decision to remain non-nuclear. Hiroshima and Nagasaki had already become international focal points for antinuclear efforts.[61] Because the LDP faced a strong leftist opposition in the mid-1950s, the party sought to hijack the nuclear issue, both to strengthen its power base and to weaken its leftist opponents. "The LDP tried to steal the agenda by making the antinuclear platform more general — advocating the cessation of all atomic experiments and global nuclear disarmament. They wanted it to be seen as a gesture that Japan was doing something in the international arena for disarmament, to show Japan's unique presence in international affairs and thus gain domestic support."[62]

Thus the LDP short-circuited leftist criticism by embracing the emerging nonproliferation norm. At the time Japan also argued before the United Nations Eighteen Nation Committee on Disarmament (ENDC) that "nuclear weapons should be should be eliminated from the earth."[63] Besides linking their domestic antinuclear sentiment to the emerging international norm, Japanese politicians faced outside pressure to conform to that norm. The United States made a number of efforts to persuade the Japanese to join the NPT, one being an attempt to include wording in the 1967 Johnson-Sato Joint Communiqué to guarantee Japan's NPT signature.[64] Japanese decision-makers were aware of the international nuclear nonproliferation norm; indeed, Japan provided support for it, through both governmental and nongovernmental channels.

In the end, it is not surprising that the report urged a "multidimensional" path to security. The Yoshida doctrine — advocated a decade before by Prime Minister Yoshida — emphasized economic growth and increased quality of life, with national security handled by the United States under the auspices of the U.S.-Japan Security Treaty. By the time of the 1968 and 1970 reports, Japan's economy was already being hailed as a miracle. Taking the nuclear route would secure both Japanese independence and, after a number of years, military strength with second-strike capability. Economically and technically, Japan could achieve this. But doing so would entail rejecting the close relationship with the United States, engendering diplomatic isolation, and risking economic growth. Japan would risk being outside the emerging nuclear nonproliferation norm that it was helping to create. Going nuclear would also entail psychological unease, rejecting the role of economic engine and U.S. partner, and embracing a new role of independent military power. The strong domestic antinuclear sentiment only made the decision easier.

Committing to the NPT, Mid-1970s

In contrast to the nuclear soul-searching of the 1960s, which was brought on by fear of a nuclear aggressor (China), the nuclear debate of the 1970s was prompted by negotiations on the NPT. While the NPT was opened for signature in 1968 and entered into force in 1970, Japan did not sign it until 1970 and took until 1976 to ratify it. These delays created suspicions in the international community about Japan's nuclear intentions. If Japan were committed to the 3NNP, it was argued, why would its leaders stall in embracing the international norm against nuclear nonproliferation? The answer lies in the difficulty Japanese politicians had in creating a consensus for ratification in a divided society. The left (JSP and JCP) argued that the NPT did not go far enough and that by allowing the five nuclear weapons states to keep their nuclear arms, it perpetuated the power of nuclear weapons. The right (conservative elements of the LDP) refused to close off Japan's nuclear option, while the center (most of the LDP) was willing to accept this. Both the right and the center were disturbed by the treaty's potential infringement on Japan's ability to run an independent, peaceful nuclear energy program. Finally, all segments of the political spectrum were unhappy with the discriminatory nature of the regime, which preserved nuclear haves and have-nots, with no firm deadline on negotiation of total disarmament. According to one news report about the NPT ratification debate, "The country is clearly troubled by the second-class political status accorded its first-class economy."[65]

For the ruling party, negotiating acceptable compromises both domestically and internationally proved to be difficult and time consuming.[66] To appease the left, the centrist government assured them of the continued commitment to the 3NNP, specifically the principle stating that nuclear weapons would not be introduced onto Japanese soil. The left had always been suspicious of the prior consultation clause in the U.S.-Japan Security Treaty, in which this principle was open to negotiation via "prior consultation" between the U.S. and

Japanese governments in an emergency situation. Repeated statements from Prime Minister Takeo Miki helped win the support of the JSP. Also contributing to the JSP's final decision to support NPT ratification was the fear of provoking nationalist elements of the LDP. The JSP realized that if they protested the inequality of the NPT too much, they might incite the national pride of the right, who believed Japan should not accept a substandard nuclear position. Such provocation could strengthen the conservative elements of the LDP and ultimately lead to an undermining of the 3NNP. Therefore, the JSP agreed to support the NPT ratification.[67]

Convincing the right took more effort. The hard-liners within the LDP did not want to tie Japan's nuclear hands for twenty-five years, as the NPT would do.[68] The U.S. withdrawal from Vietnam further eroded conservative trust in U.S. extended deterrence. An article published in the influential Tokyo monthly *Bungei Shunju* argued, "After Vietnam, the Japanese can no longer go on living in their comfortable little Douglas MacArthur world."[69] According to an English report on the article, "The heart of [the author] Kase's argument is that Japan's total trust in U.S. security guarantees since 1950 has left it living in a dream world; the English commentary was titled 'Paradise Lost.' America, Kase says, demonstrated all too clearly in Vietnam that when the national interest requires it, Washington is perfectly capable of abandoning an ally. As a result, he says, 'We can trust the U.S. no longer. We need to consider our options — including the nuclear one.'"[70]

To address the concerns of those who doubted the credibility of U.S. security guarantees, Foreign Minister Miyazawa met with Secretary of State Henry Kissinger to seek further assurances.[71] In response the United States publicly reiterated its obligation to defend Japan, with nuclear weapons if needed, should Japan be attacked with either conventional or nuclear weapons.[72] In addition, the two countries instituted a new joint body, the U.S.-Japan Defense Cooperation Committee, to coordinate emergency security plans. One report noted: "The timing of the announcement had apparently been geared toward Miki's policy stand on the nuclear nonproliferation treaty. The creation of the defense cooperation committee, sources said, was seen as a way of mollifying those in Miki's party who objected to any weakening of Japan's defense posture."[73]

The issue of nuclear energy concerned not only the right wing but also the centrist government, which some argued was the main cause of the six-year delay in ratification:

It has been the government that refused to budge — largely because it was unhappy about the proposed international inspection arrangements, which, Japan noted, would not apply to all signatories, and especially not to the members of Euratom, whose arrangements for self-inspection antedated the treaty. In February 1975, it was agreed that Japan should be treated on the same basis as the members of Euratom by the International Atomic Energy Agency — meaning that it will be allowed partly to inspect itself.[74]

Even after Japan was given privileged treatment similar to that of Euratom, conservative elements still voiced concerns about Japan's ability to maintain an independent nuclear energy program. The government reminded them that if Japan remained outside the NPT, its ability to import enriched uranium and other nuclear-related materials would be severely limited.[75] Given their desire to reduce Japan's dependence on foreign oil (in 1970, almost 70 percent of Japan's energy came from imported oil), the conservatives finally acceded.[76]

Reassurances on the nonnegotiable nature of the 3NNP convinced the JSP to support NPT ratification; security guarantees and settlement of nuclear energy concerns convinced the right wing of the LDP. What convinced the centrist elements of the government, both the bureaucracy and the bulk of the LDP? For the most part, politicians and policymakers believed that refusing to ratify the NPT was unthinkable due to the rift it would cause with the United States. Japan's defense was secured through the U.S.-Japan Security Treaty, and the United States was by far Japan's closest ally. The Ministry of Foreign Affairs (MOFA) "repeatedly emphasized the importance of Japan's ratification of the NPT as a means for further increasing the U.S.'s trust of Japan: as Japan's ratification of the NPT touched upon the fundamental issue of the level of mutual trust between the U.S. and Japan, it was felt that any further hesitation in ratifying the NPT without a clear justification would damage the friendly U.S.-Japan bilateral relationship."[77] Officially, the Japanese government issued a statement declaring that by joining the NPT, Japan would further reinforce its role as a "Peace Nation," and its support of "Peace Diplomacy," and would increase international trust in Japan.[78] Once ratification took place, the nuclear issue was considered settled. More than one Japanese defense expert commented that following ratification of the NPT, Japan's debate about nuclear weapons never approached the same intensity as beforehand, simply because the Japanese had made a commitment, and they saw it as unlikely that they would break it.

Indefinite Extension and North Korea, Mid-1990s

Japan's nuclear deliberations in the mid-1990s were spurred by two events: the North Korean attempted withdrawal from the NPT in March 1993, and the 1995 push for an indefinite extension of the NPT. Japan's closest neighbor revealed that it was working on a nuclear weapons program, and the international community was asking Japan to forswear nuclear weapons indefinitely. It should come as no surprise that Japan reassessed its nuclear status. Worries about a potential North Korean nuclear weapons program began in the late 1980s, when North Korean officials refused to allow IAEA inspectors access to its Yongbyon nuclear plant. Concern spiked in March 1993, when Pyongyang announced it planned to withdraw from the NPT. In May 1993, Japan's anxiety increased further when North Korea tested Nodong-1 ballistic missiles in the Sea of Japan.

The result was a "revival of the nuclear weapons debate" among both politicians and bureaucrats, culminating in an official review by the Japan Defense Agency (JDA).[79] An official study was requested by senior military planners, "designed to reexamine Japanese grand strategy" and in particular Japan's nuclear policy.[80] Foreign and domestic observers began to ask whether Japan was considering a nuclear weapons program of its own to counter the North Korean efforts, especially following the G-7 summit in July 1993, held in Tokyo. The summit, expected to produce a strong G-7 endorsement of the NPT's indefinite extension, instead resulted in a weakened declaration due to Japanese opposition. One newspaper reported: "This was an apparent compromise between Japan, which asserted that a reduction of nuclear arms should come first and objected to a permanent extension of the treaty, and other G-7 nations which wanted the permanent extension."[81]

Editorials around the region speculated about whether Japan's position meant it wanted to keep a nuclear option open, and the South Korean ambassador to Japan urged that Tokyo explain why it thwarted the endorsement of indefinite extension.[82] The Japanese government responded by issuing statements denying that Japan was trying to preserve a nuclear option and claiming that "some political forces in Japan demand that the nuclear powers fulfill their obligations under the NPT before any indefinite extension."[83] Foreign Minister Kabun Muto acknowledged the government's trouble in gaining domestic consensus for indefinite extension but argued that Japan was prepared to support extension for a number of years, after which indefinite extension could be considered again. Some Japanese government officials privately complained about the U.S. demand for making the NPT permanent; one source said, "It's a little selfish that countries with nuclear arms call on non-nuclear nations to give up nuclear weapons forever."[84] In particular, some in MOFA believed that indefinite extension would mean that Article 6, which called for the nuclear weapons states to work toward disarmament, would become obsolete.[85] In addition, others in the government called for strengthened IAEA inspections and plutonium controls before indefinitely extending the NPT. Japanese politicians who opposed the indefinite extension because they wanted to preserve a nuclear option were a small minority, mostly in the right wing of the LDP.[86] The issue was abruptly resolved in September 1993, when a newly elected government declared its support for making the NPT permanent.[87]

The Japanese change of heart likely came about for a number of reasons. Negative domestic and international reaction to Japan's opposition to indefinite extension was stronger and more pronounced than expected. U.S. pressure influenced the decision, especially given the lead role the United States was playing in diffusing the nuclear crisis in North Korea. Finally, the North Korean crisis was being managed, with negotiations and diplomatic efforts involving the United States, South Korea, the IAEA, and the United Nations. The quick and global response to the North Korean situation reassured the Japanese and enabled them to mollify conservative elements of the LDP. However, while publicly the Japanese had settled the issue, internally questions lingered. As mentioned, in 1995 the Japan Defense Agency (JDA) conducted a review of a potential Japanese nuclear weapons program, benignly titled "A Report Concerning the Problems of the Proliferation of Weapons of Mass Destruction."[88] According to JDA sources, "the 31-page internal document was drawn up by three members of the Defense Agency internal bureaus, the Joint Staff Council and the National Institute for Defense Studies under the instruction of then vice minister of defense, Shigeru Hatakeyama."[89] The text of the report has not been released, but it apparently contained a plan for a potential nuclear weapons program, for a JDA spokesman told reporters that "the plan was scrapped due to fears it would violate the Nonproliferation Treaty, undermine the U.S. military presence in the region, and cause a backlash from Asian nations."[90] Japanese efforts to develop nuclear weapons would signal a loss of trust in the United States, which would hurt the diplomatic and political relationship, as well as potentially undermining the credibility of U.S. security guarantees. With a majority of states agreeing by consensus at the 1995

NPT Review Conference to extend the NPT indefinitely, the defense analysts feared that a Japanese decision to violate the treaty would both weaken the nonproliferation regime and cause a severe backlash over Japanese hypocrisy. One of the foremost Japanese experts on nuclear issues noted that part of the JDA reasoning in saying no to a nuclear weapons program was awareness that such a program "would deal a serious blow to the international nuclear non-proliferation regime."[91]

North Korea Redux, Current Period

Japan's latest round of nuclear introspection does not have a clear start date or a single occurrence that set it off. The North Korean nuclear crisis beginning in October 2002 clearly added fuel to the fire, but the Japanese were anxious before this. A combination of factors—North Korean aggressiveness, doubts about U.S. reliability, and confusion and unease about Japanese identity—ignited the latest questions about nuclear status. One of the most important events was the North Korean launch of the Taepodong missile over the Japa-nese mainland in August 1998, delivering a Sputnik-like shock to the Japa-nese: "The very fact that North Korea launched a missile that actually flew over the main island of Japan and splashed down into the Pacific Ocean was enough to send shivers up just about every Japanese spine. The possibility that North Korea, viewed by most Japanese as the most enigmatic and unpredict-able country in the region, had the capability to attack Japan with its ballistic missiles was horrifying."[92]

Months later, in March 1999, the Japanese Coast Guard (JCG) found and pursued North Korean spy ships that had intruded into Japan's territorial wa-ters. In December 2001 JCG chased a heavily armed North Korean spy ship that had violated Japan's territorial waters and, in returning hostile fire, ended up sinking it.[93] Hoping to improve relations with Pyongyang, the Japanese participated in the first Japan–North Korea summit in September 2002. In-stead, the North Koreans revealed that they had abducted Japanese citizens in the 1970s and 1980s, several of whom died at early ages in North Korea. The Japanese public was outraged and demanded a hard line from their govern-ment.[94] Thus when the North Korean nuclear crisis restarted in October 2002 (Pyongyang informed the U.S. government that it had been working on a secret uranium enrichment program), both the Japanese government and the citi-zenry felt cheated and disillusioned. North Korea's continued confrontational behavior — such as attempting to "ban" Japan from the talks to resolve the nuclear crisis and then declaring that Japan should be dealt with "with arms, not words" — has only further hardened the populace against their neighbor.[95]

On top of the aggressively bizarre North Korean behavior, Japan began to wonder about U.S. reliability. North Korea claimed that the test firing in August 1998 was not a ballistic missile but a satellite launch. The United States agreed, announcing that "what was initially suspected as a two-staged ballistic missile was more likely to have been a three-stage rocket carrying a very small satellite (contained in the nose cone), whose third stage failed to launch."[96] However, JDA analysts believed the data were inconclusive. The U.S. decision to interpret the event in the least threatening way provoked what some have called the "perception gap," in which the United States does not take certain security issues as seriously as Japan does. Because the missile or satellite was fired on the same day a key document of the Korean Peninsular Energy Development Organization (KEDO) was to be signed by representatives of all parties involved, some Japanese officials believe that the United States was more interested in preserving the non-nuclear arrangements than in reacting to a potential immediate threat to Japan. In response to the missile firing, Japan cut off both KEDO funds and food aid to North Korea. But one month later, U.S. secretary of state Madeline Albright put intense pressure on Japan to resume the KEDO funding. Reluctantly, Japan did so. Japanese critics argued that the United States had accepted North Korea's way of "doing business" and was too quick to neglect Japan's security concerns.[97] According to one newspaper report:

> The missile launching also served to renew doubts here about American guarantees of Japanese security. Japanese complained bitterly that Washington failed to share its reconnaissance intelligence and gave the country no warning of the North Korean launching. In response, Japan accelerated development of its own costly spy satellite program, and politicians began discussing the need for something beyond American guarantees to defend their country. "Simply put, we doubt the United States would sacrifice Los Angeles for Tokyo," said Taro Kono, a member of Parliament.[98]

Japan's plan for reconnaissance satellites drew criticism from the United States. A senior U.S. Defense Department official told the Japanese: "The 1960 U.S.-Japan Security Treaty, under which the U.S. provides its satellite-collected information to Japan, is sufficient for Japan's present and future security needs."[99] However, suspicions lingered that the United States did not provide "unadulterated information; rather they are manipulating the information in order to serve the U.S.'s national interests."[100]

Finally, many in the Japanese government grew concerned about the new U.S. emphasis on nuclear weapons, emphasized in the 2001 Nuclear Posture Review. Japanese policymakers, including some in MOFA, were worried about U.S. president George W. Bush's nuclear policy because of the greater dependence on nuclear weapons.[101] One defense expert said, "The Japanese government depends on debate within the United States. They hope the Bush policies don't go too far or any further."[102] Another argued, "American foreign policy increases confusion because its consistency has declined. It's clear they think nuclear weapons are a key linchpin of American military strategy."[103] Some criticized the Nuclear Posture Review outright, one saying: "If the U.S. emphasizes that nuclear weapons are important, it will have a negative effect on the NPT and serve as an incentive to other countries. If the U.S. crows about their nuclear weapons, other countries will also desire them."[104] American unilateralism in handling Iraq unnerved the Japanese, not only because of the war but also because they saw it as undermining the United Nations. "They fear it doesn't work anymore. The deep respect for the U.N. has been eroded because of the Iraq situation."[105] The Japanese have staked their security on the United States; if U.S. reliability erodes, more Japanese are likely to want to reassess their security options.

The third main issue provoking Japan's recent consideration of nuclear weapons development is confusion and unease about Japanese identity, about Japan's place in the world. Once the initial concerns about the reliability of the U.S.-Japan Security Treaty were answered in the 1950s, Japan had a well-defined role in the international system, at which it was very successful. The country's economic growth was the envy of the world, and Japan served as a valued partner in the American-led Western bloc during the Cold War. Its defense was secured by the United States, and security guarantees were seen as reliable due to the bipolar world that no one wanted to disrupt for fear of triggering a nuclear holocaust. One defense analyst noted, "After World War II, Japan defined international relations through economic relations and prosperity, under U.S. extended deterrence. Our most important goal was to keep the U.S. engagement in Asia Pacific."[106] When Japan's security was threatened (such as in the late 1970s, when the Soviet Union began a military build-up in the Far East, including ss-20 missiles), the Japanese elite responded by seeking even greater political intimacy with the United States.[107]

But the end of the Cold War began to erode the roles Japan was accustomed to playing. Its economy slowed down and sputtered to a halt. With the break-up of the Soviet Union, Japan was no longer a critical link in the West's Far East defense, and it began to feel eclipsed by a rising China.[108] The Gulf War also shook Japanese identity when Japan was not able to commit peacekeeping troops to the multinational un force in Iraq due to Article 9. Instead, their "checkbook diplomacy" — a $13 billion contribution — garnered ridicule instead of the respect anticipated.[109] Hence since the Gulf War, Japan has channeled its desire for a greater international role into a norm of international cooperation. One defense analyst noted: "Japan certainly found pride and dignity through their economy, at least until the 1990s. Since the 1990s and the Gulf War shock, we couldn't find dignity by clinging on to economic strength. So Japan has been putting more emphasis on diplomatic and international engagement."[110] Today the Japanese public feels frustrated about the economy and society. A security expert observed: "Japan used to be a very coherent society, but not so much anymore. Now many foreigners move in, the crime rate has gone up, and Japan has the highest suicide rate among developed countries — over thirty thousand commit suicide each year."[111] Anxiety built up about Japanese security, especially in light of North Korean behavior. All these social and economic and security frustrations have led a small minority to bring up the nuclear option as a "solution" for Japan's identity crisis.

North Korean aggression, doubts regarding U.S. reliability, and general unease with Japan's place in the world have combined to result in more militaristic stances from Japanese politicians, a number of whom have raised the possibility of a Japanese bomb. The most recent crop of comments started in 1999, when Shingo Nishimura, newly appointed vice-minister of jda, made a series of alarming statements to a popular magazine about Japanese nuclear armament. He argued, "A place that does not have nuclear weapons is endangered the most. Therefore, Japan must also arm itself with nuclear weapons, and this issue must be discussed at the Diet."[112] He compared a nuclear deterrent to the deterrent of punishment for rape, saying that just as men refrain from becoming rapists because punishment is a deterrent, so countries avoid provoking those with nuclear armaments.[113] The public outcry against Nishimura was so strong that he was forced to resign the next day, but the comments sparked a wave of suspicion throughout the region. Also in 1999, an advisor to the Japan Atomic Energy Commission raised the nuclear specter when he referred to Japan as a "virtual nuclear weapons state," due to its plutonium stockpile and nuclear technical expertise. The advisor apologized and said his comments were misinterpreted.[114] For a few years such comments stopped, but they resumed in April 2002. A prominent opposition politician, Ozawa Ichiro, revealed in a lecture that he had told a member of the Chinese Communist Party that Chinese military build-up was unacceptable. He said he told the visitor, "If you get too inflated, Japanese people will get hysterical. It would be easy for us to produce nuclear warheads. We can produce thousands of nuclear warheads overnight. We may have enough plutonium at nuclear power plants for 3,000 or 4,000 rounds." He added, "I told that person that if we rise to the occasion, we will never be beaten even in terms of military power."[115] Japanese news commentators connected Ozawa's comments to the growing insecurity in Japan:

> It would be easy to dismiss Ozawa's comments as the rantings of a sidelined opportunist trying to deal himself back into the game as Prime Minister Ju-nichiro Koizumi falters. But there's more to it than that. Ozawa's comments are evidence of a growing nuclear attraction. This results from an increasing sense of insecurity. China is a rising great power with an assertive, authori-tarian government. That makes Japan nervous. . . . Moreover, the Japanese know that although China still wants Japanese aid and investment, in the longer term it intends to exact revenge on all who preyed upon it when it was weak. Japan is at the top of that list.[116]

Ozawa was pressured to retract his remarks, but other public officials soon fol-lowed suit.[117] Less than a month later, Deputy Chief Cabinet Secretary Shinzo Abe told students that nuclear weapons and ICBMs do not violate the Japanese Peace Constitution.[118] When questioned about his aide's remarks, Chief Cabi-net Secretary Yasuo Fukuda said, "The [three non-nuclear] principles are just like the Constitution. But in the face of calls to amend the Constitution, the amendment of the principles is also likely."[119] He was also reported to have said, "If international tension is intensified, some citizens might even argue that Ja-pan should possess nuclear weapons."[120] The comments touched off waves of domestic and international criticism. Fukuda's remarks were originally attrib-uted to a "senior government official," but after China, South Korea, and Rus-sia filed official protests, Fukuda was named.[121] Both Abe and Fukuda issued apologies and retractions and reiterated the Japanese government's commitment to the 3NNP. Fukuda appeared before the Diet to express regret, while Abe held a personal interview with the leading newspaper *Asahi Shimbun* to explain the context of his comments.[122] Months after the comments, the Japanese media was still focusing on the remarks.[123]

In February 2003 JDA released a report to the media to notify the public of the 1995 study examining a potential nuclear weapons program.[124] The announcement was likely intended to remind North Korea that Tokyo occasionally reconsidered its nuclear stance. In August 2003 the president of Japan's National Defense Academy warned in a *Washington Post* editorial that if the United States negotiated a non-aggression pact with North Korea, "Tokyo could no longer rely on its alliance with Washington and thus might decide to develop its own retaliatory nuclear weapons."[125]

The concern escalated after the North Korean nuclear test in October 2006. In response, fears of a Japanese nuclear response spiked — especially when high-level LDP officials openly called for discussion of an indigenous nuclear option.[126] While Prime Minister Shinzo Abe responded to these calls by declaring Japan's commitment to the Three Non-Nuclear Principles, he refused to dismiss the officials and argued that in a democracy, he could not quash debate on the matter.[127] In addition, the Japanese government conducted a secret study about the possibility of going nuclear; the report was leaked to the press in late December. Titled "On the Possibility of Developing Nuclear Weapons Domestically," the report examined the technical feasibility of producing tactical nuclear weapons. Because of the multitude of technical problems, analysts estimated it would take at least three years and between 20 and 30 billion yen to create a small stockpile of tactical nuclear weapons.[128] Japan has not responded to the North Korean tests with a nuclear deterrent of its own, yet it is clear that the crisis sparked serious internal deliberations.

JAPAN'S NUCLEAR DECISION-MAKING: INFLUENCE OF THE INTERNATIONAL SOCIAL ENVIRONMENT

In chapter 2 I argued that the influence of the nuclear nonproliferation regime of state elites could be understood through the lens of social psychology: how norms are transmitted, how actors process norms, and conditions that affect the influence or potency of norms. Reviewing the details of the Japan case study through this framework does indeed give us greater insight into how and in what ways the international social environment created by the nuclear nonproliferation regime influenced Japanese decision-making.

Norm Transmission: Descriptive Norms

Descriptive norms describe the normative messages actors understand when observing the behavior of those around them. I have argued that descriptive norms influence elite decision-making: the greater the number of states publicly forgoing the nuclear option — or even surrendering it — the more likely it is that outlying states will do the same. Conversely, when NPT member states hedge or withdraw, it becomes more likely that other states will do the same. As we have seen, Japan signed the NPT early on (in 1970) but delayed ratification until 1976. Neither the signature nor the ratification decision seemed particularly influenced by the descriptive norm; that is, by the number and stature of countries that had already signed and ratified. In other words, evidence does not show that the Japanese were concerned about being an awkward outlier from the regime.[129] This was likely due to the fact that several dozen states had not yet acceded to the NPT; a year before Japan joined, only ninety-six states were members, and several prominent states were not — including China. However, the more recent weakening of the descriptive norm has influenced the debate in Japan. A number of events qualify as weakening the norm: India and Pakistan's nuclear tests in 1998 (and the mild international response), the U.S. refusal to ratify the CTBT and new emphasis on nuclear weapons as outlined in President Bush's Nuclear Posture Review, North Korea's withdrawal from the NPT in 2003, and recent struggles with Iran over IAEA inspections. As a high-ranking MOFA diplomat warned a former U.S ambassador, "Japan signed onto an NPT with five nuclear weapons states, not six, seven, or eight."[130] The Japanese elite is clearly disturbed by the high profile the Bush Administration has given nuclear weapons, arguing that the more Americans talk about nuclear weapons, the more desirable they will be to other states.[131]

Norm Transmission: Injunctive Norms

Injunctive norms are clear normative messages, typically delivered orally or in writing, proscribing or prescribing certain behavior, often with rewards and punishments attached. I argue that the more a state is admonished to forgo a nuclear weapons option, the more likely it is to do so. However, this is not the only or the most important cause-effect relationship that can be theorized regarding injunctive norms. In particular, the effect the NPT had in laying out a clear, injunctive normative message is important to note; the hypothesis might be stated as: "States were less likely to start a nuclear weapons program after the NPT entered into force than before."

For Japan, the creation of the NPT did influence nuclear decision-making. After the Chinese nuclear test in 1964, the Japanese elite considered whether to acquire a nuclear option. Officials knew that the United States was negotiating for a global nuclear arms control agreement and that a Japanese nuclear weapons program would not go over well.[132] In broader terms, the NPT certainly sent out a powerful injunctive message. "Before the NPT, a nuclear weapons program was an act of national pride. After the NPT, a nuclear weapons program was an act of international outlawry," one former U.S. ambassador noted.[133] Given that Japanese experts agreed that their international credibility would be damaged if they withdrew from the NPT, this perspective is more than just an American one.

Norm Transmission: Subjective Norms

Subjective norms are actor interpretations of the opinions of their reference group. That is, if North Korea believes China does not oppose a secret nuclear weapons program (despite Chinese rhetoric to the contrary), then that interpretation will likely influence North Korean nuclear decision-making. The concept of subjective norms is important because actors do not always believe or properly interpret descriptive and injunctive norms. In addition, when descriptive and injunctive norms collide, actors have to interpret what results. In the case of Japan, subjective norms did not seem to play a large or even minor role in periods of nuclear decision-making. Nevertheless, recent statements by the Bush Administration and Republican congress members have suggested that the United States would not object to, and might even prefer, a nuclear-armed Japan. So far the official Japanese response has been silence, but as one Japanese expert said, "The Bush Administration has been influential in making Japan unsure about the nuclear option."[134] As Katsuhisa Furukawa notes, "US arguments suggest to a small number of extremists in Japan that the acquisition of nuclear weapons could possibly be Japan's alternative national security policy."[135] Thus, U.S. statements may create the perception of a subjective norm that Japanese nuclear weapons are permissible.

Norm Processing: Linking

By what processes do norms go from being transmitted to being acted upon? Before actors decide to act based on a norm, they must first identify the norm as one worth considering. One of the ways this consideration is triggered is by linking, or the connection of the norm to well-established values. In Japan, linking has been raised to an art form by domestic NGOs in the peace movement. Since the Lucky Dragon incident in the mid-1950s, both grassroots activists and left-wing political parties have run well-organized campaigns linking the atomic bombings of Hiroshima and Nagasaki to Japan's nuclear decision-making. For the Japanese, before the NPT, the antinuclear norm was Japan-specific. After the NPT entered into force, the norm was enlarged to include international disarmament. "The majority of the public identifies with the non-nuclear norms, and these were created by the NPT; they were not in existence before the NPT, because those who tried to acquire nuclear weapons were not blamed or accused of being ethically bad. Now it's a totally different story," one Japanese government expert said.[136] The internationalization of the non-nuclear norm strengthened domestic antinuclear groups and gave them added legitimacy as well as additional platforms. A significant amount of money and energy is spent by these groups to link Japanese nuclear policy with the wartime experience of Hiroshima and Nagasaki. For example, the city of Hiroshima spends approximately 2 billion yen each year (approximately U.S. $18.4 million) on outreach and education efforts through its Peace Cultural Foundation, including a number of international initiatives: a new multidisciplinary set of courses on the effects of nuclear war held at universities around the world, special traveling museum exhibitions, and non-nuclear lobbying through the Conference of Mayors.[137]

An impact of these linking activities has been to create a taboo on the discussion of a nuclear option for Japan. Each year, the Japanese prime minister participates in the commemoration activities at Hiroshima and Nagasaki, declaring that Japan, as the only victim of atomic weapons, will continue to promote disarmament around the world. While such talk may be mere rhetoric, the effect has nevertheless been to constrain Japanese policymaker options. Prime Minister Sato lamented the fact that public opinion kept his government from pursuing the nuclear option.[138] Even after the North Korean nuclear tests in 2006, the effect continues. A senior defense expert who believed the nuclear allergy was weakening in Japan still concurred that raising the nuclear option is dangerous for politicians: "Pacifist public opinion is not organized, just very vague, just 'atmosphere.' But if politicians are regarded by the general public as hawkish on nuclear weapons, they could lose their seats."[139] Hughes's analysis leads him to conclude in a similar vein that "Japanese public opinion is likely to remain a significant constraint on policy change [on nuclearization] even in the absence of Japan's bilateral alliance with the United States."[140]

Beyond creating a general atmosphere that makes it difficult for politicians to raise the question of a nuclear option, the groups rally and protest when a politician does choose to raise it. Clearly, the NPT has allowed domestic groups to create links between the atomic bombing of Hiroshima and Nagasaki and the need to maintain Japan's non-nuclear posture. Thus, the NPT strengthened these groups by giving them an international platform with which they could lobby. Many of the groups have international connections, and some members have participated in antinuclear demonstrations in the United States; in return, people outside Japan have joined in local efforts to lobby the Japanese government to do more regarding nuclear nonproliferation.[141]

Norm Processing: Activation

At any given point in a decision-making process, numerous norms — even contradictory ones — could be applied. In nuclear decision-making, both the norm of self-help and the norm of nuclear nonproliferation are relevant. How do actors decide which norm or set of norms should guide their actions? Social psychology research suggests that norms that have been activated — that have been highlighted or made focal — have an edge. The problem with testing this concept in political science is that because so many norms can be relevant, and more than one can be activated at a time, it is hard to establish for sure that activation of any particular norm influenced policymakers. However, for Japan, activation of the nuclear nonproliferation norm — or a norm linked to it — did seem to happen in ways that suggest such activation was relevant to the decision-making process. Domestic activation of nuclear nonproliferation at critical points has clearly influenced debate on the issue. As already described, nuclear weapons are the political "third rail" in Japan — any politician who brings up the topic meets with a firestorm of domestic protest and ends up either retracting a statement or resigning. These protests clearly activate the nuclear nonproliferation norm, linked with Japan's Peace Constitution and unique experience as the only country to have suffered atomic bombings.

More recently, domestic groups are activating the NPT norm even more specifically. The Peace Depot, a small NGO based outside Tokyo, documented official Japanese pledges made during the 2000 NPT review conference. Then it published explicit reviews of Japanese government actions, measuring actions taken versus actions promised. The compilation was used to lobby the Japanese government and was disseminated widely to the media and peace groups, in hopes that other domestic NGOs would use the information as well. Within five years, moderate and progressive newspapers have run more than a hundred articles on Peace Depot, illustrating how the group's influence is magnified through media attention.[142] Without the NPT, this group's "activation" would not be possible, for there would be no NPT review conference with specific Japanese commitments for the group to document and monitor.[143] How effective is this "activation"? A conservative defense expert argued that these groups have the power to focus public attention and can sway the opinion of the general public.[144] Thus, he concluded, they did have an impact on the policy process, since Japanese politicians do not want to be branded as "pro-nuclear." A senior MOFA official argued that peace groups tie the hands of the government and limit the options that can reasonably be considered.[145] A former Japanese ambassador expressed the sentiment more bluntly, saying, "Those peace groups practically dictate our policies!"[146] This may be an overstatement, yet officials agreed that because of their ability to generate media coverage, peace groups can focus public attention on the non-nuclear norm and thus limit government policy choices.

Norm Processing: Consistency

Social psychology has found that the need to appear and to be consistent is a powerful motivator. This need is often engaged through making commitments; once they are made, people tend to behave in ways consistent with them. For Japan, the need to appear consistent did not seem to motivate the initial decision to sign the NPT. However, once the country signed the NPT, the nuclear option was largely closed. Cialdini argues that commitments "grow their own legs"; that is, people create other reasons to support commitments so that external inducements are no longer necessary. An analogous process happens in states, in terms of the creation and growth of disarmament bureaucracies with budgets and organizational power to redefine and reframe issues. Within Japan, that meant a disarmament division within MOFA, which exercised leadership internationally on the nuclear nonproliferation issue — for example, in the CTBT negotiations.[147] In fact, the disarmament division even spends money on nonproliferation education programs for school children in Japan; one could argue (cynically) that officials are attempting to ensure continued citizen support for division goals. Recent reforms led to elevation of the issue within MOFA: "the arms control and nonproliferation section was elevated to the divisional level, and within this division, arms control and nonproliferation functions were given prominence over nuclear energy compliance," reflecting "the prominence of multilateral arms control and nonproliferation within Japanese foreign policy."[148]

In addition to the consistency that the disarmament bureaucracy has brought, the Japanese elite feels tied to its record of active engagement in international nonproliferation issues.[149] A senior Japanese defense expert summarized the point: "If Japan took the nuclear option, we would lose all credibility in the international community. We would have to break our agreements with the NPT, the IAEA, and all of the associated bilateral agreements. Japan will not take the nuclear option, not only because of our domestic policy but also because of our commitments and our relationships with other countries."[150] A former Japanese ambassador argued that breaking these agreements is extremely unlikely: "We might be sanctioned by the IAEA and the United States. We would face severe international criticism and isolation. We would never try to do that, because it would lead us back to the 1930s, when Japan withdrew from the League of Nations."[151] Thus, while consistency did not seem to influence the initial decision to forgo nuclear weapons, it does seem to have reinforced that decision, with its influence growing over time. This is important to note because the decision to forgo nuclear weapons does not occur only once. As described, Japan has considered the nuclear option four times.

Norm Potency: Uncertainty

Regardless of how norms are transmitted and received, the conditions under which these processes take place also matter. Social psychology indicates that uncertainty increases norm "potency," the likelihood the norm will be accepted. Whether a task itself is unclear, or the results of a decision are hard to predict, the uncertainty generated makes actors more open to outside influence. A cost-benefit equation in flux—when costs and/or benefits seem to be rising or falling—would meet this definition. The NPT dramatically changed the cost-benefit equation for nuclear weapons acquisition. Certainty of the value of nuclear weapons was replaced by uncertainty over whether nuclear weapons were worth the new economic and social costs as well as uncertainty about whether they were needed, given the commitment of nuclear weapons states not to use such weapons against non-nuclear weapons states. For Japan, their first consideration of a nuclear weapons option—in the 1960s—was marked by uncertainty. Could Japan trust the United States to fulfill its security commitments? How would states in the region react to a Japanese nuclear weapons program, especially with the ongoing negotiations for the NPT? Could Japan secure prestige by developing a small nuclear weapons program similar to that of France? In the end the Japanese decided to forgo a nuclear weapons program because they could not be sure its benefits would outweigh its political costs.

Norm Potency: Similarity

When norm transmitters are similar to us, or are entities with which we desire a good relationship, we are more open to their normative influence. The similarity effect goes beyond the expectation of receiving something from a relationship; positive feelings about someone created by similarity or the desire to be similar to someone make a person more open to normative influence. In the case of Japan, it is likely that the similarity effect did make decision-makers more open to normative influence. However, teasing out the effect of similarity in these cases is somewhat difficult. For the Japanese, the postwar U.S. occupation and restructuring was much more positive than many expected. "After losing the war, the Japanese thought the Americans would eat them alive. That didn't happen."[152] As John Dower argues, American "gifts," from food to democracy, led to a warm acceptance of the occupiers. Popular cartoonist Kato Etsuro illustrated the sentiment:

> Like the hand of God reaching down from heaven, the United States, in another illustration, made a present to Japan of the "key to freedom" that unlocked restrictions on speech and expression. As if wielding giant scissors from the sky, America cut the chains that had bound ordinary Japanese and

granted them civil liberties. With the arms of a great deity, MacArthur's headquarters levered the crushing burden of the old *zaibatu* — the gigantic financial and industrial oligopolies that dominated the presurrender economy — off the backs of the exploited people. While Japan's leaders slept, the Americans — again, godlike hands extended from on high — provided food for the near-starving people.[153]

This positive view of and desire for a close relationship with the United States likely made Japan more open to the American normative messages to forgo nuclear weapons. However, at the same time, the Japanese were concerned that a nuclear weapons program would ruin the relationship, potentially causing the United States to renege on its security commitments to Japan. Sorting out the different weights of these motivations is difficult, but it is probable that the similarity effect did provide some motivation, even if security concerns provided some as well.

Norm Potency: Conflict

Polarizing conflict normally leads actors to reject normative influence from those outside their group membership, and especially those with whom they are in conflict. This proposition is difficult to test in the Japan case study. The United States was the main external source of normative pressure for Japan to forgo the nuclear option as well as to sign and ratify the NPT. Yet the relationship has not suffered from polarizing conflict to any great degree, and not during any major periods of nuclear decision-making. Domestically, little open conflict has taken place on the nuclear weapons issue, at least not since the 1950s. At the time the LDP was in conflict with antinuclear parties on the nuclear issue and suffered for this at the polls.[154] The LDP quickly learned its lesson, according to one Japanese security expert: "In late 1955, the LDP tried to take the nuclear issue for their political agenda to weaken the left — to steal the issue and advocate nuclear disarmament."[155] In this instance conflict led not to polarization but to convergence.

What was the overall effect of the international social environment created by the nuclear nonproliferation regime on Japan's nuclear decision-making? During the first major decision-making period — after the Chinese nuclear test in 1964 — the elite faced strong pressure from two dimensions: domestic antinuclear sentiment, and the U.S. desire for Japan to remain non-nuclear. With such strong pressure already in place, it is hard to argue that the emerging nuclear nonproliferation regime exerted a great deal of influence on the Japanese decision. Nonetheless, it is important to note that the emerging regime likely strengthened the domestic antinuclear NGOs by giving them an international platform and increased legitimacy. In addition, the Japanese government was involved in the regime negotiations, expressing support for it. With Japan's signature of the NPT in 1970, the international social environment became more influential. First, domestic groups used Japan's regime membership to link its atomic devastation to the powerful nonproliferation regime, and they became adept at activating the norm through protests, letter-writing campaigns, and publishing documents that called on the government to live up to its formal regime commitments. Second, once Japan began to tangle itself in the nuclear nonproliferation regime, backing out became harder because of bureaucratic pressures and the fear of losing international credibility. As a Japanese defense expert noted, reversing Japan's non-nuclear policy would require withdrawing from not only the NPT but also IAEA agreements and associated bilateral agreements.

JAPANESE NUCLEAR DECISION-MAKING: THEORETICAL ANALYSIS

What explains Japan's nuclear forbearance, a robust policy that has withstood both external testing—nuclear testing, nuclear-armed missiles, and nuclear-laced threats from its neighbors—and internal dissent, including more than one prime minister who lamented the Japanese nuclear allergy? On the surface, a plausible argument could be made for any of the three main theoretical perspectives: realism, neoliberal institutionalism, or constructivism. Because Japan's security concerns were met through the U.S.-Japan Security Treaty and U.S. extended deterrence, Japan had no need for nuclear weapons, and in fact an independent nuclear weapons program would have hurt the relationship most needed to secure Japan's defense, the U.S.-Japanese relationship. Or one could contend that the exorbitant costs associated with a nuclear weapons program, in contrast to the remarkable rewards of being able to focus on the economy and let the United States pay for defense, made the decision easy for Japanese policymakers. Finally, an argument could be made that the antinuclear sentiment unique to Japan has, over time, been so strongly reinforced by domestic events and international expectations that it is now central to Japanese identity and will not be easily overcome. All these propositions contain some truth, and none can stand alone. Nor must the explanations be mutually exclusive (although some would argue that the theories generating them are).

I contend that although security and economic factors were important to the Japanese on each of the four occasions when they considered the cost-benefit equation of nuclearization, in the long term, it is only because of the role they embraced that they conceptualized costs and benefits as they did, leading to decisions for continued nuclear forbearance. During the 1950s, the Japanese formed an identity around three concepts: an antinuclear Peace Nation due to Article 9 and Japan's unique experience, the spirit of international cooperation through the United Nations, and the Yoshida doctrine of the "trading state."[156] (It is important to note that the United States pressured Prime Minister Yoshida to invest more in defense after the Korean War broke out. Yoshida forcefully rejected the pressure, arguing that due to the war devastation, Japan could not afford both military build-up and economic development. He chose economic development.)[157] One international relations specialist commented that "this trinity was, and still is, very strong in Japan. It means that a state can maintain an important position in the international system without resorting to military means."[158] Given this identity, security was conceptualized in terms of "comprehensive security," which encompassed human and economic security but did not reject the role of the military, especially as related to the trading state, such as in sea-lane defense. This set of core ideas about what Japan was all about guided the conceptualization of costs and benefits in the debates about nuclear weapons options. To explore this further, the following sections examine each set of expectations against the case study evidence.

Realist Expectations

Realist expectations outlined in chapter 1 indicate that a state may forgo nuclear weapons for five potential reasons: lack of threat, lack of regional threat, presence of security guarantees, the possibility of weakened security, and achievement of an alternative means of deterrence. Expectations regarding lack of threat and lack of regional threat fail for Japan. Japan is surrounded by nuclear-armed neighbors; having defeated them all militarily within the past hundred years, Tokyo has cause to believe those states are less than friendly toward it. Actions by China, the Soviet Union, and North Korea have all prompted Japan to debate a nuclear option (although in the Soviet case with ss-20 missiles, concerns were settled quickly and are not included in the major periods of debate). The next realist expectation, proposing that a state might forgo nuclear weapons because they could make it a target, is also not confirmed by the Japan case. In each of the four decision periods, Japanese decision-makers did argue that nuclear weapons would weaken their security. However, this was not due to becoming a nuclear target (I found no record of this being a particular concern; U.S. bases in Japan meant the Japanese already accepted that they could be a target) but rather because a nuclear weapons program would disrupt regional and international relations. In this way, "comprehensive security" would be threatened and economic and diplomatic relations could be harmed. Another realist expectation — alternative means of defense — does not apply to Japan, since in the post–World War II era it has never sought biological or chemical weapons, and in fact Japan has used international fora to fight against their spread.

The most promising realist expectation is security guarantees, since the guarantees provided by the United States certainly played a major role in Japan's nuclear decision-making. To what extent? Three issues arise to answer this. First, the fact that the Japanese would accept a security guarantee from the nation that had just dropped atomic bombs on it is illustrative. Once Japan was able to formulate its own nuclear deterrent, it should have done so, according to the most basic tenet of realism, the self-help principle.[159] Indeed, this is what Prime Minister Sato desired to do, but he was thwarted by the public's enthusiastic embrace of his own 3NNP. The cost-benefit analysis of the 1968–70 reports shows that the Japanese believed they could have developed their own nuclear armament, but the political and economic costs were too high. The question becomes how high a cost is too high to secure a nation's defense, and especially to liberate it from those who defeated it just a few years prior? What the 1968–70 report meant was that the cost was too high given the Japanese prioritization of national goals. A nuclear deterrent could be obtained, at the cost of funds necessary for economic development and at the cost of important international relationships. As discussed earlier, some argued in the Diet that the U.S. nuclear umbrella was full of holes that could subject Japan to nuclear rain. The only sensible alternative, it was argued, was for Japan to develop its own second-strike capability. A realist may suggest that not all states will develop their own nuclear weapons, particularly weak states that can negotiate credible security guarantees from more powerful allies. However, it is hard to understand how Japan was weaker than France; as the 1968–70 reports indicated, the technical barriers were not insurmountable, and the cost could have been borne by the state if the political decision was made for nuclear weapons.

Second, numerous high-level policymakers, including prime ministers, have been less than satisfied with the U.S. security guarantee, arguing forcefully for an independent Japanese nuclear deterrent. This indicates that U.S. extended deterrence is not enough in itself to explain Japan's nuclear forbearance; earlier discussion documented the desire among numerous politicians for an independent nuclear force and their concern over U.S. lack of reliability in time of need. Hughes documents further concern from Prime Ministers Yoshida and Ikeda, among others. Kurt Campbell and Tsuyoshi Sunohara note that both past and present members of the LDP leadership have questioned whether U.S. extended deterrence is sufficient. For example, after the Chinese nuclear tests, a number of high-ranking officials felt that Japan should acquire its own nuclear capability *even with the continuation of U.S. security guarantees.*[160] Again in the late 1960s, the LDP secretary-general argued, "Liberal Democrats see the need to outgrow the 'nuclear allergy.'"[161] More recently, a Foreign Ministry official argued that the "United States would be highly unlikely to use its nuclear arms to defend Japan unless American forces in Japan were exposed to extreme danger."[162] Interviews with numerous high-level government bureaucrats and defense experts confirmed that most believed former Prime Minister Abe would prefer an independent nuclear deterrent, though such a preference would likely remain unexpressed due to concerns over public reaction. As a senior Ministry of Defense official said, "Abe probably does want nuclear weapons privately, but he would never express it."[163] If U.S. extended deterrence by itself explained Japan's nuclear forbearance, one would not expect generations of Japanese policymakers to be gnashing their teeth at the lack of a Japanese nuclear deterrent.

What kept these politicians from pursuing the nuclear weapons option they desired? Domestic public sentiment played a large role, and this points to a third issue with the relative importance of U.S. security guarantees. Without U.S. extended deterrence, would public sentiment have been enough to restrain policymakers? Arguing counterfactuals is difficult, but both logic and evidence seem to point to "no" — U.S. security guarantees did seem to be a necessary, though not sufficient, condition for Japan's non-nuclear posture. First, the majority of policymakers have genuinely accepted a transformed view of security and success for Japan. Could they have done so without credible U.S. security guarantees? Japan was able to focus on its role as a trading state precisely because the United States guaranteed its defense. Without U.S. extended deterrence, it is possible that the decades-old consensus for a peaceful, prosperous national identity could not have been formed or maintained. Second, for decades, Tokyo has sought reaffirmation of U.S. guarantees after major security crises, from the Chinese nuclear denotation in the mid-1960s to the North Korean tests in 2006. These reassurances, which the United States has continued to provide, serve two purposes: to satisfy moderate policymakers who want to focus on trade and diplomacy instead of military build-ups, and to placate right-wing politicians who prefer an independent Japanese military. Without explicit U.S. security guarantees, and their continued reaffirmation, Japanese vulnerability might have led many participating in the national consensus for peace and prosperity to rethink their positions. In addition, without these guarantees, right-wing politicians might have decided it was worth the severe political costs of pursuing a robust military, including nuclear weapons, in the face of what they would perceive as complete vulnerability. Finally, regional neighbors might have pursued a more aggressive approach to diplomacy with Japan if the country were left unprotected by U.S. extended deterrence, an outcome that could have shifted not only moderate but even leftist opinions on the need for an independent nuclear force. Thus, evidence points toward the conclusion that while U.S. security guarantees were not sufficient for Japanese nuclear forbearance, they were likely necessary.

Both the benefits and the limitations of realism are even more stark in the current period. After the North Korean nuclear tests, the Japanese sought and received confirmation of U.S. extended deterrence. Within the Ministry of Defense there has been a greater push for closer security cooperation with the United States — for example, for the creation of a joint U.S.-Japanese nuclear planning group so that Japan does not have to rely blindly on U.S. extended deterrence.[164] This indicates that, as realism would predict, Japan does indeed count on security guarantees from the United States. Nevertheless, prospects for closer nuclear cooperation, particularly an actual NATO-like nuclear planning group, are unclear. For example, at what point can Japan count on a counterattack from the United States? What level of attack is required for a U.S. response, and what type of U.S. response can Japan expect? This type of clarity is currently lacking, and while some Japanese policymakers and bureaucrats are unhappy about it, they are not pursuing the issue forcefully. Indeed, realists would likely not predict high-level efforts aimed at mitigating security concerns: instead of developing its own nuclear weapons or demanding clarification of U.S. commitments, Tokyo is focusing on regional integration and diplomacy.

> Perhaps even more importantly [than strengthening its alliance with the United States], Tokyo today aspires to enhance its diplomatic standing in the world in order to balance against China's rising influence. To do so, Japan is seeking a permanent seat on the UN Security Council and trying to foster regional integration and institutionalization in Asia, with the aim of shaping rather than reacting to the global and regional security environment. . . . Japan is currently embarking on a new major diplomatic initiative to build an "arc of freedom and prosperity" around the outer rim of the Eurasian continent through diplomacy that emphasizes values. Tokyo decision-makers regard Japan's international reputation as an asset the country has nurtured since the end of World War II. They regard it as too valuable to throw away simply for the sake of establishing its own nuclear deterrent against North Korea's nuclear weapons program.[165]

In other words, the Japanese elite values reputation, diplomacy, and leadership in international institutions above having its own nuclear deterrent. While this is possible due to U.S. extended deterrence, it also points to the need for explanations beyond traditional realism.

Neoliberal Institutionalist Expectations

Expectations generated by neoliberal institutionalism focus on how institutions can change states' cost-benefit calculations to discourage going nuclear but cannot change states' essential desire to have nuclear weapons. The first neoliberal expectation proposes that states forgo nuclearization to gain the material benefits offered by the NPT. In some ways, the Japan case seems to fit these predictions. With limited indigenous sources of energy and heavy dependence on imported oil, Japan sought to develop a nuclear energy program to provide greater energy independence. During debates about ratification, moderates reminded conservatives that unless Japan ratified the NPT, they would likely find the supply of enriched uranium and other nuclear-related materials severely restricted. In other words, hard-liners decided to forgo keeping the nuclear option open in exchange for easy access to fuel and supplies for the country's nuclear energy program. In addition, Japan has been working hard to develop a complete plutonium-based fuel cycle so that nuclear fuel imports would no longer be needed.

However, these arguments paint only a small part of the picture. When the discussions about NPT ratification and indefinite extension took place, both centrist and conservative elements of the government were concerned about Japan's ability to operate a nuclear energy program. The main issue was their wish to ensure that if Japan signed up with the NPT, it would not be overly restricted by IAEA limitations on nuclear energy programs. In other words, they wanted to join the NPT but feared that membership would hurt, not help, their nuclear energy program (as opposed to the predicted expectation that states would join only because of the assistance provided to nuclear energy programs). In addition, while LDP hard-liners were convinced to ratify the NPT because they wanted easy access to needed fuel and supplies, they represented only a small segment of the Japanese government. LDP moderates, the largest group, believed that NPT ratification was necessary to preserve the relationship with the United States. Finally, if Japan's officials agreed to ratify the NPT solely to maintain access to nuclear fuel until their own fuel cycle could be built, they would not likely be one of the major supporters of disarmament, even pushing the United States to do more for nonproliferation.

The next neoliberal expectation posits that states join and adhere to the NPT to escape the security dilemma. It is fair to say that most states joined the NPT at least in part because they recognized it as the best way to keep nuclear weapons from spreading. In addition, Japanese policymakers indicated in debate over both NPT ratification and indefinite extension that they did not want to undermine the NPT, in part because it could trigger an Asian arms race. An arms race would divert resources from economic development and would also disrupt the good relations needed for trading. However, the premise of this expectation is that a state agrees not to seek nuclear weapons because others also agree not to, and the state is satisfied with compliance and verification. Should a state question the reliability of others' compliance, it is not likely to continue to abide by the NPT while others may be secretly building nuclear weapons. Therefore, many states should have been ready to exit the NPT after the Gulf War, after the Libyans came forward with their nuclear program, after the North Korean nuclear test—because each incident made it clear that it is possible to develop a nuclear weapons program in secret. Movements to strengthen verification measures have been slow and halting.

Constructivist Expectations

In explaining why states choose to forgo the nuclear option, constructivism looks to the international social environment and the roles states play in it. The first constructivist expectation proposes that changes in the way the political elite thinks about state interests lead to nuclear forbearance. Here, persuasion (defined in chapter 1 as "transformation of state interests") works in two ways. First, a significant segment of the Japanese population, including many politicians and large portions of the Ministry of Foreign Affairs, has been persuaded specifically that nuclear weapons are morally wrong and thus can never be considered a legitimate political or military tool. Utilizing the media and well-organized peace groups, this "persuaded" segment has essentially shut down any serious discussion of a nuclear option, often by activating the international non-nuclear norm through protests, rallies, and letter-writing campaigns. As outlined earlier, government officials believe that peace group activities do limit government actions because of the public pressure they create. This meshes with the evidence; any politician who openly advocates a nuclear weapons program meets a harsh public outcry and is forced to retract or at least "reinterpret" the remarks; some have been forced to resign. Defense experts agree that nuclear weapons are the political "third rail" in Japanese politics, a topic to be handled carefully and best avoided if at all possible. According to a senior Japanese policymaker, "No politician dares to take this up! Antinuclear sentiment is so strong. Some may think it in their heart but would never express it."[166]

Second, an even larger portion — the great majority of politicians and citizens — has accepted transformed definitions of security, power, and prestige in today's international system. Elliot Walker argues:

Popular Japanese nuclear pacifism is as steadfast as ever. As of a year ago, 55 percent of polled Japanese even stated that the U.S. nuclear umbrella is unnecessary for Japan's defense. But opinions can change, can't they? Such must be the rationale for questioning Japan's non-nuclear policy. Japan's democratic system will keep in check any nuclear militarism — for now. But Japan's security environment is changing, and so is Japanese military policy. The dispatch of Japan's maritime Self Defense Forces abroad punctuated changes that have been going on for some 10 years, and have accelerated since 9/11. How should Japan deal with national security, post–Cold War and post-9/11? The question inevitably suggests that Japanese pacifism must undergo at least some changes, or else be at odds with Japan's national interests. Then, if pacifism can change, why not nuclear pacifism? There is a fundamental problem with this line of argument, however. What are Japan's national interests?[167]

Walker's question — *What are Japan's national interests?* — is at the heart of the matter. For Japanese decision-makers and the public, independence means economic independence and international engagement to maintain friendly relations. National interest does not include military might; in fact, MOFA often stresses that it is a "Peace Nation" that conducts nonmilitary diplomacy. One defense expert asked, "Given that the U.S. was paying for our defense, why wouldn't we take advantage of that and focus all our resources on our economy and improving our standard of living?"[168] Such a question illustrates the shift in Japanese thinking. A realist answer would be: "Because why in the world would you trust those who just defeated you with your very defense and security? You must secure your own borders because alliances are fleeting." Only a small minority of Japanese thinks in this way. Instead, most do not question that alliances can be trusted with the defense of their nation, and gladly focus on economic growth and international engagement, especially on nuclear disarmament issues. In both finances and policy one can see the emphasis that the Japanese government places on non-nuclear diplomacy. The Comprehensive Test Ban Treaty negotiations were funded in large part by the Japanese. Tokyo funds training for personnel from developing countries in arms control and nuclear nonproliferation.[169] In 2004 organizational changes to MOFA gave the arms control and nonproliferation division more prominence and more clout.[170] Subsequently, MOFA has boosted funds allocated to supporting the nonproliferation regime.[171] As noted earlier, MOFA funds peace education for Japanese school children. The priority placed on negotiations can likewise be seen in policy. After the North Korean nuclear tests, Japanese policymakers initiated not a nuclear weapons program but several programs designed to strengthen both regional integration and Japan's diplomatic standing. As already indicated, Tokyo decision-makers have nurtured Japan's international reputation as an asset too valuable to sacrifice for the sake of a nuclear deterrent against North Korea.[172]

The next constructivist expectation predicts that states forgo nuclear weapons not because they believe it is the best choice for their security but rather because of the cost-benefit calculations of the social costs and rewards. This outcome describes the right-wing politicians who favor an independent Japanese nuclear deterrent. As discussed, the impact of the nuclear allergy in Japan, reinforced by the international norm against proliferation, was likely significant in silencing the nuclear hopes of these politicians. After declaring that if the Chinese should have nuclear weapons, Japan should also have them, Prime Minister Sato explained why it was not possible for Japan to acquire a nuclear option immediately: "Japanese public opinion will not permit this at present, but I believe the public, especially the younger generation, can be 'educated.'"[173] Sato's hopes for "education" were not realized; the blunt impact of public opinion on Japanese nuclear policy has continued for decades, with any public official's statements that could be seen as pro-nuclear creating public outrage and demands for retractions. Even after the North Korean nuclear tests, conservative and liberal defense experts agreed that politicians who express pro-nuclear sentiments face a very real risk of losing their seat in the Diet. Current scholarly analyses agree that public opinion is a serious restraint on Japan's nuclear policy. Campbell and Sunohara argue that the depth of antinuclear sentiment among the Japanese public "is such that only major changes in the international or domestic environment, and probably only a combination of such changes, could engender a domestic political environment more permissive toward Japan's acquiring nuclear weapons."[174] Hughes takes the argument further, positing that even without the U.S. security guarantees, "Japanese public opinion is likely to remain a significant constraint on policy change."[175] Thus social conformity does likely explain the relative silence on the nuclear option, both in the Diet and in the bureaucracy.

Additionally, Japanese policymakers believe that even if they did wish to go nuclear, the diplomatic and social costs internationally would be very high. Several agreed with the sentiment expressed by a senior defense analyst that Japan would not take the nuclear option because it would compromise all credibility in the international community by breaking the NPT, IAEA, and other agreements. "Japan will not take the nuclear option, not only because of our domestic policy but also because of our commitments and our relationships with other countries."[176]

The final constructivist expectation proposes that states valuing a relationship with a high-status NPT proponent forgo nuclear weapons to maintain that relationship (the outcome of identification). The Japanese leadership gives much weight to the relationship with the United States, to the point of going along with expensive policies with which they do not agree, solely to preserve friendly relations.[177] Some may argue that the Japanese interest in maintaining a strong relationship is only to maintain the U.S.-Japan Security Treaty. Certainly U.S. extended deterrence plays a role in this, but especially in later years, it has become much more than a set of utilitarian calculations in which the Japanese determined the need to remain cordial. Instead, the Japanese seek what has been described as "political intimacy" with Americans. The Japanese response to Soviet ss-20 ballistic missiles being placed in the Far East was to strengthen the personal relationship between Prime Minister Nakasone and U.S. president Ronald Reagan and to embed themselves further into the "West." Prime Minister Nakasone argued that Japan and the United States shared an "inseparable destiny."[178] The affective component of the relationship is demonstrated by Japanese response to several perceived slights by U.S. president Bill Clinton. One analyst noted that when Japan received not a single mention during the ninety minutes of Clinton's State of the Union address, Tokyo's political district of Kasumigaseki "was devastated."[179] When Clinton failed to visit Japan on his way to meetings with the Chinese in August 1998, the media erupted with reports of the "Japan passing," noting that while the U.S. president did not have time to meet with Japanese leadership, he did manage a short holiday in Hawaii on his way home. Because Japan was mentioned twice in the Clinton 1999 State of the Union address, some Japanese expressed hope that this was the beginning of the end of the "Japan passing," even though one of the two references was negative.[180]

Interviews with Japanese experts confirmed that politicians and bureaucrats are extremely sensitive to U.S. treatment of Japan, and they often couched their language in affective terms. One Japanese journalist argued that the LDP should and probably could put more pressure on the United States on nuclear disarmament issues, but they do not because "they are very afraid of being disliked by the U.S. government; it would be very awkward for them."[181] Others described the tension in MOFA's disarmament and North American sections, because disarmament section officials know they need to promote nuclear disarmament but hesitate to push too hard for fear of American displeasure.[182] The North American section, meanwhile, "is a little nervous about MOFA's promotion of nuclear disarmament because it might hurt the relationship with the U.S."[183] One defense analyst with close connections to MOFA said, "We are very reactive to U.S. policy. The Japanese government is very, very sensitive to any policy changes, or even hints of policy changes, in the United States."[184] Another defense expert said the Japanese government is "always concerned

Table 4 Japanese Nuclear Decision-Making

EXPECTATION	OUTCOME/ANALYSIS
Realism	
Lack of threat	*Fails* (Japanese elite faced two nuclear neighbors with whom it has fought wars in recent years.)
Lack of regional threat	*Fails* (Japanese elite faced two nuclear neighbors with whom it has fought wars in recent years.)
Security guarantee	*Necessary but not sufficient* (Many Japanese elite wanted nuclear weapons despite U.S. extended deterrence, but it did allow the country to forgo a peace and prosperity consensus that ended up allowing most Japanese to trust the promises of their most recent conqueror.)
Nuclear weapons make state a target	*Fails* (This issue never came up in any of the four main periods of debate on the nuclear option.)
Alternative WMD provides deterrent	*Fails* (Japanese elite renounced all forms of WMD.)
Neoliberal Institutionalism	
NPT's material benefits	*Fails* (Japanese elite feared the NPT would hinder their civilian nuclear program by restricting their plutonium-based fuel cycle; they were so far advanced, they did not need the technological assistance.)
Escaping the security dilemma	*Fails* (Japanese elite hoped other states would abide by the NPT but recognized that not all states were members and states could withdraw at will. North Korea confirmed this.)

Table 4 Japanese Nuclear Decision-Making (*continued*)

EXPECTATION	OUTCOME / ANALYSIS
Constructivism	
Changed thinking about security (persuasion)	*Passes* (Japanese elite reconceptualized security along the lines of the Yoshida doctrine, rejecting the self-help principle and embracing economic and diplomatic strength. In addition, significant portions of society are persuaded specifically about the undesirability of nuclear weapons.)
Calculation of social costs and rewards (social conformity)	*Mixed* (Domestic social costs kept conservative Japanese elite from pursuing nuclear option, but without security guarantee, this many not have been enough to keep them from pursuing nuclear weapons. Today, Japanese elite do recognize international social costs—loss of legitimacy—that would come with abandoning nuclear nonproliferation regime.)
Desire to create or maintain important relationship (identification)	*Important but not sufficient* (Japanese elite value relationship with the United States above and beyond pure instrumental reasons. However, identification with one's recent conqueror requires additional explanation.)

about what U.S. leaders are thinking about; they are too timid as a result."[185] A government bureaucrat admitted that officials "do not want to annoy the U.S. too much" and therefore tone down their disarmament work.[186] This pervasive sense of dependence is not what one would expect if Japan were interested in maintaining relations with the United States for solely strategic reasons. However, it is consistent with what one would expect in identification. Indeed, Japanese identification with the United States has influenced its nuclear policy. In each of the four periods of debate about the nuclear option, including today, Japanese decision-makers have understood the consequences of going nuclear against the wishes of the United States, and in both the NPT ratification and indefinite extension debates, the centrist governments argued that any further hesitation in supporting the NPT would alienate the United States.

What does this analysis tell us about the reasons for Japan's nuclear forbearance? Early on, political elites clearly did want an independent nuclear deterrent despite the U.S. security guarantee, but they could not pursue this because of high domestic costs — especially the linking and activation efforts of peace groups. However, the security guarantee provided enough security to allow the majority of Japanese to settle into a "trading state" role with a focus on diplomacy, not the military. Over time, the vast majority of Japanese have accepted a redefinition of security — one that does not include nuclear weapons. As T. V. Paul notes, "Japan's rethinking of the value of nuclear weapons has resulted from its changed view of power and influence since its defeat in 1945. To some Japanese scholars, nuclear weapons have not elevated the power and prestige of second-tier states. Japanese views about power and prestige differ in some sense from those of the traditional realpolitik school."[187]

Despite recent events including the North Korean nuclear tests and threats, Japan is today still quite unlikely to develop nuclear weapons — and some argue that it would not do so even without U.S. extended deterrence. Although changes in the security and material position of Japan might seem likely to drive Tokyo from cooperation, forbearance continues because the Japanese are persuaded. Indeed, the 1995 JDA report on possible nuclearization asks whether its conclusion that Japan should refrain from nuclear weapons would still hold true if the alliance with the United States disintegrated and the nuclear nonproliferation regime collapsed. The answer was still yes, nuclear forbearance is still in the best interest of Japan.[188] Hughes concludes that even "a hollowing out of the U.S. nuclear deterrent is unlikely to automatically translate into the inclusion of a nuclear deterrent within Japan's force structure."[189]

Such judgments illustrate the depth to which Japan has accepted both the international norm against nuclear weapons and its changed view of prestige and status. As one defense expert noted, "Acquiring nuclear weapons would change Japan's identity. If pro-nuclear elements want to convince the people of Japan to accept nuclear weapons, they must come up with a compelling vision as to what kind of country this would be to live in. They must have an alternative paradigm for Japan's diplomacy."[190] Thus, while a combination of realist and normative factors provides the best explanation for Japan's early nuclear forbearance, the long-term transformation in thinking about goals a modern state should pursue is best understood as persuasion.

CHAPTER FOUR

Egyptian Nuclear Decision-Making

O f all the countries that might have developed nuclear weapons but instead refrained, Egypt is the most curious case. All "typical" signs point to an Egyptian bomb. Egypt fought and lost four wars with a nuclear-armed neighbor, Israel. Although Egypt and Israel signed a peace treaty in 1979, most describe it as a "cold peace," and Egypt spends much of its political capital in international fora criticizing its neighbor. Moreover, Israel is not Egypt's only nuclear concern. Its neighbor to the west, Libya, was known to have been working on a nuclear weapons program for decades. Two of Egypt's competitors for regional leadership — Iran and Iraq — had serious nuclear weapons programs. For many years, Egypt's political elite also faced internal pressure for nuclear weapons development. Public opinion supports an Egyptian nuclear bomb, as do the former government elite, some current members of the military, and parts of Egypt's nuclear establishment.[1] In addition, with smaller oil reserves than many of its Arab neighbors have, Egypt faced severe energy crises more than once, prompting calls for nuclear power reactors.[2] Despite all these factors, Egypt never acquired nuclear weapons capability and instead embraced the Nuclear Nonproliferation Treaty.[3]

To understand Egypt's counterintuitive choice, this chapter first examines the country's security and social environments, a grasp of which is essential to understanding its nuclear stance. Examined next are the main period in which Egyptian decision-makers considered the nuclear option, the shift to abandoning that option, and the gradual consolidation and strengthening of Egypt's support for the NPT. Then I discuss how the international social environment influenced Egyptian nuclear forbearance. Finally, findings are compared to the theoretical expectations presented in chapter 1 to see which the evidence supports, and in what ways. The evidence supports the conclusion that both realism and constructivism help us understand Egypt's nuclear forbearance better: an alternative form of WMD (chemical weapons) undercut the need for a nuclear weapons program, and Egypt's forbearance also derived from changes in the way the elite thought about security and calculated social costs and benefits associated with going nuclear.

EGYPTIAN SECURITY AND SOCIAL ENVIRONMENTS

Before investigating Egypt's nuclear decision-making, an explanation of the Egypt-specific security and social environments influencing elite perceptions is in order. As with the Japan case study, this examination of relevant security and social factors helps us understand the landscape of nuclear decision-making.[4] In contrast to the Japanese case, in which all discussion of nuclear issues begins with Hiroshima and Nagasaki, the Egyptian perspective on nuclear weapons is defined by the opaque nuclear posture of Israel. Discussion of the Egyptian security environment is focused on two issues: Egypt's past wars with Israel, and Egypt's initiatives for peace with Israel and their implications. This section is not meant to be a comprehensive account of Egyptian-Israeli relations but rather gives an overview of the hot wars and cold peace between the two countries. Egypt's social environment also exerted influence on its nuclear decision-making. In particular, the chapter examines two closely related aspects of the social environment: the Egyptians' belief in their nation's leadership of the Arab world, and the Egyptian embrace of the United Nations and international law, particularly as related to the nuclear nonproliferation regime.

Israeli-Egyptian Conflicts

Between 1948 and 1973, Egypt and Israel fought against each other in four wars, all of which Egypt lost militarily. The first occurred as a result of the declaration of the state of Israel on May 14, 1948. The next day a combined Arab force (made up of Egyptian, Syrian, Jordanian, Lebanese, and Iraqi military personnel) attacked Israeli forces. The Arab armies fared poorly, and after several months of fighting, Israel had defeated the invasion and held not only the land given to it in the UN partition of 1947 but additional land as well.[5] The second major conflict, known as the Suez War, involved an invasion by Israeli, French, and British forces in response to Egyptian president Gamal Abdel Nasser's nationalization of the Suez Canal and blockade of all Israeli ships in July 1956. In an emergency session of the UN General Assembly, both the United States and the Soviet Union demanded withdrawal of the Anglo-

French-Israeli troops from Egypt.[6] While the Egyptians lost on the battlefield, Nasser saw the event as a tremendous political victory.[7] He was able to keep the Suez Canal nationalized, and Israeli forces withdrew to be replaced by a special UN peace force.

Trouble continued to brew, however, and by 1967, Nasser refused to allow Israeli ships to pass through the Gulf of Aqaba. Since Israel had withdrawn from the Sinai only because of explicit promises by the Western powers that Israeli ships would not be blockaded again, the Israeli leadership reminded the United States, Britain, and France of their assurances, to no avail. With no help forthcoming, Israel launched what is now known as the Six Day War in June 1967. In six short days, Israel attacked and defeated the forces of Egypt, Syria, and Jordan, resulting in Israeli occupation of the Sinai, the Gaza Strip, the whole West Bank of Jordan, the entire city of Jerusalem, and the Golan Heights. Territory under Israeli control had tripled, at a cost of 15,000 Arab fatalities and only 676 Israeli fatalities. The fourth and last major conflict involving Egypt and Israel took place in 1973 and is known as the Yom Kippur War or the Ramadan War. Egyptian and Syrian forces launched surprise attacks on Israeli-controlled territories. It took a full week for Israel to stem the Arab onslaught, which fractured the image of Israeli invincibility. Israel eventually rolled back the Arab armies and was well on its way to defeating them when the superpowers intervened to force a cease-fire. While Egypt had lost on the battlefield, its president, Anwar Sadat, certainly won politically. He had turned the Israeli occupation of the Sinai into an international concern as well as winning back Arab honor with the Egyptian military's strong performance in the first several days of the war.

Israeli-Egyptian Peace

By the end of the 1973 war, Sadat had realized that Israel was not going to disappear and likely would not be defeated militarily. Under Soviet and U.S. pressure he agreed to meet with the Israelis at a Geneva peace conference in December 1973. With the help of U.S. secretary of state Henry Kissinger's "shuttle diplomacy," the Egyptian-Israeli rapprochement began. The peace process took a giant leap forward when Sadat visited Jerusalem and addressed the Israeli Knesset in 1977. Although neither Sadat nor Israeli prime minister Menachem Begin "made any substantive concessions during that first face-to-face encounter in Jerusalem, both leaders made a solemn pledge never again to go to war with each other. The Sadat mission was widely heralded as a major turning point in the 30-year-old conflict between Arab and Jew."[8] The two nations met at the historic Camp David summit in September 1978, when the two leaders signed both the "Framework for Peace between Egypt and Israel" (which promised an Israeli withdrawal from the Sinai) and the "Framework for Peace in the Middle East," which dealt with the larger Arab-Israeli issues, including the Palestinians. The Egypt-Israeli peace treaty was signed in 1979.

Around the globe Sadat was lauded as a strategic visionary, but in his own country and in the Arab world, he was seen as a traitor. Iraq led a drive against Egypt in the Arab League, which expelled Egypt in 1979 and did not readmit it until a decade later. Sadat was assassinated by a Muslim extremist from his own country. Hosni Mubarak replaced Sadat as Egypt's president, and while he maintained the agreements Sadat had made, he did not pursue peace as vigorously as Sadat did. Relations between Israel and Egypt cooled with the transition to Mubarak, a situation that persists to the present.

Egyptian Perspectives on Arab Leadership

A sense of history and conviction in their regional leadership color the Egyptian perspective on recent developments. These closely linked aspects of the Egyptian identity were brought up a number of times by both Egyptian and non-Egyptian diplomats. As one of the oldest of civilizations, Egypt "views itself as the strongest country in the Arab world, enjoying a clear national identity forged over millennia of rich history."[9] One prominent Egyptian diplomat said, "Egyptians have a psyche and sense of security that is so strong, almost to a fault, which leads them always to look to the long term. Others in the region with short, troubled histories look to the short term."[10]

Under Nasser the drive for regional leadership manifested itself in a form of Pan-Arabism, in which Egypt sought to lead the Arab countries down a "radical-nationalist" road and throw off remaining Western domination.[11] The Suez War in 1956 made Nasser a hero in the Arab world, for he not only nationalized the Suez Canal but also successfully stood up against Britain, France, and Israel. The merger of Egypt and Syria in 1958 to form the United Arab Republic (with Nasser at its head) was a personal triumph for Nasser; Syria's pullout from the union in 1961 was just as much a personal embarrassment for him. Egypt's costly participation in the Yemeni civil war, which depleted both Egypt's military and its treasury, was largely a manifestation of Nasser's desire to see his vision of Pan-Arabism win out: "And as Nasser attempted to export his vision of politics to other parts of the Arab World, he was confronted by conservative Arab states, notably Jordan and Saudi Arabia, who did not share his conception of Arab politics. The most violent manifestation of this clash of ideologies was the Yemen War from 1962 to 1967, with Nasser sponsoring the Royalists against the Saudi-backed Monarchists."[12]

Egypt's humbling loss in the 1967 Six Day War, and the resulting Israeli occupation of the Sinai, dulled Nasser's quest for Pan-Arab leadership as he focused on regaining Egypt's lost territory and pride. After Nasser's death, Sadat also sought to exert Egyptian leadership, but in a very different way. Whereas Nasser appealed to the masses with his Pan-Arabism, Sadat focused on an "Egyptian" Egypt that would lead the region by taking bold steps for peace and prosperity.[13] In fact, Egypt lost all standing in the Arab world after signing the Camp David accords, but after being accepted back in to the fold in the late 1980s, Egypt again quickly sought to dominate regional agendas, this time largely through using international diplomacy.

Egyptian Embrace of International Laws and Regimes

A related aspect of the Egyptian social environment is Egypt's strong attachment to the United Nations (UN) and international law, especially as related to the nuclear nonproliferation regime. This attachment likely springs from the Egyptian perspective that such engagement is a way to show regional leadership as well as from the success Egypt experienced in influencing the nonproliferation regime. When the first stirrings of a global effort to control nuclear proliferation were occurring, Egypt was there.[14] "We had a very active role from the beginning. Egypt was a member of the eighteen-member Committee on Disarmament — in 1961, Egypt was a member of this committee, but China wasn't," one Egyptian expert said. "Then, in 1965, a ten-nation committee under the Disarmament Committee created the NPT. Egypt was an active participant in this group, and in fact proposed articles for the NPT."[15] A senior Egyptian diplomat said, "We did a lot of work in the UN. To deal with the conflict in the region, we needed a new art, and therefore put a lot of imagination into how to make the region free of all WMD with verification and compliance."[16] Indeed, to show its goodwill, Egypt signed the NPT the very first day it opened for signature.[17] Egypt was absolutely essential to bringing the rest of Arab states into the NPT, according to an Arab League official: "Egypt has always been the leading state. They have the greatest expertise on the topic of nuclear nonproliferation, not just in the region but also internationally."[18]

Egypt's active participation in international regimes is not limited to the NPT; indeed, Egypt is known for its engagement and leadership in the UN. One U.S. official heavily involved in the Middle East peace process noted: "Back in the 1960s, the [Egyptian] diplomatic side was cutting its teeth, learning how to use the UN to gain leadership in the Arab world. The Foreign Ministry took the lead in such things as issuing international proclamations, which were and still are a source of pride for Egyptians. Egypt likes to be involved in every decision possible in the UN."[19]

Most significant is the fact that Egypt's international diplomacy is a source of both pride and regime legitimacy.[20] A U.S. expert noted "a great sense of pride in Egyptian diplomacy and leading the way, moving nuclear nonproliferation forward themselves and providing leadership to the Arab world. They are proud not to be a pariah state, to instead be pushing a positive agenda. Egypt is still very keen to play a leadership role and to be seen as a 'good guy.'"[21] When Egypt was readmitted to the Arab League in 1990, it was quick to reassert its diplomatic leadership:

> The peace process began in earnest in October 1991 in Madrid with Egypt resuming its desired central role. Egyptian political commentator Salama Ahmed Salama has echoed Cairo's views on its pivotal position in the peace process by stating "no one can deny Egypt its historical regional role, particularly after the machine guns fall silent and negotiations are concluded." Other Egyptian commentators have argued that Egypt "is one of the few countries whose foreign role surpasses its human and material potential" and as an example of this, have cited that since 1990, "Egypt has shouldered the responsibility of sponsoring the peace process."[22]

Egypt's role in the nuclear nonproliferation regime is especially important given that Egypt relinquished its nuclear option. Instead of seeking the glory of the Arab bomb, Egypt sought the glory of leading the nuclear nonproliferation effort in the Middle East. A U.S. diplomat said: "Some say that states pursue nuclear weapons for the glitter factor. For Egypt, the glitter factor was transferred over to using the UN and taking a leadership role diplomatically, especially with regard to the nuclear nonproliferation issue."[23]

The power and competence Egypt has shown in the United Nations is seen as a source of leverage and credibility not only by the government elite but also by the public at large, enhancing regime legitimacy. A former Egyptian military officer said, "Egypt's leadership role in the Middle East is of real interest, even to the public. It's as important to them as economic development."[24] Some believe that Egypt's activist stance on nuclear nonproliferation is part of a calculated attempt to improve Mubarak's standing both regionally and domestically:

> Leading the charge on the nuclear issue may have been an attempt to restore Egypt's leadership in the Arab world by making it appear as the guardian of the Arab states' security interests. Egypt's tough position also made Cairo a central address for appeals for indefinite extension of the NPT. Thus, Egypt's militant position may have been intended to compensate for its domestic troubles and diminished standing in regional affairs. This became increasingly apparent as the NPT campaign evolved; Egypt's position evoked strong nationalist sentiments, increasing domestic support for the Mubarak government.[25]

More recently, Egypt has shown extreme rigidity on nuclear nonproliferation, particularly in the Working Group on Arms Control and Regional Security (1992–96), as well as in both the 1995 and 2005 NPT Extension and Review conferences. Some point to the fact that Egypt felt its regional leadership role was threatened by the thaw in Arab-Israeli relations, which "would make less relevant Egypt's position as the key Arab interlocutor with Israel."[26]

EGYPTIAN NUCLEAR WEAPONS DECISION-MAKING

Given the social and security context, how did the Egyptian elite make the decision to remain non-nuclear? While Egyptian officials could have decided to reassess their nuclear weapons policy at any time, instead, they seem to have considered a nuclear program only in the 1960s, shutting that door entirely in the early 1970s. Understanding the influences on Egypt's nuclear decision-making process requires review of the major periods in that process: 1954–59, when Egypt was interested in nuclear energy but not weapons; 1960–67, the main period when Egypt pursued a nuclear weapons option; 1967–73, when the nuclear program was stalled but not yet dead; and 1974 to the present, when Egypt embraced the NPT regime and energetically participated in it to force Israeli movement on the nuclear issue.

Details of Egypt's nuclear deliberations are less well documented than for Japan, for a number of reasons. First, Japan considered a nuclear option a number of times, some quite recently, whereas Egypt's main contemplation took place decades ago, making information harder to access. Second, Japan conducted formal studies with paper trails, and in some cases defense officials gave details to the media. Egypt, on the other hand, never conducted any formal cost-benefit analyses and never had a detailed written plan for its nuclear weapons option.[27] The following timeline for the Egyptian program was developed through independent interviews with a number of senior officials (scientific, military, and diplomatic) who either were involved with the nuclear program in the 1960s or were very close to those who were. In most cases senior officials independently gave complementary or overlapping details on the main issues related to the nuclear weapons program.

Entering the Nuclear Age, 1954–1959

The Egyptian nuclear program began in 1954, just two years after the overthrow of King Farouk and in the same year Nasser took power as president. Nasser had a strong interest in developing Egypt's technological capabilities, and at the same time nuclear science was being promoted internationally. "In the 1950s, after the establishment of the IAEA and Eisenhower's Atoms for Peace, many developing countries began talking about the peaceful uses of nuclear power. It was like joining the scientific elite, and countries thought, 'Why don't we jump in?' Whether they needed it or not, they just wanted to get on board," one senior science bureaucrat said. "That's why Egypt did it."[28] In particular, an invitation to the UN Conference on the Peaceful Uses of Atomic Energy in 1955 spurred the Egyptians on. "We received the invitation in late 1954, so we started the Atomic Energy Establishment (AEE) to prep for the conference in Geneva," said another high-level science bureaucrat. "The secretary-general of the Council of Ministers, Professor Ibrahim Hilmy Abdel Rahman, led the effort—he was a scientist but also a politician. He wrote a memo to establish the AEE, and then put together the delegation to the Geneva conference."[29] Concerned to ensure that Egypt developed its scientific expertise, Nasser backed the efforts, saying, "We missed out in the steam age, and also in the electricity age, but we ought not to allow ourselves under any circumstances to be left behind in the atomic age."[30]

While the potential for military applications of nuclear power was not explicitly ruled out, several Egyptian officials agreed that military purposes were not the main force behind the creation of the AEE. "The establishment of the

AEE was not associated with any Israeli activity. We wanted to get on board with the new trend, nuclear power," one senior science bureaucrat said.[31] In addition, Nasser was fascinated with the potential for medical uses. "A favorite lady singer in Egypt developed thyroid problems, and she went to the Walter Reed hospital in the United States to be treated with radiation therapy. After she came back, she told Nasser, and he was very impressed."[32] A senior science bureaucrat reported that he spoke with Rahman a number of times, and when he asked about the military applications being planned in the early years, Rahman told him none were planned. "He said at that time there were no nuclear activities with military significance."[33] Another former high-level official concurred. "At that point there was no differentiation between peaceful and nonpeaceful uses — we just wanted to acquire the capacity. Our main goals were for electricity generation, desalination of water, medical uses, and generally learning the technology. While some scientists may have considered the nonpeaceful applications, it was not Egyptian policy."[34] Reports from the founding of the AEE confirm that nuclear weapons were not a top priority at the time:

> The AEE's governing council had five members, with Rahman serving as its Secretary General. One of the five members was an army officer; a second was an intelligence officer. When the program was just getting under way, Rahman asked these two board members whether the nuclear program should be set up to pursue weapons or for peaceful uses. Rahman's inquiry moved up the chain of command. He was later told that, for the time being, the focus should be on peaceful applications, but that the program should be organized in a way that would preserve a military option.[35]

One Egyptian expert on the topic agreed. "When Egypt first approached the Soviet Union for our first nuclear reactor in 1956, we were not displeased with what they proposed: a 2-megawatt (MW) reactor. In addition, the agreement between our countries was that all spent fuel from the reactor would be taken back to Moscow."[36] Such a small reactor would be militarily insignificant.[37]

The question remains: why did Egypt not pursue military applications of nuclear technology more vigorously? At this point, the first stirrings of the nuclear nonproliferation regime were only just beginning, so international disapproval would not have been overwhelming. Egypt had the strongest cadre of scientists of any Arab nation, and the Egyptian desert would have provided excellent testing grounds.[38] Nasser's bid to lead the Arab world could have been significantly strengthened with nuclear weapons. While Nasser was not aware of Israel's nuclear weapons program until 1959, the threat Israel posed became real in the 1956 Suez War. It was rumored that on at least two occasions, foreign experts approached Egypt with an offer to help with nuclear weapons technology and material, but both times the Egyptian government declined.[39] Egypt's lack of progress was not for lack of strong leadership of the program. The AEE's director, Ibrahim Hilmy Abdel Rahman, had a close relationship with Nasser, who appointed him as secretary-general of the Council of Ministers and secretary-general of the Board of Atomic Energy. Rahman was effective in a number of areas, from negotiating a nuclear protocol with the Soviet Union in 1957 to arranging for Soviet construction of Egypt's first research reactor and persuading the Soviets to train Egyptian science graduates.[40] When Rahman left the AEE in 1959, he was replaced by another strong proponent of nuclear research, Salah Hedayat, a former Free Officer who had helped make bombs for Nasser before the 1952 revolution. Nasser founded the Free Officers, a junior group of army officers, to overthrow the Egyptian monarchy. Associated with the army and with Nasser's friend Field Marshal Abdel Hakim Amer, Hedayat was also more outspoken on the desirability of a nuclear weapons program, a message that should have found favor with Nasser in late 1959 after the Dimona revelations.[41]

Finally, one might argue that in such a short window, creating a nuclear weapons program would have been untenable. However, Israel went from a political decision to acquire nuclear weapons in 1956 to a fully functional reactor capable of producing weapons-grade plutonium in 1963.[42] The obvious explanation for Egypt's lack of rapid progress in developing a nuclear weapons program during this period is that no political decision had been made to create one. Why not? The best answer to that question is most likely another question: why should it have? Egyptian leadership did not become aware of Israel's nuclear program until late 1959. Nasser's main preoccupation was with inter-Arab rivalries, even after the 1956 Suez War. While a nuclear bomb would have garnered him prestige, he would not have used it against other Arab countries, so it was not a high priority. In addition, Egypt's nuclear program had been progressing, with students receiving training in the Soviet Union and plans for a research reactor firmly in place. More important, the program was designed so that it could be used to create a military option if necessary. Thus, while Egypt's nuclear program did not progress rapidly, it was nevertheless moving forward in a timely manner.

Taking Military Applications Seriously, 1960–1967

After Egypt became aware of the Israeli nuclear program at Dimona in late 1959, and after the public revelation about Dimona's nuclear purpose in 1960, Nasser directed the AEE to look into military applications of the nuclear program. One expert said, "In 1960, for the first time, Nasser said we should consider a nuclear weapons program, because of Dimona. It wasn't for prestige or for positive usage to attack, or for regional dominance. It was to match Israel. Nasser would not accept being second-rate in this area."[43] In his famous speech on December 23, 1960, Nasser declared that if Israel acquired nuclear weapons, Egypt would certainly acquire them as well.[44] He later said he would send four million soldiers to tear down Dimona.[45] Nasser told the United States that if Israel acquired nuclear weapons, there would be war, "no matter how suicidal for the Arabs."[46] It is not known at what point the Egyptian leadership was convinced that Israel had serious nuclear capability, but it is likely they knew as early as 1963.[47] As discussed later, Nasser did not give the nuclear weapons program the resources or political priority it needed, leading some to conclude that his declarations were rhetoric for consumption by the Israelis and his Arab competitors. Indeed, the response within the AEE was mild; military applications were added onto the list of nuclear projects but did not seem to be given special priority. Prior to the 1960 revelation concerning Dimona, the main AEE projects included a nuclear power reactor, a desalinator, a small research reactor, and a fuel fabrication facility.[48] After the 1960 revelation, the biggest change seemed to be an emphasis on ensuring that the nuclear power reactors acquired were heavy-water reactors. "These reactors were designed to be a plutonium route to nuclear weapons," said one former military official.[49]

Because the Soviets were unwilling to transfer critical technology, and because the Egyptians were unhappy with the quality of the nuclear technology that was transferred, the Egyptians asked for bids for a nuclear power plant from Western companies.[50] By 1964 Egypt had completed negotiations with Siemens, a West German company, for a natural-uranium-fueled, heavy-water-moderated reactor.[51] Because this type of reactor had the potential to create fissionable material, the United States was concerned.[52] However, due to Egyptian anger over the West German sale of tanks to Israel, the deal was canceled a year later.[53] Egypt turned to Westinghouse, which had placed a bid at the same time as Siemens. Westinghouse had proposed a light-water reactor, which would require imported enriched uranium fuel, and in which it would be harder to produce weapons-grade nuclear material.[54] The reactor project never went forward though, due at first to financing troubles and then due to all nuclear programs being frozen as a result of Egypt's loss in the 1967 war.[55] In addition to efforts to acquire a power reactor, the AEE was busy on a number of other fronts as well. In 1961 the Soviets constructed a 2-MW research reactor at the Inchas Nuclear Research Center, forty kilometers outside Cairo. On other activities, Robert Einhorn reports:

> During the early 1960s, the Egyptian government boosted its budget for nu-
> clear programs, stepped up its efforts to recruit and train nuclear scientists,
> approached a wide range of countries for assistance, examined prospects for
> mining thorium and uranium in Egypt, and explored elements of the nu-
> clear fuel cycle that could eventually enable it to produce fissile material for
> nuclear weapons. In this latter connection, Egypt made initial attempts to
> produce heavy water, conducted experiments in fabricating uranium fuels,
> and approached the United States and Soviet Union, both without success,
> to acquire a radiochemistry laboratory that would have helped Egypt learn
> how to extract plutonium from spent reactor fuel.[56]

In addition to indigenous development, the Egyptians sought to purchase nuclear weapons components or entire devices.[57] The first such attempt is the least documented. According to Shai Feldman, during the early 1960s the Nasser regime "attempted to buy a nuclear capability by recruiting German scientists who played a role in Nazi Germany's nuclear program during the Second World War. This effort was soon aborted by sabotage operations carried out by Israel's security services."[58] Egypt also approached both the Soviet Union and China not only for technical assistance but also for the purchase or transfer of a nuclear device.[59] The Soviets were approached in 1965, but they declined to provide nuclear weapons or fissile material.[60] The Egyptians approached the Chinese as well. After China conducted a nuclear test in 1964, Nasser was delighted that a Third World country had broken the nuclear monopoly. He sent a delegation to China to congratulate them and, according to a former AEE official, to ask for China's help with Egypt's nuclear weapons program. The former AEE official said, "I knew people in the delegation that went to China after their detonation. The team went and inquired about prospects for a nuclear device. The Chinese took them to various facilities, but then told them, 'You have to build your own infrastructure.'"[61] After defeat in the 1967 war, Nasser is reported to have contacted both the Soviets and the Chinese again. The Soviets advised him to give up a nuclear weapons ambition and sign the NPT.[62] The Chinese again told the Egyptians that self-reliance was the best route.[63] In any case, the crushing defeat Egypt suffered in the Six Day War in 1967 put what would become a permanent hold on their nuclear weapons program.

Even more than during the previous period, questions arise about why Egypt did not make further strides in developing a nuclear weapons capability. The reasons seem to involve other upheavals. Internally, the AEE lacked stable leadership, mainly because Hedayat came under fire from a number of different quarters. Both Hedayat and his mentor Amer, Nasser's defense minister, believed that Israel would acquire nuclear weapons and Egypt must try to match their effort.[64] However, when Syria pulled out of the United Arab Republic (UAR) in 1961, Nasser blamed Amer, who served as his special commissioner to Syria.[65] As a result the relationship grew hostile, with rumored coup attempts by Amer's army forces.[66] Hedayat's connection to Amer may have influenced his fortunes at the AEE; between 1964 and 1965 he was removed from his positions as minister of science and chairman of the AEE. Hedayat also had other personality and personnel problems at the AEE that likely contributed to his removal.[67] One former military officer alluded to the issue: "We didn't want to create heroes in the system that a nuclear bomb would create."[68] Interestingly, it was after Hedayat's departure that the AEE turned to Westinghouse for a nuclear power plant — a light-water reactor from which it is far more difficult to produce weapons-grade nuclear material. There is no conclusive evidence that Nasser believed a nuclear weapons program would strengthen Amer's position, but it is a possibility.

In addition to political maneuverings, the nuclear program suffered from management issues. While Egypt did have a strong cadre of nuclear scientists and technicians, it lacked experienced program managers.[69] As one former military officer claimed:

The people had not worked together before, and there wasn't a lot of harmony. . . . The Egyptians were scientific experts but not program leaders. With any technology project, you need both substantive expertise and administrative expertise. But the administrative need was not clear to people in the Third World. In Egypt, they thought that if you have the technology and the material, that's all you need. But you also need someone to lead the program administratively. This was lacking in Egypt, the knowledge of how to lead a program to get results.[70]

Although poor program management may have delayed the Egyptian nuclear effort, it likely would not have derailed the work if the program had had strong political support. It may be that infighting and delays arose because the program did not have strong, consistent support from Nasser. According to one Egyptian security expert, "The program was very modest, and it suffered from a number of administrative and bureaucratic problems: engineering versus non-engineering, military versus non-military. But Nasser was not resolved to have a nuclear weapons program, so the problems never really got solved."[71]

The evidence points toward the conclusion that before the 1967 defeat, Nasser was never seriously determined to develop a nuclear weapons capacity. According to a former AEE official who started his employment there in 1965, the military applications portion of the nuclear program never had a separate budget: "You can tell it wasn't taken seriously because there was never any fund set aside specifically for the project." This correlates with the claim by another senior science official who said that Egypt never had a written plan for nuclear weapons development. "It was never put on paper or in any official form that we wanted to go in that [military] direction. There was never a written plan."[72] Additionally, there was never any official cost-benefit analysis of developing a nuclear weapons program.[73] A senior Egyptian diplomat agreed: "In the 1960s, Nasser was never completely serious about it. He wanted to see the possibilities and keep the option open. But he did not commit serious resources that would have been needed."[74]

One might argue that the real problem was Nasser not having enough resources to devote to a nuclear program, given Egypt's relative poverty and the high cost of nuclear technology. However, at the time Egypt did seriously consider a nuclear program, it had "equal or greater resources when compared with either Israel or Pakistan at the time these countries opted to go nuclear."[75] In addition, although the nuclear weapons project did not have separate funds under the AEE, James Walsh notes that Nasser did choose to spend enormous sums of money on a number of pet projects: "How is it that Egypt had the money for three new army divisions, an $80 million a year jet program, over $100 million for intervention in Yemen, and a 'particularly expensive' missile program at the same time it lacked the monetary resources for atomic research? The funds spent on any one of these programs would have allowed Egypt to significantly upgrade its nuclear infrastructure."[76]

If Egypt did not develop a nuclear weapons capability because Nasser did not want one, the next question arising is why Nasser felt that way. Even with fragmentation of the Egyptian political elite, he still retained enormous personal power and had the ability to pursue his chosen policies.[77] Some cite a missed opportunity, suggesting that Nasser did not see the importance of a nuclear weapons program until it was too late (after the defeat in the Six Day War).[78] This argument rings true, especially in light of the fact that after the 1967 war Nasser asked both the Soviet Union and China for nuclear weapons; he likely realized he no longer had time for their indigenous development.[79] Perhaps Nasser feared that a strong nuclear weapons program would strengthen his rival Amer and waited until Amer was removed from power in 1967 before making it a priority. However, even before problems between Nasser and Amer surfaced, Nasser was not giving nuclear weapons priority; twice before 1960 the Egyptian government had been offered foreign help on this, and Nasser declined.

Another potential explanation is that Nasser had other priorities. A typical realist expectation would be for Nasser to examine the material capabilities of hostile states around Egypt and base threat perceptions on that examination. Such analysis would lead to the conclusion that Israel was by far the biggest threat to Egypt, and one would expect military planning and acquisition (including a nuclear program) aimed at meeting that threat. However, Nasser did not see Israel as his greatest threat until after the 1967 war. With his vision of Pan-Arabism, he devoted most of his attention to inter-Arab conflicts. Michael Barnett notes that Nasser's cautiousness toward the Israelis "stood in direct contrast to, and was a result of, the turbulence in intra-Arab politics. . . . Such intra-Arab struggles left Nasser with little time or energy to concentrate on the Israelis."[80] In other words, Nasser gave leadership of the Arab world his highest priority and made his threat assessments accordingly. Yet a nuclear weapons program would not have hurt or detracted from Nasser's bid for Arab leadership — quite the opposite. Stephen Walt argues that the "cardinal principle of Nasser's foreign policy" was "preserving his own leadership of the Arab revolution."[81] Janice Stein argues that Nasser's heavy engagement in seeking Pan-Arab leadership makes Egypt's non-nuclear stance quite puzzling, since a nuclear weapons program would have accorded him great status in the Middle East.[82] Indeed, nuclear weapons would have given Nasser significant leverage over his rivals as well as greater international stature. Thus his drive for Pan-Arab leadership does not explain Egypt's non-nuclear stance but only makes it more perplexing.

One potential explanation for Nasser's reluctance to pursue a nuclear weapons program seriously after 1960 is the influence of the international norm against nuclear proliferation. At first glance this may seem implausible, given that the NPT was not open for signature until 1968 and did not come into force until 1970. But closer analysis shows otherwise. From the beginning Nasser hoped to use the nuclear issue as another way to extend his leadership over the Arab world. Israel's nuclear potential was brought up repeatedly at meetings of Arab leaders; the Egyptian government suggested that an Arab nuclear research effort take place.[83] Arab states could contribute funding for the research, while Egypt would house the facility and provide the bulk of the scientists. However, the effort never got off the ground, due in part to the inter-Arab rivalry. "There was some reluctance to pay for an Egyptian nuclear program, when the question remained whether these weapons would be turned against them at some point."[84] Instead, through 1965, the main result of high-level Arab discussions of Israel's nuclear potential seemed to be agreements to raise the issue at the United Nations and through other diplomatic channels.[85] Some Arab states criticized Nasser for his political and diplomatic approach to the Israeli nuclear issue — they preferred a military response — but Nasser continued to call for "sustained political pressure against Israel and the consolidation of Arab unity."[86]

When little came of these efforts, he turned to the prospect of using the emerging nuclear nonproliferation regime as another way to assert Egyptian leadership via the Israeli nuclear issue. Egypt had already gained prominence due to its early and active involvement in disarmament issues.[87] As one American expert noted, "Back in the 1960s, the [Egyptian] diplomatic side was cutting its teeth, learning how to use the UN to gain leadership in the Arab world."[88] A senior Egyptian diplomat concurred, saying that by the mid-1960s, Egypt began to "put a lot of faith and influence into international negotiations."[89] In the meantime, U.S. president John F. Kennedy had engaged Nasser in personal correspondence, in part to ask Egypt to abide by the spirit of the emerging nonproliferation regime. In both 1962 and 1963, Kennedy specifically asked for a pledge from Nasser that Egypt would remain non-nuclear.[90] Nasser responded positively to Kennedy's requests: "Nasser declared that the UAR does not think of bringing that terrifying danger (nuclear terror) to the region she lives in."[91] At least one Egyptian scientist believes that those communications strongly influenced Nasser's position.[92] By 1966 Egypt began to use diplomatic tools to confront the Israeli nuclear issue. Mostafa Elwi Saif notes: "The Arab Summit is said to have discussed, in 1966, deep Arab concerns regarding the potential Israeli nuclear threat, and passed a resolution providing for Arab states to undertake general discussion of nuclear dangers in Geneva and in UN meetings the following fall. [In a public forum], Nasser stated that Egypt agreed to join the IAEA safeguards system and he wanted Israel also to be part of that agreement."[93]

At the same time, Nasser warmed to the idea of a nuclear-weapon-free zone in the Middle East.[94] As mentioned, after the 1967 war Nasser did ask both the Soviets and the Chinese for nuclear weapons. These requests were likely last-ditch efforts to salvage a humiliating situation — (Nasser was so shamed by losing the Sinai in only six days that he resigned, but he returned to power after a public outcry calling for his return) — as opposed to being part of a grand plan for an Egyptian nuclear weapons program. Indeed, after the 1967 defeat, the nuclear program was frozen completely. When the Soviets declined Nasser's request for nuclear weapons, they instead urged him to sign the NPT, which he did shortly thereafter. One senior official noted, "Nasser didn't really argue with them, because he had already assessed the situation and he was not serious about acquiring nuclear weapons."[95] Instead, even before the opening of the NPT for signature, the Egyptian leadership had been exposed to the international norm against nuclear nonproliferation. More important, they saw it as an opportunity to oppose Israel and expand their leadership in the Arab world. Had the NPT not come to fruition, this diplomatic option would not have been available to Egypt.

Closing the Door, 1968–1973

On July 1, 1968, Egypt joined fifty-nine other countries to sign the NPT the first day it opened for signature.[96] Many in Egypt thought Nasser's decision to sign the NPT was "very strange."[97] Although the Egyptian delegation had been active in the NPT negotiations, Egypt had just lost a war to Israel, a neighbor with a suspected nuclear capability.[98] The decision was explained as an alternate way to handle the nuclear dilemma: that with the Egyptian signature, the United States would exert pressure on Israel to give up its nuclear weapons program.[99] To what extent was Egypt's signing of the NPT a critical juncture in their non-nuclear policy? As noted, some suggest that it merely confirmed what Nasser had already decided. But some Egyptian officials noted that the signing of the NPT officially shut the door on the nuclear option. "If Egypt had wanted to play with the option, we would not have signed. We would not have signed as a cover and then done something else. Signing said, 'That's it, that's the end.'"[100] Egypt's signing of the NPT not only closed the door to the nuclear option but, as already argued, opened the door to the new way Egypt would handle the Israeli nuclear problem: through diplomacy. The NPT gave Egypt a different way to fight against an Israeli bomb. Nasser also wanted to garner international credibility; by signing, he intended to make the statement "Egypt is part of the international community—Israel is not."[101]

If the 1967 war shut down the nuclear option, and Nasser's signing of the NPT signaled a serious intent to forgo nuclear weapons for the long term, then Sadat's vision of Egyptian economic development and peace with Israel sounded the final death knell. As Egypt's first vice president, Sadat succeeded Nasser when he died of a heart attack in 1970. Many thought Sadat had remained as Nasser's vice president only because he was pliable and did not represent a threat to Nasser's rule. As a result, few expected that Sadat would remain president for long. Surprisingly, Sadat brought to the presidency a robust agenda that he would pursue with passion. His short-term goal was to regain the Sinai, as well as Egypt's pride, which had been badly damaged in the 1967 war. In the longer term Sadat wanted to focus on Egypt's development. He believed that war with Israel only drained Egypt's national coffers and attention; peace with Israel was necessary to see Egypt develop.

A strong relationship with the United States was also important, not only because that would give Egypt leverage in its negotiations with Israel but because Sadat believed an alliance with America had greater promise for the Egypt of the future. "Sadat was very much determined that the relationship between Egypt and the United States should be a fundamental dimension in Egypt's future," one official observed.[102] In this context nuclear weapons would only be a liability and would provide few assets, if any. The money for nuclear weapons development could be better spent on conventional weapons to help take back the Sinai and on economic development. Nuclear weapons development would also make it very hard to establish a strong relationship with the United States.

The 1973 war only confirmed for Sadat that Egypt did not need nuclear weapons. First, Sadat asked Soviet advisors to leave Egypt in 1972, which left some wondering how Egypt would regain the Sinai without Soviet help. Then Egypt and Syria launched the October 1973 surprise attack against Israel. "In 1973, we knew that Israel had nuclear weapons, missiles with armed nuclear warheads," said a former military official. "So there was some gambling that Israel would not go nuclear unless we crossed their borders. That was not in our plan, or even in our capacity."[103]

With the October war, Sadat had several goals. Militarily, he hoped to gain back the Sinai, or portions of it, as well as destroy the myth of Israeli invincibility. Politically, he wanted to bring the Arab-Israeli conflict back into superpower focus and thus "obtain a lever to move to a diplomatic settlement."[104] He also intended to use the war to reach out to the United States. "Sadat's commanders were astonished that he called the United States after only one week into the war," a former military officer said.[105] While Egypt ended up losing on the battlefield, Sadat clearly won politically, using the war to get the attention of the United States. And he was prepared to offer the nuclear issue as an incentive to the United States. "Sadat knew that the U.S. would not come to Egypt without incentives. The nuclear issue was one of those issues we were ready to abandon. It was a tool, something we could give to the U.S. as a present, even though Sadat knew that the nuclear program was already closed and it wasn't really much of a present."[106] A former AEE official agreed that although the nuclear weapons program was halted in 1967, it was 1973 that marked the true total abandonment of any nuclear weapons option for Egypt.[107]

Why Sadat rejected the nuclear option is somewhat of a puzzle. His anti-Israeli views were well known, and for years he argued that Egypt could never negotiate with Israel while it occupied Arab territory.[108] Several months before Nasser's death Sadat said of Israel, "Don't ask me to make diplomatic relations with them. Never. Never. Leave it to the coming generation to decide that, not me."[109] Ibrahim Karawan noted, "For years Sadat refused to negotiate with Israel as long as it occupied Arab land, and he characterized negotiating under these conditions as total capitulation."[110] Thus Sadat did not pursue peace with his neighbors because of any affection toward them but because war kept Egypt from development and international integration. Under such circumstances, a secret nuclear weapons program under the guise of a nuclear power reactor would have made sense. In this way, Sadat could have reaped the peace dividends he sought while preserving the nuclear option and his country's security. While discovery of a secret nuclear weapons program could

have harmed Egypt's relationship with the United States, enough overlap between civilian and military applications existed for Sadat to have protested
that no military applications were planned. In addition, Egypt was critical to
the U.S. effort in the Middle East, and hence the likelihood of too strident an
American response was low.

To understand Sadat's nuclear forbearance, we need to understand his larger
strategic decision to pursue peace and engagement with the United States.
When Sadat took power, he declared his intention to continue to fight in col-
laboration with other Arab states against Israel.[111] Resources were funneled
into the military to prepare for a war to liberate the Sinai; but the economy was
in shambles and continued to deteriorate, in large part because the loss of the
Sinai cost Egypt between $400 and $500 million each year.[112] Without greater
resources, Egypt could not launch a serious military effort to regain the Sinai.
However, the domestic consequences of "no war, no peace," as the strategy
was called, were also untenable, given the internal instability and frequent
agitation for war with Israel.

Egypt could have embarked on a new wave of radicalism, opting for greater
Soviet assistance and total mobilization of society for war. Such a plan would
have been welcomed by Sadat's chief rival, Ali Sabri, a Free Officer who advocated heavy industrialization, state socialism, a militant stand against Israel,
and friendship with the Soviet Union.[113] Instead, Sadat purged his opponents
in the May 1971 "Corrective Movement" and continued the limited economic
opening that Nasser had begun after the 1967 war. He launched the October
1973 strike against Israel not only to resolve the Sinai occupation but also because he believed it would spur foreign economic aid, both from Arab states
to thank Egypt for their attack on Israel and from the West as an incentive to
stop the fighting.[114]

Despite the fact that only an international settlement prevented Israel
from crushing the Egyptian troops, Sadat enjoyed enormous domestic popularity from the 1973 war, earning the title "Hero of the Crossing." He realized, however, that after six years of war preparation, the Egyptian military
had made only slight inroads against the Israeli army. Armed conflict would
not solve Egypt's problems. Some in Egypt still advocated leftist policies, including "continued cooperation with the USSR, increased solidarity with the
Arabs with a view toward confrontation with Israel and toward external finance, a search for arms and markets in the European West, and continued

alienation from the U.S."[115] Instead, Sadat broke with all past policies and chose diplomacy:

> By deciding to seek a negotiated solution, Sadat placed himself at odds with the dominant Arab thinking, and certainly with Syria, his compatriot in the 1973 War, who continued to sponsor a rejectionist stance. Consequently, Sadat had to abandon a comprehensive settlement of the Arab-Israeli conflict and seek a separately negotiated agreement with the Israelis. In general, before 1973 Egypt's Israel strategy was premised on a collective Arab effort and the adoption of confrontational actions and policies; after 1973, however, Sadat opted for a solitary diplomatic stance.[116]

Essentially, Sadat had internalized a number of lessons he had learned during Nasser's regime. Pan-Arabism led to involvement in wars like the Yemeni conflict, which bankrupted Egypt's economy and contributed to the devastating loss in the 1967 war. In addition, Sadat and others felt that the Arab states did not appreciate Egypt's contributions to the Arab movement, nor did they provide Egypt with appropriate financial assistance. Since the Soviets would not provide Egypt with enough assistance to deal Israel a decisive blow, their help would not solve Egypt's burning issues.[117] Decades of conflict led Sadat and his inner circle to long for the ability to move Egypt forward; they had "lost all stomach for continuing conflict and yearned for a Western diplomatic solution."[118] These lessons, combined with Sadat's own view of himself "as a heroic man of action with the mission to bring peace and prosperity to his country," resulted in several shocking moves on Sadat's part, including expelling Soviet advisors, turning to the United States, negotiating with Israel, and the surprise move of visiting Israel and delivering a speech to the Israeli Knesset.[119]

Given Sadat's strategic choices, his decision to declare publicly that the nuclear option was dead is not surprising. Egypt had decided it wanted U.S. support, and the United States would expect closure of the nuclear option. However, the original question posed — why Egypt did not pursue a secret nuclear program, as Iraq, Libya, and Iran did — remains unanswered. A lack of finances might seem an appropriate answer, except that after the 1973 war Egypt's military spending continued to increase. According to Barnett, Egypt spent three times as much on arms in the six years from 1975 to 1981 as it had in the previous twenty years. A covert nuclear program was not out of reach economically. The most probable explanation for Sadat's nuclear forbearance is that he believed the diplomatic solution would provide both the peace and the prosperity he was seeking for Egypt, making it unnecessary to balance the Israeli nuclear program. As Barnett argues, the 1967 war triggered an ideological crisis that created "policy elasticity": "Crises discredit old policies that failed to confront the present challenge and instigate a search for new solutions. In sum, state and societal actors recognize that crisis politics demand a deviation from the routine to satisfactorily confront the exceptional challenge."[120] As a result Sadat rethought Egypt's security dilemma, including who his friends and foes were, thus opening the door to Egyptian policies that no longer valued a nuclear weapons option. In addition, Sadat knew that continued adherence to the NPT would allow Egypt to use the regime to prod Israel toward nuclear forbearance.

Nuclear Power and NPT Diplomacy, 1974–Present

After 1973, with the U.S.-Egyptian and Israeli-Egyptian rapprochement, Egypt's nuclear policy began to evolve. This period was marked by serious attempts to acquire civilian nuclear power reactors to meet Egypt's rapidly growing energy needs. In addition, Egypt became proficient in using the NPT and associated international instruments to put pressure on Israel to end its nuclear weapons program. It is interesting that as Israel's muscular nuclear program came to light, Egypt responded by adhering more firmly to the NPT and being quite clear that all nuclear power plants would be placed under IAEA inspections.

During U.S. president Richard Nixon's state visit to Cairo in 1974, he offered the Egyptians assistance with building nuclear power reactors. Sadat enthusiastically accepted, fully agreeing to nuclear safeguards, but the reactors were never built, for a number of reasons. Nixon also offered Israel help with nuclear reactors, but after the Indian peaceful nuclear explosion later in 1974, the U.S. administration added stringent safeguards on the technology for both countries.[121] Israel declined to participate, in part because the U.S. offer was contingent on both countries accepting, and the Israelis did not want Egyptians developing nuclear technology.[122] Thus the Egyptian deal was canceled. When Egypt sought help with reactors from the Soviet Union, the United States relented and renewed talks for nuclear assistance. Negotiations began, but progress was slow.[123] In the interim Egypt was investigating other nuclear projects as well. For example, in 1975 the AEE began exploring the possibility of using nuclear explosives to excavate "a 70-kilometer canal from the Mediterranean to the Qattara Depression. An artificial lake also was to be created and filled with water up to 70 meters deep from which Egypt might generate nearly 10,000 megawatts of electricity."[124] The Egyptians contracted with a German firm for surveying, but the project never progressed beyond that point.

The U.S. reactor deal hit a serious roadblock in 1978, when the United States passed new legislation requiring even stricter safeguards on all nuclear technology. Egypt therefore sought help from other foreign sources, including the French and the Germans. However, because the Egyptians had not ratified the NPT, they were not able to find a company that would sell them a power reactor.[125] At the time, Egypt was suffering from a severe energy shortage. "In the late 1970s, the need for power became even more pressing. In those days, we had gray outs all the time. Factories were only operating at half capacity. The telephone situation was terrible," one senior government official said.[126] Hence Egypt rethought its stance on ratification of the NPT. By this point Egypt was not trying to preserve a nuclear option; rather, refusal to ratify was a form of protest against the Israeli refusal to join the regime.[127] For decades Israel showed no signs of relenting on the nuclear issue, and it was not likely to reverse its stance any time soon.

Egypt's energy crisis, meanwhile, was growing; a joint report at the time by the Egyptian Ministry of Industry and the U.S. Department of Energy estimated that by the year 2000, Egypt's energy needs would be 105 billion kilowatt hours a year, while capacity in 1980 provided only 16 billion kilowatt hours annually.[128] As a result Sadat decided to ratify the NPT in January 1981. The appropriate legislation was pushed quickly through the government, and Egypt entered into a number of nuclear cooperation agreements, with India and Indonesia (February 1981), France and the United States (March 1981), Germany (1981), Canada (1982), Britain (1982), and Switzerland and Belgium (1984).[129] A high-level science official noted that in all these agreements, "we made it clear that we were seeking nuclear power for civilian purposes, and that was it. We agreed to put all installations under safeguards as appropriate for a country that had ratified the NPT, because we wanted to comfort the whole international scene about our intentions."[130] Negotiations for a hot cell laboratory had begun in 1977 with a French engineering firm, and once the Egyptian NPT ratification took place, installation began. It was completed in 1982, giving the Egyptians two hot cells with which AEE scientists could gain experience in nuclear waste management.[131]

Sadat was assassinated in 1981, whereupon the issue of pursuing nuclear power fell to President Mubarak. There was a great deal of controversy over the selected nuclear power plant site near Alexandria, and in the end an alternate site farther away from the populated area was chosen. The controversy, along with the risks associated with nuclear power, made Mubarak very cautious. "In early 1986, there was a big meeting with the president—he gathered many scientific advisors to talk about the question of nuclear power, because there was some opposition from political parties," said a former high-level official. "I told the president, 'You are a pilot. If a plane falls down from the sky, would you cancel the air force?' Sophisticated technology has risks. You just need to understand and minimize those risks."[132] At the urging of his science advisors, and painfully aware of Egypt's severe energy crisis, Mubarak decided to move ahead on nuclear power.

A month after the meeting, the Chernobyl nuclear accident put all plans on hold. "Mubarak told us that we needed to study the situation and see about the safety implications," the former official said.[133] Public concern over nuclear power had dissipated by 1989, but by then Egypt had discovered an abundant source of energy, natural gas. The Egyptian electricity minister said: "After the Chernobyl disaster and the strong international reaction that followed, we started to think of an alternative and especially during the economic crisis in Egypt in the 1980s. The government started to reconsider the major projects, which require huge finances, including the atomic projects. The discovery of natural gas in great quantities came as an alternative to the nuclear installations, which require foreign funding."[134]

A former Egyptian diplomat said, "With the gas we found offshore and in the Delta, we have reserves sufficient for the next fifty years. So there's no rush to develop nuclear power." But the diplomat noted that not everyone was happy with Mubarak's decision to keep nuclear power shelved:

The president is afraid of the peaceful use of nuclear energy. He very reluctantly accepted the proposal for peaceful use of nuclear power, only because of the energy shortage. When the decision was made to keep the program shelved due to finding the gas reserves, a lot of people said it was a big mistake to stop investing in nuclear power. Why not save the gas reserves for future generations? Or sell it? In addition, technicians and others were not happy, because they wanted to maintain their technical know-how. A peaceful nuclear program could be a deterrent against Israel, just in that it would have given Egypt deterrence by having advanced technology. But the real debate all this time has been whether to invest in peaceful nuclear power or not—not about whether to have a military aspect to any nuclear program.[135]

Egypt did acquire a 22-MW light-water research reactor from Argentina, which became operational in 1997. The reactor, under full IAEA safeguards, is used to train technical staff and create radioisotopes for industrial and medical uses.[136]

Egyptian efforts to acquire nuclear power were less than successful, but they did enable Egypt to capitalize on the other important benefit of seeking rapprochement with the United States and ratifying the NPT: using the nuclear nonproliferation regime as a way to blunt Israel's nuclear advantage.[137] Avner Cohen notes:

> The establishment of the nonproliferation regime, with the NPT as its centerpiece, opened a new political opportunity for the non-nuclear Arabs to score political points against Israel on the nuclear issue. Israel's reluctance to sign the treaty was, certainly from an Arab perspective, an issue that placed Israel in defiance of an emerging international norm. Given this situation, the Egyptian-Arab basic interest was clear: first, to force Israel to sign the NPT and to place its nuclear program under the eye of the international community, and second, if Israel refused to sign the treaty, to make the utmost political gain out of it.[138]

Egypt has not been successful in pressuring Israel into nuclear disarmament, but it has achieved progress in highlighting the continued existence of the Israeli nuclear program and in keeping the matter on the international radar. In 1974 Iran submitted and Egypt sponsored a resolution to the General Assembly of the United Nations calling for a nuclear-weapon-free zone in the Middle East. Each year since then, Egypt has sponsored—and the UN General Assembly has adopted—such a resolution. Starting in 1980, the annual resolution was adopted by consensus, meaning that it was supported by Iran, Israel, and all Arab states.[139] Starting in the 1990s, the Egyptians began raising the issue even more forcefully. In 1990 Mubarak proposed a WMD-free zone in the Middle East.[140] To complement the bilateral tracks of the Madrid Peace Process, which began in October 1991 after the conclusion of the Gulf War, five working groups were formed to provide multilateral fora to support the process. The Working Group on Arms Control and Regional Security (ACRS) was formed to handle security concerns.[141] While ACRS made important progress, the forum broke down by 1995. Bruce Jentleson and Dalia Dassa Kaye attribute this to a number of factors, "the main one being the dispute between Egypt and Israel over the nuclear issue. While this was a long-standing issue, Egypt now went even further in essentially linking the entirety of the ACRS agenda to the nuclear issues, and consequently bringing ACRS to a halt."[142]

With the 1995 NPT Review and Extension Conference, "Egypt hit the high pitch on nuclear nonproliferation," said a former U.S. diplomat. "Egypt saw it as an opportunity to push Israel to take steps to join the NPT."[143] Because the NPT was originally created with an expiration date of twenty-five years, the review conference was critical to maintaining the nuclear nonproliferation regime. Two options were possible: that the NPT would be extended again for a certain period of time, with another review and extension conference to take place at that expiration date; or indefinite extension. The United States lobbied hard for an indefinite extension, but some states opposed indefinite extension since they feared it would freeze the nuclear status quo, undermining the nuclear weapons states' promise to work toward disarmament. Egypt used this opportunity to argue for movement from Israel on the nuclear issue. By pressing Arab states to create a common position through the Arab League, Egypt exerted a great deal of influence, according to a disarmament expert in the Arab League: "Before the 1995 review conference, the Arab League created a committee to advise the Arab states on what position they should take. The committee included diplomats, military officers, legal advisors, and more."[144] He relayed the experience of the Arab states:

> We created a common Arab position: we would agree on the indefinite extension and the rest of the Arab states would sign the NPT, so long as Israel also joined the NPT. Western diplomats visited us, and when they said they could not talk about Israel, we said that we could not support indefinite extension. They were quite upset, and they tried to strike a deal with us. They said, if we approved the extension, that would embarrass Israel and put pressure on Israel, because once the remaining Arab states joined, Israel would have no reason not to. While I advised against it, for political reasons the Arab states agreed to join and support indefinite extension, in exchange for the Middle East Resolution, which would call on all states in the region to join the NPT. Egypt was very important in bringing in the rest of the Arab states.

So by the year 2000, all 22 Arab states had joined the NPT. But in the 2000 NPT Review Conference, the Americans wanted to ignore the Middle East Resolution. Egypt helped us force the issue, but we still only got a resolution with no enforcement mechanisms. The Egyptians gave away their leverage and brought in the rest of the Arab states. In exchange, they only got the Middle East Resolution, which in practical terms is useless.[145]

In 1996 Mubarak hosted the signing of the Pelindaba Treaty, which codified the African NWFZ.[146] Egypt signed the treaty but has not yet ratified it, in protest of Israel's continued refusal to join the NPT. Then in 1998 Egypt joined with seven other states to form the New Agenda Coalition (NAC), which demanded greater progress from the nuclear weapons states on disarmament and, notably, called on the three nondeclared nuclear-capable states to join the NPT as non-nuclear states.[147] The NAC declaration took the nuclear weapons states by surprise, and the NAC has had a strong influence on subsequent NPT review conferences. In addition, the NAC's resolution "Toward a Nuclear-Weapon-Free World: The Need for a New Agenda" found overwhelming support in the UN General Assembly. Involvement in the NAC placed Egypt at odds with the United States, but as Egypt illustrated during the 1995 Review and Extension Conference, pressing the Israelis on the nuclear issue can take precedence over keeping the Americans happy.

Today Egypt continues to use diplomatic channels forcefully to apply pressure to Israel about its nuclear program.[148] A senior Egyptian diplomat said: "We use diplomatic initiatives in many arenas: disarmament conferences, the review conferences, preparatory sessions for the next review conference. We are hammering on the importance of getting Israel to adhere to the NPT, or the Middle East NWFZ, or the Middle East WMDFZ, or to accept mutual inspections between Israel and Egypt. We are trying to use diplomacy to push Israel to accept the NPT, in all fora that we are involved in."[149] A former Egyptian diplomat who later became involved with the Egyptian Council on Foreign Relations, a security-related NGO, described with great enthusiasm his work on challenging Israel to adhere to the NPT: "We are approaching a review conference, and there's a very active role played by the Egyptians. We've been doing a lot of work, and we have some new ideas to put forward. The Egyptian government is interested and will support our ideas."[150] The Arab League, under the leadership of an Egyptian secretary-general, is also moving forward with diplomatic efforts. In 2000 the Arab League created a disarmament department so as to look at the issue in a holistic way. "Arab states are moving into these norms and conventions, and they need advice. For the 2005 review conference, we are preparing papers on issues not solely relevant to Arab states, but also larger issues as well. We need to keep knocking on the door."[151] Along with the disarmament department, a committee was established to monitor and document Israeli activities that are contrary to the NPT.[152]

The Iranian nuclear crisis, along with increasing criticism within Egypt of Israel's nuclear program, has resulted in Cairo reopening the door to nuclear power. In September 2006 Mubarak's eldest son and presumed heir, Gamal Mubarak, proposed a revival of Egypt's nuclear power plans, calling for plants to be operational in ten years.[153] His father publicly supports those plans — a reversal of his long-standing caution on nuclear issues.[154] In October the Egyptian Parliament gave its stamp of approval to the plan for building nuclear power plants. In addition, the government has begun recruiting Egyptian scientists from overseas to work on the project.[155] Egypt has been engaged in a flurry of preliminary negotiations with a number of countries, including the United States, Russia, and China, for the plants.[156] The goal is to build three power plants along the Mediterranean coast by 2020, to provide 1,800 megawatts of energy.[157]

The external motivations for the revived nuclear energy plans are clear. For the current Egyptian leadership, Iran's nuclear program is an unacceptable bid for regional leadership.[158] If Iran succeeds, Egypt needs to be able to show that it too has the capability to develop nuclear weapons. Otherwise, Egypt fears that Iran will attempt to assert hegemony over the region and fears losing its ability to lead the Arab world, paving the way for Saudi Arabia or another Arab country to balance Iran.[159] In addition, Cairo likely realizes that it would no longer be the prime negotiator with Israel — that would fall to Iran, which would have much more leverage. Thus a successful Iranian nuclear weapons program, without an accompanying Egyptian capability, would relegate Egypt to the sidelines — something Cairo does not relish.

However, for the main opposition force within Egypt, the Muslim Brotherhood, Iran is not the concern. In fact, the Muslim Brotherhood has publicly stated that an Iranian nuclear weapon will be an Islamic deterrent against Israel.[160] Rather, they want Egypt to develop nuclear energy — and nuclear weapons — to balance Israel. As the spokesperson for the Muslim Brotherhood parliamentary caucus said in July 2006, "We are ready to starve in order to own a nuclear weapon that will represent a real deterrent and will be decisive in the Arab-Israeli conflict."[161] Additionally, the Muslim Brotherhood argues that Egypt "should have nuclear weapons as a matter of national right and prestige."[162] Indeed, for both the current elite and the opposition, a nuclear power program represents the best way for Egypt to reassert its leadership of the Arab world.[163]

A number of internal factors have contributed to the plans for nuclear power as well. First, Mubarak feels the need to deflect domestic criticism. The Egyptian populace is unhappy with Israel's monopoly on nuclear weapons; in fact, a majority almost certainly supports an Iranian nuclear weapons program, not to mention an Egyptian nuclear weapons program.[164] The Muslim Brotherhood attacks on the current regime have motivated it to respond. It is no coincidence that Gamal Mubarak's proposal came just a few months after the Muslim Brotherhood's calls for a nuclear weapons program. Given that the current regime has concerns about stability, this is one way to gain public support while undercutting opposition criticism. Gamal Mubarak is widely seen as being groomed to take over from his father in 2011, for which he must shore up public support, and the nuclear proposal is an excellent way to do that; the tactic has been extremely successful.[165] As the *Economist* noted in reporting the event, "By announcing Egypt's nuclear-power drive at a party conference, during a period of high regional tension over Iran's nuclear ambitions, the younger Mubarak was clearly staking out a more assertive role, both for himself and for Egypt."[166] Even though Mubarak has been quite clear that the program is for peaceful purposes, the public does not distinguish between civilian and military nuclear activities — a nuclear program of any sort conveys a sense of balancing Israel.[167] Moreover, Mubarak has wrapped the nuclear program in anticolonial sentiment, arguing that Egypt would "offer a new vision for the Middle East based on our Arab identity" and "explicitly rejecting the 'New Middle East' that outside powers are actively seeking to advance in the region."[168] Finally, Egypt does have real energy needs. Its natural gas supplies are expected to run out within thirty-five to forty years.[169] Hydroelectric power, the other main indigenous source of energy, cannot plug the gap. Even though energy production has increased almost 10 percent in the past several years, consumption has increased by 21 percent during the same period.[170]

Whether this surge of interest in nuclear power represents a new period in Egyptian decision-making is unclear. Even one power plant would take a decade or more to build, and any new facilities will be under IAEA inspections, making cheating difficult. The country will have to rely on external financing, and where this will come from is not clear.[171] It is difficult to gauge whether Mubarak is simply hoping to deflect internal criticism and match Iranian technical capabilities or truly intends to pursue a nuclear weapons program. At this point, the first seems more likely, but until or unless the Iranian nuclear crisis is defused, the Egyptian nuclear power program is likely to continue.

EGYPT'S NUCLEAR DECISION-MAKING: INFLUENCE OF THE INTERNATIONAL SOCIAL ENVIRONMENT

In chapter 2, it was argued that influence of the nuclear nonproliferation regime on state elites could be understood through the lens of social psychology: how norms are transmitted, how actors process norms, and conditions that affect the influence or potency of norms. Reviewing the details of the Egypt case study through this framework does indeed give us greater insight into how the international social environment created by the nuclear nonproliferation regime influenced Egyptian decision-making.

Norm Transmission: Descriptive Norms

To reiterate the parameters in chapter 2, descriptive norms are those normative messages actors understand when observing the behavior of those around them. This study hypothesizes that descriptive norms influence elite decision-making: when more states publicly forgo or surrender the nuclear option, other outlying states are more likely do the same. On the other hand, NPT member states hedging or withdrawing make it more likely for other states to do the same. As we have seen, Egypt signed the NPT the first day it opened for signature, in 1968, but delayed ratification until 1981. When Egypt signed the NPT, Nasser deliberately wanted to make use of descriptive norms to embarrass Israel. He wanted to send the message that Egypt was a member of the international community, while Israel was not. However, neither in signing nor in ratification did the number and status of states that had already signed seem to influence Egypt's decision-makers. This is probably due to the fact that many states were still outside the treaty (111 states had ratified before Egypt, leaving several dozen — including China, France, and many in the Middle East — yet to accede).

Yet the more recent weakening of the descriptive norm has influenced the debate in Egypt. Events weakening the norm since 1998 include nuclear tests in India and Pakistan, new U.S. emphasis on nuclear weapons, North Korea withdrawing from the NPT, and complications with IAEA inspections in Iran. Egyptian leadership is under increasing pressure from opposition parties and the public in general to reverse its non-nuclear stance, in part due to Israel's continued refusal to give up its nuclear option but also in part due to the strides Iran and North Korea seem to be making.[172] Emily Landau notes that while Egyptian officials believe the United States would not look favorably on an Egyptian nuclear weapons program, "on the other hand, looking at what has happened more recently with India and Pakistan since they became declared nuclear states, Egypt could conclude that the implications of going nuclear might not be that serious, especially in light of American-Pakistani cooperation since September 11. In this context, Egypt will most likely be very interested in U.S. policy toward North Korea in the coming months."[173]

In addition, disarmament experts within the Arab League have called on Egypt and the rest of the Arab states to reconsider their adherence to the NPT. At this point, weakening of the descriptive norm does not seem to have pushed any state into reversing its non-nuclear position (unless one counts North Korea's withdrawal as a delayed reaction to the India-Pakistan tests). However, it is not out of the realm of possibility. Considering the prestige that Egypt derives from its leadership in the nonproliferation regime, if a number of states (even outside the Middle East) went nuclear, it could shift Cairo's cost-benefit calculations significantly.[174]

Norm Transmission: Injunctive Norms

Clear normative messages specifying behavior, rewards, and punishments are injunctive norms. The hypothesis arising is that the more states are admonished to forgo nuclear weapons, the more likely they are to do so. Another cause-effect relationship involves the clear injunctive normative message of the NPT — the expectation that once it entered into force, states were less likely to start a nuclear weapons program.

In the case of Egypt, the creation of the NPT did influence Nasser's nuclear decision-making. "When the program started in the early 1960s, we had complete freedom because there were no treaties against it," one Egyptian expert said.[175] Once the international treaty was created, however, Egypt felt pressure to sign, and signing marked a halt to its nuclear weapons program. The NPT did not have to enter formally into force in order to exert influence on elite decision-making. The understanding that the treaty was being created and had the backing of a majority of states was enough. In broader terms, the NPT certainly sent out a powerful injunctive message: once the NPT was in place, a nuclear weapons program was no longer an act of national pride but "an act of international outlawry."[176] Mubarak himself said it would damage Egypt's international credibility to withdraw from the NPT.

Norm Transmission: Subjective Norms

Actor interpretations of reference group opinions are subjective norms: a North Korean belief that China does not oppose secret nuclear weapons is likely to influence North Korean decision-making. Actors may not interpret descriptive and injunctive norms properly, and they must also interpret what results when descriptive and injunctive norms collide. In the case of Egypt, subjective norms did not seem to play a large or even minor role in periods of nuclear decision-making. Of the major groups by which the Egyptian leadership might have been influenced (the United States, Soviet Union, radical Arab states such as Iraq and Syria, and conservative Arab states such as Jordan and Saudi Arabia), there were no reports of the Egyptian elite believing that one of these groups secretly supported an Egyptian nuclear weapons program while publicly saying the opposite.

Norm Processing: Linking

The processes whereby a norm moves from transmission to being acted upon require that actors identify the norm as worth considering. Such consideration can be triggered by linking—connecting the norm to well-established values. In Egypt, the influence of linking is evident. One of the first incidents of linking took place when Nasser approached the Soviet Union after the 1967 war, asking for help with nuclear weapons. The Soviets declined and instead recommended that Nasser sign the NPT, saying it would embarrass Israel and enhance Egypt's international credibility. As described, Nasser had already made the connection between using the non-nuclear regime for these very two goals—it is likely that hearing it from one of the two superpowers confirmed the value of such a strategy. From the creation of the Arab Republic of Egypt, engagement in international affairs was important to the Egyptian elite. Egypt had already been actively engaged in disarmament negotiations in the

1960s. By linking signature of the NPT with increased international legitimacy, the Soviets made this important step toward ending Egypt's nuclear weapons program more palatable to Nasser. This same type of linking — garnering international prestige while highlighting Israel's isolation — was suggested to Egypt by the United States during Egypt's decision-making on ratification of the NPT and the 1995 NPT Review and Extension Conference.

Norm Processing: Activation

Numerous norms, some contradictory, can apply at any point in a decision-making process. The norms of self-help and of nuclear nonproliferation may both be relevant. How do actors select which should guide their actions? The norms that have an edge are those that have been activated (highlighted or made focal), according to social psychology research. Testing this concept in political science is problematic in that multiple norms can be relevant and activated, making it difficult to establish whether activation of a particular norm influenced policymakers. Yet in Egypt, activation of the nuclear nonproliferation norm — or one linked to it — seems to have occurred in ways suggesting that such activation was relevant to decision-making. Unlike in Japan, in Egypt few domestic groups called for continued support of the nuclear nonproliferation norm; the Egyptian Council on Foreign Relations is one of the few NGOs to do so. Instead, norm activation came from influential outside sources. In the early 1960s, U.S. president John F. Kennedy initiated correspondence with Nasser, asking him to remain non-nuclear and activating the norms embedded in the emerging nuclear nonproliferation regime (a regime Egyptian diplomats were actively engaged in creating). Later in the decade, the Soviet Union activated the nonproliferation norm embedded in the NPT and linked it to international legitimacy, as previously discussed. Without the agreements hammered out in the NPT, the Soviets might not have felt the same way about controlling nuclear proliferation, and even if they did, they would not have had a legal instrument to ask the Egyptians to sign.

Norm Processing: Consistency

In social psychology findings, the need to appear and be consistent is a powerful motivator. Once commitments are made, people tend to remain consistent with them. Although the need to appear consistent did not seem to motivate

Egypt's initial decision to sign the NPT, once Egypt did sign, the nuclear option was largely closed. More than one Egyptian expert has argued that signing the NPT shut down the nuclear option totally. I have argued that signing the NPT was an important milestone toward that end, but it was not the final end to the nuclear weapons program. While we cannot know if Egypt would have reversed course had it not been for Sadat's reconceptualization of Egyptian security, the Egyptians signing the NPT did represent an important commitment that would have been hard to break. Commitments "grow legs," causing people to invoke other reasons for them, Cialdini argues, and removing the need for external inducements. States do something similar: disarmament bureaucracies spring up and use their budgets and organizational power to redefine and reframe issues. Within Egypt, the effect of the NPT-related bureaucracy is striking because officials were given a seat at a very small table. No longer were military and scientific personnel the only people providing input on nuclear issues; those at the table now included the diplomatic elite who served in Geneva and devoted themselves to international order. While they undoubtedly had Egypt's best interests at heart, they thought about Egypt's best interests in very different ways than did military officers who had fought on the battlefield against Israeli soldiers.

The influence of the diplomatic corps on nuclear nonproliferation issues is magnified because it does not appear that the decision on the nuclear option has been rethought since Mubarak took power.[177] One former military officer said, "There's been no formal study. It was not as though Mubarak asked those for and those against for arguments, and each side made their case, and Mubarak decided. It was already decided."[178] As Robert Einhorn notes: "All available evidence points to the conclusion that Egyptian leaders decided long ago to renounce nuclear weapons and have stuck to that decision."[179] Since the Foreign Ministry has authority over the issue, and the issue has not been seriously reconsidered for at least twenty years, their power is truly consolidated. This was confirmed by a former senior diplomat, who said with an air of absolute confidence, "Some are interested in matching Israel's nuclear weapons capability. But we are not interested. In the government and those involved in negotiations in the NPT, no, for us it was not a concern."[180]

His claim is substantiated by a report regarding Mubarak's rejection of a potential nuclear option in the early 1980s. Allegations arose that "the Ministry of Defense went to Mubarak in 1984 and requested permission to start a nuclear weapons program. Mubarak is said to have 'rejected the idea completely.' Mubarak, it is said, pointed out that Egypt had made a commitment under the NPT and argued that a nuclear program, if discovered, would undermine Egypt's credibility internationally. We are now in a period of peace, observed Mubarak. Israel's nuclear arsenal had to be addressed politically, not militarily."[181]

In addition to the consistency that disarmament bureaucracies have brought, Egyptian officials may feel tied to their record of active engagement in international nonproliferation issues. Egypt has made considerable investments, politically and financially, in its international diplomatic role. As one Egyptian expert noted:

> A good part of the Egyptian elite is legalistic, with a belief in an organized world. It's in our political culture, and it's very strong. And the more we are involved, the more important our involvement is. Because of Egypt's status as a founder of the UN, global treaties are important to us. You don't sign it if you aren't going to abide by it. Egypt is a believer — when things like UN resolutions aren't obeyed, we are astonished, as though we have a world government. You can see this reflected in our behavior: our best caliber go to the UN; the number two diplomat in the Foreign Ministry is head of our UN delegation. In most international fora, Egypt is overrepresented.[182]

Reversing course on nuclear nonproliferation would mean abandoning decades of work as well as international credibility, something the Egyptians prize. In discussing obstacles to an Egyptian nuclear option, Landau observes: "Not only does Egypt have obligations to the NPT, but it has built itself up as the major regional advocate of a WMDFZ and even sought to advance its leadership role by promoting this agenda."[183] A former U.S. diplomat concurred: "The Egyptians have gained power because of their competence in using the UN system. If they violated the NPT, they would lose that."[184] While consistency did not seem to influence the initial decision to forgo nuclear weapons, it does seem to have reinforced that decision, with its influence growing over time.

Norm Potency: Uncertainty

Conditions under which norms are transmitted and received also have bearing, and social psychology indicates that uncertainty raises norm "potency," or the likelihood of norm acceptance. Uncertainty makes actors more open to outside influence when a task is unclear or results of decisions are difficult to predict—as happens when costs and benefits are rising or falling. The cost-benefit equation for nuclear weapons acquisition changed sharply with the NPT. Gone was certainty about the value of nuclear weapons. In came uncertainty over whether they were worth the new economic and social costs and even whether they were needed, now that nuclear weapons states had made commitments not to use such weapons against non-nuclear weapons states. For Egypt, uncertainty over the utility of nuclear weapons and awareness of their political and financial costs also shaped elite decision-making. Using nuclear weapons against a neighbor would wreak havoc on Egypt's environment as well. While a nuclear option could provide political leverage, military deterrence, and national pride, it would hurt Egypt's ability to get the conventional weapons needed to regain the Sinai. With the creation of the NPT, a nuclear weapons program became more difficult logistically and would also cost Egypt international credibility.

In addition, the NPT created a significant benefit for Egypt by providing a diplomatic route to increasing international legitimacy, highlighting Israel's noncompliance, and strengthening Egypt's claim to regional leadership. A U.S. diplomat commented, "Some say that states pursue nuclear weapons for the glitter factor. For Egypt, the glitter factor was transferred over to using the UN and taking a leadership role diplomatically, especially with regard to the nuclear nonproliferation issue."[185] The NPT transformed the costs and benefits of the nuclear option from making acquisition harder and more costly to making nuclear forbearance a diplomatic tool and source of pride.

Norm Potency: Similarity

We are more open to the influence of norm transmitters similar to us or with which we want good relations. Beyond the expectation of receiving benefits from the relationship, similarity or the desire to be more similar creates positive feelings and makes us more receptive to normative influence. The similarity effect likely made Egyptian decision-makers more open to normative influence, but it is not always easy to pinpoint the effect of similarity. Sadat's decision to close with finality the nuclear option — as part of his strategic choice to pursue a relationship with the United States and peace with Israel — was also likely influenced by the similarity effect. As one former military officer argued, "Under Sadat, Egypt was transformed from East to West, from war to peace, from socialist to a more open economy."[186] Sadat's desire to transform likely made him more open to normative influence by those he wanted to emulate, including the normative message to exercise nuclear forbearance.

Norm Potency: Conflict

Conflict is polarizing, usually leading actors to reject outside normative influence, especially from the opposing side in the conflict. The Egypt case study presents mixed results for this expectation. Well before the U.S.-Egyptian diplomatic rift in 1965, U.S. president John F. Kennedy had personal communications with Nasser, including on the topic of nuclear nonproliferation. At least one Egyptian scientist believes that those communications strongly influenced Nasser's position, despite the falling out with the United States. Of course, Sadat shocked the world by responding to the military defeat in 1973 by pursuing peace with Israel, which would also seem to undermine the proposed effect of conflict. More recently, polarization did occur in the ACRS forum, in which unresolved conflict over Israel's undeclared nuclear capability led to a breakdown in the talks.[187] However, some have suggested that the polarization was as much of a function of Egypt's concern over its regional leadership role as over unresolved conflict.

Even before the nuclear nonproliferation regime was formalized through the opening of the NPT for signature, its influence shaped the way the Egyptian elite thought about the opportunities and risks offered by nuclear weapons. By creating economic and social costs for going nuclear, as well as diplomatic incentives and opportunities for prestige through forgoing nuclear weapons, the nonproliferation regime made the decision for nuclear forbearance an easier one. After Egypt committed to the regime, the diplomatic corps gained a seat at the decision-making table and eventually consolidated its influence, because Sadat and Mubarak never felt the need to reopen formal debate over the nuclear option. Instead, Egyptian diplomats used the NPT to highlight Israel's unsafeguarded nuclear complex, providing them with prestige both in the Arab world and among domestic constituents. Without the NPT and associated agreements, such a strategy would not have been possible.

EGYPT'S NUCLEAR DECISION-MAKING: THEORETICAL ANALYSIS

Not only has Egypt forgone a nuclear option in the face of a nuclear-armed neighbor against which it has lost four wars, but the state has also become one of the international leaders in the global nuclear nonproliferation regime. What accounts for such counterintuitive behavior? To examine the matter, each set of theoretical expectations is compared to the case study evidence.

Realist Expectations

Realist expectations outlined in chapter 1 indicate that a state may forgo nuclear weapons for five potential reasons: lack of threat, lack of regional threat, the presence of security guarantees, the possibility of weakened security, and achievement of an alternative means of deterrence. The expectations of lack of threat and lack of regional threat disappoint in the Egyptian case. As defined in chapter 1, threat can be constituted by a nuclear-armed adversary, an adversary with nuclear potential, or an adversary with overwhelming conventional forces. Egypt became aware of Israel's outstanding conventional forces in the 1948 war, knew of Israel's nuclear potential by 1960, and believed Israel had nuclear-armed missiles by the early 1970s. Besides the situation in Israel, Egypt was alarmed by the nuclear progress of other neighbors: Iran, Iraq, and Libya. Contrary to some reports, the Egyptian political elite was unhappy with the prospects of any of these states acquiring a nuclear capacity.[188] The concern over Iraq and Iran was that if either of these states went nuclear, it would attempt to exercise regional hegemony, curtailing Egypt's leadership role.[189] Libya, in contrast, was seen as potentially unstable: "The Egyptian elite see Libya acquiring nuclear weapons as equal to Israel in terms of threat."[190]

The third expectation also does not find a great deal of support in the Egyptian case, because Egypt never had a formalized security guarantee from a nuclear power. As noted previously, while it is rumored that the Soviets gave some sort of security guarantee, there is no evidence for it. Even if promised, a secret, informal security guarantee would likely not be enough to quell a country's fears.[191] Some may question whether Egypt's bilateral relationship with the United States would be a quasi security guarantee that could serve in place of an Egyptian nuclear deterrent. However, as Einhorn notes, the United States has not provided officials in Cairo with any formal agreement to come to their aid should Egypt be attacked: "Cairo understands that strong U.S. ties with Israel preclude Washington's providing Egypt the kind of security guarantee that other close U.S. friends and allies have received (that is, to come to an ally's defense if it is threatened or attacked)."[192] Certainly the United States has an interest in maintaining peace in the Middle East and wants to see Egypt thrive because of the role Cairo plays in moderating tensions in the region. However, if war between Egypt and another country did break out, that country would most likely be Israel — and Egypt is under no illusion that the United States would side with Cairo. Indeed, Egypt's most devastating wars were fought against Israel, and Israel is the only country in the region with nuclear weapons. If Egypt has not received any formal security guarantee from the United States and knows that Washington would side with Tel Aviv over Cairo, the argument that Egypt relies on an informal U.S. security guarantee is less than convincing. In addition, senior Egyptian policymakers have argued that if the political decision were made to pursue nuclear weapons, the relationship with the United States would not stop them.[193]

The potential of nuclear weapons making Egypt a target (Expectation 4) is also not borne out by the evidence. The issue was not brought up in any report or analysis and was not mentioned by any interviewee. The only time the question of becoming a target was raised involved whether Egypt would want to start a secret or non-IAEA nuclear facility after the 1981 Israeli bombing of Iraq's Osirak reactor. But Egypt had already consolidated its non-nuclear stance by this time. In addition, this expectation refers not to specific nuclear installations being targeted but rather to the fact that by going nuclear, a state could find itself drawn into a potential nuclear war.

The fifth neorealist expectation, which posits that states may not seek nuclear weapons because they instead seek other forms of WMD for deterrence, finds more support. Egypt is known to have begun both chemical and biological weapons programs by the early 1960s, in part as a response to the Israeli nuclear threat. Evidence about the biological weapons program is sparse, and Egypt likely relegated it to a secondary role early on.[194] The Egyptian chemical weapons program, however, has been more serious. Egypt was the first country in the Middle East to use them on the battlefield, during the Yemen civil war (1963–67), likely using stocks left behind by the British. Although Egypt currently denies that it has any stocks of chemical weapons, Western intelligence agencies believe that Egypt maintains supplies of a number of chemical agents and that members of the military receive training in chemical warfare.[195] Adding to the suspicion is the fact that Egypt refuses to sign the Chemical Weapons Convention despite having played a leadership role in its negotiation, citing Israel's refusal to join the NPT. To what extent does Egypt's chemical weapons program explain its decision to forgo nuclear weapons? First, chemical weapons are often called the "poor man's WMD" because they are less expensive. But they are also less destructive, less effective, and more problematic to deploy than nuclear weapons. "There is little question that the lethality of chemical weapons — as measured by per unit weight of delivered munitions — is lower by many orders of magnitude than it is for nuclear weapons or the undemonstrated and inherently uncertain potential of biological weapons. Thus, it is misleading to include chemical weapons in the category of WMD; 'weapons of indiscriminate destruction' or 'weapons of terror' might be a more appropriate designation."[196]

Whereas both passive and active countermeasures can be taken against chemical (and biological) weapons, the only protection against a nuclear strike is to prevent it from being launched.[197] Thus chemical weapons are not in the same league as nuclear weapons, and whether they provide an adequate deterrent against nuclear weapons is questionable. Khan notes, "Chemical weapons are not equivalent to nuclear weapons even though they inflict a high cost. . . . Chemical weapons are not effective deterrents against Israeli nuclear weapons, even though they may be used to enhance the bargaining position of the possessor."[198]

However, this does not mean that Egypt did not consider its chemical weapons as an attempt to match Israel's WMD capabilities. What it does mean is that chemical weapons are not a full deterrent to nuclear weapons, and that states facing a nuclear-armed adversary are not likely to feel satisfied with only a chemical weapons capability. Michael Siler argues that although Egypt "was alleged to have had chemical weapons of mass destruction, Sadat felt that this kind of deterrence was not credible in a future confrontation with Israel."[199] This was borne out by Egypt's behavior; while they had an operational chemical weapons stock in the early 1960s, the Egyptians continued exploring the nuclear option, including seeking nuclear weapons from the Soviet Union and China. Then, after acceding to the NPT, Egypt expended enormous effort to pressure Israel into giving up its nuclear weapons. The Egyptians' reliance on chemical weapons may have blunted their desire for nuclear weapons but did not erase it. As one former military officer said, "Egypt worked in two tracks: we tried to get rid of Israel's nuclear weapons through diplomatic efforts, and we sought military alternatives such as strong conventional forces, surface-to-surface missiles, and chemical weapons options."[200] Nevertheless, the presence of an alternative form of WMD may have helped assuage both security concerns and psychological needs: Egypt would not be left without any defense against a WMD attack and in fact could launch one of its own.

Neoliberal Institutionalist Expectations

How institutions can change a state's cost-benefit calculations to discourage going nuclear is the pivot of the expectations invoked by neoliberal institutionalism; a state's essential desire to have nuclear weapons is not at issue here. Under the first neoliberal expectation, it is to gain the material benefits offered by the NPT that states forgo nuclearization. At first glance this seems to describe the case of Egypt exactly. Egypt had refused to ratify the NPT for thirteen years, citing Israel's failure to join the regime. Severe energy crises had led Egypt to seek nuclear power reactors, but their efforts to acquire civilian nuclear power plants were blocked because they had not yet ratified the NPT. As a consequence, Sadat pushed through domestic opposition and completed Egypt's accession to the NPT, immediately afterward signing several nuclear cooperation agreements with foreign governments. The problem with this line of reasoning is that at the time this cost-benefit analysis was made, Egypt had already closed its nuclear option. In other words, it did not decide to shut down its nuclear weapons program so that it could acquire help with civilian power plants. The decision Sadat did face was whether to give up the diplomatic leverage of not having ratified the NPT in order to secure help with civilian nuclear technology.

Recognizing the NPT as the best way to keep nuclear weapons from spreading is part of the reason most states joined. The next neoliberal expectation posits this wish to escape the security dilemma as what causes states to join and adhere to the NPT. It is unclear whether Nasser felt that signing the NPT would make Egypt safer, but he likely hoped that Egypt's signature would create pressure on Israel to join, as the Soviets suggested it would. During the 1960s, when the nuclear option was being considered the most seriously, the danger of a nuclear arms race was probably not a major concern for Nasser, given the immediate dangers he was facing with the attempted annexation of the Suez Canal, occupation of the Sinai, and more. But the potential for a nuclear arms race probably became clearer in the 1970s, when both Iraq and Iran started their nuclear programs. By the late 1970s, the logic was clear to the Egyptians: "We saw that if we were to [open the nuclear option], this would trigger a dangerous arms race. In the end we would also lose. Therefore, the strategy was, instead of getting in the race, try to get Israel out of the race."[201] As mentioned in chapter 3, the premise of this hypothesis is that a state agrees not to seek nuclear weapons because others also agree not to, and the state is satisfied with compliance and verification. Aware of the "cheating" by Iraq, Iran and Libya (all members of the NPT), as well as facing a neighbor who refused to join, Egypt is probably more aware of the limitations of the NPT than any other state. Egypt joined and ratified the NPT not because its political leaders believed they would no longer face any nuclear threat or intimidation after accession — on the contrary, they initially refused to ratify the NPT because they believed that until Israel joined, the NPT could not provide a secure framework. They acceded to the NPT because they believed it gave them the best set of tools for handling the Israeli nuclear threat without threatening the international legitimacy necessary to achieving their other goals of economic development and engagement with the United States.

Constructivist Expectations

Constructivism invokes the international social environment and the roles states play in it as the explanation for forgoing the nuclear option. The first constructivist expectation proposes that nuclear forbearance derives from changes in the way the political elite think about state interests. In many ways, this describes Sadat. Egypt had lost four wars, and its economy was in a downward spiral. Sadat looked at the Egypt he now had to lead and did not like the future he saw. Hence he decided to change strategy in order to take Egypt to a better future. Numerous interviewees — Western and Egyptian, military and diplomatic — commented on Sadat's vision for the Egypt of the future: peaceful and prosperous. But to implement his change in strategy, Sadat had to change his own thinking about who Egypt's enemies and friends were. Israel could no longer be demonized, and Sadat could no longer characterize negotiation with Israel as "total capitulation." To encourage Egypt's development, Sadat believed he needed to seek peace with Israel and create a close relationship with the United States. Recall a former military officer's summary of Egypt's transformation "from East to West, from war to peace," and to a more open economy.[202]

Because of this fundamental shift in state interests, nuclear weapons could no longer be part of Egypt's strategy. "The decision to ratify the NPT was a direct derivative of the grand strategy decision to base Egypt's future on a close relationship with the United States. Sadat was educated to the fact that given U.S. nuclear nonproliferation policy, both close relations with the U.S. and a nuclear weapons program were incompatible. The priority was the relationship with the United States."[203] Why would a relationship with a potentially fickle superpower — one that supplied your enemy with arms and political backing — be preferred over a nuclear weapons program? Given the shift in national priorities, nuclear weapons had little value. "If we had nuclear weapons, what would we do with them?" a high-level diplomat asked. "We have a peace treaty with Israel, and we are slowly developing that relationship. We have no other enemies, and we have no ambitions to become the preponderant power in the region. Egypt's power relies on rebuilding our economy after so many years of war. Egypt wants to become a model for the region, instead of boasting about a weapon that we would never use."[204] A former military officer agreed:

> We had no national reason to need them with the Sinai back and no hostilities or bilateral disputes with Israel. The financial cost would be an obstacle, and especially with our relationship with the United States, the political cost would be really high. And how would we use it? Would we hit Israel and destroy the Palestinians? Even if Israel hit Egypt, would we strike back and take out the Palestinians, as well as some of Jordan and Syria? No. This can be dealt with through diplomatic tools. The main dilemma is Egyptian prestige, but the regional environment has helped Egypt maintain its leadership role and in persuading other Arab states to give up nuclear weapons.[205]

While Sadat's decision to make peace with Israel, and the accompanying devaluation of nuclear weapons, may seem like an obvious choice, at the time it was totally counterintuitive. Sadat's move from the Soviet Union to the United States shocked both superpowers.[206] His 1977 trip to Jerusalem shocked the world. His bold moves did win him political support domestically, at least for a short time. But there were many other ways for him to win political support domestically without shifting superpower alliances and declaring Egypt's enemy a friend. In essence, Sadat decided to gamble that peace with the nuclear-armed adversary that had defeated Egypt four times was worth the potential payoff of a better future for his country. Some in Egypt would argue that he lost his gamble. Many Egyptians have made the argument that relying on a peace treaty to protect Egypt's national existence is folly.[207] Nonetheless, Sadat clearly changed the way he thought about Egypt's allies and adversaries, rejected the self-help principle, and instead embraced diplomacy as the way to secure Egypt's future.

In addition to being persuaded about new state goals and new ways to achieve them, there is also the matter of being persuaded specifically about the merits of the NPT and the nuclear nonproliferation norm.[208] In Japan, one might not be surprised if members of the elite truly believe in halting nuclear nonproliferation, given their country's unique experience. In Egypt, one might not expect the same. However, some portions of the diplomatic corps and the Foreign Ministry do seem to have embraced the nuclear nonproliferation norm fully due to the NPT. It is impossible to estimate what percentage, but it is likely at least a moderate amount. One Western expert who has worked with the Egyptians noted: "Egypt has strongly associated itself with international law and international norms. There's a whole generation of Egyptian Foreign Ministry guys who were brought up and trained in the nuclear nonproliferation regime. They are not going to go against the norms underlying the regime."[209] Speaking of one of Egypt's most senior diplomats, a U.S. expert said, "Violating the NPT would undermine every personal value he holds. He spent a career supporting nuclear nonproliferation."[210] Because the NPT took the issue of nuclear weapons out of the military's domain and into that of the Foreign Ministry, the beliefs and assumptions of these diplomats matter a great deal in Egypt's nuclear decision-making.

Egypt's leadership role in the New Agenda Coalition substantiates the Foreign Ministry's commitment to nuclear nonproliferation. The NAC issued a direct challenge to the United States and other nuclear weapons states about their lack of progress in nuclear disarmament. (Japan, on the other hand, declined to join the NAC because of concerns over American reaction.) Egypt's participation in the NAC is based on the desire to see Israel join the NPT, but it also shows in some measure that Egypt is committed to furthering the nuclear nonproliferation norm. Finally, the Egyptian decision to reject an opportunity to restart a secret nuclear weapons program confirms that officials do not see the value in a nuclear deterrent. In the late 1990s the Egyptian government was approached by nonstate parties from a former Soviet republic with the offer of nuclear material and nuclear technology.[211] Here was a perfect opportunity for Egypt to balance Israel's nuclear program — which at that point many Egyptians argued was not just for Israeli defense but also for psychological and political domination.[212] Instead, Mubarak declined, and Egypt continues to rely on diplomacy to balance Israel's nuclear weapons. After the India-Pakistan nuclear tests of 1998, Mubarak argued that the proper response was for Egypt to work even harder to promote a non-nuclear Middle East.[213]

The second constructivist expectation predicts that states forgo nuclear weapons not because they believe it is the best choice for their security but rather because of the cost-benefit calculations of the social costs and rewards. This position seems to describe Nasser's eventual position on the nuclear issue. By 1967 the Egyptian leadership had been exposed to the nuclear nonproliferation norm through a number of avenues: UN negotiations, personal communications from Kennedy, and dealings with Soviet allies. The Egyptians had begun to use the UN to highlight Israel's unsafeguarded nuclear complex. By 1968 Nasser was ready to sign the NPT so that he could garner international credibility for Egypt and place a spotlight on Israel's refusal to join the regime — both of which enhanced Egypt's claim to regional leadership. In other words, Nasser did not seem to be convinced of the inherent immorality of nuclear weapons, nor did he seem to have changed value systems so as to be ready to embrace Israel as a friend. Instead, he saw the utility of the nuclear nonproliferation regime — to embarrass his enemy, to enhance his nation's credibility, and to further Egypt's leadership in the Arab world. The cost of such benefits was nuclear forbearance, which Nasser found to be an acceptable price. Such a cost-benefit calculation would only be possible in an international social environment with strengthening nonproliferation norms.

The final constructivist expectation proposes that states valuing a relationship with a high-status NPT proponent forgo nuclear weapons to maintain that relationship (the outcome of identification). While Egypt considers its relationship with the United States critically important, identification is not the best way to describe the Egyptian attitude toward nuclear nonproliferation. When Sadat first ratified the NPT, it was in part a simple cost-benefit calculation. Because Sadat knew that he could not have a close relationship with the United States and have a nuclear weapons program, he simply chose to close the nuclear option for good. His decision was not based on a desire to imitate or garner praise from the United States; rather, it was a calculated move. In fact, Egypt is one of the few countries to have submitted a statement with its instruments of ratification, in which it rebuked the United States and Soviet Union for lack of progress on disarmament: "Egypt wishes to express its strong dissatisfaction at the nuclear weapons states, in particular the two superpowers, because of their failure to take effective measures relating to the cessation of the nuclear arms race and to nuclear disarmament."[214] Today those supporting the nuclear nonproliferation regime do so with a sense of great frustration toward the United States, as opposed to identification with the United States. As noted earlier, Egypt had no concerns about participating in the NAC, which essentially issued a challenge to the United States and the other nuclear weap-

---

Table 5 Egyptian Nuclear Decision-Making

EXPECTATION	OUTCOME / ANALYSIS
Realism	
Lack of threat	*Fails* (Egypt lost four wars to nuclear-armed neighbor.)
Lack of regional threat	*Fails* (Egypt lost four wars to nuclear-armed neighbor.)
Security guarantee	*Fails* (Egyptian elite did not receive any credible security guarantee.)
Nuclear weapons make state a target	*Fails* (The only "target" concerns relate to potential targeting of nuclear facilities—and this arose in 1981 when Israel bombed Iraq's Osirak reactor, after Egypt's nuclear option was already closed.)
Alternative WMD provides deterrent	*Important but not sufficient* (Egyptian elite did rely to some extent on chemical weapons capability but still aggressively pursued other ways to counter the Israeli nuclear program.)
Neoliberal Institutionalism	
NPT's material benefits	*Fails* (Egypt did not ratify the NPT, and thus become eligible for its material benefits, until after the nuclear option was closed.)
Escaping the security dilemma	*Fails* (Egyptian elite recognized more than perhaps any other state the limits of the NPT, given Israel's refusal to join and the fact that three neighbors were all members of the NPT yet were known to be working on nuclear weapons programs.)

ons states to stop stalling on nuclear disarmament and hold up their end of the bargain.

What does this analysis of expectations tell us about the reasons for Egypt's nuclear forbearance? First, some explanations can be ruled out. Lack of threat — regional or otherwise — does not satisfy as an explanation. A reassuring security guarantee is not what kept Egypt from developing nuclear

Table 5 Egyptian Nuclear Decision-Making (*continued*)

EXPECTATION	OUTCOME / ANALYSIS
Constructivism	
Changed thinking about security (persuasion)	*Passes* (Sadat reconceptualized Egyptian security, including what constituted a legitimate way to deal with an enemy, leading to a devaluation of nuclear weapons. In addition, some part of Egypt's diplomatic corps is likely convinced that nuclear weapons are truly not the best route for Egypt.)
Calculation of social costs and rewards (social conformity)	*Passes* (Nasser realized that the emerging nuclear nonproliferation regime created new benefits for nuclear forbearance—including the ability to shame Israel and gain status in the Arab world. This allowed him to recalculate costs and benefits of Egypt's nuclear weapons policy, likely leading him to sign the NPT. However, Sadat went beyond a strictly utilitarian cost-benefit calculation, changing the value of a nuclear program, and thus requiring additional explanation beyond social conformity.)
Desire to create or maintain important relationship (identification)	*Fails* (Egyptian elite never seemed to place great emphasis on "friendship" with the United States; in fact, they joined the New Agenda Coalition, which blasted the nuclear weapons states for lack of disarmament progress.)

weapons, for it never received a convincing one (and most likely never received any at all). Fear of becoming a target became pertinent only after Israel's bombing of the Iraqi Osirak reactor in 1981, when Egypt's nuclear option had already been closed for years. Trading the nuclear option for guaranteed access to nuclear energy also does not seem to be a main motivation factor, for similar reasons: Egypt made this trade in 1981, long after any nuclear weapons program had been active. Egypt likely hoped its accession to the NPT would help it escape the security dilemma, but decades of Israeli refusal to join the regime have shattered that illusion. Indeed, if the Egyptian elite ever believed that the regime could ensure satisfactory compliance even among those who joined it, the revelations of Iraq's nuclear program in 1991 would have disabused them of that notion. Finally, Egypt's nuclear forbearance did not seem to result from identification with the United States. Sadat's rapprochement with the United States was based more on the realization that America could provide what Egypt needed (economic aid, conventional weapons, additional leverage against Israel, international credibility) as opposed to a desire to establish a friendship.

Potentially persuasive explanations include an alternative form of WMD to provide deterrence, a change in the way Egyptians thought about security, and the calculation of social costs and benefits. Egypt's chemical weapons program has been a dedicated one and is still considered active even today. Statements by Egyptian officials indicate that they consider (or at least would like others to consider) their chemical weapons program as a deterrent against the Israeli nuclear program. However, Egyptian actions confirm that they did not consider their chemical weapons as a full deterrent to Israel's nuclear program. They attempted to build their own nuclear weapons program, even seeking nuclear devices from the Soviet Union and China. After choosing to abandon the nuclear route, Egypt then exerted extensive efforts diplomatically to balance the nuclear equation by bringing Israel into the NPT. A former military officer acknowledged that Egypt pursued two tracks: one diplomatic, one military (convention arms, missiles, and chemical weapons). Nonetheless, the chemical weapons program gave Egypt a sense of security and pride that it could respond to an Israeli nuclear attack with WMD of its own. Both Feldman and Einhorn note that this is part of Egypt's decision-making calculus.[215] The chemical weapons program likely made it somewhat less urgent for Nasser to pursue a nuclear capability, and somewhat easier for Sadat to close the door totally on the nuclear option. Because the Egyptians did continue to pursue other ways to match or negate Israel's nuclear weapons program, it is unlikely that the chemical weapons program was sufficient in and of itself to create Egypt's nuclear forbearance. Yet it should not be dismissed as an inconsequential factor.

Social conformity — Egyptian calculation of social rewards and costs associated with being inside or outside the NPT — also offers promise as an explanation. This is the best explanation for Nasser's eventual acceptance of the NPT, for it allowed him to use the regime to draw international attention to Israel's unsafeguarded nuclear complex and to advance Egypt's international legitimacy — both of which enhanced Egypt's claim to regional leadership.

The price of such a bargain was nuclear forbearance, which Nasser was willing to pay. Thus, in the international social environment fostered by the emerging nuclear nonproliferation regime, these social and diplomatic rewards were seen as greater than the military benefit of a nuclear weapons program. Without the emerging regime, these rewards would not have existed.

However, one must also note that Nasser accepted the use of the regime as a substitute for his own nuclear deterrent only after failing to achieve a nuclear option. Israeli sabotage, difficulty securing needed technology to produce and reprocess plutonium, and lack of help from current nuclear powers all seriously hindered the Egyptian nuclear weapons program, raising the incentives for Nasser to conform. Had these roadblocks not slowed him down, Nasser may have been less willing to do so. Of course, there is some question about whether Nasser was ever really serious about a nuclear weapons program. In addition, other countries have faced even more serious obstacles and yet have pursued the nuclear option in secret for many decades. Both of these facts would mitigate the importance of these roadblocks. But it seems reasonable to conclude that while social conformity best describes Nasser's eventual acceptance of the NPT, he was strongly encouraged to select that option because of serious material obstacles on the path to nuclear weapons.

One might also classify Sadat's decision to continue Egyptian nuclear forbearance as a result of social conformity. Sadat's original decision to seek a relationship with the United States was based in large part on his belief that it could give him what he needed to pursue Egyptian development. Knowing that American assistance would not be forthcoming should Egypt have an active nuclear weapons program, he made a trade-off. However, by looking only to social conformity, this analysis ignores one thing: Sadat was willing to make this trade-off because his changed priorities devalued nuclear weapons. I argue that it was persuasion — a changed view of security and status — that even allowed such a cost-benefit calculation. Sadat's dramatically different vision for Egypt changed what nuclear weapons meant to Egypt. As mentioned, a senior military officer observed that with Egypt ready to abandon the nuclear option, it became a tool — "something we could give to the United States as a present . . . and it wasn't really much of a present."[216] The phrase "it wasn't really much of a present" is striking. For a country facing a nuclear-armed adversary against which it had lost four wars, and knowing of secret nuclear weapons programs of three other neighbors, a nuclear capacity sounds like the perfect present. But as a senior Egyptian diplomat reframed it, "Nuclear weapons weren't part of the future as we saw it, with Arabs and Israelis living together. Why would you need the ultimate weapon when you are living peacefully with your neighbors?"[217] Indeed, Sadat's change of heart led him to reconceptualize Egypt's security dilemma: who Egypt considered a friend, who Egypt considered an enemy, and the acceptable methods by which one deals with enemies.[218] One of the results of this reconceptualization was that nuclear weapons were no longer necessary or even valuable.

The nuclear nonproliferation norm was important to this reconceptualization in a number of ways. When Sadat came to power, Egypt had already signed the NPT, setting a precedent for forgoing the military option of matching Israel's nuclear weapons program and instead relying on diplomatic tools to handle this security issue. Nasser had already reconceptualized the value of the nuclear issue: not as a rallying point for a preemptive military strike against Israel's nuclear facilities or for an equivalent Egyptian nuclear weapons program, but rather as a way to force Israel's unsafeguarded nuclear program into the international spotlight and to gain status regionally. The emerging nuclear nonproliferation regime added these rewards to Nasser's cost-benefit calculation, and in the end he decided that the rewards made it worth giving up the nuclear option. For Sadat, the nuclear option in itself lost value, making the equation more lopsided. As the Egyptian diplomatic corps became more experienced and more successful in using the regime to shame Israel and enhance Egyptian status, the benefits side of the equation only strengthened — benefits that would not exist without the NPT and the associated international social environment.

The lesson of Egyptian nuclear decision-making is that a number of factors combined to produce the long-lasting nuclear forbearance we see today. First, material impediments to the nuclear program created a climate that strongly encouraged Nasser to sign the NPT and use it as a method to shame Israel and gain status in the Arab world. Thus realist obstacles created the environment for Nasser to choose social conformity. In addition, the chemical weapons program gave Nasser policy space to reject nuclear weapons. Sadat, facing these same challenges and then some, went further than Nasser: instead of strategically using the regime to advance his goals, he radically rethought what success meant for Egypt. Conflict with Israel, and the nuclear weapons program needed for it, were no longer the goals Cairo would pursue. Instead, peace with Israel and total abandonment of the nuclear option were the new path for success. As with Japan, over time this commitment became embedded into Egyptian government—and in fact even more so, since a nuclear option has not been seriously considered by the Egyptian leadership for decades. Indeed, despite public and opposition calls for an Egyptian nuclear program, diplomatic frustration with Israel's continued nuclear status, and a complete inability to get Israel to move at all on its nuclear program, Egyptian leadership remains on a non-nuclear path today.

CHAPTER FIVE

Nuclear Decision-Making in Libya, Sweden, and Germany

The cases of Japan and Egypt highlight critical lessons in the search for understanding how countries decide whether to pursue a nuclear weapons capability. State elites certainly consider security needs — but how security is defined is much broader and more inclusive than might be predicted by traditional approaches. In both cases, top leadership did want to acquire nuclear weapons, and only after assessing the obstacles (for Japan, a norm-driven domestic populace and for Egypt, foreign and technical interruptions) did they acquiesce to nuclear forbearance. Over time, however, the nuclear nonproliferation regime helped change the perception of what security would look like for Japan and Egypt, as well as the perception of the value of nuclear weapons. In addition, we see specific ways in which the international social environment pressured and in some cases persuaded policymakers that they should not seek nuclear weapons.

To what extent can these lessons be generalized to other countries? Are the findings anomalous and not likely to apply elsewhere? Or are the cases of Japan and Egypt likely to open up new insight for a number of other states? To address these questions, this chapter examines the case histories of three more countries that have abandoned the nuclear option: Libya, Sweden, and Germany. Each is important in helping assess the value of lessons learned from Japan and Egypt. Libya is a critical case for a number of reasons. Libya's recent abandonment of the nuclear option is the only known case in which the same person made both the decision to acquire and then the decision to abandon a nuclear weapons capability. The policy implications are tremendous: What would convince Libya to give up a potential nuclear deterrent? What is the current value of the nuclear nonproliferation regime? Does the NPT still persuade?

Sweden is a critical case because the country originally intended to acquire a nuclear deterrent. As the emerging nuclear nonproliferation regime took shape, however, Sweden had to struggle with what nuclear weapons meant for its security and identity. Thus the Swedish case gives us a clear picture of how, early on, the regime helped to transform thinking about the value of nuclear weapons. Germany's importance springs from the fact that the country was the critical case for the nonproliferation regime. In the formative days of the regime, a number of other countries (including Sweden) indicated that they were not willing to give up a nuclear option unless Germany did. Success of the nonproliferation norm in Germany can therefore be seen as success for the norm worldwide. In addition to this historical significance, Germany is one of only a few countries today that could develop nuclear weapons in a very short period. Thus assessing Germany's commitment to the regime is important for policy's sake.

To develop each case, I examine the history of the country's nuclear program and the decision-making process that eventually led to a choice against nuclear weapons. Then the evidence is compared against my larger findings to see to what extent — and why — they mesh.

LIBYA

For decades, Libyan leader Muammar Qadhafi pursued nuclear weapons — along with other types of WMD — to balance Israel and to exert leadership in the Arab world. When the Libyan government announced the decision to give up those WMD programs in December 2003, the world was stunned. What could have convinced the Middle East's "bad boy" to give up his weapons and cooperate with the international community? The Libyan case of nuclear rollback is significant for a number of reasons. It is the first and only case in which the same person made the decision to acquire *and* the decision to forgo nuclear weapons. In addition, if we understand what would persuade an Arab dictator to give up his nuclear weapons program at the same time others in his region are pursuing them, we may be able to halt further proliferation. Finally, at a time when the nonproliferation regime is severely stressed, the Libyan case provides some cause for optimism. To understand why Libya gave up its substantial nuclear weapons program, we must first review how Libya built up that program.

Libya gained its independence in 1951 under King Idris al-Sanusi, under whose leadership Libya signed the NPT in 1968. A year later, twenty-nine-year-old

Qadhafi led a successful coup against the monarch and quickly began his quest for WMD, including nuclear weapons.[1] In 1970 Tripoli tried unsuccessfully to purchase nuclear weapons from China.[2] Libya then began negotiating with the Soviet Union for a nuclear reactor, but the Soviets first wanted the Libyan government to ratify the NPT. Tripoli ratified the NPT in May 1975, although Qadhafi had told the Sudanese newspaper As Sahafa just a month beforehand that he wanted Libya to become a nuclear weapons state: "'Nuclear weapons are no longer a secret,' he told the paper."[3] Thus ratification of the NPT likely meant little but rather was done to gain access to the technology needed to produce nuclear weapons indigenously. In June 1975 the Soviets and Libya signed an agreement for the Soviets to provide a ten-megawatt research reactor to Libya, housed at Tajura. The reactor came on line in 1983 and has always been under IAEA inspections.[4]

Libya reached out to other countries as well in its quest for nuclear weapons. In the early 1970s Qadhafi reportedly made a pact with Pakistan to create an "Islamic Bomb," funded by Libya's oil money and produced by Pakistani scientists.[5] By the end of the decade Libya had reportedly provided Pakistan with more than a hundred tons of yellowcake, which it had purchased from Niger.[6] Qadhafi also tried to procure nuclear weapons from India after that country's successful nuclear explosion in 1974. Abid Hussain, the Indian ambassador to the United States, reported the Libyan proposal in 1991: Qadhafi "offered in the late 1970s to pay India an amount comparable to its foreign debt in exchange for nuclear weapons technology, but India declined."[7]

By 1980 it was clear that Libya would not be able to purchase outright a nuclear weapon or the technology to create the full fuel cycle, so Qadhafi started to focus on building an indigenous bomb:

> After concluding nuclear accords with India, the Soviet Union and possibly Argentina that are expected to give Libya a nuclear research capacity, Colonel Qadhafi has opted for a "home-grown" Libyan nuclear capacity. Industrial sources report that rather than trying to emulate Iraq or Brazil by buying a complete system, the Qadhafi approach will be to obtain bits and pieces. Included will be a nuclear-fueled electric power generating plant from various Western firms, a reprocessing plant to make plutonium from Niger, and Chad uranium. Libya meanwhile is sending thousands of students to the United States, West Germany, and France to study nuclear physics.[8]

However, obstacles continued to surface. Several attempted purchases of nuclear technology from Western countries were scuttled, in part due to pressure from the United States. Nuclear suppliers tightened export controls to prevent countries such as Libya and Pakistan from gaining access to sensitive nuclear technology.[9] Under Ronald Reagan, the U.S. government instituted new rules to stop Libyan students from studying nuclear science in the United States.[10] Saudi Arabia reportedly supplanted Libya as the financier (and thus potential recipient) of Pakistan's nuclear weapons program.[11] After the fall of the Soviet Union, Libya saw a possible way to reinvigorate its ailing nuclear program and began a campaign to recruit Soviet nuclear scientists.[12] The campaign was largely unsuccessful, but Libya continued its nuclear quest: during the mid-1990s, Western police and customs agents intercepted a number of nuclear-related technologies apparently on their way to Libya.[13] And yet during the 1990s Qadhafi also began to give signs that he might be willing to give up his quest for nuclear weapons. In 1992, he met with IAEA Director-General Hans Blix and agreed to "cooperate fully with the agency in implementing safeguards against diversion of nuclear technology to military uses."[14] Qadhafi made a number of statements declaring that Libya was not seeking nuclear weapons, and he signed the African Nuclear Weapons Free Zone Treaty in 1996. However, after Israel's conservative Likud Party declared it would never relinquish Israel's nuclear weapons, Qadhafi urged all Arab countries to seek nuclear weapons.[15]

Especially beginning in the late 1990s, Qadhafi's security policy began to be pulled in two directions. On the one hand, the Libyan economy was straining under the UN sanctions in place to punish Libya for the 1988 bombing of the Pan Am flight over Lockerbie, Scotland. As a result, a "growing chorus of voices" inside Libya, including Qadhafi's son Saif Aleslam, began advocating for change in its approach to foreign policy.[16] On the other hand, acquisition of sensitive nuclear materials continued, including preassembled L-1 centrifuges for uranium enrichment.[17] This somewhat schizophrenic approach persisted. Libya began working on reconciling its relationship with the British, including ending support for the Irish Republican Army and accepting responsibility for killing a British police officer in 1984. Britain's trust in Qadhafi's intentions grew, leading London to lobby on behalf of Tripoli to end UN sanctions.[18] In May 1999 Libya offered to give up its WMD programs to the United States, which began a process of secret on-and-off negotiations culminating in the

December 2003 announcement that Libya had renounced its nuclear weapons program.[19] During this period, however, Libya continued to receive sensitive nuclear technology from the black market A. Q. Khan network, including additional centrifuges, thousands of parts for centrifuges, and a blueprint for nuclear weapons.[20] However, with Libya's public announcement in December 2003, all suspect trading has stopped, and Libya turned over millions of dollars' worth of nuclear equipment to the United States and the IAEA. Both the IAEA and the United States report that Libya has been cooperative and its nuclear program has been dismantled.

Understanding Libya's Nuclear Forbearance

Libya's nuclear rollback shocked and delighted the international community. The country's nuclear program was much more advanced than Western analysts suspected; the IAEA estimated that Libya could have had a nuclear weapon within three to seven years. While Tripoli would not have had a large-scale program that could produce hundreds of nuclear weapons a year, Qadhafi also knew that only a few nuclear weapons are needed to increase one's leverage dramatically. Why would the same man who had invested massive amounts of money, time, and prestige in developing his nuclear program now make the decision to give it up?[21] How did this unexpected transformation occur?

Some argue that the best explanation for Libya's nuclear rollback is security — namely, Qadhafi believed he would be invaded, just as Iraq was, if he did not relinquish his WMD programs. As America prepared for war against Iraq in late 2002, Qadhafi reportedly grew nervous that he might be next. "Italian press accounts quote then–Prime Minister Silvio Berlusconi as saying that Col. Qadhafi had called me to say he feared he would be America's next target. 'Tell them I will do whatever they want,' said one diplomat, recounting the call."[22] Libyan diplomats contacted the British shortly before the March 2003 invasion to reiterate Qadhafi's willingness to negotiate. A few months later, in October, Western agents interdicted a German ship bound for Libya with thousands of centrifuge parts. With the war going well in Iraq, according to this line of argument, Qadhafi cracked under the pressure and agreed to make an official announcement in December 2003 of his WMD rollback.

This argument is problematic for two reasons. First, Qadhafi had been trying to negotiate with the United States since the early 1990s. Tripoli agreed in 1997 to tear down its chemical weapons factory in Tarhunah and offered in May 1999 to give up its WMD programs.[23] Second, the Americans and particularly the British had been conducting secret negotiations with Libya before George W. Bush took office — that is, well before the invasion of Iraq. The problem may not have been that Qadhafi did not want to give up his WMD programs; rather, the Americans were not interested in talking with him about those — they were more concerned about Libya claiming responsibility for Lockerbie. Perhaps Qadhafi's frantic comment to the Italians was not a sign that he had suddenly changed his mind but rather a reflection of his concern that the Americans would continue to ignore his requests for negotiations. Judith Miller notes:

> Clearly, Col. Qadhafi's decision, which Libyans say predated the Iraqi invasion, was part of a broader shift prompted by the miserable failure of his socialist experiment at home, the collapse of the Soviet Union abroad, and his growing conviction that the sanctions which prevented him from expanding oil production — and which isolated him — were jeopardizing his rule. A canny survivor, Col. Qadhafi first signaled a willingness to negotiate in the early 1990s, soon after the Soviet collapse, officials say. But Washington had little interest in dealing with him then, given his monstrous record on terrorism. Subsequent feelers to the Clinton administration went nowhere because they preceded a financial settlement with the families of the victims of the bombing of Pan Am 103 over Lockerbie.[24]

Former Clinton Administration official Martin Indyk confirmed that Qadhafi had been trying to capture the attention of Washington but making little headway: "From the start of President Bill Clinton's administration, Mr. Qadhafi had tried to open back-channels, using various Arab interlocutors with little success. Disappointed, he turned to Britain, first settling a dispute over the shooting of a British policewoman in London and then offering to send the two Libyans accused in the Lockerbie Pan Am 103 bombing for trial in a third country."[25] At this point the United States still did not want to deal with Qadhafi, but his cooperation with the British gave him momentum in lobbying the United Nations to drop the sanctions. The campaign pressured the United States into negotiating with Libya because Washington feared it would be the only voice against dropping the sanctions and would likely be isolated in the Security Council.[26] Rather than simply veto any Security Council measure, Clinton decided to begin negotiations with Libya to see if the United States could "graduate" the rogue state into the international community.

Washington, however, was focused on Libya's terrorist activities, especially the Lockerbie bombing, and thus told the Libyans that WMD would wait. As Sammy Salama notes, "It was assessed that Libya's modest chemical weapons arsenal and infant nuclear program were not an imminent threat, and as a result, there was no urgency driving the U.S. to accept Libya's offer to surrender its WMD."[27] In other words, fear of invasion is not what motivated the Libyans to surrender their nuclear weapons program, given that they offered to give it up four years before the United States invaded Iraq. Rather, the reason Libya gave up its nuclear weapons program after the U.S. invasion of Iraq is that only at that point was the United States interested in negotiating.

If fear of regime change was not what motivated Libya to give up its nuclear program, what did so? Many experts point to the heavy toll sanctions took on the Libyan economy. The United States placed sanctions on Libya in 1986 for being a state sponsor of terrorism, resulting in the loss of American oil business and, more important, oil technology. Six years later the United Nations imposed sanctions, including "universal oil and travel sanctions," against Libya for the 1988 Lockerbie bombings.[28] These sanctions meant that Tripoli could not sell its most profitable export — oil. Tripoli also could not import the oil-field technology needed to increase efficiency and expand oil production. By all accounts, the sanctions led to serious economic stagnation and even depression. By settling the Lockerbie dispute and giving up its WMD, Libya could end the sanctions, develop its oil fields, and increase its economic growth. Salama estimated that lifting of sanctions would mean "a several billion dollar infusion into the Libyan economy and new jobs for thousands of Libyans."[29] A number of analysts have argued that the sanctions, in conjunction with poor management of the Libyan economy, created such dire economic conditions that Qadhafi had no choice but to give up his WMD programs.[30] As Indyk says, "The only way out was to seek rapprochement with Washington."[31]

Clearly sanctions did put pressure on Libya. What is not clear is whether sanctions were the critical component in motivating Libya to give up its WMD. In fact, the historical timeline does not support this. UN sanctions against Libya were suspended in April 1999, and Tripoli made its first offer to give up its WMD programs to the United States in May 1999 — and made the offer again in October 1999.[32] Had getting rid of the sanctions been the motivation behind giving up its WMD programs, one would expect that the events should have been played in reverse. That is, Tripoli should have offered to give up its WMD, and then the UN would have suspended the sanctions. Rather, the sanctions were suspended and then Tripoli offered to abandon WMD efforts. Thus the offer to give up its WMD programs could not have been motivated by a desire to lift the sanctions, since that had already occurred. (The sanctions could have been reinstated, but there was little support within the Security Council for doing so.)[33] The same is true for Libya's actual disarmament in 2003. The UN sanctions were permanently lifted in September 2003, and in December, Tripoli announced it was giving up its WMD programs.[34] Clearly, having the UN sanctions lifted was not the motivation behind Qadhafi's decision to give up his nuclear program.

The argument can perhaps be made that the offers following each UN move were intended to encourage the United States to follow suit with its own unilateral sanctions. However, the effectiveness of both the UN and U.S. sanctions against Libya has been questioned. Some European companies never adhered to the UN ban and continued their business with Libya throughout the 1990s. According to one report, "The end of sanctions will not have an immediate impact on Libya's lifeblood, oil, because the industry is already producing at full capacity and the embargo never stopped a number of European companies from working on the oil fields. 'I don't think the Italian companies ever stopped doing business with Libya,' said Jan Stuart, the head of energy research at FIMAT USA, a brokerage unit of Societe Generale, in New York."[35] In addition, the formal lifting of the UN sanctions in 2003 cleared the way for other European companies interested in developing Libya's oil fields — companies that had been hesitant to do so while the UN sanctions were still in place. Thus the UN move would have "a substantial effect on [Libya's] oil industry in three to five years, according to Roger Diwan, a departmental head at PFC Energy in Washington."[36]

Without a doubt, Libya also wanted the United States to lift its sanctions. But with new investment and technology flowing in from Europe, Libya could expect improving economic conditions. Even before the UN permanently lifted the sanctions, Libya began making new awards granting access for exploration to European companies — and announcing that they hoped soon to award over a hundred more.[37] For fear of losing out to Europeans in the race for Libyan oil, American businesses began calling for the United States to lift its sanctions. "With the UN sanctions gone, Tripoli has been getting impatient and last year threatened to cancel the operating licenses of U.S. companies if they don't return to Libya within a year. Losing those licenses would likely lead to losing their wells and assets to European companies. Germany's Wintershall has already asked Libya for permission to drill oilfields previously owned by U.S. companies."[38] Thus the U.S. sanctions remaining in place hardly seem to have created a dire situation that would have forced someone committed to acquiring nuclear weapons to give up that nuclear weapons program.

In fact, even if the sanctions had not been lifted, Qadhafi certainly had other options. A rich and extensive literature on the effectiveness of sanctions provides little conclusive evidence on whether sanctions actually work.[39] As William Kaempfer and Anton Lowenberg note, sanctions can damage a country's economy, but that does not mean the political leadership will bend: "It is just as likely that economic hardship will cause citizens of the target nation to rally to the defense of their government."[40] The North Korean case serves as a foil to Qadhafi's choice: despite famine, a dilapidated economy, and severe energy crises, Kim Jung Il has not felt rapprochement with Washington to be his only answer. From a number of vantage points, then, it is clear that sanctions do not provide a satisfactory answer to the question of why Libya gave up its nuclear weapons program.

If neither fear of invasion nor pressure from economic sanctions was the primary motivation behind Qadhafi's decision to abandon his nuclear program, then what was? I contend that as with Sadat, Qadhafi rethought what it meant to be a successful country — a process that began in the 1990s — and this process has led to many changes in Libyan outlook, including the decision to give up its nuclear ambition. Without the economic sanctions, Qadhafi likely would not have had the motivation to rethink success. However, without the decision to create a new path for Libya, economic sanctions likely would not have led to WMD abandonment.

Qadhafi came to power in the late 1960s as part of the struggle against colonialism and imperialism. His identity was based on "being the bad boy on the block," as one Egyptian diplomat put it.[41] He took pride in supporting liberation and revolutionary movements as well as in attacking Western interests wherever possible. As Ray Takeyh notes, Qadhafi's worldview "convinced him of the inherent iniquity of the international order, and led him to the conclusion that Tripoli should be unfettered by international conventions or rules."[42] The end result of such a course was Libyan involvement in terrorist activities such as the Lockerbie bombings, which led to U.S. and UN sanctions.

The 1990s became a period of struggle over Qadhafi's — and Libya's — identity. The collapse of the Soviet Union left Libya isolated in a global environment with the United States as the only superpower. Pan-Arabism was no longer in style, and some of the revolutionaries whom Qadhafi had supported — including Nelson Mandela and Yasir Arafat — were now engaging the West diplomatically. In addition, Libya's command economy was inefficient, especially in light of the wave of market liberalizations taking place around the world. Simply put, Qadhafi — and Libya — were behind the times; a redefinition of state interests was needed. The question was: what direction would that redefinition take — renewed revolutionary, conciliatory peacemaker, or something entirely different?

This question created an "extraordinary dispute" in Libya's political elite in the mid- to late 1990s, as Takeyh notes: "The pragmatists in the bureaucracy — led by the late General Secretary Umar al-Muntasir and Energy Minister Abdallah Salim al-Badri — stressed the need for structural economic reforms and international investments to ensure Libya's long-term economic vitality and political stability. The hard-liners — including long-time Qadhafi confidant Abdelssalem Jalloud — wanted to continue defying the West, for they saw Libya's past radicalism as the basis of the regime's legitimacy."[43]

Two different types of motivations drove the coalition for reform: a desire to see the Libyan economy improve, and a desire to see Libya leave behind its pariah status and become a constructive member of the international community. These motivations overlapped to some extent, but the first focuses specifically on the need for economic reforms, while the second looks to transform the broader meaning of what a successful Libyan state would be. The desire to reform in order to improve economic conditions was strongly voiced by Shukri Ghanem, who became Libyan prime minister from 2003 to 2006. An American-educated economist, Ghanem "emerged in the mid-1990s as a growing chorus of voices [was] advocating changes in cash-strapped Libya."[44] Ghanem argued that the only way for Libya to survive was to disentangle the government from the economy, because "it proved that whatever it touches it spoils."[45] To achieve this Libya would need to reengage with the outside world, specifically the United States.

It would be a mistake, however, to conclude that the reformers wanted change only for the sake of improving the economy. The reforms for which they were calling go far beyond economic restructuring to include a free media, protection of human rights, and direct democracy. The number one proponent of such reforms is Qadhafi's eldest son, Saif Aleslam al-Qadhafi. A Western-educated engineer, Saif Aleslam has pushed for a much broader view of the need for changes in Libyan society. In addition to arguing for

Libya's nuclear disarmament, Saif Aleslam has publicly called for a wide array of domestic and foreign policy reforms, from releasing political prisoners to ending conflict with Israel. The younger Qadhafi has called for Libya to engage constructively with the United States as well as to "be the spearhead of all positive changes in the Middle East, in cooperation with the rest of the world."[46] When Saif Aleslam was only fourteen, he and two of his brothers were seriously injured in the U.S. attack on Qadhafi's compound in Tripoli — and his adopted sister was killed.[47] Remarkably, he did not seem to internalize hatred of the United States but rather seemed to accept America as a nearly invincible force with which cooperation was necessary. Indeed, the futility of Libya's decades-old policy of conflict was not lost on Saif Aleslam, nor were the potential gains from diplomacy. In explaining why Libya gave up its WMD, he said, "We have seen that the armed struggle of the Palestinians, which lasted 50 years, did not produce results such as those obtained by means of negotiations that lasted five years. They told the commander [his father] that they had given up the rifle and taken the path of negotiations, and obtained what they had not obtained in 50 years."[48]

The conflict between the reform-minded and revolution-minded continued until 1998, when Qadhafi made a clear decision for reform and against revolution. As Takeyh notes, "A series of articles in the official daily *Al-Jamahiriya* began to criticize the intransigence of the hard-liners and their inability to recognize prevailing global realities. The Revolutionary Committees — informed groups of zealots . . . that served as the hard-liners' power base and had dominated Libyan politics since the late 1970s — were purged and relegated to the margins of society."[49] A year later Qadhafi surrendered the two Lockerbie suspects and offered to give up his WMD programs.

While Qadhafi's son may have been convinced of the value of diplomacy, it is unclear why Qadhafi himself would have been. The Libyan leader's reputation for stubbornness and resisting change was well known throughout the Arab world.[50] Changing course meant more than just a change in tactics; in some ways, it meant that Qadhafi's platform of the past several decades was now discredited.[51] Given that Libya was only a few years away from nuclear weapons, why did Qadhafi not simply stay the course a little while longer — especially considering how European oil companies were lining up to develop Libya's petroleum resources?

A number of reasons seem to stand out. First, despite public denials of succession planning, Qadhafi likely wants to hand off a stable, successful government to his son. He realizes that reform would be difficult for his son to implement after Qadhafi's death; leading the effort himself now helps ensure the success of both the reforms and the succession. Second, the rise of Islamic fundamentalism around the world did not leave Libya untouched, and radicals who saw Libya as too secular began to pose some level of threat to regime stability. Poor economic conditions only added fuel to that fire. Third, Qadhafi's quest for nuclear weapons had met obstacle after obstacle; it was an expensive and less-than-fruitful endeavor. At almost every turn, his attempts to pursue technology, get training for his scientists, and make outright nuclear weapons purchases were blunted by foreign — often American — intervention. Decades of persistence had paid off somewhat, as is shown by the IAEA's estimate that when it gave up the nuclear pursuit in 2003, Libya was within three to seven years of producing a weapon. Nonetheless, in face of such roadblocks, the enormous effort required to inch the program along likely led Qadhafi to question the wisdom of his pursuit.

Finally, Qadhafi has always shown a desire to exert leadership regionally and even globally. The failure of his drive for Pan-Arabism, and repeated rebuffs from other Arab countries, led Qadhafi to feel rejected and embittered.[52] He began to search for a new paradigm, as is illustrated by Libya's new insistence on African — not Middle Eastern — identity. The rejection stung Qadhafi so deeply that in 2001 he declared, "Africa is closer to me in every way than Iraq or Syria." In 2003 Qadhafi directly repudiated Arab nationalism, saying: "The times of Arab nationalism and unity are gone forever. These ideas which mobilized the masses are only a worthless currency. Libya has had to put up with too much from the Arabs for whom it has poured forth both blood and money."[53] His son later proclaimed, "The new Libya is black, because we are African now."[54] Settling the terrorist disputes and giving up WMD would allow Qadhafi to take on a new leadership role and give him the international acceptance he had desired for so long. Libyan state newspapers declared that in "making such a courageous decision, Libya would serve as a role model that would be emulated by great and small powers alike, in order to bring about a more civilized world free of the threat of WMD."[55] A number of analysts have noted that Qadhafi "craved recognition" and desperately wanted to "rejoin the family of 'civilized nations,'" and giving up his WMD allowed him to do just that.[56]

These factors led Qadhafi to wholesale rejection of his decades-long approach to foreign policy and complete acceptance of a new one. Instead of branding Arab leaders who deal with Israel "sellouts," Qadhafi's son now says that Israel is not a threat to Libya, and Libya no longer desires confrontation with Israel.[57] Instead of plotting attacks against U.S. interests, Qadhafi invites the U.S. president and secretary of state to visit.[58] Instead of enforcing a command economy, the Libyan leader praises the free market and argues that his country should follow the example of Japan to become an economic power.[59] And of course, instead of secretly developing a nuclear weapons program, Qadhafi offered it up as a "gift" to the United States. These are the actions of someone who has rethought what security means. Security is no longer obtained through conflict and confrontation; instead, diplomacy and cooperation are the path to a secure state. Instead of nuclear proliferation, nuclear nonproliferation is seen as the better choice. In discussing Libya's nuclear disarmament, Saif Aleslam shows the extent of this reconceptualization of security: one reason Libya gave up nuclear weapons was "we were on a dangerous path, and had problems with the West. When the West came and told us that it didn't want to fight us, but to be partners with us—why persist in being hostile to it?"[60]

Securing one's state through nuclear armament does not lead to safety, according to this line of reasoning—rather, it is a dangerous path. The way to safety is instead to trust your enemy when its leaders say they do not want to fight. In other words, Libya had rejected the self-help world and embraced the international community. Because a requirement of rejoining the international community was to forgo nuclear weapons, Libya did so.

Lessons Learned

How the international social environment can put pressure on policymakers to forgo nuclear weapons is discussed in chapter 2, which also outlines nine mechanisms that can increase the potency of the nuclear nonproliferation regime.[61] We saw that in both Japan and Egypt, these mechanisms did affect how policymakers valued nuclear weapons. Does the same hold true for Libya? With regard to descriptive, injunctive, and subjective norms, at the time of Libya's offer to disarm in 1999, the pressure created by all three norms was toward nonproliferation. In 1999 the descriptive norm (that is, the norm created by what countries actually do) was in some ways weakened but also in some ways strengthened. During the 1990s a number of countries gave up nuclear programs and/or nuclear weapons (Brazil, Argentina, Ukraine, Kazakhstan,

Belarus, and South Africa). Numerous holdout states finally joined the NPT. Of course, in 1998 both India and Pakistan conducted nuclear tests, weakening the descriptive norm against nuclear nonproliferation. However, the international outcry against those tests, including sanctions from the United States, Japan, and other countries, helped to limit the damage to the descriptive norm. The injunctive norm (that is, the norm created by what countries say) was still quite strong despite the nuclear tests in India and Pakistan — in fact, if anything, countries were more vociferous in condemning nuclear proliferation. In terms of subjective norms (that is, what Libya thought others believed it should do about its nuclear program), no evidence shows that Libya thought it was receiving mixed signals from other countries about nuclear proliferation. In other words, it is likely that Libya took both the descriptive and injunctive norms at face value and believed that other countries wanted it to forgo nuclear weapons.

The most remarkable thing about analyzing Libya's internalization of these three types of norms is the fact that during the 1990s, Libya changed the focal point from which it "received" norms. Libya had formerly aligned itself with revolutionary movements and had been determined to overthrow the existing international system. In company with states like Syria and Iraq, Libya accepted normative messages from anti–status quo groups and rejected normative messages from the large majority of states adhering to the international nonproliferation norm. But as documented, during the 1990s Libya went through a period of rethinking its national interests, its definitions of security and success, and its identity. Coming out on the other side of this rethinking process, Qadhafi wanted to rejoin the international system and thus began to pay attention to normative messages from the international community on nuclear nonproliferation. These normative messages about nuclear nonproliferation are not what caused Qadhafi to change his vision for Libya. However, once he changed his vision, had these normative messages not been present, Qadhafi would have felt far less pressure to give up his nuclear weapons program.

In terms of the processes of consistency, linking, and activation that affect the potency of norms, two of three seem to have made an impact. Consistency did not — that is, Libya is not non-nuclear today because Qadhafi was consistent. The opposite applies: only because Qadhafi was willing to make a dramatic break with past behavior is Libya non-nuclear today. Linking, however, was clearly evident: the British and the United States both told Tripoli that to be accepted back into the international community, it must give up its WMD program. These links harmonized with the links established by the NPT, which declares that peaceful states will adhere to their promise to forgo nuclear weapons. Because Qadhafi was "desperate to have the country rejoin the family of civilized nations," the link meant he needed to give up his nuclear weapons program — which he was willing to do.[62] In terms of activation, the nuclear nonproliferation norm was activated consistently by Western nations over the decades, as they alternated between encouraging and threatening Libya to give up its nuclear aspirations. As discussed, the activation of these norms meant little to Qadhafi when he reveled in attacking the international system. But once he decided he wanted to become part of that system, the activation of the nuclear nonproliferation norm reminded him that Libya's nuclear program was a barrier to acceptance into the community of nations.

The conditions affecting norm potency — uncertainty, similarity, and conflict — all seem to have influenced Libya's calculations regarding its nuclear program. After the collapse of the Soviet Union in 1991, Qadhafi no longer had superpower backing, and now he had to face the hegemon he had been attacking for decades — and face it alone. Additional UN sanctions were imposed against Libya in 1992 and 1993, preventing the sale of airplane, arms, and oil technology, among other things. U.S. pressure in particular, including interdictions, made it clear that pursuing a nuclear weapons program would be extremely difficult. The costs of Qadhafi's revolutionary strategy were climbing dramatically. During the same time frame, the value of nuclear weapons was in question. As we have seen, several states gave up nuclear weapons during the 1990s, all but three outlier states joined the NPT, and the NPT was indefinitely extended in 1995. On the other hand, both India and Pakistan tested nuclear devices in 1998. The effect was that utility of Qadhafi's strategy had come into serious question. This uncertainty helped pressure the Libyan dictator into rethinking his security strategy. Similarity also likely helped Qadhafi decide to give up his nuclear program. When we perceive a norm transmitter to be similar to us, or to be an entity with which we desire a good relationship, we are more open to its normative influence. As discussed, during the 1990s Libya went through a transition process in which its interests and goals shifted dramatically. As a result, its role models and those it viewed as worthy of emulation also changed. No longer praising radical fundamentalists working for the liberation of Palestine, Qadhafi has become increasingly critical of these groups, and in fact called Islamists "medieval."[63] No longer modeling the Libyan economy after the command-and-control structure of the Soviets,

Qadhafi has been working hard to inject more free-market strategies into Libya and even expressed a desire for Libya to be more like Japan.[64] He also heard the message that to succeed diplomatically, he would need to emulate the behavior of the more than 170 states that had truly forsworn nuclear weapons. As Michele Dunne notes, "Libya craves the recognition and normalization of its status that can come only when it is removed from the U.S. list of state sponsors of terrorism, when there is a full-fledged U.S. embassy in Tripoli, and when senior Libyan officials are welcome in Washington."[65] To this end, Qadhafi was willing to give up Libya's nuclear program.

The last condition that affects norm potency—conflict—again shows a counterintuitive result. The original expectation from social psychology was that conflict would create polarization, leading to the rejection of outside norms. In each case so far, however, conflict has ended up creating openness to outside norms. The same is certainly the case with Libya. Libya's support, both direct and indirect, of revolutionary and liberation movements brought it little except grief, culminating in the U.S. bombing of Tripoli and U.S. and UN sanctions. As a result, Libya learned that cooperation is more fruitful than conflict. As Qadhafi's son noted, the Palestinians obtained more in five years of diplomacy than they did in fifty years of war. Qadhafi himself announced that "his confrontation with the superpower is a thing of the past, it is a time for reciprocal interests."[66]

Having explored the Libyan decision to give up the nuclear option, and the impact of the international social environment on that decision, we must now address whether Libya's nuclear forbearance is best characterized as persuasion, conformity, or identification. Conformity clearly does not describe the Libyan case, whereas both identification and persuasion offer better explanations. Conformity would mean that Qadhafi still wanted a nuclear program but gave it up because of outside pressure. His actions would have changed, not his fundamental attitude toward nuclear weapons. If this were the case, we would expect to see only minimum compliance with U.S. and UN inspectors, less than full disclosure, and potential hedging behavior (trying to retain some elements of the nuclear complex). Instead, we have seen the opposite. Due to Libya's forthright compliance, the A. Q. Khan nuclear black market was exposed. IAEA Director Mohamed El Baradei complimented Libya on "full cooperation, the readiness to answer all questions we have and to satisfy technical requirements."[67] British officials have also praised Libya's openness in revealing the full scope of its nuclear program.[68]

Another indication that Qadhafi was not merely accepting begrudgingly the conditions forced upon him is that the Libyans were eager to negotiate regarding their nuclear program. The Libyans first proposed to give up their WMD programs in May 1999, even though UN sanctions had already been suspended. When negotiations began, a number of initial conditions had been set by the United States, which kept adding conditions throughout the negotiations. Surprisingly, the Libyans accepted the additional requirements without complaint.[69] This indicates that the Libyans likely wanted to give up their WMD in exchange for full acceptance into the international community. These negotiations were not without risk for Qadhafi. While secret talks toward rapprochement took place, U.S. officials continued to lambaste Libya, calling it a "rogue state" and threatening to "do what is necessary" to guarantee American security.[70] Thus Qadhafi had to tread carefully to ensure that the negotiations were not a cover for larger plans for regime change. Indeed, this is probably part of the explanation for why Libya continued to pursue nuclear technology up until 2003. Because Washington had been less than interested in responding to his overtures, Qadhafi was pursuing a two-track strategy in case the United States eventually rejected his attempts to cooperate.

In summary, Libya not only made the initial offer to give up its WMD programs but also accepted risks in negotiations and, once these were completed, lived up to its end of the bargain completely and thoroughly. This behavior does not describe conformity.

Identification also does not offer a good explanation for Libya's nuclear forbearance. As a reminder, identification takes place when an actor wants to be like another and changes actions to mimic those admired. It can take place when a friend agrees with another friend, not because of a real change of mind but because it is important to a significant other. In some ways, this does sound like the Libyan case: Libya wanted to be accepted by the international community and was therefore willing to accept the international community's judgment on nuclear weapons. However, the reason identification does not fit the Libyan case is because Libya's preferences clearly changed. In identification, preferences do not change. Rather, as Kelman notes, "the individual actually believes in the responses which he adopts through identification, but their specific content is more or less irrelevant. He adopts the induced behavior because it is associated with the desired relationship."[71] For Qadhafi, the content of his responses was relevant, and preferences did change. He did not endorse free-market measures simply because this was expected, but rather because he believed they could help lift Libya's economy out of depression. He did not give up his WMD because he had no opinion on the topic, but rather because he came to believe that cooperation would take his country much further than conflict. Indeed, the number of areas in which Qadhafi reversed course is astonishing — indicating a deeper change in beliefs, and thus persuasion.

Qadhafi clearly has fundamentally changed his vision for Libya. In April 1999 (the same month he agreed to release the Lockerbie suspects for trial, and one month before he offered to give up his WMD to the United States), Qadhafi declared: "The world has changed radically and drastically. The methods and ideas should change, and being a revolutionary and a progressive man, I have to follow this movement."[72] In numerous areas, Qadhafi has backed up his words with action. With regard to terrorism, Libya has provided helpful information to the United States. Before 2001, Libya expelled terrorist organizations from its borders, broke ties with other radical groups, and extradited suspected terrorists to other countries.[73] Efforts were stepped up after September 2001: "Literally on the 12th of September, the head of Libyan intelligence, Musa Kusa, who has also been involved in negotiating on the WMD issues, was meeting in Europe with people from the CIA, saying, 'This is our list of suspects. These are the terrorists that we know that are connected to al Qaeda, who are operating out of Europe, and so forth.'"[74]

In the economic realm, the Libyan government has introduced sweeping reforms to streamline government operations, privatize government holdings, and attract foreign investment. To do so, Qadhafi invited numerous Western experts to Libya to analyze the current system and advise on the best ways to reform; the government also hopes to bring in advisers from the World Bank and International Monetary Fund.[75] The eventual goal is for Libya to serve as a regional trading hub, similar to Hong Kong or Dubai.[76] "As a sign of the times, the regular procession of visitors to the colonel's tent no longer includes guerilla leaders and terrorists, but instead features investment consultants and Internet executives."[77] On the diplomatic front, Tripoli has worked hard to exert leadership in Africa and has contributed constructively on a number of fronts, from aiding in conflict resolution in several African countries, to hosting an Organization of African Unity meeting to investigate the creation of a "United States of Africa."[78]

Foreign policy has also changed dramatically. Qadhafi recently invited George W. Bush to visit, and his son met informally with members of the Israeli parliament, saying that Israel is no longer a threat to Libya.[79] This is in stark contrast to past Libyan behavior; Qadhafi was famous for accusing any Arab leader who negotiated with Israel of being a sellout. Most indicative of a true change of course are the extensive domestic reforms that Saif Aleslam has laid out for Libya, including private ownership of media, freedom of the press, release of political prisoners, abolition of secret courts, movement toward free elections, and tracking human rights violations. These goals will not be met quickly, and Libya has faced obstacles even in the small baby steps it has taken. But the range and depth of the proposed reforms shows that Libyan leadership has rethought what it means to be a successful country and is making changes accordingly. As described, Qadhafi's decision to transform Libya and chart a new future for his country directly impacted his thinking on nuclear weapons. As Lisa Anderson notes, the decision to dismantle WMD programs "is consistent with a whole set of things the Libyans have been doing for the last couple of years, all of them intended to bring Libya back into the family of what we call 'civilized nations.'"[80] Because of the NPT and associated nuclear nonproliferation regime, the expectations for Qadhafi were clear: for Libya to come back into the fold, the WMD programs must end. Because of Qadhafi's rethinking of what it means to be a successful state, nuclear weapons were no longer required. Instead of focusing on weapons, revolution, and conflict, Libya now looks to improve economic development and diplomatic relations. Nuclear weapons would only hinder those goals.

As indicated, however, Qadhafi's persuasion was helped along by factors that made it much harder for him to continue pursuing a conflictual, revolutionary strategy and much easier for him to turn to a more cooperative approach. In this way, Libya's nuclear forbearance resembles Egypt's. For Libya, decades of obstacles made it clear that obtaining nuclear weapons would be quite difficult: unsuccessful attempts to pair with states with more advanced technology (e.g., Pakistan and India), blocked efforts at training Libyan students in Western nuclear science programs, Western interdictions of dual-use materials, and more. Without these roadblocks, Qadhafi never would have felt the need to rethink what success meant. In the same way, Nasser faced obstacles in his pursuit of nuclear weapons, from Israeli sabotage to unsuccessful attempts to procure assistance from the Soviet Union and China. Nasser's response was conformity; he decided to use the NPT as a tactical measure to shame Israel and gain status regionally. But over time and with Sadat's reformulation of Egyptian grand strategy, Egypt's acceptance of the nonproliferation norm has become more genuinely a case of persuasion. In Libya's case, Qadhafi's son and other reformists helped the leader shift his frame and move from outright rejection of the norm to acceptance. Thus, without traditional realist tactics, Qadhafi would have been unlikely to give up his pursuit of nuclear weapons, but without a change in thinking about state security, even the obstacles Qadhafi faced probably would not have led to a change in strategy.

SWEDEN

In the 1950s and 1960s Sweden had a serious nuclear weapons program and came close to a nuclear weapons capability.[81] As Jan Prawitz notes: "In the early days, the issue was when rather than if Sweden should acquire its own atomic bombs."[82] Military planners saw tactical nuclear weapons as essential to deterring a Soviet invasion, and political leaders believed joining the nuclear club would underscore Sweden's reputation as a technologically advanced state. Yet in 1970 Sweden ratified the NPT and it has become one of the most forceful voices for nuclear nonproliferation and arms control. To understand the Swedish transformation from near-nuclear power to disarmament advocate, an understanding of both domestic and international environments is critical.

Shortly after the United States used atomic weapons to end World War II, the Swedish began to consider acquisition of nuclear weapons. "The Swedish research program initially was motivated primarily by the need to keep pace with other technologically advanced countries. During World War II Sweden's armed forces, with the exception of its air force, had been cut off from Western technological developments. After the war ended, the armed forces consequently were eager to move ahead with research on jet aircraft, missiles, rockets, and atomic 'wonder weapons.'"[83] Because the Swedes had little in the way of natural energy supply but large deposits of natural uranium, the government decided to pursue a nuclear power program based on heavy-water reactors. This would allow the country to generate energy based on Sweden's natural resources, helping to provide energy security, while also making it easier to produce weapons-grade plutonium than with light-water reactors. As Mitchell Reiss notes, "While Sweden's interest in heavy-water reactors was originally rationalized in terms of its expected benefits for civilian purposes, Swedish officials were not unaware of the potential military applications of this choice of technology."[84]

By 1952 the military was already holding public discussions about the necessity of Sweden acquiring nuclear weapons—specifically, tactical nuclear weapons. Once nuclear warheads could be miniaturized, military analysts around the world assumed that technologically advanced countries would add tactical nuclear weapons to their military repertoire. No longer did a nuclear exchange have to mean all-out war; rather, nuclear weapons could be used in a limited way on the battlefield by commanders. In addition, the Swedish military believed that the main threat to their state was the Soviet Union, with which they could not hope to compete in a strategic nuclear arms race. The goal of their tactical nuclear weapons would be to "wage a tactical battle until the United States stepped in with strategic forces."[85] Swedish analysts believed a Soviet attack could come as part of a larger incursion into Europe or, less probably, as an isolated attack. In either case, the two main routes for a Soviet invasion would be from the south (by sea) or from the north (over land), and "it was thought that only a few nuclear weapons would be required to deter either a ground or amphibious invasion. The level of destruction which even a small nuclear arsenal would have granted Sweden would be sufficient to escalate the potential cost of the conflict, and thus deter the Soviet Union."[86]

Early on, a large number of those within the Swedish elite believed that they faced a nuclear threat from the Soviet Union and that Sweden would eventually acquire or produce its own nuclear weapons for defensive purposes. In 1954 the Swedish prime minister acknowledged that Sweden needed to be prepared to defend itself from a country likely to use nuclear weapons against it.[87] By 1955 three of the four main parties in Sweden supported some sort of funding for nuclear weapons research.[88] And by 1957 a majority of the fourth party, the Social Democrats, supported a nuclear weapons research program.[89] Swedish military planners strongly believed that Sweden would be safer with nuclear weapons than without, as explicated in planning statement ÖB 57, issued in 1957:

> It would be difficult to find an example where the aggressor refrains from using an effective weapon only because the defender does not have the same military capability. . . . There are also examples which can be produced where a warring state has used a weapon for the sole reason that the

other side didn't possess that weapon or was not able to use it. Therefore, there are strong reasons to believe that if the Swedish armed forces did not have nuclear weapons, it would increase rather than decrease the likelihood that an aggressor would use such a weapon against it.[90]

A year later the Swedish Parliamentary Commission on Defense recommended that a decision on a nuclear weapons option be postponed, but it proposed that funding and personnel for nuclear research should be given high priority. Reiss notes that the commission's report "marked a clear trend toward great acceptance of a national nuclear force."[91] By 1957 a majority of the Swedish populace supported a nuclear weapons option.[92]

Rather than commit to immediate nuclear weapons procurement (which would have been practically difficult anyway) or funding for nuclear weapons research, the Swedish government decided on a course of keeping the nuclear option open without making any clear commitment to a weapons program. This allowed the ruling party, the Social Democrats, to avoid a split in their ranks over the nuclear issue, since some members advocated a nuclear weapons program while others were vociferously opposed to this. Over time, however, Sweden's "decision not to decide" became increasingly untenable, especially as the country took on a leadership role in the emerging nuclear nonproliferation regime.[93] As the left wing of the Social Democrats gathered strength, the government worked hard to turn the public tide against nuclear weapons. By 1967, 69 percent of Swedes were *against* nuclear acquisition, in large part due to "the government's efforts to encourage a negative attitude toward nuclear weapons among the Swedish population. The government established in the public consciousness a link between non-nuclear defense and the traditional (and nearly sacred, by some estimates) policy of 'nonalignment in peace' that would lead to neutrality in time of war."[94] The next year Sweden signed the NPT, which it ratified in January 1970. Despite an increasing Soviet threat during the Cold War (including a Soviet naval build-up and stepped-up incursions into Swedish territorial waters), Sweden has abided by its international commitment to forgo nuclear weapons.[95]

Understanding Sweden's Nuclear Forbearance

To understand Sweden's nuclear decision-making, we must understand the Swedish commitment to neutrality. Paul Cole notes: "Swedish history is replete with examples that suggest Sweden fares better when it stays out of great power political struggles. Over the past four hundred years, whenever Sweden became engaged in the struggle for the mastery of Europe, it paid a heavy price in the end. Sweden's aloofness and neutrality in the East-West conflict during the twentieth century reflect, in large measure, the lessons of what Swedes refer to as the 'Great Power era.'"[96] On the other hand, neutrality has been quite successful for the Swedes — since 1815, Sweden has not engaged in armed conflict. Thus it is no surprise that the Swedish have developed an ethos of an armed and neutral peacemaker, requiring both a strong defense capable of deterring and repelling invaders and strong diplomacy to resolve regional tensions and promote peace. This ethos provides a strong sense of national identity for Swedes — as strong as the Peace Constitution in Japan or the "right to life, liberty, and the pursuit of happiness" in the United States.

The question for Sweden, then, was: how did nuclear weapons fit in with this national identity? The ethos of neutrality did not automatically rule out a nuclear-armed Sweden, for two reasons. First, the Swedish prided themselves on their sophisticated military technology, and going nuclear would have allowed them to enhance that image. George Quester explains:

> Like other countries, Sweden would not have been indifferent to the prestige arising from the ability to manufacture nuclear weapons. A first-rate aircraft industry not only facilitates military defense within a framework of neutrality; it makes other people think more highly of Swedish economic and industrial prowess. Having the largest air force per capita in the world (indeed for many years, one of the four or five largest absolutely) only bothers a few Swedes; to most it has given pleasure. Other things remaining equal, similar considerations might have applied with regard to nuclear weapons.[97]

Second, armed neutrality did require Sweden to have a capable and credible defense — something that a small stockpile of tactical nuclear weapons would certainly provide (as Israel felt). Cole notes: "Nuclear weapons could still be compatible with the national ethos if they were perceived as an indispensable asset for national defense. In the 1950s and 1960s, Swedish scientists were capable of producing nuclear weapons, and military analysts made a compelling assessment of how these weapons could contribute to national security requirements. For two decades, this was enough to allow pro-acquisition sentiments to flourish."[98]

Why did the Swedish elite turn against nuclear weapons development, given that it was compatible with their national identity, and the military leadership believed it was required for national security? Two main causes collided to create conditions ripe for redefining the value of nuclear weapons and making them incompatible with the Swedish national identity: domestic politics and the emerging nuclear nonproliferation norm.

First, the Social Democrats finally gained enough seats in parliament not to have to worry quite so much about creating a rift in the party (and thus losing power) over the nuclear issue. On the question of whether Sweden should become a nuclear weapons state, the party was split between the "pragmatists, who supported measures that would contribute to Swedish interests in the world as it existed and thus were willing to contemplate acquisition of an independent nuclear capability, and the more ideological component of the party that sought to use Swedish foreign policy as a vehicle for advancing a vision of how the world should be and therefore roundly rejected a nuclear role for Sweden."[99] The ideological side won out, and because that group now had enough seats in parliament not to need to preserve party unity, they were able to impose their antinuclear policies.

Why did the left-leaning faction triumph? In part, because of the shifting international milieu — which leads us to the second reason Swedes rejected a nuclear weapons program. As discussed in chapter 2, by the middle of the 1950s worldwide opinion was turning against nuclear weapons. In August 1955 the world's first conference protesting nuclear weapons was held in Hiroshima.[100] The next year the U.S. Democratic presidential candidate, Adlai Stevenson, proposed an end to aboveground nuclear tests.[101] Eisenhower dismissed the proposal, but when he was reelected, "considerable pressure by powerful popular movements" prodded him to begin expert talks with the Soviets on the possibility of an enforceable test ban.[102] By 1958 more than eleven thousand scientists had signed petitions to ban nuclear tests; the petition was delivered to the United Nations secretary-general.[103]

This international normative movement against nuclear weapons was felt in Sweden as well. The Social Democrats' Women's Organization led the charge against nuclear weapons in Sweden, emphasizing in its May 1956 conference that nuclear weapons posed a grave danger not just to Sweden but to all of humanity. In January 1957 the military leadership announced that nuclear weapons could be produced within six to seven years. The next day

Swedish radio broadcast a number of responses, including a fiery one by the head of the Social Democrats' Women's Organization, Inga Thorsson. As a result, "Thorsson and her association became one of the most influential actors in the debate. After her radio presentation, the debate intensified and various politicians, writers, artists, and journalists participated in the debate and often they had long newspaper dialogues."[104] By 1958, unions, peace groups, and large numbers of unaffiliated individuals were engaged in protests against a potential nuclear deterrent as well as against increased military budgets.[105] These protests sparked the formation of a new, influential group called the Action Committee Against Swedish Nuclear Weapons (AMSA).[106] As Eric Arnett argues, "Anti-nuclear actors succeeded in stopping Sweden's nuclear weapons program completely, despite the influence of the nuclear establishment and the popularity of the nuclear option among the electorate."[107]

This emerging international norm, the negotiations being conducted to support it, and the Swedes' own involvement in these negotiations had an impact on Swedish decision-making. With its desire to help reduce international tensions, Sweden had a history of working through international fora to promote peace. Thus trust in international organizations and treaties was higher than it might otherwise have been. This trust — and a corresponding desire not to harm the negotiations that could solve the nuclear problem peaceably — led the Swedish elite to put off acquiring nuclear weapons. The Social Democrats' official report in 1958, *Neutrality, Defense, Nuclear Weapons*, emphasized this point: "Negotiations between the great powers about banning nuclear weapons tests are presently taking place. . . . It would be in accordance with Sweden's own national interest as well as in the interest of the international peace efforts . . . if these negotiations were to be successful. It might have a negative impact on the disarmament efforts if Sweden now decided to manufacture nuclear weapons."[108] In addition, the Swedish elite became convinced that the only way for the country to "defend against nuclear weapons is by trying to reduce the risk that such weapons will ever be used."[109] Thus the international negotiations to stop the spread of nuclear weapons were seen as the best way to strengthen Sweden's security.

The Swedes sought to engage the international negotiations, both to strengthen the norm and to use it to help their own domestic antinuclear efforts. Cole notes: "Opponents of nuclear weapons began to look to the UN for a formula that would offer Sweden the opportunity to forgo acquisition in the name of international law."[110] Sweden quickly became involved in international fora to this end. In 1955 Swedish expert Dr. Sigvard Eklund chaired the first international Conference on Peaceful Uses of the Atom in Geneva; he became director general of the IAEA in 1961.[111] In 1958 Foreign Minister Östen Undén proposed a nuclear test ban treaty in the United Nations General Assembly.[112] After the Soviets ended their moratorium on testing in 1961, Undén proposed to the First Committee of the UN General Assembly a plan for the creation of a "non-nuclear club" to pressure nuclear weapons states to end testing and to encourage other states to stay non-nuclear.[113] By 1962 Sweden joined the newly created Eighteen Nation Disarmament Committee (ENDC), giving the country's diplomatic corps a powerful voice for nuclear nonproliferation. Sweden signed the Partial Test Ban Treaty (PTBT) in 1963, shortly after it was opened for signature. As the ENDC entered into negotiations for a treaty banning the spread of nuclear weapons, Swedish officials made a number of important contributions, including three modifications that ended up in the final draft of the NPT.[114] Sweden signed the NPT in 1968 and ratified it in 1970. Quester argues that the engagement of the antinuclear faction in international negotiations did indeed end up strengthening antinuclear sentiment in the country; in fact, he argues that this may be the most important factor in Sweden's decision to forgo nuclear weapons:

> Sweden's position as one of these eight [neutral countries appointed in 1962] to the ENDC has indeed had a significant impact on national considerations of military policy. The international role of Sweden in effect shifted from passive and circumspect neutrality to honest-broker arbitration, and public opinion adjusted to the change. First on the test ban and then on other disarmament steps, the Swedish delegation at Geneva saw itself as an independent source of expertise as well as spokesman for the other seven less economically developed nonaligned states. With this kind of vested interest in prodisarmament positions, a fuller national exploration of bomb options could well be forgone. If the Irish General Assembly resolution (and the antiproliferation implications of the test moratoriums and test ban) had not already reduced the legitimacy of Swedish nuclear weapons, Sweden's role at the ENDC had made them decisively obsolete in terms of prestige considerations. Rightly or wrongly, Swedes today see themselves as having worked for all forms of disarmament at Geneva, as having been against proliferation all along.[115]

In effect, the emerging international norm against nuclear proliferation coincided with the growing dominance of the left wing of the Social Democrats in Sweden, creating a powerful combination that led the Swedish to reverse course completely on the nuclear issue. Arnett argues that "Sweden was concerned not only with domestic constitutive norms when deciding about nuclear weapons, but also with international norms."[116] The Social Democrats did this by using the international nonproliferation norm to delegitimize nuclear weapons and thus to redefine what nuclear weapons would mean to Sweden. For example, the Social Democrats emphasized their role as a mediator between East and West in the ENDC, a role they could not play if Sweden developed independent nuclear force. To emphasize the importance of nuclear nonproliferation, parliament member Alva Myrdal was named to the Cabinet in 1967 as minister of disarmament.[117] The Social Democrats also promoted their nuclear nonproliferation work as a way that Sweden could be a role model for the rest of the world. Cole explains how the Social Democrats used their international disarmament work to transform the image of nuclear weapons from being viewed as a technologically sophisticated way to preserve armed neutrality into being seen as an aggressive, immoral factor incompatible with Sweden's peaceful nature:

> This [antinuclear faction of the Social Democrats] carefully cultivated an image of Sweden, both at home and abroad, that perfectly complemented the country's collectively shared ethos. It was an image that depicted Sweden as a nation of peace and disarmament, whose commitment to nuclear forbearance could set a standard for the world. In creating the myth of Swedish anti-nuclearism, they transformed a latent public wariness of nuclear weapons into a real political constraint on the acquisition of an independent nuclear arsenal. In a country where the most important barrier against nuclear acquisition — then as now — is political will, the importance of national beliefs and images should not be undervalued.[118]

Arnett notes that in the Swedish case, domestic politics and international norms coalesced in a powerful way to keep the state from going nuclear despite security threats and initial political and public support for a nuclear weapons program.[119]

Other reasons informed the Social Democrats' desire to forgo nuclear weapons as well as their ability to win over the public. The cost of a nuclear weapons program concerned the ruling party, especially because of its commitment to an extensive social welfare program. However, the Swedish military did spend large amounts — "at a rate seen in few other countries" — on both conventional defenses and civil defense programs designed to protect against nuclear and chemical attacks.[120]

More important, some argue that the Swedish government believed Sweden would be protected under the NATO nuclear umbrella, despite the fact that extended deterrence was never offered by the United States. The logic of this argument is that the United States would never allow a Soviet incursion into Western Europe, and that the Swedish leadership knew it. Thus they felt they could rely on a tacit nuclear guarantee. This indeed may have placated more conservative elites who would have preferred an independent nuclear deterrent but were blocked by domestic sentiment. This argument does have some problems, however. The relationship between the United States and Sweden was more ambivalent than that with many other U.S. allies. For example, Sweden criticized the United States heavily for much of the Cold War, at one point leading to the U.S. ambassador being withdrawn from Stockholm.[121] In addition, there is no indication that the United States ever even informally or secretly made the promise to protect Sweden with nuclear forces. As Arnett notes about the argument that Sweden did not develop nuclear weapons because of an informal U.S. security guarantee, "such an explanation does not explain how Sweden — a non-aligned country that lost its last war with Russia and has a close relationship with Finland, a part of Swedish territory conquered by Russia in the 19th century which had fought and lost a war with the Soviet Union as recently as 1945 — could be adequately reassured by such a tacit guarantee, when full NATO allies often were not reassured even by a formal guarantee."[122] Hence while it is likely that the Swedes did place some trust in a U.S./NATO response to a Soviet incursion, additional explanations are necessary.

Another reason often given for Sweden's nuclear forbearance is that decision-makers believed nuclear weapons would weaken, not strengthen, their national security. This was the case, it is argued, because nuclear weapons would make Sweden a target for the Soviet Union, whereas a non-nuclear Sweden would have a better chance of staying neutral and out of the fray. The problem with this argument is that Sweden's military leadership clearly did not believe it. As late as 1959, "the armed services presented their case that nuclear weapons would enhance Sweden's ability to resist aggression, even going so far as to Xerox a chapter of Kissinger's 1957 book advocating tactical nuclear weapons for defense, and distributing copies to all the members of the panel."[123] The supreme commander explicitly rejected the argument that a small number of tactical nuclear weapons would make Sweden a target, and in fact he argued that remaining non-nuclear would increase the probability that the Soviets would use a nuclear weapon against Sweden.[124]

Military leadership had given detailed, thoughtful arguments in favor of acquiring tactical nuclear weapons. Since the Soviets would have to invade either by land from the north or by sea from the south, tactical nuclear weapons would have raised the cost of such an invasion, especially considering Sweden's neutral, non-NATO status. In addition, tactical nuclear weapons would disperse the enemy's forces, making it easy to engage them in conventional combat. Military leadership was so certain Sweden would acquire nuclear weapons that in 1957, the supreme commander "did not submit a non-nuclear option among his four long-term defense plans."[125] The interest of the air force began to wane in 1960, when it began prioritizing funds for the new, state-of-the-art Viggen fighter aircraft. Only after loss of support from the air force did military planners begin publicly discussing security drawbacks to nuclear weapons.[126] Nonetheless, even as late as 1965, the military argued that tactical nuclear weapons would strengthen Sweden's security and that funds for exploratory research and fissile material stockpiling should be made available.[127] In other words, before the decision to forgo nuclear weapons was made, the only voices saying that nuclear weapons made Sweden less safe were political voices — those arguing that Sweden should serve as a model for the rest of the world by promoting and practicing disarmament. Not even all politicians agreed; as late as 1959, some Social Democrats continued to argue that nuclear weapons would be helpful in Sweden's quest for armed neutrality.[128] Thus fear of Swedish nuclear weapons making Sweden a target was not likely the real motivation behind nuclear forbearance; those making that argument were already committed to Swedish nuclear forbearance. Indeed, using the "target" argument may have been a way for the left-wing Social Democrats, sensitive to accusations that they were weak on defense, to beef up their security image — they wanted to send the message that their opposition to nuclear weapons was based on a security rationale rather than an ideological one.[129]

Prawitz offers a similar security argument, suggesting that "flexible response" made nuclear weapons less relevant for Swedish security. Flexible response meant that nuclear weapons were less likely to be used in a European conflict, and thus Sweden had to be prepared to defend its territory with conventional forces. If Sweden opted to spend less on conventional defense and instead invested in tactical nuclear weapons, it might have to escalate to nuclear use if attacked with conventional forces. Because the Swedes refused to engage in first use of nuclear weapons, they instead decided to forgo nuclear weapons and focus on conventional forces. However, this cannot be why Sweden gave up its nuclear weapons program. Sweden's decision to drop the nuclear program had already been made well before NATO adopted flexible response in 1967. Analysts estimate that the Swedish nuclear weapons program was dead between 1960 and 1962 (some say as early as 1959).[130] The United States did not even begin to discuss flexible response until late 1961. These security arguments are post-hoc rationalizations. The military did not fully give up its hopes for nuclear weapons until 1965.[131] Eventually the military elite did begin to argue that nuclear weapons would hurt Sweden's security. But this was after a budget for a nuclear weapons program had been denied for several years, and after the Social Democrats consolidated their grip on power and took on a leadership role in the international nonproliferation movement. Did the military elite really change their minds, or were they adapting to political realities? Either way, their arguments at most served only to put the last nail in the coffin of the Swedish nuclear weapons program.

The puzzle should be stated clearly: by 1957 all major political parties and a majority of the voting population supported moving forward on funding for nuclear weapons research, at the very least. Sweden perceived a serious threat from the Soviet Union and received no security guarantees from any state. And yet the vociferous antinuclear wing of the Social Democrats was able to overrule these pressures toward nuclear weapons, and less than a decade later, the nuclear option was ruled out. This happened because the antinuclear faction of the Social Democrats, through public debate, was able to cast nuclear weapons as a "square peg in the round hole of Swedish society."[132] This group used "images and metaphors that expressed a sense of 'Swedishness' without reference to nuclear weapons," and "made these weapons the symbol of 'anti-Swedishness.' In a highly homogeneous society such as Sweden's, images that express 'Swedishness' carry a great deal of social weight."[133] To make the task of the antinuclear faction even easier, pronuclear advocates often adopted the language and logic of Western defense analysts, making their case harder to sell to the public. Cole notes: "The anti-nuclear weapon faction in the government took its ideological case against nuclear weapons to the general public through party newspapers and speeches. On the international slate, it launched a series of initiatives intended to establish firmly Sweden's anti-nuclear credentials. Without a plan to influence public opinion in their favor, the pro-nuclear strategists and planners were destined to lose the fight."[134] From 1957 to 1959, pronuclear support among the public increased from 40 percent to 57 percent.[135] By publicly defining the fight *against* nuclear weapons as a fight *for* "Swedishness," the Social Democrats managed to turn the tide completely against the nuclear option. In 1967 only 30 percent of Swedes favored the acquisition of nuclear weapons — 69 percent were opposed.[136] As public sentiment turned against nuclear weapons, their acquisition became less and less feasible. Cathleen Fisher observed: "Over time, Sweden's disarmament rhetoric and neutral ideology helped to create a national anti-nuclear ethos among the Swedish population. When the time came to move forward with the production, assembly, and deployment of nuclear weapons, Sweden's leaders, afraid to pay the political price of weapons acquisition, balked. Nuclear weapons were simply incompatible with Sweden's image of itself as the model peaceful state."[137]

Lessons Learned

Sweden's case is an excellent example of how the international social environment surrounding nuclear nonproliferation can have a real impact on state nuclear decision-making. After Hiroshima and Nagasaki, the Swedes assumed they would develop nuclear weapons, as would other modern, developed states. As the Cold War began, tactical nuclear weapons were envisioned as the best way to deter the Soviet Union from invading Sweden, a state so committed to neutrality that it rejected membership in NATO. Thus nuclear weapons would enhance Sweden's self-image as a securely armed, neutral, and technologically sophisticated state. Only one faction of one main party disagreed. What happened to stop this seemingly irresistible press toward nuclear acquisition?

The main cause was the Social Democrats' antinuclear faction, which first managed to keep the government from anything more than a "decision not to decide" and then turned an antinuclear agenda into policy after gaining control. The group was able to accomplish this in part by hooking into the emerging international norm against nuclear proliferation. Of the nine processes through which the international social environment could exert influence, eight do seem to help us understand how the international interacted with the domestic.[138] The descriptive norm for nuclear nonproliferation — that is, what the Swedes gathered about expectations for nuclear decision-making by observing others' behavior — changed dramatically between the early 1950s and mid-1960s. Instead of countries planning to acquire nuclear weapons, within the space of a decade a number of countries spoke out against nuclear proliferation and committed to nuclear forbearance (including West Germany). The injunctive norm — that is, the public message being transmitted worldwide about nuclear nonproliferation — changed even more dramatically, as identified in earlier discussion of Libya. In 1955 Hiroshima hosted the world's first conference protesting nuclear weapons.[139] More than eleven thousand scientists signed a 1958 petition delivered to the UN secretary-general to ban nuclear tests.[140] Even Eisenhower was pressured into test-ban talks with the Soviets by the force of "powerful popular movements."[141] Subjective norms — what you think others think you should do — also seem to have played a role. Swedish elites were painfully conscious of how their decisions could impact other states; they seemed to feel pressure to behave "properly" because of expectations from others. Lars Van Dassen notes: "The nuclear bomb was thought of as an 'unclean,' immoral possession and that much more could be achieved nationally and internationally by focusing on welfare — and if necessary — conventional defense. Politicians and the government increasingly used the argument that the rest of the world would think very little of Sweden as an international citizen, should it proliferate."[142]

The antinuclear norm was activated in Sweden as news of worldwide antinuclear protests was reported alongside news of Swedish activities to help stop the spread of nuclear weapons. Most important, the antinuclear wing of the Social Democrats created a powerful link between the concept of Swedishness and a non-nuclear weapons state. Without the emerging international norm against nuclear weapons, this link could not have been made. In other words, had nuclear weapons been seen merely as another type of weapon, instead of a deadly threat to all humanity, the left would not have been able to construct a convincing argument that nuclear weapons would erode Sweden's peaceful, neutral stance. This is especially pertinent considering that a strong defense was considered essential to Sweden's belief in armed neutrality. Consistency played a role in Sweden's nuclear forbearance in at least two ways. First, the Swedish elite clearly wanted to be seen as representing a peaceful, neutral state that favored cooperation over conflict. Once international negotiations started on nuclear nonproliferation, the Swedes believed that they needed both to be a part of and to adhere to these negotiations. Appearing consistent was important. In addition, once Sweden made its commitment to forswear nuclear weapons, that decision seemed to cement its policy. Quester noted in 1973 that "Swedish public opinion today would severely punish any party that explicitly endorsed nuclear weapons, in large part because a respectable status quo has gradually developed, which now seems to leave no role for such weapons."[143] Other actions in this realm were judged by whether they were consistent with Sweden's non-nuclear policy.[144] For example, a decade after its ratification of the NPT, Sweden faced a serious security threat in October 1981 that could have undermined its commitment to the treaty. Van Dassen reports:

> A Soviet Whiskey-class submarine U-137 had stranded near the navy base of Karlskrona situated in the archipelago of southeastern Sweden. The stranded submarine was hardly the accident the USSR claimed it to be. . . . It would have been virtually impossible for the U-137 to enter the archipelago as far as it did with its navigation instruments in disarray as the official Soviet explanation framed it. From the outside of the submarine, experts from Sweden's National Defence Research Establishment measured the ionizing radiation and concluded that there were between 10 and 20 kg of U-238 on board, and this could conceivably only serve one purpose: as the tamper in one or two nuclear warheads in either a torpedo or mine.[145]

The Swedes were disturbed and apprehensive, since the Soviets had brought nuclear weapons into the territory of a neutral, non-nuclear NPT signatory. The Soviets were clearly more of a menace than the Swedes had thought. The most shocking part of the incident, van Dassen notes, was that during and after the crisis, not a single person either inside or outside government called for Sweden to restart its nuclear weapons program. The non-nuclear principle had become so embedded into Swedish thinking and policy that a restart simply was not even considered.[146]

Regarding conditions that affect norm potency, two of the three (uncertainty and conflict) shed light on Sweden's nuclear forbearance. Arms control negotiations clearly created uncertainty about the value of nuclear weapons for Sweden. In fact, Swedish negotiators told the Americans and Soviets that they would refrain from building nuclear weapons if a global treaty could be worked out, but they would not otherwise be able to make that promise.[147] In other words, the value of nuclear weapons would be different with a treaty than it would be without; with a treaty, they would not be worth pursuing, but without one, they might be. This uncertainty generated by the international negotiations is what helped lead to the Swedish "decision not to decide" during the late 1950s. Conflict also seems to have helped create the Swedish mindset to seek cooperation instead of power. Many researchers point to Sweden's bitter experiences in playing "great power politics" between 1630 and 1800. As with Japan, Egypt, and Libya, bitter experiences with conflict seem to have shaped the national consciousness to avoid armed conflict as much as possible and instead to seek diplomatic paths to peace.

Having explored the Swedish decision to give up the nuclear option and the impact of the international social environment on that decision, we must now address whether Sweden's nuclear forbearance is best characterized as persuasion, conformity, or identification. Simply stated, neither conformity nor identification describes Sweden's decision to forgo nuclear weapons: persuasion is the most compelling explanation. If conformity were the reason for Sweden's nuclear forbearance, we would expect policymakers to drag their feet on each and every commitment required, hoping to forestall and perhaps negotiate down commitments. Instead, Sweden signed and ratified the PTBT almost immediately, signed and ratified the NPT quickly, began cooperation with nuclear export controls in the late 1960s, and became a staunch supporter of numerous nonproliferation initiatives.[148] In addition, conformity would mean a state abided by the treaty only because it had to; one would not expect a conforming state to propose new, more restrictive additions to the treaty that would bind signatories even further. And yet this is exactly what Sweden has done. For example, Sweden was a leading player in the creation of the "Model Additional Protocol" in the 1990s, which includes the possibility of more intrusive inspections that would assist the IAEA to catch countries working on secret nuclear programs.[149]

Identification also does not "fit" the Swedish case. First, Sweden did not closely identify with the United States (or any other major power) after World War II. The Swedish elite rejected membership in NATO and had a number of confrontations with the United States throughout the Cold War, as noted earlier. In addition, identifying states are not expected to harass or confront the states with which they identify. Yet Sweden has taken pride in doing so.[150] The *Washington Post* reported Swedish satisfaction with assertively promoting disarmament: "'Lots of people hate the Swedes,' said Defense Ministry spokesman Bo Eriksson. 'They think we're a pain in the ass, always bragging at nonproliferation conferences and arms control negotiations.'"[151] Another sign is Sweden's leadership (along with Egypt) in the New Agenda Coalition, the group of seven states banding together in 1998 to demand that nuclear weapons states take disarmament more seriously.[152]

Rather, Sweden's behavior seems like that of a persuaded state. The domestic debate of the 1950s and 1960s left the large majority of Swedes—elite and citizen alike—convinced that nuclear weapons were not compatible with Sweden's ethos and that such weapons were immoral and could very well destroy humanity. This passion comes through in Sweden's numerous and diverse diplomatic efforts to constrain nuclear weapons. The depth of this persuasion is illustrated by the Swedish response to the stranded Soviet submarine—no one even thought to question Sweden's non-nuclear policy. Sweden commits a great deal of energy and diplomatic effort to promoting nuclear nonproliferation, and its commitment seems to grow stronger as states such as the United States seem to back away from their commitments. This persuasion likely would not have happened without a dedicated core group in Sweden willing to argue vociferously for it in public debates. However, this persuasion also was not likely to happen without the international norm against nuclear proliferation, which allowed Sweden's antinuclear group to gain credibility and power.

In some ways, the Swedish case parallels that of Japan. For both countries, initially at least some political leaders wanted nuclear weapons, but they were blocked by domestic groups that used the international norm to bolster their case at home. In addition, in both countries, the presence of a U.S. security guarantee (formal in the Japanese case, tacit in the Swedish case) likely helped mollify conservative elements unhappy with the outcome of the domestic fight. However, over time, the large majority of the population, including political elites, became persuaded that nuclear weapons were not the best way to secure the state and found nuclear weapons incompatible with state identity.

GERMANY

With an advanced nuclear power infrastructure, large amounts of excess stored plutonium, and nuclear-armed neighbors, Germany seems to be a perfect candidate for a nuclear weapons program. However, Germany does not have an independent nuclear force and in fact has led efforts both to prevent the modernization of NATO's nuclear forces and to induce NATO to consider a no-first-use pledge. The German public is strongly antinuclear, and the prospects for a German bomb in the near to mid term are quite low.[153] Explaining the puzzle of German nuclear forbearance requires a review of German nuclear decision-making and of the factors that contributed to Germany's current non-nuclear state. The main time frame in which Germany seriously considered a nuclear weapons program was 1955–63. During this period a number of conservative political and military leaders argued that Germany needed its own nuclear deterrent, but they faced considerable opposition from leftist parties and the public. With the signing of the Partial Test Ban Treaty in 1963, most serious hopes of West German nuclear capability died out. Germany signed the NPT in 1969, and in time the German elite gradually took on the same antinuclear outlook as that of the German populace.

After the end of World War II the West German government was required to forswear nuclear weapons in the 1954 Paris Agreements, which brought the country into the Western European Union. The Germans were protected by U.S. nuclear weapons, based on German soil since 1953. However, German elites believed that once they had proved themselves a reliable and civilized state, they would be allowed to possess their own nuclear weapons.[154] Thus they expected the renunciation to be short-lived; as Chancellor Konrad Adenauer argued, "Tactical nuclear weapons are basically nothing but the further development of artillery. It goes without saying that, due to such a powerful development in weapons technique (which we unfortunately now have), we cannot dispense with having them for our troops. We must follow suit and have these new types—they are after all practically normal weapons."[155] This motivation was fueled in part by fear of the Soviets.[156] As J. I. Coffey notes, West Germany still felt "threatened by the USSR despite the assurances provided by membership in NATO, by the presence of large numbers of American and other allied forces, by the dissemination of nuclear weapons, and by specific and repeated American commitments."[157]

Beyond the Soviet threat, the Germans had a deep fear of American abandonment: "There was a lot of anxiety about whether Germany would be admitted into the circle of Western nations and doubts that the United States was really willing to defend the country against the menace of Soviet communism."[158] The fears became more profound in July 1955, when the U.S. Radford Plan was leaked to the press: the United States planned on significantly reducing troop levels in Europe, with up to 450,000 to be withdrawn within the next few years. German military and political leaders were shocked, believing such a withdrawal would amount to "atomic isolationism" on the part of the United States.[159] The Radford Plan was dropped, but a similar program called the "New Look" was soon implemented. New Look was meant to deter Soviet incursions into Western Europe not through conventional forces but with the threat of massive nuclear retaliation. For the Germans, however, this simply meant that Germany would become ground zero for any future conflict, which would quickly turn nuclear. "A message came through loud and clear to the West Germans: the US Joint Chiefs of Staff were willing to use Bundeswehr soldiers, not American soldiers, as atomic cannon fodder along the front lines."[160] One senior military planner publicly argued that the New Look did not provide adequate protection for Germany, and he advocated that Germany withdraw from NATO and become a neutral state.[161] A later change in American strategic policy caused even more concern in Bonn: flexible response, which backed away from massive retaliation to allow for conventional responses to Soviet aggression. The German elite began to doubt American commitment to their defense:

> Talk about raising the nuclear threshold has aroused profound suspicion about the likely response of the United States President to an incursion into Germany. Hamburg is virtually on the zonal frontier, Berlin is 100 miles inside enemy territory, and even Frankfurt is only 120 miles from Thuringia: to what adventures might the Russians be tempted if they knew there was a gap before nuclear weapons would be used and that NATO policy was to bring the action to a halt by imposing a pause? This question is being very seriously asked in Bonn, and Herr Strauss and the government appear to be profoundly disturbed about the existing position. Essentially it is a crisis of credibility.[162]

This crisis of credibility led Adenauer to raise secretly the issue of whether Germany could produce its own nuclear deterrent.[163]

Because that option seemed unworkable, the Germans attempted to work with the French and Italians to create a joint nuclear program, with uranium enrichment to take place on French soil. After Charles de Gaulle came to power, though, the potential for nuclear weapons cooperation ended, since de Gaulle insisted on an independent French bomb.[164] The German elite next pursued the possibility of control over U.S. nuclear forces on their soil through an American-sponsored multilateral nuclear force (MLF). The MLF would allow the United States to retain operational control over nuclear weapons while allowing NATO members greater participation in the management of NATO's nuclear deterrent: "Among other advantages, MLF presented the French with an alternate to an independent deterrent of their own, allowed for the eventual deployment of British nuclear submarines under the aegis of NATO, granted the West Germans a larger voice in alliance nuclear policy-making, and, by preserving ultimate U.S. operational control in the form of a Presidential veto, furthered the twin objectives of nonproliferation and single unified command and control."[165] Both Britain and France objected, and other NATO countries joined in the objections, in part because they found Bonn's enthusiastic endorsement of MLF somewhat disconcerting.[166] In addition, the Soviets protested strongly, arguing that MLF would make Germany a de facto nuclear state. The Soviets used the promise of cooperation with the United States on the then-emerging Nuclear Nonproliferation Treaty (NPT) to pressure the Americans to drop MLF. In the end the United States withdrew its proposal for MLF and instead asked Germany to sign the NPT. German officials were not happy about pressure to join the NPT, for two reasons. First, some leaders were concerned that the NPT would hamper Germany's ability to maximize competitiveness in the civilian nuclear sphere. Second, conservative politicians believed the NPT would relegate Germany to second-class status forever; Adenauer described it as "a Versailles of cosmic dimensions."[167] A new, more liberal coalition took power in 1969, and only then did Germany sign the NPT. German hopes for an independent nuclear force were dashed.

During this time, however, the German opposition parties and general public did not acquiesce to elite machinations to equip the country with nuclear weapons. In 1954 the NATO field exercise Battle Royal showed that a small Soviet attack would result in extreme radioactive contamination on German territory. The Social Democratic Party (SPD) leadership used the results to attack the government, saying: "Apparently they totally ignored the civilian population and its activities during the maneuver. Hasn't anyone done any thinking at all about civilian losses caused by the use of such atomic weapons?"[168] But the response to Battle Royal was minor compared to the reaction to Carte Blanche. Held in June 1955, Carte Blanche was another NATO exercise, this one intended to simulate the results of a massive Soviet nuclear attack.[169] While technically NATO emerged as the victor, simulated German causalities were shocking: 1.7 million Germans killed, 3.5 million wounded, and extreme radioactive fallout.[170] The media publicized the simulated results extensively, and the public response was heated: "The general population reacted with shock and fear. There were public meetings; pacifist groups issued dire warnings of an apocalyptic future. If a repetition of the last terrible days of World War II was unconfrontable, this new horror to which their government had exposed them was inconceivable."[171]

Domestic opposition to a German nuclear option was strong. Jenifer Mackby and Walter Slocombe report that "each German decision on nuclear policy was marked by bitter debates in the Bundestag and often by massive demonstrations and protests."[172] By 1955, 75 percent of Germans associated even nuclear energy with war and death.[173] In 1957, after rumors of a Franco-German bomb had spread, a group of prominent German scientists issued the Göttingen Manifesto, calling for complete German renunciation of nuclear weapons (whether produced by Germany or not). In addition, the scientists declared they would not work on any nuclear program that could be used for military purposes.[174] When the German chancellor and other top government officials said the German army had to have nuclear weapons, public response grew even stronger:

> [The calls] unleashed a furious response from the German scientific and religious communities, which served to further polarize German society over the issue. Led by the SPD, this renewed opposition forced the more conservative Christian Socialist Union/Christian Democratic Union coalition to back away from its nuclear stance. The next few years brought an increase in antinuclear sentiment in Germany with a related peace movement led by leaders of the nuclear physics community, churches, and other dedicated antinuclear organizations.[175]

The peace movement quickly spread through formation of antinuclear groups, organized protests of thousands of Germans, and calls for global nuclear disarmament. As Thomas Berger notes, the ferocity of the public response forced the government to denounce publicly the possibility of a German bomb as well as make any introduction of NATO nuclear weapons dependent on Soviet-American progress in arms control negotiations.[176] In addition, the combination of domestic protest and international concern led the German elite to sign the PTBT begrudgingly in 1963. The conservative-controlled government refused to sign the NPT, and it was not until an SPD prime minister took power in late 1969 that Germany signed the treaty.

At this point, a nuclear Germany was seen as extremely doubtful, thanks to its new international commitments. Peace groups began to focus on Vietnam. Nuclear debate did not restart in Germany until more than a decade later. In

1979 NATO members agreed to pursue the development of intermediate-range nuclear forces (INF), specifically the Pershing II and cruise missiles, to counter a perceived Soviet advantage in intermediate-range ballistic missiles. This decision—combined with concern over U.S. seriousness on arms control and with growth of a new German political party, the Green Party—led to the most furious antinuclear demonstrations in German history. "Chancellor Helmut Schmidt was vilified by hundreds of thousands of West Germans for being a prime architect of the 1979 NATO decision to deploy hundreds of new nuclear missiles capable of striking the Soviet Union."[177] Enormous demonstrations—drawing several hundred thousand protestors each—took place in West Germany and across Europe in 1980 and 1981, followed by co-ordinated "widespread passive resistance measures" in 1982 and "direct action against those military bases slated to receive the Pershings and cruise missiles" in 1983.[178] By 1987, 66 percent of West Germans were opposed to U.S. bases in their country.[179]

The antinuclear sentiment was not confined to the German public; the attitude spread to German decision-makers. While German officials did not want to fold their U.S. nuclear umbrella, they did take a number of steps to curtail U.S. nuclear forces in Germany—certainly a counterintuitive strategy, at least from a realist point of view. The INF debate of the early 1980s "traumatized" the German political elite, making leaders less likely to raise the nuclear issue.[180] The INF issue also helped propel the leftist Green Party to national stature and radicalized the Social Democratic Party, helping to ensure that more elected politicians would be antinuclear.[181] In 1993 the German government proposed a Ten-Point Initiative on nonproliferation, including conclusion of the CTBT by 1995, negotiation of a fissile material cut-off treaty, an international regime to monitor plutonium, and a nuclear weapons register.[182] By 1998 the Germans raised the issue of a NATO no-first-use policy. Wade Boese reported:

Defying outspoken U.S. opposition, the new German coalition government raised the issue of a nuclear no-first-use policy at the NATO foreign ministers meeting in Brussels on December 8, 1998. . . . Most alliance members view the nuclear elements of the strategic concept as untouchable. Yet the new German government, which advocates a nuclear-free world, has voiced concerns that the nuclear powers' failure to take steps toward disarmament or reducing the role of nuclear weapons will reduce the incentive for non-nuclear-weapon states to forgo the nuclear option.[183]

From a realist point of view, such actions would be foolish and dangerous, since the Germans were in effect undermining the nuclear deterrent that protected them. After intense U.S. criticism of the German effort and reconsideration of domestic political issues, the German leadership backed down.[184] The effort was nonetheless a sincere one and showed that the Germans were trying to devalue the utility of nuclear weapons.[185] Today the likelihood of an independent German nuclear weapons program is close to zero, at least for the short to mid term. As former German foreign minister Klaud Kinkel said, "Germany is the best proof that renunciation of nuclear weapons is not a disadvantage. There can be no doubt that this decision is final."[186]

Understanding Germany's Nuclear Forbearance

With its sophisticated nuclear industry and skilled scientists, Germany could easily develop nuclear weapons if it so chose. What kept the country from doing so? Many argue that a combination of forced disarmament after World War II and the U.S. nuclear umbrella during the Cold War made it both unlikely and unnecessary for Germany to produce its own nuclear bombs. T. V. Paul sums up why Germany abstained from nuclear weapons:

> The most commonly accepted explanation is that it was forced to do so by the victors of the Second World War. Subsequently, the American nuclear umbrella and the presence of massive U.S. forces forestalled any need for it to seek a national nuclear capability. The United States acted as a pacifier and a "balancer of last resort" of Western European states such as West Germany and contained the challenger, the Soviet Union. By extending security guarantees to West Germany, the United States removed the major structural and systemic reasons for the pursuit of an autonomous defense policy.[187]

However, this perspective does not explain why the West German leadership did not feel satisfied by the U.S. security guarantee and clearly did seek a nuclear deterrent beyond what the Americans provided. Doubts about American reliability began with the Radford Plan in 1955, when it was leaked that the United States planned to withdraw up to 450,000 troops from Europe within a few years. Some argue that Adenauer felt deeply betrayed by the Radford Plan, which broke his trust in American commitments.[188] While the Radford Plan was scrapped, the policy that replaced it — New Look — was little different. Instead of stationing troops to deter Soviet conventional incursions, the United

States would rely on massive nuclear retaliation. New Look unsettled West German politicians for a number of reasons. They believed the United States was abandoning Europe, and they worried that Washington was prepared to "contain" conflict to the European continent. In other words, they doubted that the United States would trade New York for Bonn.

Finally, the U.S. plan for flexible response also undermined the trust West Germans had in U.S. reliability. Under flexible response, any Soviet incursion would not immediately be met by a nuclear response — instead, Washington could choose from any number of options (nuclear or conventional) to respond. The West Germans believed flexible response would provide a nearly irresistible temptation to the Soviets. Cathryn Carson notes that after this crisis of credibility, "Adenauer confidentially raised the idea that the Federal Republic might need to produce its own nuclear weapons."[189] Then in late 1956, West Germany began secret negotiations with the French and Italians for a European nuclear deterrent that could replace the less credible American one. Much to the dismay of West German conservatives, the election of de Gaulle put an end to those hopes. Next the West German elite turned enthusiastically to multilateral nuclear force, which would put tactical nuclear weapons into the hands of the Bundeswehr. In fact, part of the U.S. motivation for initiating MLF was to forestall German ambitions for an independent nuclear force.[190] But MLF was crushed by objections, not only from the Soviets but also from Britain and France — none of whom wanted to see the German military have control over nuclear weapons. Shortly thereafter, West Germany buckled under pressure and signed the Partial Test Ban Treaty; conservatives privately lamented that this would make it extremely hard to create an indigenous nuclear capability. Conservatives refused to the sign the NPT; it was only after the election of a coalition government led by the SPD that West Germany submitted its signature for the international treaty.

This timeline is not the timeline of a country that felt secure under the U.S. nuclear umbrella. Instead, it tells the story of a country that doubted U.S. reliability and that sought some other way to secure itself. As noted, one prominent West German military planner believed that the New Look completely undermined West German security and publicly called for the country to become an independent, neutral state. Even some American analysts have argued that West Germany would have been safer during the Cold War with its own nuclear deterrent. If Bonn was not satisfied with American security guarantees, why did Germany not produce its own nuclear weapons?

For the period between 1955 and 1963, when West Germany was most likely to pursue its own nuclear deterrent, four main factors kept the country from going nuclear. First, developing an independent nuclear capability in secret would have been have been extremely difficult because of the restrictions placed on West German scientists. If news of a serious nuclear weapons program had been made public, West Germany would have faced retaliation not only from its allies but also from the Soviet Union. Second, reunification was extremely important to West Germany, and its leaders knew an independent nuclear force would damage prospects for reunification. Third, domestic sentiment against nuclear weapons made it quite difficult for the government seriously to pursue a military nuclear program. As noted, the country's top physicists had already publicly stated their refusal to work on any aspect of a nuclear program that could be used for military purposes. The Göttingen Manifesto received a great deal of press coverage, and the government sought a meeting with the scientists to contain the damage. In the end, in response to the manifesto, government officials announced that they were not seeking an independent nuclear deterrent, nor direct control over NATO weapons in West Germany.[191] The antinuclear protests between 1958 and 1960 showed the conservatives ruling the government that a political price would be paid for any nuclear weapons program — a price that might sweep them right out of office. Fourth, the U.S. nuclear umbrella did help relieve West Germans of some of their fear of the Soviets. While it was not a sufficient condition, it no doubt played a role in Bonn's nuclear decision-making. In this case, the initial German decision against nuclear weapons was shaped in part by normative antinuclear sentiment domestically but also by important security calculations that fit realist predictions.

In the late 1960s, however, attitudes in the West German elite toward an independent nuclear capability began to change. Beginning in the 1960s, Bonn's policy of *Ostpolitik* — rapprochement with the East — placed greater emphasis on diplomatic cooperation with East Germany and the Soviet Union. West Germany was seeing the results of cooperation with neighbors economically and diplomatically, and officials realized "they could gain more by being a responsible member of the Western alliance than by pursuing an independent nuclear venture."[192] Instead of focusing on its own nuclear option, Bonn began to focus on arms control and disarmament.[193] Integration with its European neighbors became a much higher goal, making the costs of a West German nuclear program much steeper and in fact making nuclear weapons less useful (since they would hurt, not help, integration efforts).

In addition, West Germany's rapid economic growth led the elite to conclude that the country did not need to function as a "great power player" to succeed. Harald Müller notes that the government "viewed civilian — particularly economic and social — achievements as equally or more important than being on a level playing field with France and Britain in military terms."[194] When détente was broken by Soviet aggression in Afghanistan, Bonn was willing to host additional tactical nuclear weapons to guard against any potential Soviet incursions into Europe. However, the government soon found out that the West German public would not permit it. Indeed, the INF debacle of the 1980s taught policymakers that the nuclear issue could create extreme public discontent and thus needed to be avoided at all costs. In the 1990s, after the end of the Cold War and reunification, the German elite no longer showed any desire for its own nuclear weapons and, in fact, began to call for the removal of U.S. nuclear weapons from German soil. Thus, whereas up until the early 1960s West German leaders did not develop nuclear weapons because they could not, later they simply no longer wanted these weapons, due to a change in goals. Paul notes, "West Germany's own ambitions regarding power and influence changed over time. Traditional military power seemed to have limited relevance to the creation of a stable, unified Europe."[195]

Lessons Learned

To what extent did the international social environment created by the nuclear nonproliferation regime help shape elite attitudes and decisions regarding nuclear weapons? A number of these influences did seem to shape the way the German leadership approached the question of an independent nuclear deterrent.

With regard to the way norms are transmitted — that is, descriptive, injunctive, and subjective norms — all three played a role in German nuclear forbearance. Descriptive norms — what the West Germans understood about nuclear nonproliferation by watching the behavior of other states — certainly helped persuade Bonn to remain non-nuclear. Adenauer was keenly aware of the discriminatory nature of the Paris Accords as well as of the PTBT and the NPT. The sting of Britain and France having nuclear weapons was sharp; but it was made less so by the fact that no other European country had independent nuclear forces. Both the PTBT and NPT were universal in nature and intent, which made German signature easier to secure. Germany was not the only country being asked to forswear nuclear weapons — this applied to all countries that did not already possess them. In fact, without the universal nature of the PTBT and NPT, it might have been impossible to secure West Germany's signature.

The injunctive norm — the norm clearly communicated through verbal and written means — also impressed upon the West German elite that nuclear proliferation was strongly discouraged. Because of German aggression in World War II, many countries feared the possibility of revival of an armed and nationalistic Germany. For West Germans to show that they rejected the Nazi mentality, they needed to act in nonaggressive ways. Because the injunctive norm was so strong for Bonn, the cost of rejecting it would have been high. Subjective norms — what the West German elite believed other countries thought Bonn should do — seemed to reiterate that the country was expected to forgo nuclear weapons. No evidence shows that Bonn thought it was receiving mixed signals from other countries about nuclear proliferation. West German leaders likely took both the descriptive and injunctive norms at face value and believed that other countries wanted Germany to forgo nuclear weapons.

How West Germany processed the nuclear nonproliferation norm also pressed the state into compliance. Linking was particularly noticeable, both internationally and domestically — actors both external and internal to the state made it clear that due to Hitler's aggression, Germany must now behave responsibly, including forgoing nuclear weapons. In other words, being a responsible member of the civilized world was directly linked with staying non-nuclear, especially for Germany. The United States, Great Britain, and France linked full return of West German sovereignty to Bonn's pledge to renounce weapons of mass destruction. Because of Germany's past, these links were especially emphasized.

The same linkages were made domestically. "[Domestic] opponents of German access to nuclear weapons generally shared a fear of the resurrected Bundeswehr. Since a prodemocratic German army able and willing to subsume itself completely to civilian authority had never existed, concerns arose over the specter of ex-Nazi generals with direct control of such powerful arms."[196] Thus domestic groups pushed for their government to reject not only an indigenous nuclear weapons program but also shared control of U.S. bombs. Domestic groups also linked West German nuclear policy to the atomic devastation in Japan, arguing that the same devastation could be replicated on German soil. For example, the SPD ran television broadcasts against nuclear weapons in Germany, using footage from Nagasaki.[197] Protesters declared at peace marches, "No Euroshimas!" Another historical link made by domestic groups was between the horrors of World War II and the potential horrors of nuclear warfare.

Acutely aware of the suffering Germany had caused, many West German citizens saw nuclear weapons as even worse than what Hitler had wrought—and wanted nothing to do with it. They argued that the pronuclear elite was continuing Hitler's campaign of mass murder: "At some of the protest marches, anti-nuclear campaigners carried banners with the slogan, 'first Bergen-Belsen, now Bergen-Hohne.' Bergen-Belsen, the concentration camp, and Bergen-Hohne, the nuclear missile range, were equated as symbols for mass murder."[198] Later on, it would be the German government linking good international citizenship to nonproliferation—directing the norm to the United States. In the 1990s Berlin pressured the United States to ratify the CTBT and to reconsider NATO's nuclear policy.

In terms of activation, we can see clear evidence that activation of the global nonproliferation norm helped fuel antinuclear sentiment in West Germany. After the Carte Blanche exercises in 1955 (the simulated exercises predicting 1.7 million Germans killed and 3.5 million wounded), 88 percent of Germans supported an international agreement to ban nuclear weapons outright.[199] German scientists active in the antinuclear movement in West Germany drew motivation and ideas from their participation in international antinuclear groups, such as the Pugwash movement.[200] For example, Nobel Prize winner Albert Schweitzer (from Alsace, part of Germany when Schweitzer was born) broadcast his "Declaration of Conscience" in April 1957, appealing to citizens around the world to join together to ban nuclear testing. Schweitzer's radio appeal was heard in more than fifty countries, and newspapers all around the world carried news of the physician's appeal. The message was especially resonant in West Germany, where nearly all the newspapers commented "at length on Schweitzer's statement and warned against continued nuclear tests."[201] Shortly afterward, the West German legislature passed a resolution to urge the superpowers to stop testing and to continue arms control efforts.[202] The fact that negotiations for an international test ban treaty were under consideration allowed Schweitzer, the SPD, and German peace activists of all types to activate the emerging norm to influence Bonn's policymaking.[203] Activation of the nuclear nonproliferation norm took place during the INF crisis as well. From 1980 to 1983, hundreds upon hundreds of articles, books, and reports were published by West German peace groups, many of which argued for disarmament instead of missile deployments.[204]

In terms of consistency, we see both direct and indirect evidence that the desire to be consistent influenced policymakers. After World War II Bonn set out to project the image of a peaceful state and carefully acted in ways consistent with that image. To maintain consistency with its "good neighbor" ethos, West Germany needed to remain non-nuclear. Additionally, we see consistency at work in that after West Germany signed the NPT in 1969, talk of an independent nuclear force simply disappeared. Once West Germany ratified the NPT in 1975 (by a wide margin in the Parliament), bureaucracy settled into its role of adhering to the treaty and later took on new roles of promoting additional arms control and disarmament.[205]

Regarding conditions that affect the potency of norms, all three conditions seemed to affect West Germany's nuclear decision-making. Uncertainty over the costs of an independent nuclear force caused Adenauer and his defense minister Franz Josef Strauss to back away from the option and make public declarations that they were not seeking a West German bomb. As noted, scientists published the Göttingen Manifesto to pressure the government into rejecting an independent nuclear deterrent (or one created with France and Italy). The public response to the manifesto, Schweitzer's broadcast, and other antinuclear messages substantially raised the costs of Bonn pursuing its own nuclear deterrent, thus creating uncertainty about its viability. In the end, the conservative government signed the PTBT because it lacked certainty that rejecting the treaty and producing its own nuclear weapons would be worth the cost.

The condition of similarity, interestingly enough, created pressure both for pursuit and for rejection of a West German nuclear program. Because of Germany's historical role as a great power in Europe, Adenauer and other conservatives felt a pull to mimic the behavior of Germany's two European rivals, France and the United Kingdom. These countries' independent nuclear forces clearly fueled the desire among conservatives for West Germany to gain similar status through a nuclear weapons program. On the other hand, the desire to integrate into Europe and be accepted back into the community of nations was also quite strong—and to achieve that goal, Bonn had to reject nuclear weapons. Conditions of conflict were originally expected to create polarization and thus reduce the impact of global norms. However, as we saw with Egypt and Japan, conflict actually promoted the acceptance of global norms in West Germany. Germany's devastating defeat in both world wars was deeply imprinted on the West German public, leading people to embrace a culture of antimilitarism.[206]

Having explored how the international social environment created by the nonproliferation regime influenced West Germany's nuclear decision-making, we next need to address whether German nuclear forbearance is best characterized as persuasion, social conformity, or identification. Initially, the West German elite's decision to refrain from a military nuclear capability was not because they did not want nuclear weapons. Rather, the decision to forgo nuclear weapons was based on a calculation of costs and benefits, with uncertainty over the high costs leading the elite to refrain from a nuclear program. Such an outcome is best characterized as conformity. With its high level of industry and skilled scientists, West Germany clearly could have developed its own nuclear deterrent as early as the French, or earlier. It would have been easier to do this after the French, since Bonn could have claimed to be following the French lead. In fact, security concerns did push West German decision-makers to consider their own independent nuclear force as a deterrent to the Soviets. With the fear of communism spreading worldwide, one could argue that the United States would have accepted (however begrudgingly) an independent German bomb.

What compelled the Germans to refrain from a nuclear weapons program was, in part, a desire to avoid being seen as — and in fact acting like — an aggressive, militaristic neighbor. Germans had no desire to rekindle fears of Nazi Germany. A self-help attitude would likely have led to the French route of an independent nuclear force. Because of recent German history, Bonn was not willing to adopt such an attitude even though Germany had more to fear from the Soviets than did France. Domestic political opposition also forced the West German elite to accept a non-nuclear status. As mentioned, after the German leadership publicly called for German control of nuclear weapons (either through NATO or independently), public reaction was immediate. Thus, early German nuclear forbearance can best be seen as social conformity, since the elite clearly did want nuclear weapons but was not willing to accept the costs. As Leonard Beaton and John Maddox note of West Germany in 1962, "No non-nuclear power says with more determination that it must have nuclear weapons for its defense; yet none (except possibly Israel) must make a more perilous leap to get them. Its political reasons for holding back are at present decisive."[207]

However, once Bonn signed and ratified the NPT, elite attitudes began changing. In contrast to the events of the 1950s and 1960s, we find no record of official government investigations into an independent nuclear force during the 1970s and beyond. For the West Germans, the NPT settled the matter. Indeed, from the 1970s, arms control and disarmament became part of the West German foreign policy plate.[208] As NATO settled into a workable security arrangement, and as West Germany experienced remarkable economic success, policymakers realized that security alliances did indeed protect Germany and allowed them to focus attention on economic growth. The Germans, as with the Japanese, learned their lessons from history. A militaristic and aggressive national strategy had failed them utterly. Thus they were willing to try an integrated, alliance-based strategy to protect their security. What they found was that not only was their security protected, but they were also able to focus on economic growth, leading to unprecedented economic development and economic power.[209] As Berger notes, "In the past, Germany and Japan sought to remedy this vulnerability [to interruptions in international commerce] through the creation of autarchic empires. The spectacular failure of those efforts has led them to rely instead on diplomacy and cooperation in the postwar period."[210] The German leaders initially abided by the NPT norm out of social necessity and ended up internalizing that norm and even promoting it against their own best security interests (at least as defined in traditional realist terms). Currently, "nuclear weapons are not seen as desirable for a Germany that has so convincingly demonstrated both its economic and moral superiority."[211] This outcome is best characterized as persuasion. Even within nationalistic circles, nuclear weapons are scorned: "Indeed, those publications that adopted the most nationalistic pose in the reunification debate tended to be especially contemptuous of nuclear weapons, the possessors of which were portrayed as the 'losers' in the recent political upheavals."[212]

Germany's nuclear weapons policy clearly goes beyond traditional realist considerations. As Mark Gose notes about German motivations, "These motivations include not only traditional security concerns but, perhaps, intensified nonsecurity influences as Germans redefine what it means to be 'German.'"[213] This is especially clear in light of German behavior after the collapse of the Soviet Union and after German reunification. A number of analysts predicted that as soon as the Soviet threat dissipated, Germany would begin acting like a "normal" state and exert its great power status in Europe once again — including the acquisition of nuclear weapons.[214] Not only have we *not* seen Germany flex its military muscles, we have seen Germany seek to strengthen the nuclear nonproliferation regime at the expense of its own security (as traditionally defined). Such moves make no sense to a realist but make great sense to a state that defines its security through its integration into economic, military, and political institutions.

How can we be sure that German nuclear forbearance is not simply identification — that is, based on loyalty to the United States as opposed to its own decision that nuclear weapons are not needed or valued for security? A state that identifies would not go out of its way to strengthen the nuclear nonproliferation regime, but Germany has done so. In 1990 Germany significantly strengthened its own export controls, leading the way for the Nuclear Suppliers Group (NSG) to strengthen its own policy. Müller notes: "Germany further helped improve the NSG guidelines, notably by including dual-use equipment and technology in its control list and adding a catch-all clause. Within the EU, the previous laggard Germany became a driving force in the negotiations on a joint export control policy, a major achievement of EU common security policy in the early nineties."[215] In addition, if a state forgoes nuclear weapons based on identification, then its highest priority is the relationship with the state it identifies as critical. This has not been the case with German nuclear politics, especially after the end of the Cold War. Berlin has encouraged the United States to ratify the CTBT, pushed NATO to consider a no-first-use policy, and argued that NATO nuclear weapons should be withdrawn from Europe.[216]

Rather than reflecting identification, German attitudes about what it means to be a successful state have undergone a complete transformation. "The old revisionist and power-hungry Germany had cascaded from a large territory covering central and central eastern Europe through two world wars to a middle-sized state squeezed at the center, and ended as the pariah of Europe."[217] In contrast, by embracing the role of an economically successful, peaceful state, at the conclusion of the Cold War West Germany ended up with larger territory (through reunification), the largest economy in Europe, and powerful diplomatic influence. As in the four preceding case studies, the Germans learned and came to internalize that security is best achieved without, rather than with, nuclear weapons.

However, as with the other democratic case studies, this persuasion took time to develop. Like their counterparts in both Japan and Sweden, German political leaders did not fully trust the U.S. security guarantee and wanted their own independent nuclear deterrent. In the German case, the restrictions were even more severe: the U.S. allies France and Britain were strongly against a German bomb, and the Germans also had to fear a Soviet response to any nuclear weapons program. As in both Japan and Sweden, the political elite also faced an antinuclear populace, fueled in part by the emerging antinuclear norm, making the political costs for the nuclear option quite high. Thus, as indicated, the initial German decision against nuclear weapons was shaped by a number of factors, including security calculations. However, again as with Japan and Sweden, once this decision was made, Bonn internalized the antinuclear sentiment over time, and today its nuclear forbearance is based on a normative commitment to antinuclear principles.

CHAPTER SIX

Reflections on Theory and Policy

One of the great mysteries in international politics today is why so few states have developed nuclear weapons. Cases such as North Korea, Pakistan, and Iran only underscore the point: if a country has the political will, not even poverty or underdevelopment can keep it from building a nuclear weapons program. While we can understand why a state such as Costa Rica or Tahiti does not seek an atomic bomb, it is less clear why states with both the motive and the means would fail to do so. For example, why did the forty states listed in chapter 1 (table 3) — all of which have nuclear-armed neighbors and nuclear facilities — choose to forgo nuclear weapons? It seems that not all states are motivated by the traditional, realist definition of threat. Perhaps, as neoliberal institutionalism posits, the new costs and benefits imposed by the nuclear nonproliferation regime have given states enough incentives to overcome their nuclear ambition. If so, then we would expect states to remain members of the NPT long enough to take advantage of the material benefits, only to cheat or withdraw afterward. A system of rewards and punishments is not likely to take away states' motivation for the nuclear option — that is, if state elites define security with the traditional self-help focus on material capabilities. Only when state decision-makers expand their view of security to go beyond material capabilities will they even be interested in regime incentives beyond a purely instrumental attitude ("How long before I can leave or cheat?").

While these two theories contribute in important ways to understanding nuclear forbearance, the fact that a large majority of states has joined and adhered to the nuclear nonproliferation regime says that elite definitions of security are broader than both realists and neoliberals might predict. The fact that states have remained members of the NPT despite changes in national leadership and other domestic conditions indicates that something systemic is at least partially at work (as opposed to an idiosyncratic set of beliefs held by a specific set of decision-makers).

This book has argued that the international social environment, supported by first an emergent and then a full-fledged nuclear nonproliferation regime, has helped to provide that systemic impetus toward nuclear nonproliferation. The emerging antinuclear norm led to the development of the nuclear non-proliferation regime, which set forth a clear injunctive norm against nuclear proliferation; and then as states acceded to the treaty, the expanding regime established a descriptive norm against nuclear proliferation as well. The negotiations to create the regime, and the regime itself, communicated that a nuclear weapons program was a violation of international norms, instead of an act of national pride. In addition, international legitimacy was linked to nuclear non-proliferation; members of the international community were expected to comply. From the beginning, the emerging regime nourished the international norm that actors of all types—governmental and nongovernmental, domestic and foreign—could rally round and activate their own drive to further nuclear nonproliferation. Over time, nuclear proliferation became more costly—economically, technically, and diplomatically—whereas nuclear nonproliferation became more rewarding. In changing cost-benefit analyses, the regime created uncertainty about whether security benefits would be worth the high political and financial costs. Although the terms of the NPT allow states to withdraw for reasons of national security, only one—North Korea—has done so in more than three decades. That is in part because once states accede to the regime, they are tethered to it in a number of ways: a domestic bureaucracy is created and empowered to advocate for the NPT, nuclear decision-making becomes no longer solely a function of security advisors but also involves those in the foreign ministry, and elites fear that backing out of the NPT would result in a loss of international credibility and legitimacy.

The case studies provide an informative look at the ways in which the international social environment interacts with other variables to create nuclear forbearance. From the five case studies, two sets of patterns emerge—one for democratic states, and the other for authoritarian states. In the three democratic regimes—Japan, Sweden, and Germany—significant elements of the political elite wanted an independent nuclear deterrent. However, in each case, portions of the domestic population lobbied heavily against an indigenous nuclear weapons program, activating the emerging international norm against nuclear weapons to strengthen and add credibility to their arguments. Thus the domestic political costs for going nuclear rose sharply. Given these costs, conservative elements decided to give up the battle, a decision enabled in part because their security concerns were alleviated at least somewhat by the security assurances provided by the United States, either explicitly (Japan and Germany) or tacitly (Sweden). It is important to note that the security guarantee by itself is not what led to nuclear forbearance, since the elite in all three states did seek nuclear weapons despite extended deterrence. But it is just as important to note that because of the security guarantee, the conservatives who wanted nuclear weapons likely found it much easier to accept non-nuclear status. Over time, however, elite attitudes in all three countries changed to reflect a transformed view of security, one in which nuclear weapons were devalued rather than valued.

In the two authoritarian cases — Egypt and Libya — another pattern prevailed. Both Nasser and Qadhafi sought nuclear weapons but were blocked by foreign intervention, export controls, and great power pressure. These obstacles eventually led both to give up their nuclear ambitions. Also in both states, the political elite eventually recast the notion of success, with the new definition excluding rather than including nuclear weapons. The process took place in different ways in Egypt and Libya. In Nasser's case, he decided to use the international norm against proliferation in a tactical way: by signing the NPT, he could shame Israel and gain status in the Arab world. Then Sadat consolidated the lessons from Nasser's reign and dramatically reenvisioned Egypt's future, redefining what success meant and reinterpreting who friends and enemies were. Part of this process meant forsaking the nuclear option for good — a decision strongly encouraged by the existence of the NPT. For Qadhafi, the process took much longer and was inspired in part by his son, who encouraged him to see decades of conflict and losses as a signal that Libya needed to try a different path. As mentioned, without the roadblocks presented by the United States and others, Qadhafi would not have needed to try a different path. But as with Egypt, the end result has been a redefined vision of what it means to be a successful state, a vision that does not include nuclear weapons.

ANALYTICAL REFLECTIONS

Chapter 1 spells out the major arguments regarding nuclear forbearance, and each of the case studies includes discussion of the relevance of facts to theories. But in a more general sense, what does the larger theoretical discussion tell us about nuclear decision-making? This section identifies potential generalizations that were overlooked in chapter 1 but were suggested by the facts, and it addresses the broader implications of the theories to our understanding of the topic.

Realism and Security

For decades, much of the default thinking about nuclear weapons has been under the rubric of realism, or at least security. Clearly, the material capabilities of other states did influence both Japanese and Egyptian decision-making on nuclear weapons. In the Japanese case, three of the four periods of nuclear rethinking were caused at least in part by neighbor states' nuclear maneuvering: China in 1964, North Korea in the 1990s, and North Korea in the current period. The Egyptian program unquestionably started in response to the revelations about Israel's secret nuclear project at Dimona. Both the West German elite and the Swedish military believed that the Soviet threat warranted investigation of a nuclear option. But while adversarial nuclear programs caught the attention of these countries, they did not prove to be enough of a threat to create a lasting motivation for a matching nuclear weapons program. Or at least they did not prove to be a threat that required an indigenous nuclear response.

These countries also sought security-related measures to address their regional nuclear imbalance. Japan relied on U.S. extended deterrence, Egypt sought balance through conventional weapons and a chemical weapons option, the West Germans had U.S. nuclear weapons stationed on their soil, and the Swedes beefed up their conventional forces. As discussed previously, in the long term these alternative measures would not have been sufficient to ensure forbearance if national elites had not changed the way they thought about security. However, it is important to note that just because these states did not embrace the neorealist self-help attitude, they did not ignore the security needs. Rather, they thought in a different way about security needs and how to fulfill them — a way not predicted by neorealism.

One potential realist argument is that because it is so unlikely that nuclear weapons would be used, their utility is limited, and states would rather seek more useful ways of strengthening their security. Both Japanese and Egyptian experts raised the question: if we had nuclear weapons, what would we do with them? However, nuclear weapons do not need to be used to make a country more powerful. Egypt is concerned about the political leverage that nuclear weapons could give to Iran: one former Egyptian diplomat said, "We are worried about Iran—can you imagine an Iranian nuclear bomb? They may want to assert hegemony over the whole Gulf area."[1] The Israeli nuclear arsenal clearly limited Egyptian war aims in the 1973 war. Facing a potential nuclear holocaust if they invaded Israel, the Egyptians could no longer participate seriously in the Arab goal of ending the existence of the state of Israel. Some elements of Japanese society, confronting China's rise and uncertainty concerning American abandonment, argue that Japan should have a nuclear weapons capability because "nuclear development is a kind of insurance, a card Japan can use against the United States, a means to increase Japan's autonomy with regard to the United States. The nuclear option is their answer to this uncertain situation."[2]

Neoliberalism and Economics

Neoliberal institutionalism offers two main types of arguments with regard to nuclear decision-making: the ability of institutions to provide a means for states to escape the security dilemma, and the economics of nuclear weapons programs. On the surface the institutional argument is quite compelling. States do not want nuclear-armed neighbors, and the best way to avoid that is by joining the NPT. Through international export controls, and through verification and compliance measures, everyone can feel fairly assured that the neighbors are not secretly developing nuclear weapons. The first problem with this argument, however, is that it took time for everyone to jump on the bandwagon. After ten years, 110 states had joined the NPT, which meant dozens had not. In addition, the NPT gave states an escape clause, allowing them to opt out in a matter of months if they believed their national security demanded it. Furthermore, until 1995, the NPT was not a permanent treaty: it was in place for only twenty-five years, with the option to renew. Thus in the first few decades of the NPT, the regime did not offer states a firm guarantee about the nuclear posture of their neighbors. And in the last few decades, the news grew worse; it became evident that cheating while a member of the NPT was possible. After the Gulf War, UNSCOM's discovery of the secret Iraqi nuclear weapons program made it clear that membership in the NPT did not mean a state was abiding by its non-nuclear commitment. Discoveries concerning the A. Q. Khan network only reiterated this message.

The second type of neoliberal argument—focusing on economics—deserves more attention. This project examined one variation of the argument:

that states forgo nuclear weapons in order to gain the material benefits offered by the NPT (technology transfer, financing for civilian nuclear projects, etc.). In all five case studies, this did not prove to be true. The Japanese and West Germans were concerned that the NPT would actually interfere with their civilian nuclear programs, which were plutonium based. The Egyptians finally acceded to the NPT because they wanted technology transfers for nuclear power plants — but this decision was made long after the nuclear weapons option had been closed. Libya signed the NPT before Qadhafi took power and started his secret program. The Swedes did not sign the NPT because of the need for technology; rather, they were motivated by antinuclear sentiment.

Two other variations of the economics argument deserve attention. The first is whether a nuclear weapons program was simply out of reach financially for the states in question. For Japan, being able to afford a nuclear weapons program was never an issue. Even back in the mid-1960s, the time when Japan would have been least able to afford it, a government study concluded that while it would be expensive, it was feasible. In the German debate the question of cost was not raised as a significant issue, considering that Germany was already investing in the nuclear fuel cycle. In Sweden the issue of cost was raised — but the question was, how do we provide generous welfare benefits and fully fund both conventional and nuclear forces? In other words, the Swedes had the money to pay for a program, but they chose to allocate the resources to their welfare state. For oil-rich Libya, cost was also not an issue, as is shown by the millions that Qadhafi spent on advanced nuclear technology. For Egypt, a developing nation with a rapidly expanding population, the cost issue might be more relevant. However, at the time Egypt seriously considered a nuclear program, it had "equal or greater resources when compared with either Israel or Pakistan at the time these countries opted to go nuclear."[3] In addition, while the nuclear weapons project did not have separate funds under the AEE, Nasser did choose to spend enormous sums of money on a number of pet projects.[4] In other words, had the political will been behind the bomb, an economic way could have been found to pay for it.[5]

The second variation in the economic argument is that states were willing to forgo nuclear weapons to gain the benefits of foreign investment and better integration into the international economy. This argument is worth examining. For Japan, it does not seem to hold. When Japan first seriously considered a nuclear weapons program (in the mid-1960s), the country had already embarked on a period of economic growth starting a decade prior with the advent of the Yoshida doctrine. Forgoing nuclear weapons was not needed to jumpstart the economy or provide access to international markets, since both had already happened by this time. A nuclear weapons program could potentially have hurt Japan's economy, in that the United States might have withdrawn from the U.S.-Japan Security Treaty and Japan would have had to shoulder the burden of defense by itself. However, this was not a major consideration in its cost-benefit calculation. Rather, the loss of international integration — diplomatic, political, and economic — seemed to be the main concern to Japanese decision-makers. Neither Germany nor Sweden raised the issue of losing foreign investment if they chose to go nuclear.

With regard to Egypt, it may seem that Sadat made the decision to shelve the nuclear weapons program permanently in order to gain U.S. economic aid. Indeed, Etel Solingen makes the argument that it was Sadat's desire to liberalize the Egyptian economy and attract foreign investment that led him to give up the nuclear option. She notes: "That *infitah* (economic liberation) was launched in 1971, the same year Egypt advanced, for the first time, the idea of a NWFZ, is quite suggestive."[6] This argument has a number of problems, however. First, Egypt's signature of the NPT would seem to mean more than its sponsorship of an Iranian call for a Middle East NWFZ. But because Egypt's signature of the NPT took place in 1968, under Nasser, it does not fit neatly into Solingen's argument. No reports or interviews indicate that Nasser signed the NPT for potential economic benefits; instead he most likely signed because the NPT would give him a platform to embarrass Israel and strengthen his own claim to Arab leadership. Second, although Sadat did reason that an officially closed nuclear option would help him win over the Americans, he sought more from the United States than just help with liberalizing his economy. He hoped for greater leverage against Israel, assistance with civilian nuclear power, and U.S. conventional arms, in addition to economic aid. But as noted in the Egypt case study, by the time Sadat engaged the Americans, the nuclear option had already been largely shut down. Nuclear weapons were already devalued because given his vision of peace with Israel, Sadat did not see a need for them. Regarding Libya's nuclear decision-making, many have pointed to the prospects of sanctions being lifted and greater foreign economic investment as critical to the decision to disarm. Clearly, reformers within Libya wanted the country to be opened up to international investment and trade. However, as noted, Libya offered to give up its WMD after UN sanctions had already been suspended. Thus if Qadhafi still wanted a nuclear weapons program, he would not have had to sacrifice it on the altar of economic gain, given that sanctions no longer kept foreign investment out. It was Qadhafi's change of heart, rather than sanctions, that led him to give up his nuclear weapons program.

Constructivism and the NPT

The pivot of this study is how the international social environment, nurtured and sustained by the NPT and associated agreements, has influenced states' thinking about nuclear weapons and security in general. Evidence has been presented for this influence, yet it is important to note the nuclear nonproliferation regime was not the sole force in elite thinking about the value of nuclear weapons. Instead, the NPT and associated agreements were likely a necessary but not sufficient cause for today's nearly global nuclear forbearance. For both Japan and Egypt, probably the most critical factor in the decision to stay nonnuclear was a changed view of state goals. The Japanese elite in the mid-1960s decided to trust in U.S. extended deterrence because they had redefined what security meant, and the new definition was more about economic strength than military strength. One Japanese defense expert explained: "Security is the issue of the survival of the nation. So the economy is vital to security, which is in essence the Yoshida doctrine. Japan didn't have the capacity to have a full-scale military because it would damage the pace of economic recovery. Japan chose to make minimal military commitments while expanding economic capabilities."[7] It was not that a full-scale military would *destroy* Japan's economy — that people would have to "eat grass," as the Pakistanis declared they would, if necessary, to secure nuclear weapons — or even that it would damage economic recovery. It would damage the *pace* of economic recovery.

After the humiliating defeat in World War II and the atomic bombings of Hiroshima and Nagasaki, Japan essentially rejected the military path, along with the self-help principle, and instead focused on economic growth and doubling the national income. The case of Egypt tells a similar story. The nuclear weapons program had already been basically shut down when Sadat came to power, but the nuclear ambition was not necessarily gone, as evidenced by Nasser's requests to China and the Soviet Union for nuclear devices. When Sadat became president, Egypt had fought and lost in a number of conflicts, not only against Israel but including its intervention in the Yemeni civil war. The economy had been ravaged, the population was suffering, and after one more loss on the battlefield in 1973, Sadat decided to change strategies. He made the strategic decision to transform Egypt, as one Egyptian expert said, from East to West, from war to peace, from socialism to a more open economy. With this decision Sadat promised the United States to end once and for all Egypt's nuclear weapons program. It was an easy promise to make because from the new Egyptian standpoint, "Why would you need the ultimate weapon when you are living peacefully with your neighbors?"[8] As discussed in chapter 5, we can see the same change of interests in Libya, Sweden, and Germany.

Such wholesale transformation of state interests cannot be easily explained by the NPT, but constructivism does provide avenues for explanation. The case study evidence offers a potential clue as to why Japan and Egypt would so dramatically reprioritize state goals. The fact that both countries had experienced degrading, large-scale military losses likely made them reluctant to contend with further conflict and led them to seek alternate paths to state success. For Japan, this path was set in part by the constitution created by the United States, but it was also due in large part to deep-seated public mistrust of the military. As Thomas Berger notes:

> The majority of Japanese also felt victimized by their own military for having dragged them into a war that rationally could only end in tragedy, and for conducting that war without regard for the suffering that was inflicted on the Japanese people. Consequently, the military was seen as innately inclined to take matters into its own hands, and hostile towards human rights and democracy. The profound Japanese distrust of its own military has consistently been reflected in the Japanese debate over defense and national security throughout the postwar era.[9]

It was because of mistrust of the military that the Yoshida doctrine was even allowed to take root. One Japan expert argued that Prime Minister Yoshida, with his emphasis on economic growth and refusal to build up military capabilities, was in the minority at the time.[10] But because security issues so inflamed the public and opposition parties, Yoshida was able to implement his policies. After Japan's economy launched into its miraculous growth, with both the left and right mollified (the left with the LDP's capitulation on nuclear issues and the right with the renewed U.S.-Japan Security Treaty), Japan's identity as a peaceful, non-nuclear trading state became established.

War devastation likewise led Egypt to seek other alternatives. "For us, we lost four wars. Our focus became: how do you remove the problem of war?"

one former military officer said. "So we started a new attitude, to solve the security dilemma in the region through a different way."[11] In fact, of the four wars
that Egypt lost against Israel, two were actually political wins: the Suez War in
1956 (Nasser was able to retain control of the Suez Canal) and the Yom Kippur War in 1973 (which shattered the image of Israeli invincibility). Both these
political wins for Egypt were secured only through internationalization of the
conflict. The Suez War was resolved through an emergency session of the UN
General Assembly, in which the United States and Soviet Union called for
withdrawal of the Anglo-French-Israeli troops from Egypt. In the closing days
of the Yom Kippur War, the Israelis had encircled Egyptian troops on the Sinai, intent on finishing them off, when again superpower intervention forced
the Israelis to withdraw. Perhaps a potent lesson for the Egyptians was that
while they lost four wars on the battlefield, they won two of them politically —
in the court of international diplomacy. Their winning strategy — what Sadat
called "diplomatic science" — would allow them not only to make peace with
their enemy but also to focus on Egypt's sadly neglected social and economic
development. Of course, not all Egyptians grasped or accepted these lessons; it
was an Egyptian who assassinated Sadat. One Egyptian expert noted the irony
of Sadat's legacy: "Sadat was not popular in Egypt, even though he liberated
the Sinai. On the other hand, Nasser lost the Sinai, but many millions of Egyptians went to his funeral."[12] Egypt's economy never performed miraculously,
and vocal elements of domestic society reject their government's non-nuclear
policy, yet Egypt has managed to establish an identity as an important international diplomatic player.

Conflict also helped changed the way Libya, Sweden, and Germany
thought about the value of a cooperative approach to international relations.
For Libya, Qadhafi saw that his years of revolution led to isolation and loss,
whereas the revolutionaries he had supported were engaging in negotiations
with the West — and being rewarded for it. Qadhafi's son saw that the Palestinians reaped more rewards in five years of diplomacy than in fifty years of
fighting. This understanding of how conflict failed to pay off led the regime
to rethink its approach to the international community, including pursuit of
WMD. In Sweden, a history of playing — and losing — in great power games led
people to conclude that neutrality was a much better strategy. When the Social
Democrats were able to define nuclear weapons as an affront to the Swedish
national identify of neutral peacemaker, that effectively ended Sweden's bid
for a nuclear weapons program. In Germany, the horror of World War II still

lingered as the public reacted to the idea of a German military with nuclear weapons. Many West Germans felt their state needed to stay out of great power politics and focus on integration and economic development. Two world wars had stripped a large and "power-hungry" Germany of much territory and made it "the pariah of Europe."[13] As the post–World War II West German economy took off, many felt the path of cooperation paid better dividends than a militant strategy would.

Domestic Politics

The appropriateness of including domestic variables in explanations of international relations is still a matter of debate.[14] Etel Solingen's accounts of nuclear decision-making, reviewed in chapter 1, broke new ground by advancing domestic politics as a key component in moving fence-sitters. The nature of the present work — investigating the effects of the international social environment on elite decision-making — renders it amenable to including domestic variables, given the focus on policymakers. Unlike Solingen, I do not argue that domestic politics was the primary factor. However, the case study evidence makes it clear that domestic politics and the international social environment do interact in important ways, shaping how environmental influence is channeled. This pertains particularly for the democracies: Japan, Sweden, and Germany. For example, in Japan, the nuclear nonproliferation regime empowered domestic antinuclear groups, giving them greater legitimacy as well as more opportunities to pressure the government. Groups gather not only for the anniversary of the atomic bombings but also before NPT review conferences. While peace groups are dissatisfied at being unable to force their government to work harder for disarmament, the groups do influence policy by raising the costs of discussing a nuclear option — hamstringing discussion and thus action.

The impact of domestic politics is also clear in Sweden. Because the Social Democrats were able to activate the emerging nonproliferation norm and cast the disarmament effort as a function of "Swedishness," public support for a nuclear option dissipated. Even in Germany, domestic groups influenced nuclear policy. Early on, they raised the cost of discussing a nuclear option; later, during the 1980s, West German protests against intermediate-range nuclear weapons rocked the country and traumatized the political elite. That the international social environment created by the nonproliferation regime — or any systemic effect — is shaped and filtered by domestic conditions is clear when one considers that not every state has reacted to the environment in the same way, as the cases of Israel, North Korea, and Iran illustrate.

One may question to what extent normative influences shaped policy decisions in the democratic case studies (Japan, Sweden and Germany), especially in the initial decision to give up the quest for the bomb. Domestic political pressure was an important component in all three cases, but the question is, how is this normative influence? The answer is because in all three cases, the domestic political pressure was fueled by a normative commitment against nuclear weapons — and was strengthened by activating the emerging international norm against nuclear weapons. As Eric Arnett argues in the case of nuclear programs, "Domestic politics and norms are inextricably intertwined. Domestic politics reflect norms, and norm-building can be a powerful argument in domestic politics, even when nuclear weapons have popular support."[15] Indeed, in these three case studies, evidence points not toward a simple domestic political struggle but rather toward a norm-driven crusade against nuclear weapons.

POLICY IMPLICATIONS

A poster hanging in the metro system in Washington, D.C., reads: *Osama Bin Laden said getting nuclear weapons is a religious duty.* Reports about A. Q. Khan's nuclear proliferation network appear in the *Washington Post* and *New York Times.* IAEA inspectors report less than full, unencumbered access to nuclear facilities in Iran and Brazil. After more than a decade, the North Korean nuclear crisis remains unsolved and in fact grows worse. The question of why states do or do not seek nuclear weapons is not simply an academic exercise but one with critical policy implications. To explore practical lessons that be gleaned from this study, policy prescriptions are examined through the lens of the nine different mechanisms through which social influence is funneled.

Strengthen Normative Messages—Descriptive, Injunctive, and Subjective

Focusing only on technical denial while ignoring the normative content of the NPT may simply lead to better ways to hide nuclear weapons development. (After Israel bombed the Osirak reactor in 1981, an Israeli official was rumored to have said, "We have put the nuclear genie of Baghdad back in his bottle."

Ten years later, UNSCOM officials found out differently.) The heading of this section reads "strengthen normative messages," but a better description might be "stop weakening normative messages," for today many are concerned that the NPT's normative weight is being seriously eroded. In terms of injunctive norms, the Arab states in particular are discouraged by the U.S. refusal to call on Israel to join the NPT or even to name Israel specifically in resolutions on Middle East nuclear nonproliferation. For example, Egypt brokered a deal during the 1995 NPT Review and Extension Conference whereby the rest of the Arab states would join the NPT, and in return, the conference issued a resolution to call on all parties in the Middle East to comply with the regime. (The United States refused to name Israel.) An Arab League disarmament expert explained that what the Egyptians truly ended up with "in practical terms is useless": all twenty-two Arab states had been persuaded to join the NPT, but the Egyptians had given away their leverage and had received only the Middle East Resolution, with no enforcement mechanisms.[16] As a result, there are growing calls for Arab countries to reverse policy and work toward a nuclear weapons capability.

The weakening of the descriptive norm seems to be having even more of an effect. Obviously, North Korea and Iran fuel concerns that the NPT cannot survive many more "unofficial" nuclear weapons states. But the United States has also been accused of weakening the regime through its actions. Events at a gathering in advance of the 2005 NPT review conference highlight the debate. A representative of the New Agenda Coalition referenced the U.S. Nuclear Posture Review, arguing that "plans to develop new nuclear weapons or rationalizations for their use contradict the spirit of the NPT." Another spokesperson said "nuclear weapon states' refusal to pursue disarmament creates a permissive attitude for proliferators."[17] The United States rejected such talk; U.S. Undersecretary of State for Arms Control and International Security John Bolton said: "We cannot divert attention from the violations we face [in North Korea and Iran] by focusing on Article Six issues that do not exist. If a party cares about the NPT, then there is a corresponding requirement to care about violations and enforcement."[18] NAC members noted with dismay the U.S. attitude toward its NPT commitments, since Article 6 (disarmament) issues clearly do exist. Not only has the United States ignored its Article 6 commitments, but it openly flaunts its disregard by planning for new nuclear weapons and making them a linchpin in security planning. In essence, the United States is propagating a new descriptive norm, which may persuade some or at least give an opening to those who refrained only for social conformity. If the social costs of a nuclear weapons program decline, then those who refrained because of those social costs may rethink their decision. The potential effects are quite serious. According to a former U.S. ambassador, a senior Brazilian politician told him, "What Brazil needs is respect, and the way to get respect in the world is to have nuclear weapons."[19] Unfortunately but unsurprisingly, in 2004 Brazil refused entry to IAEA inspectors.[20]

In other words, the United States needs to send injunctive and descriptive normative messages that are consistent with each other and consistent over time. Consistency is needed because these messages shape subjective norms—how a particular actor believes another actor wants the first to act. The case of Japan illustrates the point. What does Tokyo believe the United States feels about an independent nuclear deterrent? Because of mixed signals—such as messages from both Dick Cheney and John McCain—some in Japan believe that the United States privately would not mind if Japan acquired its own nuclear deterrent. In fact, some Japanese analysts feel that such talk emboldens conservatives who would like to pursue a nuclear option. If the United States does want to limit nuclear proliferation even among its allies, consistent injunctive and descriptive normative messages against nuclear proliferation will in turn shape a clear subjective norm, making it obvious that new nuclear weapons programs are not acceptable.

Encourage Linking, Activation, and Consistency

In the case studies, linking, activation, and consistency all proved to be important tools in either pushing the elite toward a non-nuclear stance or consolidating that non-nuclear stance. In the same way, U.S. policymakers can use these processes to encourage continued non-nuclear positions and discourage nuclear proliferation.

Linking allows policymakers to connect the value of nonproliferation to values already held by those we seek to influence. For almost all countries, the linkage between nuclear nonproliferation and being a civilized, responsible member of the international community is likely to be a useful one. In reverse, linking violations of the NPT to rogue behavior could also be useful. Analysts have noted that states are not lining up to be the next "rogue" state after North Korea or Iran. In addition, to be particularly effective, U.S. policymakers need to understand what specific states value, and then link compliance with the nonproliferation regime to what is valued. For Brazil, that might be international status; for Japan, it might be recognition of contributions to global peace. Another lesson from linking is that we should be careful what positive values we attach to nuclear proliferation, and what negative values we attach to nuclear forbearance. For example, the proposed U.S. deal with India for nuclear technology and supplies is likely to link, at least indirectly, increased global status with rejection of antinuclear principles. During a trip to Delhi, Bush called India a "global leader" and "described it as an example for the rest of the world" for its democratic society.[21] Given India's decades-long rejection of the NPT and its holding of nuclear tests in 1998, it is not inconceivable that the U.S. nuclear pact with and effusive praise for India may suggest to some that nuclear weapons are a route to greater international prestige.

Activation can also be used to promote nuclear forbearance and discourage proliferation. Such activation can be as simple as reminding countries of the near-global commitment to nuclear nonproliferation. Policymakers can encourage activation by citizen groups or NGOs as well. In all three democracies studied, antinuclear groups played important roles in keeping the state on a non-nuclear course — mainly by raising the cost for politicians of broaching the topic of a nuclear option, accomplished in part by activating the emerging global norm against nonproliferation. The role of antinuclear groups is less important today in Sweden and Germany, mainly because state elites show little interest in nuclear weapons.

However, in Japan a small but vocal group of politicians is interested in exploring a Japanese nuclear program. When they raise the issue of an indigenous nuclear deterrent, the peace groups activate the antinuclear norm by protesting, holding marches and sit-ins, and contacting the government directly to express their outrage. Because the media covers such protests extensively, most politicians refrain from making inflammatory remarks about a Japanese bomb. In addition, at least one NGO, Peace Depot, directly activates the international norm by tracking Japanese government disarmament commitments made at NPT review conferences and then publishing detailed critiques of government follow-through. Some fear that the antinuclear groups in Japan are weakening due to deaths of atomic bomb survivors as well as to lack of funds. Should these groups weaken significantly, public space for discussion of a Japanese nuclear deterrent may grow, lowering costs for pronuclear politicians. Hence strengthening peace groups can help keep the costs high for policymakers who might prefer an independent nuclear capability. Such strengthening could take place in a variety ways, from financial support by foundations to official recognition from international organizations. Indeed, in any democracy that might be considering a nuclear program, strengthening antinuclear groups may play the same role as in Japan—raising the political costs of a nuclear capability. Activation need not take place through direct U.S. comments but can work through support of groups already interested in highlighting the international norm for political purposes.

The psychological principle of consistency also provides some policymaking lessons. We learned especially from Egypt that once a commitment to the nonproliferation regime is made, it brings the diplomatic corps to the table, helping to ensure that another set of opinions is considered in nuclear decision-making. We also saw from Japan that numerous international commitments led the country to feel bound to these undertakings and concerned about the reputational effects of backing away from them. As Kurt Campbell and colleagues note, "Decisions to renounce nuclear weapons are not so easy to reverse. Embarking on a nuclear weapons program after a lengthy period of abstinence would require a new aspirant to overcome years of non-nuclear inertia, both political and technical."[22]

Linking, activation, and consistency could be helpful in global efforts to disarm North Korea. In the North Korean case, linking, activation, and consistency all currently reinforce the same bad behavior. Because North Korea has worked on a nuclear weapons program for over a decade, in defiance of the international community, its track record leads to defense and rationalization of its behavior. The principle of consistency means that dramatic change from past patterns is difficult, and this applies to North Korea as well. In addition, activation of the nuclear nonproliferation norm in the North Korean case often goes hand-in-hand with detailed descriptions of its long-term rebellion against that norm, again reinforcing the impact of consistency. Kim Jong Il's other negative behavior, such as crushing dissenters and ignoring the basic needs of citizens, is often linked with nuclear defiance. Making these connections is not incorrect in any way, but the end result paints a picture of an intractable dictator who cannot possibly do what is right. In other words, such rhetoric on the part of the West can reinforce the effects of consistency, making it less likely that North Korea will want to or feel able to change its behavior.

If the United States were to use consistency, activation, and linking differently, it might be able to encourage rather than discourage North Korea's disarmament. To use the principle of consistency to advantage, the United

States needs to look for patterns of cooperative North Korean behavior and stress those in negotiations. Instead of declaring North Korea part of the axis of evil, not to be trusted, public emphasis could be placed on having been able to make agreements with North Korea in the past and on the belief that this is possible again. Allowing North Korea to be consistent with a more cooperative type of behavior would mean its cooperation could be linked to positive benefits that could develop, and norm activation could take place in a positive manner through these links. This type of approach would allow North Korea to save face. Instead of Pyongyang having to say, "Yes, we have been irresponsible and destructive members of the international community, but we want to turn around," this approach would allow North Korea to say, "We have been willing to negotiate and cooperate in the past, and would like to do so again." The latter is much more feasible than the former. Such framing is not likely to lead to a dramatic breakthrough, but it could be helpful in overall negotiation tactics.

Take Advantage of Uncertainty, Similarity, and Conflict

U.S. policymakers can take advantage of situations that increase the potency of norms and, in some cases, can help create those conditions. The condition of uncertainty offers a number of ways for policymakers to help foreign elites value nuclear forbearance. First, hard tactics count because they raise the costs of nuclear weapons programs, which puts the decision-making calculus into flux. This point became clear in both the Egyptian and Libyan cases: foreign interventions and export-control policies both stymied these countries' nuclear programs, helping to contribute to rethinking of the value of nuclear weapons. Stronger denial policies change the cost-benefit equation for states, creating uncertainty about the difficulty of procuring the necessary materials and equipment and making it more likely that states will abandon the effort. Thus, supporting ratification of the Additional Protocol, fortifying export controls, and strengthening the Proliferation Security Initiative are valuable efforts, not only because of actual additional inspections and interdictions, but also because they raise the costs for proliferators and generate uncertainty about potential payoffs. In this way, material disincentives help to create nonmaterial disincentives.

The second policy lesson of uncertainty is that soft tactics count because they lower the value of nuclear weapons. As Campbell and coauthors note, a healthy global nonproliferation regime "encourages nuclear abstinence."[23] A number of experts have argued recently that the United States should do more to promote, rather than undermine, the value of security without nuclear weapons. For example, George Bunn and Jean du Preez argue that the recent change in U.S. policy, voting against legally binding negative security assurances by nuclear weapons states, is a mistake because it "encourages additional countries, including U.S. enemies, to acquire nuclear weapons."[24] Indeed, while U.S. policymakers had always opposed negative security assurances, such a bold and public statement against them is surprising because the vote was not necessary for Washington to continue its long-standing policy. Analyst Joseph Cirincione has argued that the Bush Administration's publicly released Nuclear Posture Strategy, which offered "detailed plans to build new, more usable 'low-yield' nuclear weapons and created missions for them," again sent a public message that nuclear weapons are valuable today.[25] Campbell and colleagues argue that the United States should instead find ways to "reduce the salience of nuclear arms" because "a long-term strategy to devalue the role of nuclear weapons in the international system is fundamentally in American interests."[26] If policymakers can avoid giving the impression that nuclear weapons are a component critical to American security, and can instead use soft tactics to devalue nuclear weapons (such as cooperation in review conferences and avoiding deliberate and clear announcements of our reliance on nuclear weapons), then the relative benefits of nuclear weapons are more likely to decrease and less likely to increase.

A final lesson from uncertainty is that when states do change direction and comply with the nuclear nonproliferation regime, they should be rewarded in explicit, public ways. Such measures give clear value to the benefits of nuclear forbearance and thus can help change the cost-benefit calculation. If such rewards are not forthcoming, their absence only increases uncertainty about whether a non-nuclear stance is worth it. A case in point is Libya, which Qadhafi feels has not received all the rewards promised. The United States restored diplomatic relations with Libya in May 2006 and removed Libya from the list of state sponsors of terrorism a month later, but Qadhafi has decried the lack of real progress on assistance with nuclear energy. He argued: "This should be a model to be followed, but Libya is disappointed because the promises given by America and Britain were not fulfilled. And therefore those countries said we are not going to follow Libya's example because Libya abolished its program without any compensation."[27] The Libyan diplomatic corps has taken this message to nonproliferation meetings; for example, at the UN Meeting on Disarmament Issues in August 2006 in Yokohama, the Libyan representative's prepared speech focused on the disappointment the Qadhafi regime felt because of unfulfilled promises. While the Libyan reaction may be in part an attempt to gain more foreign investment, it also serves as a lesson to policymakers: make nonproliferation as profitable as possible. The model of Libya's disarmament should be one that encourages other countries, not one that dismisses nonproliferation incentives as weak promises. By creating explicit, public rewards for nonproliferation, we can add benefits to the decision-making calculus, increasing the likelihood of decisions for nuclear forbearance.

Similarity also offers opportunities for policymakers. As discussed, decades of social psychology research have documented that people are much more open to normative influence from those they consider similar to themselves or those to whom they want to be similar. When it comes to exerting normative influence, the United States should be sensitive to this fact and be willing to use countries that might be better able to reach out to potential proliferators. For example, North Korea clearly does not see itself as a follower of the West — it rejects both capitalism and democracy and periodically issues statements attacking the United States. Thus the likelihood that the United States can use norms to pressure North Korea in the same way Washington might pressure Brazil or Japan is very low. In fact, such pressure may add incentives to do the opposite of what the United States wants; rebels gain status by opposing authority figures. How can understanding of this principle be used to achieve the goal of North Korean disarmament? The answer is twofold.

First, rather than expecting norms from the United States to be especially effective, the focus should be on other alternatives. Second, an actor that North Korea sees as similar to itself is needed to press the normative message that nuclear weapons are not acceptable. Given that North Korea is China's client state, China would be an obvious choice. An option would be to work closely with the Chinese to have them deliver normative messages to the North Koreans about nuclear weapons: nuclear weapons are not the best way to achieve security, monies devoted to economic development can ensure a more stable regime than those devoted toward nuclear weapons, and nuclear weapons without a second-strike capability actually make a state less safe. Another potential "similar" state might be Libya, which recently gave up its nuclear weapons program. The Libyans could be encouraged to explain to the North Koreans how giving up nuclear weapons has improved both their economy and their safety. Obviously, should North Korea see Libya as America's patsy, such an approach would be less likely to work. Other states not as closely connected to the United States, but still interested in nonproliferation, could also take a lead in the effort: Sweden, Egypt, and Ireland would all qualify.

Conflict as a condition that affects norm potency also offers valuable lessons. First, as previously discussed, in all five case studies, states learned from losing in conflict that cooperation is a better path to security. Policymakers should recognize this as a window of opportunity: if we see a fence-sitter that has accrued losses due to conflict, there is potential for changed thinking about security. In particular, cooperation can be linked with success to persuade a state to reject conflict.

The second lesson is that conflict can polarize and lead to the rejection of normative messages; case study evidence indicates that this is probably more likely when a state has won a conflict, or at least has not clearly lost. This lesson could be applied to North Korea today — it would not be painted as a winner in terms of economic or political stability, but it could be seen as a victor in conflict with the West over its nuclear weapons program. If the United States would like to have any normative influence on North Korea, U.S. leadership should avoid creating new, additional polarizing points of conflict while already trying to sort out conflict over North Korea's nuclear stance. It is not that Washington should avoid a conflict over North Korea's nuclear stance, but rather that U.S. leadership should avoid introducing new areas of conflict. Thus, George Bush's statement that he "loathes" Kim Jung Il was likely counterproductive in solving the crisis. Instead, Washington should look for areas of agreement with Pyongyang while asking for cooperation on the nuclear issue. Of course, doing so requires that the United States place the highest priority on disarming North Korea and that the United States be willing to set other issues aside for the time being. Such a strategy could invite criticism of coddling dictators. If promising cooperation leads to a greater likelihood of disarmament, is such coddling worth it? That is a value judgment for policymakers; the point here is that excoriating Kim Jung Il only polarizes sides further and makes a diplomatic solution less likely.

CONCLUSION

This book has entertained one of most interesting theoretical puzzles and serious policy issues today: why have so few states acquired nuclear weapons? To address the question, I have argued that we need to examine states' social environments as well as security environments. If the international social environment created and supported by the NPT exerts influence on elite perceptions and decisions, then the security environment cannot be understood without understanding the social environment. This proposition led to two main insights. First, not all nuclear forbearance is alike. Some state elites may be persuaded, others may be constrained by social conformity, and still others may identify with important allies. Second, it is important to identify and understand the mechanisms through which the social environment exerts influence.

These issues are examined through in-depth analysis of Japan and Egypt and briefer assessments of Libya, Sweden, and Germany. While these case studies provide a great deal of insight, more countries need to be studied to confirm or counter findings categorically. However, some conclusions can be drawn. All five of these countries faced inhospitable security environments, and yet all ended up exercising nuclear forbearance. Their decision-makers did this not because of adequate security substitutes for nuclear weapons (although these helped), but because they redefined state goals in such a way as to devalue nuclear weapons. Without the norms and denial policies embedded in the nuclear nonproliferation regime, Egypt and Libya would have acquired a nuclear option, and Japan, Germany, and Sweden might have done so as well. But while the NPT and associated agreements were an important factor in these states' nuclear forbearance, they were not the only cause of leaders' redefinition of security and success, and this is a critical topic for further study.

For all five states, the shock of humiliating defeat in war may have jump-started this transformation of state interests. This is not likely the cause, however, in states such as South Africa, Argentina, Australia, Switzerland, and numerous other countries that once had nuclear weapons programs. Nevertheless, the international social environment created powerful forces to guide state decision-makers into making a public commitment against nuclear proliferation, and then to lock them into that commitment and even persuade important portions of the elite to embrace the spirit of the NPT.

Policy implications flow easily from the findings. The nuclear nonproliferation regime has provided a powerful influence for state elites to exercise nuclear forbearance, and it should be strengthened, not weakened. At this point, the difference between a realist and constructivist interpretation could not be starker. For realists, the NPT gives countries access to nuclear technology and diplomatic cover to develop secret nuclear weapons programs, which they are likely to do to satisfy their security needs. Its "norms" are useless, and the money would be better spent on other programs. For constructivists, "security needs" is an empty expression that cannot be understood outside a state's social environment. Because the nuclear nonproliferation regime does shape how states interpret the value of nuclear weapons, upholding and strengthening it is critical to stopping future proliferation. In addition, by understanding the mechanisms through which the international social environment influences elite decision-making, we can better understand the value of that social environment and the best ways to maximize its effectiveness against nuclear proliferation.

Finally, the case studies provided persuasive evidence that we need a multitude of tools to discourage proliferation and encourage nuclear forbearance. Foreign intervention, great power pressure, and export controls hampered Egypt and Libya's nuclear programs, whereas security guarantees opened up enough policy space for conservatives in Japan, Sweden, and Germany to allow for nuclear abstinence. In short, realist measures made a difference. But in democratic countries, antinuclear peace groups leveraged the emerging international norm to strengthen their own position, making it too costly politically for conservatives to pursue a nuclear option. In all five case studies, over time, most state elites absorbed and accepted the normative message of the nuclear nonproliferation regime during the course of rethinking what a successful state looked like. Thus the regime has also served as a critical tool in the quest for nuclear nonproliferation. While traditional realist explanations do not offer a complete answer as to why so few states have developed nuclear weapons, they clearly provide pieces to the puzzle. Likewise, while constructivist interpretations help us understand why states remain non-nuclear despite changed material circumstances, they do not provide a complete explanation of why the original decision to forgo nuclear weapons was made. In solving the puzzle of nuclear nonproliferation, both scholars and policymakers must be willing to step outside neat theoretical boxes to understand the value of both security and norms in encouraging nuclear forbearance. Indeed, if we want to control nuclear proliferation, we must start honestly addressing how states conceptualize the value of nuclear weapons.

NOTES

CHAPTER ONE. Exploring Nuclear Restraint

1. Dr. Jermone Wiesner, science advisor to President John F. Kennedy, predicted that up to twenty states could acquire nuclear weapons by the mid-1980s. See "The Bomb: From Hiroshima to . . ." *Newsweek*, 9 August 1965, 53. See also "Prospects for Further Proliferation of Nuclear Weapons," *CIA Memorandum* 55-1, DCI NIO 1945/74, 4 September 1974. For additional discussion, see Long and Grillot, "Ideas, Beliefs, and Nuclear Policies."

2. The four new nuclear powers are India, Pakistan, Israel, and North Korea — though Israel has never formally declared its nuclear capability. While South Africa developed the bomb, it is not included because it voluntarily disarmed and remains non-nuclear today.

3. Sagan, "Why Do States Build Nuclear Weapons?" 56.

4. "More Than 40 Countries Could Have Nuclear Weapons Know-How," *Global Security Newswire*, National Journal Group (September 22, 2004).

5. For discussion of why we might expect some states that once reversed their nuclear weapons program to rethink those decisions, see Levite, "Never Say Never Again."

6. By elites, I refer to those with decision-making authority or substantial influence over decision-making.

7. I follow Stephen Krasner in defining regimes as "principles, norms, rules, and decision-making procedures around which actor expectations converge in a given issue area." Krasner, "Structural Causes and Regime Consequences," 1.

8. A great deal of research is being done on strengthening constructivist methodology, including by Alastair Ian Johnston, Jeffrey Checkel, Martha Finnemore, Kathryn Sikkink, and Thomas Risse.

9. See, for example, Ogilvie-White, "Is There a Theory of Nuclear Proliferation?"; Sagan, "Why Do States Build Nuclear Weapons?"; Flank, "Exploding the Black Box"; and Chafez, "The End of the Cold War."

10. Waltz, *Theory of International Politics*.

11. Mearsheimer, "False Promise," 12.

12. Samaddar, "Thinking Proliferation Theoretically," 440.

13. Waltz, *The Spread of Nuclear Weapons*.

14. Paul, *Power versus Prudence*, 8.

15. Benjamin Frankel, "Brooding Shadow," 38.

16. Ibid., 60.

17. Mearsheimer, "Back to the Future," 37.

18. John Mearsheimer, Lecture at the George Washington University Political Science Department, October 31, 2002. Mearsheimer said, "Our very powerful conventional forces are giving states very powerful incentives to seek nuclear weapons. If we invade North Korea or Iraq to prevent their acquisition, that gives even more incentive for states to seek nuclear weapons."

19. Israel acquired nuclear weapons capability in the late 1960s to early 1970s. India tested a nuclear device in 1974. However, one could also argue that Pakistan and North Korea achieved nuclear status before the end of the Cold War. Pakistan is rumored to have had all the components for nuclear weapons before the end of the Cold War. See "Pakistan's Nuclear Weapons." North Korea is known to have separated plutonium by 1990 and likely had enough nuclear material by 1991 for one or two bombs. See Albright and O'Neill, "North Korean Nuclear Program."

20. Typically, the threat of being targeted due to a nuclear weapons program is related to being drawn into another's conflict because of one's nuclear status. As an example, during the Cold War, a nuclear-armed ally of the United States might fear that if war broke out between the United States and the Soviet Union, the ally might be targeted by the Soviet Union because the ally's nuclear weapons would be seen as a threat to the Soviets. More recently, one might argue that Iraq is a state that was targeted solely due to its nuclear weapons program, given that the United States invaded in 2003 with the stated intent of destroying Iraq's WMD. However, there has been a great deal of debate on the true U.S. motivations for the invasion and regime change, especially given that Iraq had allowed IAEA inspectors to search facilities and no WMD were found. Revelations from Bush Administration staff also cast doubt on the official U.S. justification of ridding Iraq of WMD, including from former Treasury Secretary Paul O'Neill and former intelligence official Richard Clarke. See Suskind, *Price of Loyalty*, and Clarke, *Against All Enemies*. In addition, even if the 2003 invasion of Iraq did count as a legitimate case of a country being targeted because of its nuclear weapons program, it would be the first, and before 2003 no such case existed for states to reference.

21. As Mearsheimer notes, "There is little room for trust among states. Although the level of fear varies across time and space, it can never be reduced to a trivial level. The basis of this fear is that in a world where states have the capability to offend against each other, and might have the motive to do so, any state bent on survival must be at least suspicious of other states and reluctant to trust them." "False Promise," 11.

22. Legro and Moravcsik, "Is Anybody Still a Realist?" 15.

23. Hymans, "Theories of Nuclear Proliferation," 456.

24. Ibid., 456.

25. Mearsheimer, "False Promise," 11.

26. Alexander Wendt notes that both realism and neoliberalism are rooted in rationalism and argues that "rationalism offers a fundamentally behavioral conception of both process and institutions: they change behavior but not identities and interests." Wendt, "Anarchy Is What States Make of It," 393.

27. Keohane and Martin, "Promise of Institutionalist Theory," 42.

28. Solingen, "New Multilateralism," 210, 214.

29. Solingen, Nuclear Postures, 1.

30. Solingen, "Political Economy of Nuclear Restraint," 140.

31. Ibid.

32. Ibid., 131.

33. Solingen, "New Multilateralism," 210.

34. Ottaway, "South Africa Agrees."

35. Paul, Power versus Prudence, 152.

36. Ibid., 28.

37. Hymans, "Isotopes and Identity."

38. Ibid., 2.

39. Hymans argues that a specific type of national identity, in combination with a serious threat perception, can lead states to seek nuclear weapons. However, the argument could be made that national identity could lead states to reject nuclear weapons, even in the face of a serious threat perception. For example, Egypt has sought status by associating itself with the NPT and as the leader of the Arab world against Israeli nuclear weapons.

40. Long and Grillot, "Ideas, Beliefs, and Nuclear Policies."

41. Ibid., 27.

42. Checkel, "The Constructivist Turn," 325.

43. Bordens and Horowitz, Social Psychology, 3.

44. Some notable examples include Tetlock and Goldgeier, "Human Nature and World Politics"; Mercer, "Anarchy and Identity"; Young and Schafer, "Is There Method in Our Madness?"; Crawford, "The Passion of World Politics"; and Jervis, "Political Psychology."

45. Payne, "Persuasion, Frames, and Norm Construction," 45.

46. Constructivists often construe the effect of multilateral institutions as that of changing a state's conception of its national interest. While that is an important effect to investigate, it is also crucial to recognize that this is not the only "nonmaterial" way through which states' behavior may change. In other words, it does not have to be all-or-nothing: either states transform their attitudes and behavior (validating constructivism) or they don't (validating realism or neoliberal institutionalism). Constructivism allows

us to explore ways in which the social milieu created by regimes can influence state behavior without "converting" states. Social conformity is one conceptualization of this influence short of conversion. Another example is the cooperative process documented by Dalia Dassa Kaye in her study of the Middle East peace process, which she shows to help states gain common understandings without necessarily undergoing wholesale transformation of state preferences. See Kaye, *Beyond the Handshake*.

47. Levite, "Never Say Never Again," 85. Of course, such behavior could be something other than social conformity, which indicates external compliance with norms without internal acceptance. Nuclear hedging could also indicate nuclear ambivalence or fear about future changes in the security environment.

48. Kelman, "Compliance, Identification, and Internalization," 51.

49. Identification differs from a commonly used construct in social psychology — identity — in a number of important ways. Identification describes the result when an actor accepts influence from an important other. Identity, on the other hand, describes beliefs one has about oneself. As Alexander Wendt notes, "To have an identity is simply to have certain ideas about who one is in a given situation, and as such the concept of identity fits squarely into the belief side of the desire plus belief equation. These beliefs in turn help constitute interests. Politicians have an interest in getting re-elected because they see themselves as 'politicians'; professors have an interest in getting tenure because they see themselves as 'professors.'" See Wendt, *Social Theory of International Politics*, 170. Certainly we can expect identities to influence which relationships might make an actor wish to "identify" with another, resulting in an outcome of "identification."

50. Kelman, "Compliance, Identification, and Internalization," 53.

51. Identification as defined here is distinct from "mimesis" or "mimicry," which typically denotes deliberate strategies on behalf of actors to mimic those whose success they wish to reproduce. For example, an actor may note that rich, powerful countries perform actions X and Y; to improve chances of also becoming rich and powerful, the actor then performs actions X and Y. Identification focuses, rather, on the social context of a relationship; to improve or preserve a relationship, an actor may perform actions X and Y. There is clearly potential for overlap between mimesis and identification, for example, if the goal of strengthening a relationship is to please a powerful friend. In some cases, it is likely that the deliberate mimicking of behavior purely to gain rewards will result in internalization of that behavior over time. In addition, psychology research has documented that mimicry can have a strong affective component, resulting in unwitting imitation, which approaches what is defined here as "identification." See Lakin and Chartrand, "Using Nonconscious Behavioral Mimicry."

52. Brewer and Brown, "Intergroup Relations," 561.

53. Within the same state, some policymakers could be motivated by identification while others are motivated by social conformity.

54. Note that identification can be based on the desire to receive approval and acceptance from the in-group, in which case continuing U.S. rhetoric against nuclear acquisition would likely keep Ally Y from changing policy.

55. The example does not indicate that I believe all or even most members of the military adhere to nuclear nonproliferation norms due to social conformity. The majority of uniformed military likely has very practical reasons to be concerned about proliferation and to want to reduce the salience of nuclear weapons.

56. As a reminder, *persuaded* indicates those who have embraced nonproliferation because of the merits of the nonproliferation argument. *Conforming* refers to those who, internally, have not rejected the nuclear option but publicly forgo it only because of social pressure against it.

57. For the sake of theoretical clarity, I have categorized expectations by theory. However, I would not anticipate that only one expectation—or one set of them— would be able to explain everything about nuclear forbearance.

58. I believe this is an excellent measure of threat in realist terms, since it does not refer to relationships or perceptions—but rather to simple material capabilities. See Meyer, *Dynamics of Nuclear Nonproliferation*, 56–62. Also see Walsh, *Bombs Unbuilt*, 19–20.

59. This definition is a more limited version of that advanced in Expectation 1, in which threat was defined as having a nuclear-armed adversary, an adversary with a latent nuclear weapons capability, or an adversary with overwhelming conventional military threat.

60. Again, I set the bar higher than perhaps needed. States with a strong desire for nuclear weapons could begin a program without current nuclear facilities, so long as they had the economic and technological resources necessary.

61. The drawback of this method is that it equates nuclear activities with capability to develop a nuclear weapons program. It may be that a state has a nuclear facility built entirely by an outside entity, and in reality, the state has little to no capacity to engage in any other type of nuclear activity by itself because of its low level of economic development. To ensure this is not the case, I compared the GNP of India (which was able to develop a nuclear program indigenously) against that of the states in table 3. Only one state had a lower GNP in the time periods represented: Bangladesh.

62. Jones and McDonough, *Tracking Nuclear Proliferation*, 205–14.

63. For a thorough explanation of Israel's nuclear weapons program, see Cohen, *Israel and the Bomb*.

CHAPTER TWO. **Understanding the International Social Environment**

1. The fourth possible outcome—rejection—is not discussed since the states under question have all abided by the nuclear nonproliferation norm; that is, they have not developed nuclear weapons. Rejection is a potential future outcome, of course.

2. Wittner, *One World or None*, 3–7.

3. Tannenwald, "Nuclear Taboo," 442.

4. Price and Tannenwald, "Norms and Deterrence," 137.

5. Wittner, *One World or None*, 247.

6. Ibid., 40–42, 247–48. Wittner notes: "Following the atomic bombing of Hiroshima and Nagasaki, a movement against the Bomb rapidly took shape in dozens of countries throughout the world. Alerted to the existence of the Bomb and to its catastrophic effects, thousands of people rallied behind a loose, popular crusade to save humanity from nuclear destruction. At its center stood those pacifist groups and constituencies that had survived World War II, as well as newer, rapidly growing organizations among atomic scientists and world government proponents" (40).

7. "Secretary-General Calls for Renewed Vow."

8. Tannenwald, "Nuclear Taboo," 450.

9. Boyer, "From Activism to Apathy," 822.

10. Bunn, "Status of Norms," 23.

11. Kennedy, "Lucky Dragon."

12. Bunn, *Arms Control by Committee*, 18.

13. Müller et al., *Nuclear Non-Proliferation*, 18.

14. Tannenwald, "U.S. Arms Control Policy," 65. For thorough descriptions of the many groups protesting nuclear weapons in the United States, see Boyer, "From Activism to Apathy," 839–40. Wittner's volume in particular provides an extremely detailed account of the antinuclear activities of individuals and groups, both in the United States and around the world.

15. See "Treaty on the Non-Proliferation of Nuclear Weapons: History."

16. Interview with former senior U.S. arms control official, May 2003, Washington, D.C.

17. De Klerk, "Notes on History and Meaning of the NPT," 19.

18. Boyer, "From Activism to Apathy," 829–31.

19. Weart, *Nuclear Fear*, 377. On the 1978 Special Session on Disarmament, see *The United Nations and Disarmament: 1945–85*, 39–40.

20. Knopf, *Domestic Society and International Cooperation*, 199.

21. Scheffran, "Nuclear Disarmament," 35.

22. Tannenwald, "U.S. Arms Control Policy," 66.

23. I thank an anonymous reviewer for this insight.

24. For an excellent discussion of international organizations as social environments, see Johnston, "Treating International Institutions as Social Environments."

25. North Korea was a member until it announced its withdrawal in January 2003.

26. Jones and McDonough, *Tracking Nuclear Proliferation*, 15.

27. Ibid., 14–17. For additional background on the NPT and associated frameworks, see Roger K. Smith, "Explaining the Nonproliferation Regime," 257–60.

28. Kaye, "Europe, Syria and Weapons of Mass Destruction," 1.

29. Finnemore and Sikkink, "International Norm Dynamics," 888. Regarding the shared nature of norms, Cialdini and Trost note, "One of the most important characteristics of norms is that they do not exist if they are not shared with others" ("Social Influence," 153).

30. This categorization of norms differs from the categorization offered by social theory, which describes regulative and constitutive norms. Regulative norms tell states what to do, and constitutive norms tell states who they are. However, the difference in categorization is more complementary than conflicting. Social psychology breaks norms out according to how they are transmitted, while social theory does so according to the norms' functions. It is possible to have both regulative and constitutive functions to descriptive, injunctive, and subjective norms.

31. Cialdini and Trost, "Social Influence," 155.

32. Cialdini and Trost, "Social Influence," 157.

33. Fishbein and Ajzen, *Belief, Attitude, Intention,* 302.

34. Cialdini and Trost, "Social Influence," 159. Also see Terry and Hogg, "Attitudes, Behavior and Social Context." How are subjective norms different from descriptive norms? Descriptive norms are based on what most others are doing. Subjective norms are much more specific: what do we believe that specific people think we should do in certain circumstances?

35. Cialdini and Trost, "Social Influence," 155.

36. A good example of a subjective norm deals with teenage sex. A recent survey showed that most teens thought other teens were having sex, and they felt pressure to have sex, but they themselves were not having sex. In other words, most teens were not having sex; they just thought most were, creating pressure for them to conform.

37. For example, see Kier and Mercer, "Setting Precedents in Anarchy."

38. Jones and McDonough, *Tracking Nuclear Proliferation,* 19–22.

39. Buckley, *Canada's Early Nuclear Policy,* 80–81. See also Clearwater, *Canadian Nuclear Weapons.*

40. Ottaway, "South Africa Agrees."

41. Cialdini and Trost, "Social Influence," 161. Cialdini and Trost describe a number of different experiments and studies in which descriptive norms activated everything from littering to extradyadic sexual relations to tipping.

42. No clear hierarchy of norms can be stated; for example, we cannot say that descriptive norms will always trump injunctive norms. The matter of norm activation has rich potential for study in terms of the types of activation available, what happens when different descriptive norms compete, and more. Norm entrepreneurs are undoubtedly in the business not only of norm creation but also of norm activation.

43. Tetlock and Goldgeier, "Psychology and International Relations Theory," 93.

44. Cialdini, *Influence,* 84.

45. Tetlock and Goldgeier argue: "Most psychologists would probably agree that most political actors (psychopaths excluded) will gradually internalize the norms of fair play implicit in international institutions. These norms can become functionally autonomous from the interests that may once have inspired them" ("Psychology and International Relations Theory," 67).

46. This in turn raises another interesting question: how does a state internalize a preference or belief? While the present study examines individual policymakers, it could be argued that state internalization takes place through the creation of bureaucratic apparatus, complete with budgets and personnel to protect and defend the commitments the state has made.

47. Tetlock and Goldgeier, "Psychology and International Relations Theory," 81. Their argument is supported by social psychology research showing that when actors believe they might have to explain or justify attitudes to other people, attitude change is more likely to persist than if not. See also Petty and Wegener, "Attitude Change."

48. Payne, "Persuasion, Frames and Norm Construction," 41–42.

49. Taylor and Charbonneau, "EU Big Three."

50. Mitchell, "International Control of Nuclear Proliferation," 40.

51. Levine and Higgins, "Shared Reality." Levine and Higgins argue: "Evidence indicates that conformity is higher when group members are responding to difficult or ambiguous questions and have low confidence in their position. Moreover, conformity is greater on difficult tasks when the desire to be accurate is high rather than low" (39).

52. As Petty and Wegener note, "A great deal of work suggests that people like other people with whom they share similar attitudes (e.g., Byrne & Griffitt, 1966) or ideology (Newcomb, 1956) and dislike those with whom they disagree (e.g., Rosenbaum, 1986). This source-receiver similarity has also been shown to increase persuasion (e.g., Brock, 1965)" ("Attitude Change," 348).

53. Cialdini and Trost, "Social Influence," 158. See also Perloff, *Dynamics of Persuasion*, 146.

54. Cialidini and Trost, "Social Influence," 166.

55. Levine and Higgins, "Shared Reality," 40.

CHAPTER THREE. **Japanese Nuclear Decision-Making**

1. Interview with former senior U.S. arms control expert, Washington D.C., May 2003.

2. For the purposes of this chapter, "nuclear decision-making" refers to nuclear weapons as opposed to nuclear energy. Unless I refer specifically to nuclear energy, the term *nuclear* means "nuclear weapons."

3. Japanese Peace Constitution, Article 9, quoted in Chinworth, *Inside Japan's Defense*, 185.

4. This point was reiterated in a number of interviews with security experts. One said, "The Japanese people equate Article 9 with Japanese identity. It is the basis for Japan's identity" (interview with Japanese nuclear expert, Tokyo, July 2003).

5. Tetsuya Kataoka, *Waiting for a "Pearl Harbor": Japan Debates Defense* (Stanford: Hoover Institution Press, 1980), 5, quoted in Katzenstein and Okawara, "Japan's National Security," 103.

6. Katzenstein and Okawara, "Japan's National Security," 101–2.

7. In 1957 Prime Minister Kishi made the assessment that Article 9 did not prohibit nuclear weapons of a defensive nature. Interview with senior Japanese nuclear expert, Kyoto, July 2003.

8. In 1964, Japan's Commission on the Constitution issued an independent verdict stating that nuclear weapons were prohibited by the constitution. Maki, *Japan's Commission on the Constitution*, 100. For more examples of gradual reinterpretations of Article 9 (e.g., from individual self-defense to collective self-defense), see Katzenstein and Okawara, "Japan's National Security," 112–14.

9. Interview with Japanese nuclear expert, Tokyo, July 2003.

10. For detailed scholarly examinations of the roots of antimilitarism in postwar Japan, see Katzenstein, *Cultural Norms and National Security*, and Berger, *Cultures of Antimilitarism*.

11. Berger, "From Sword to Chrysanthemum," 135–36.

12. Dower, *Embracing Defeat*, 177.

13. More than one Japanese expert argued that the United States censored any such discussion. For example, in September 1945 the General Headquarters of the U.S. Occupational Forces (GHQ) ordered censorship of media reports on Hiroshima and Nagasaki. In May 1946 GHQ confiscated a Japanese film documenting the effects of the atomic bomb; the film was not returned until 1967. In August 1950 GHQ canceled the Hiroshima Day peace ceremony. See Nasu, *Hiroshima*, 59–60.

14. For a thorough explanation of the impact of the Lucky Dragon incident on Japanese attitudes toward nuclear technology, see Akiyama, "Socio-Political Roots of Japan's Non-Nuclear Posture."

15. Kennedy, "Lucky Dragon."

16. Kamiya, "Nuclear Japan," 64.

17. Kase, *Evolution of Japan's Security Policy*, 71.

18. Kennedy, "Lucky Dragon"

19. "No More Hiroshimas."

20. "Nuclear allergy" is the phrase widely used to describe Japanese domestic sentiment against nuclear weapons.

21. Japan's National Institute for Research Advancement (NIRA) conducted the poll in late 1999. The question posed was: "If in the near future, the U.S.-Japan Security Treaty is dissolved or becomes meaningless for some reason, what should Japan do to protect itself from being attacked by other states or parties with nuclear weapons?" Only 7 percent of the general public responded, "Should possess its own nuclear weapons," while 15 percent of the "Japanese informed people" answered this way. See *Japan's Proactive Peace and Security Strategies — Including the Question of "Nuclear Umbrella,"* 269.

22. For example, Godzilla movies reflect the fear Japanese felt over genetic mutations caused by atomic bombs. Andrew Oros notes: "While American audiences would embrace Godzilla's destruction of hapless Japanese and their cities, Japanese were well aware of what created the monster — Godzilla was the beast unleashed on Japan due to atomic experimentation, an incarnation of the force unleashed a decade earlier on Hiroshima and Nagasaki." Oros, "Godzilla's Return," 49.

23. Interview with MOFA official, Tokyo, July 2003.

24. Interview with senior Japanese defense official, Yokohama, July 2003. There are many children's books on war, in which people wrote about the sadness and hardships of conflict. In addition, there are many peace-oriented animation movies, which vividly describe the tragedies of war. Almost all Japanese children have been exposed to these media. For example, one popular cartoon series chronicles the adventures of "Barefoot Gen," an atomic bomb survivor. One expert estimated that 95 percent of Japanese students have read this comic book. A popular anime movie, *Tomb of a Firefly,* involves children who experience an air raid and later die. Interview with senior Japanese nuclear expert, Tokyo, July 2003.

25. Interview with senior Japanese nuclear expert, Kyoto, July 2003.

26. Interview with senior Japanese nuclear expert, Kyoto, July 2003.

27. Harrison, "Japan and Nuclear Weapons," 8.

28. Interview.

29. Less than a month later, Sato said, "Let me say this so that no one can misunderstand me: I do not regard it as a complete system of defense if we cannot possess nuclear weapons in the era of nuclear weapons. I will, nevertheless, adhere faithfully to the pledge I have made to the people." Harrison, "Japan and Nuclear Weapons," 10. A confidential U.S. State Department report documents that in January 1969, Sato said the Japanese government's "three non-nuclear principles were 'nonsense.'" Ota, *Will Japan Keep Renouncing.*

30. Kase, *Evolution of Japan's Security Policy,* 90.

31. Ibid., 91.

32. French, "Taboo against Nuclear Arms."

33. "Japan's DPJ Leader Hatoyama Raps Remarks against Non-Nuclear Policy," *Agence France-Press,* 1 June 2002, 1.

34. "November Opinion Polls," *Yomiuri Shimbun.*

35. Ota, *Will Japan Keep Renouncing*, 3.

36. Kyodo News, "Abe's Pledge to Afghan Mission."

37. Interview with Japanese nuclear expert, Tokyo, July 2003.

38. The term *platitudes* may be seen as derogatory, but it accurately reflects how most academics and bureaucrats felt about the level of discussion on nuclear issues in Japan, including those who are themselves passionately antinuclear. A number of analysts expressed frustration with peace activists' "low" level of dialogue, especially analysts who argued against a nuclear option. They felt that the lack of rational discussion and the emphasis on what they saw as simplistic platitudes ("nuclear weapons are evil") hurt the credibility of all arguments against a nuclear Japan. One interviewee, an academic committed to the antinuclear position, described how the Hiroshima mayor invited the North Korean leader Kim Jong Il to the ceremonies commemorating the dropping of the A-bomb on Hiroshima and Nagasaki. "If Hiroshima was serious about this, they would be working with MOFA. They are not serious. This damages the credibility of citizens' diplomacy and the legitimacy of the antinuclear movement." He argued that this was "symbolic about Hiroshima's situation—political gestures, no substance. Hiroshima's activities are becoming more and more abstract, ritualized and without substance." In addition, a number of interviewees expressed concern that the simplistic level of debate prevents the Japanese people from seeing the other reasons nuclear weapons do not make sense for Japan. As one said, "The antinuclear consensus is quite hard, which means it may be fragile, and quite broad, which means it may be thin. The consensus is powerful, but is it robust?"

39. Nabeshima, "Even Nuclear Talk Distracts."

40. Interview with senior Japanese defense official, Yokohama, July 2003; interview with senior Japanese nuclear expert, Hiroshima, July 2003; interview with former senior Japanese government official, Tokyo, July 2003.

41. Mizumoto, "Non-Nuclear and Nuclear Disarmament Policies," 10.

42. Kase, *Evolution of Japan's Security Policy*, 125.

43. President Richard Nixon, *Report to Congress* (Washington, D.C.: U.S. Government Printing Office, 1970), quoted in Van de Velde, "Japan's Nuclear Umbrella," 18.

44. Hughes, "Why Japan Will Not Go Nuclear (Yet)," 75.

45. Nabeshima, "Even Nuclear Talk Distracts."

46. Campbell and Sunohara note, "The successful Chinese atomic bomb test also prompted several senior Japanese leaders, including Yasuhiro Nakasone and Shintaro Ishihara, to call for a reexamination of Japan's policy of nuclear abstention" ("Japan: Thinking the Unthinkable," 221).

47. "Main Trends in Japan's External Relations," *National Intelligence Estimate No 41–68*, Central Intelligence Agency, January 11, 1968, p. 6.

48. Hughes, "Why Japan Will Not Go Nuclear (Yet)," 71.

49. Interview with Japanese defense expert, Tokyo, March 2007.

50. Interview with author of Japanese secret study, Tokyo, July 2003. See also Kase, "The Costs and Benefits." This section relies heavily on Kase, "The Costs and Benefits," because it is the only available resource on the report in question; Kase was given a copy of the reports by one of the study authors. I interviewed one of the study's authors but was not given a copy of the report and thus do not have knowledge of it as detailed as in the Kase article.

51. Kase, "The Costs and Benefits," 56.

52. *Asahi Shimbun*, 13 November 1994, quoted in Kase, "The Costs and Benefits," 57.

53. Interview with author of Japanese secret study, Tokyo, July 2003. The technical hurdles identified by the report are no longer relevant today.

54. Interview with author of Japanese secret study, Tokyo, July 2003.

55. Hanley, "Japan and the Bomb."

56. This point was emphasized by the study author, who wanted to distance himself from the peace groups, whose arguments he believed were based arguments on sentiment, not logic.

57. Kase, "The Costs and Benefits," 59.

58. Declassified U.S. Department of State briefing, quoted in Ota, *Will Japan Keep Renouncing*, 1. Ota notes that "the American Ambassador in Tokyo, Edwin Reischauer, privately recorded that Sato had indicated that 'he [Sato] considers it only common sense for Japan to have nuclear weapons'" (2).

59. Kase, "The Costs and Benefits," 61.

60. Ibid.

61. For example, in August 1955, the world's first conference protesting nuclear weapons was held in Hiroshima.

62. Interview with senior Japanese nuclear expert, Kyoto, July 2003.

63. Di Filippo, "Can Japan Craft an International Disarmament Policy?" 1.

64. Ota, *Will Japan Keep Renouncing*, 1, 3.

65. Willenson, "Japan: Paradise Lost?"

66. Joseph Frankel, "Domestic Politics of Japan's Foreign Policy," 262.

67. Kase, *Evolution of Japan's Security Policy*, 117.

68. "A-Pact Ratification Deferred."

69. Willenson, "Japan: Paradise Lost?"

70. Ibid.

71. The LDP hard-liners were not the only ones expressing doubt. A small group of bureaucrats with the Ministry of Foreign Affairs prepared an unpublished, informal working paper assessing possible Japanese nuclearization. Interview with author of Japanese secret study, Tokyo, July 2003.

72. Kase, *Evolution of Japan's Security Policy*, 115.

73. "Diet to Get Nuclear Nonproliferation Pact."

74. "Japan: Bombs Away."

75. "Diet to Get Nuclear Nonproliferation Pact."

76. Imai, "Post–Cold War Nuclear Non-Proliferation," 127.

77. Kase, *Evolution of Japan's Security Policy*, 114.

78. Ibid., 113.

79. Campbell and Sunohara, "Japan: Thinking the Unthinkable," 227.

80. Hughes, "Why Japan Will Not Go Nuclear (Yet)," 77.

81. *Yomiuri Shimbun*, 8 July 1993, quoted in "Japanese Papers Rap NPT Issues in G-7 Declaration," *Kyodo News Service*, 9 July 1993.

82. "South Korean Ambassador Asks Japan to Explain Its Nuclear Treaty Stance," *Kyodo News Service*, 14 July 1993.

83. "Spokesman Says Japan Not 'Preserving Nuclear Option,'" *Kyodo News Service*, 13 July 1993.

84. Quoted in Fukumoto, "G-7 Failed to Declare Indefinite Extension of NPT."

85. Interview with MOFA official, Tokyo, July 2003.

86. "Discretion Needed in Extension of NPT," *Asahi Shimbun* editorial quoted in *Asahi News Service*, 1 September 1993.

87. The new prime minister was a "mainstream nuclear pacifist," which may or may not have influenced the decision to support the NPT's indefinite extension. Interview with senior Japanese nuclear expert, Kyoto, July 2003. Nuclear pacifists typically opposed the indefinite extension because they believe it legitimizes nuclear weapons.

88. Green and Furukawa, "New Ambitions, Old Obstacles," 2.

89. "Defense Agency Sees 'No Merit' in Japan Going Nuclear," *Kyodo News Service*, 20 February 2003.

90. "Japan Debated Nuke Arsenal," CNN.com.

91. Interview with senior Japanese nuclear expert, Tokyo, July 2003.

92. Kamiya, "A Disillusioned Japan," 2.

93. Schoenberger, "Citing North Korea."

94. Kamiya, "A Disillusioned Japan," 4.

95. "North Korea Says 'Arms, Not Words' Appropriate for Dealing with Japan," *Agence France Presse*, 11 October 2003.

96. Kase, *Evolution of Japan's Security Policy*, 168.

97. Ibid., 175.

98. French, "Taboo against Nuclear Arms."

99. *Yomiuri Shimbun*, 5 September 1998, quoted in Kase, *Evolution of Japan's Security Policy*, 187.

100. *Asahi Shimbun*, 15 September 1998, quoted in Kase, *Evolution of Japan's Security Policy*, 185.

101. One MOFA bureaucrat said, "Because of the U.S.-Japan relationship, it is not convenient for us to tell America, 'You must get rid of your nuclear weapons.' But we

are afraid that some recent activities by the U.S. will ruin the international norm." Interview with MOFA official, Tokyo, July 2003.

102. Interview with Japanese nuclear expert, Tokyo, July 2003. One expert noted that since the Japanese government cannot criticize Bush's policies, they relied on the Democrats to do so. Interview with Japanese government official, Tokyo, July 2003.

103. Interview with senior Japanese nuclear expert, Kyoto, July 2003.

104. Interview with senior Japanese defense official, Tokyo, July 2003.

105. Interview with Japanese nuclear expert, Washington, D.C., May 2003.

106. Interview with senior Japanese nuclear expert, Kyoto, July 2003.

107. At the time, Prime Minister Yasuhiro Nakasone (one of Japan's most militaristic prime ministers) sought to establish a close personal friendship with U.S. President Ronald Reagan, a relationship known in Japan as "Ron-Yasu." The Japanese elite strove to be "viewed as an important member of the 'West,' with Nakasone once describing the U.S.-Japanese relationship as one where two states share an 'inseparable destiny.' For many, this was the best strategy that Japan could have adopted during the Cold War, and Prime Minister Nakasone knew that the future security of Japan lay in the continual cementing of the U.S.-Japan bilateral relationship." Kase, *Evolution of Japan's Security Policy*, 102.

108. See discussion at the end of this chapter about dismay when President Clinton bypassed Japan on a visit to China, leaving a dent in the Japanese ego.

109. Glosserman and Nakagawa, "Nuclear Taboo Remains Strong."

110. Interview with Japanese nuclear expert, Washington, D.C., May 2003. Another defense expert noted, "During the Cold War, Japan's strategy worked. After the Cold War, it doesn't work as well. Now we are seeking more autonomy in international relations." Interview with Japanese nuclear expert, Tokyo, July 2003.

111. Interview with senior Japanese nuclear expert, Kyoto, July 2003.

112. Tianri, "Maintain Sharp Vigilance," 1.

113. French, "Taboo against Nuclear Arms."

114. Hibbs, "Fukushima Links Its Critique."

115. "Tokyo Politician Warns Beijing It Can Go Nuke 'Overnight,'" *Agence France Presse*, 8 April 2002, 1. For additional analysis of Ozawa's remarks, see Paul, "Explosive Talk."

116. Lim, "Nuclear Temptation in Japan."

117. French, "Taboo against Nuclear Arms."

118. Naohito Maeda, "Shinzo Abe," *Asahi Shimbun*, 12 June 2002, 1.

119. French, "Taboo against Nuclear Arms."

120. Kamiya, "Nuclear Japan," 63.

121. Hibbs, "Fukushima Links Its Critique."

122. Maeda, "Shinzo Abe," 1.

123. The furor is in some ways puzzling, given the content of the remarks. In answering a student's direct question, Abe simply repeated the 1957 Kishi administration policy that Article 9 of the constitution does not prohibit nuclear weapons. Fukuda's statements were a bit more unorthodox but most of the excitement was generated by what some call a mistranslation (Kamiya, "Nuclear Japan," 73): "The international media failed to report or translate their statements accurately, thereby exacerbating international misunderstanding about Japan's nuclear intentions. The *New York Times*, for example, quoted Fukuda as saying that 'in the face of calls to amend the Constitution, the amendment of the [three non-nuclear] principles is also likely.' Fukada's original statement in Japanese, however, used an expression '. . . *mo* . . . *kamoshirenai*,' which is not accurately translated as 'likely.' A more precise translation should read, '. . . even the amendment of the principles could take place.' The same article reported that Abe said that Japan's possession of nuclear weapons would be legal under Japanese law if it were 'small.' Although this translation was technically accurate—the word Abe used, *kogata*, does mean 'small' in Japanese—the article failed to explain that use of the word 'small' in this context in Japan implies 'small enough to be considered strictly defensive nuclear warheads.'"

124. "Defense Agency Sees 'No Merit' in Japan Going Nuclear," *Kyodo News Service*, 20 February 2003.

125. Nishihara, "North Korea's Trojan Horse."

126. Both Foreign Minister Taro Aso and Liberal Democratic Party policy chief Shoichi Nakagawa made repeated calls for opening discussion about a Japanese nuclear weapons program. See, for example, Nabeshima, "Even Nuclear Talk Distracts."

127. Ito, "Abe Says No to Nukes."

128. Interview with senior Japanese nuclear expert, Tokyo, March 2007. See also "Report: Japan Looked into Developing Nuclear Warhead."

129. With regard to its ratification decision, MOFA was concerned that any further Japanese delay would embarrass the United States and thus create friction in the U.S.-Japanese relationship, but this was due to the lag time between signature and ratification more than to anything else.

130. Interview with former U.S. senior diplomat, Washington D.C., May 2003. The implication, of course, was that Japan would have to reconsider its adherence to the NPT if more states joined the ranks of nuclear powers.

131. Campbell and Sunohara, "Japan: Thinking the Unthinkable," 240.

132. Akiyama, "Socio-Political Roots of Japan's Non-Nuclear Posture," 81.

133. Interview with former U.S. senior diplomat, Washington, D.C., May 2003.

134. Interview with senior Japanese peace researcher, Tokyo, July 2003.

135. Furukawa, "Nuclear Option, Arms Control, and Extended Deterrence," 108.

136. Interview with senior Japanese defense official, Tokyo, July 2003.

137. Interviews with senior Hiroshima city officials, Hiroshima, July 2003.

138. Campbell and Sunohara, "Japan: Thinking the Unthinkable," 222.

139. Interview with senior Japanese defense expert, Tokyo, March 2007.

140. Hughes, "Why Japan Will Not Go Nuclear (Yet)," 96.

141. Interview with senior Japanese peace researcher, Tokyo, July 2003; interview with Japanese peace activist, Hiroshima, July 2003; interview with senior Japanese nuclear expert, Hiroshima, July 2003.

142. Interview with Peace Depot official, Tokyo, March 2007.

143. This is not to say that Peace Depot or similar groups would not be effective if not for the NPT. Rather, it points out that these particular activities by these groups require the existence of the NPT, since they are explicitly comparing commitments made in NPT Review Conferences with follow-up action by the Japanese government.

144. Interview with Japanese defense expert, Tokyo, March 2007.

145. Interview with senior MOFA official, Yokohama, August 2006.

146. Interview with former Japanese ambassador, Yokohama, August 2006.

147. It was a great embarrassment to the Japanese, who had spent both political capital and a great deal of money to conduct CTBT negotiations, when the U.S. Senate refused to ratify it. Interview with former Egyptian diplomat to Japan, Cairo, March 2004.

148. Hughes, "Why Japan Will Not Go Nuclear (Yet)," 74.

149. See, for example, Kurosawa, "Japan's View of Nuclear Weapons."

150. Interview with former senior Japanese government official, Tokyo, July 2003.

151. Interview with former Japanese ambassador to the IAEA, Tokyo, March 2007.

152. Interview with senior Japanese nuclear expert, Kyoto, July 2003.

153. Dower, *Embracing Defeat*, 68–69.

154. Akiyama, "Socio-Political Roots of Japan's Non-Nuclear Posture," 74.

155. Interview with Japanese government official, Tokyo, July 2003.

156. I owe Taku Ishikawa thanks for these insights.

157. Prime Minister Yoshida had an argument with the U.S. envoy, who said Japan had to form its own army. Yoshida refused, saying it would hurt Japan's economy. The dispute resulted in a compromise that formed a small paramilitary force, which eventually became Japan's Self Defense Forces (SDF). Interview with senior Japanese nuclear expert, Tokyo, July 2003. See also Akiyama, "Socio-Political Roots of Japan's Non-Nuclear Posture," 76.

158. Interview with Japanese nuclear expert, Tokyo, July 2003.

159. Other scholars have voiced the same issue with realism, as discussed in chapter 1. As Hymans notes, "It is hard to see why, from a realist perspective, anything less than an indigenous nuclear arsenal would be sufficient to deter outside threats. Realists spent the entire Cold War bemoaning the lack of credibility of extended deterrence: Could anyone really expect us to trade New York for Berlin?" In addition, at least one

state chose the "self-help" route, showing that it was possible. France developed its own nuclear deterrent without U.S. acquiescence, under an arguably greater threat from the Soviet Union than Japan faced from China.

160. "Japan Rethinking Security Policy," *SC No. 00767/66B,* Central Intelligence Agency, April 29, 1965; Hughes, "Why Japan Will Not Go Nuclear (Yet)," 86; Campbell and Sunohara, "Japan: Thinking the Unthinkable."

161. Campbell and Sunohara, "Japan: Thinking the Unthinkable," 225

162. Ibid., 228.

163. Interview with senior Ministry of Defense official, Tokyo, March 2007.

164. Interview with Ministry of Defense official, Tokyo, March 2007.

165. Izumi and Furukawa, "Not Going Nuclear."

166. Interview with senior Japanese policymaker, Tokyo, March 2007.

167. Walker, "Risks Preclude Nuclear Option."

168. Interview with Japanese security expert, Washington, D.C., May 2003. This sentiment was echoed by numerous other experts and government officials.

169. Hughes, "Why Japan Will Not Go Nuclear (Yet)," 73.

170. Ibid., 74.

171. Ibid., 80.

172. Izumi and Furukawa, "Not Going Nuclear."

173. Campbell and Sunohara, "Japan: Thinking the Unthinkable," 222.

174. Ibid., 241.

175. Hughes, "Why Japan Will Not Go Nuclear (Yet)," 96.

176. Interview with former senior Japanese government official, Tokyo, July 2003.

177. Interview with senior Japanese defense official, Tokyo, July 2003; interview with Japanese government official, Tokyo, July 2003.

178. Kase, *Evolution of Japan's Security Policy,* 102.

179. Clemons, "Paralysis in U.S.-Japan Policy."

180. Ibid.

181. Interview with Japanese journalist, Tokyo, July 2003.

182. Interview with MOFA official, Tokyo, July 2003; interview with Japanese nuclear expert, Tokyo, July 2003.

183. Interview with Japanese nuclear expert, Tokyo, July 2003.

184. Interview with Japanese government official, Tokyo, July 2003.

185. Interview with senior Japanese nuclear expert, Hiroshima, July 2003.

186. Interview with MOFA official, Tokyo, July 2003.

187. Paul, *Power versus Prudence,* 57.

188. Hughes, "Why Japan Will Not Go Nuclear (Yet)," 79.

189. Ibid., 96.

190. Interview with Japanese nuclear expert, Tokyo, July 2003.

CHAPTER FOUR. Egyptian Nuclear Decision-Making

1. Interview with former senior Egyptian military officer, Cairo, March 2004; interview with former senior Egyptian science official, Cairo, March 2004.

2. Egypt ranks thirtieth in the world in terms of proved oil reserves. By comparison, Saudi Arabia is number one, the United States is number fourteen, and the United Kingdom is number twenty-five. 2006 *World Fact*.

3. Saira Khan notes: "The Egyptian response to the perceived Israeli nuclear threat has been significantly muted, which calls for an explanation." Khan, *Nuclear Proliferation Dynamics*, 249.

4. While a number of factors could be highlighted, those selected are most critical to understanding the case study; for example, unless one knew about Egypt's hot wars and cold peace with Israel, the question of why Egypt would or would not want to match Israel's nuclear capability may not make as much sense. Additionally, the four topics addressed were raised, in some fashion or another, by almost every interviewee, confirming that these are critical factors.

5. Stoessinger, *Why Nations Go to War*, 196–97.

6. Stevens and Tarzi, *Egypt and the Middle East Resolution*, 2.

7. Of the Suez Canal nationalization, Sadat wrote: "It was a turning point in the history of our revolution, and in the entire history of Egypt. From that moment on, Nasser turned into an Egyptian mythical hero. The Egyptian people had been yearning for such a moment of proud achievement and self-fulfillment, after nearly a century of humiliation and oppression at the hands of British colonialists. Egypt, a small country, was at last capable of speaking loud and clear in defiance of the biggest power on earth" (el-Sadat, *In Search of Identity*, 143).

8. Stoessinger, *Why Nations Go to War*, 220.

9. Feldman, *Nuclear Weapons and Arms Control*, 209.

10. Interview with senior Egyptian diplomat, Washington, D.C., February 2004.

11. Hinnebusch, *Egyptian Politics under Sadat*, 21.

12. Barnett, *Confronting the Costs*, 94.

13. Ajami, *The Arab Predicament*, 96. See also Barnett, *Confronting the Costs*, 128.

14. Official Egyptian documents describe their involvement in this way: "Egypt played a pioneering role in laying down the basis and principles which guided the United Nations in the negotiations which led to the conclusion of the Nonproliferation Treaty. It also played a prominent role in these negotiations both in the Disarmament Committee in Geneva, and at the United Nations General Assembly in New York, and it contributed effectively to the implementation of this treaty, in particular within the Framework of the International Atomic Energy Agency in Vienna." Ministry of Foreign Affairs of the Arab Republic of Egypt, *Egypt and the Treaty*.

15. Interview with Egyptian nuclear expert, Cairo, March 2004.

16. Interview with former senior Egyptian military officer, Cairo, March 2004.

17. Interview with former senior Egyptian diplomat, Cairo, March 2004.

18. Interview with senior Arab League disarmament official, Cairo, March 2004.

19. Interview with U.S. government official, Washington, D.C., March 2004.

20. For an overview of the importance of Egypt's identity as the regional leader on security issues, see Jentleson and Kaye, "Explaining Regional Security Cooperation."

21. Interview with former senior U.S. government official, Washington, D.C., February 2004.

22. Stevens and Tarzi, Egypt and the Middle East Resolution, 3–4.

23. Interview with U.S. government official, Washington, D.C., February 2004.

24. Interview with former senior Egyptian military official, Cairo, March 2004.

25. Feldman, Nuclear Weapons and Arms Control, 221.

26. Jentleson and Kaye, "Explaining Regional Security Cooperation," 230.

27. Interview with senior Egyptian science official, Cairo, March 2004.

28. Interview with senior Egyptian science official, Cairo, March 2004.

29. Interview with former senior Egyptian science official, Cairo, March 2004. By 1955 the Egyptian government was budgeting for nuclear research and development. See Nashif, Nuclear Warfare in the Middle East, 26.

30. "Cairo Draws Up Plan for the Construction of the First Atomic Reactor in the Middle East and the Eleventh in the World," Al-Ahram, 6 December 1960, quoted in Walsh, Bombs Unbuilt, 173.

31. Interview with senior Egyptian science official, Cairo, March 2004.

32. Interview with former senior Egyptian science official, Cairo, March 2004.

33. Interview with former senior Egyptian science official, Cairo, March 2004.

34. Interview with former senior Egyptian diplomat, Cairo, March 2004.

35. Walsh, Bombs Unbuilt, 146

36. Interview with senior Egyptian nuclear expert, Cairo, March 2004. On the spent fuel agreement with the Soviets, see Pajak, "Nuclear Status and Policies," 594.

37. Pranger and Tahtinen, Nuclear Threat in the Middle East, 19.

38. Shyam Bhatia reports that in 1952, "the number of Egyptian science graduates was estimated at just under 1400, slightly more than has been assessed for China in the same year." Bhatia, Nuclear Rivals, 49.

39. Walsh, Bombs Unbuilt, 144–45.

40. Bhatia, Nuclear Rivals, 51.

41. Bhatia describes Amer as Hedayat's "friend and mentor" (Nuclear Rivals, 57).

42. Barnaby, The Invisible Bomb, 8.

43. Interview with senior Egyptian nuclear expert, Cairo, March 2004. For further discussion of Egyptian and wider Arab reaction to Dimona reports, see Flapan, "Nuclear Power in the Middle East," 34–35.

44. "Nasser Threatens Israel on A-Bomb."

45. Weissman and Krosney, *The Islamic Bomb*, 116.

46. "Need to Reassure President Nasser on the Peaceful Nature of the Dimona Reactor," Memorandum From the U.S. Department of State's Executive Secretary (Read) to the President's Special Assistant for National Security Affairs (Bundy), 11 February 1964.

47. Walsh, *Bombs Unbuilt*, 141. By 1965 one of Nasser's close friends, Mohammed Heykal, admitted to Israel's nuclear superiority in an *Al Ahram* editorial. See also Cohen, *Israel and the Bomb*, 28.

48. Interview with senior Egyptian nuclear expert, Cairo, March 2004.

49. Interview with former senior Egyptian military officer, Cairo, March 2004. The AEE originally intended to pursue a light water reactor, which would not be suitable for military purposes. Heavy water reactors produce plutonium and thus have military applications.

50. Michael Siler notes, "The small Soviet-supplied reactor at Inchas was not only incapable of producing uranium, but broke down frequently. The irregular supply of Soviet fuel for the reactor made matters worse." Siler, *Explaining Variation in Nuclear Outcomes*, 67.

51. Walsh, *Bombs Unbuilt*, 149. See also Einhorn, "Egypt: Frustrated," 4.

52. "Attempts to Purchase 150 Megawatt Nuclear Reactor by the United Arab Republic," Secret Cable, 17 January 1965, From United States Embassy in Egypt, Office of Air Attaché, to United States Air Force Chief of Staff, Digital National Security Archive, Item Number NP01098.

53. Bhatia, *Nuclear Rivals*, 55

54. Walsh, *Bombs Unbuilt*, 163.

55. Egypt's defeat in the Six Day War was so devastating that all programs outside basic military readiness were frozen. In particular, the missile program, the aircraft program, and the nuclear program were frozen. This was done so that all funds could go into rebuilding the army and basic conventional weapons.

56. Einhorn, "Egypt: Frustrated," 45–46.

57. In late 1965, an associate of Nasser's was rumored to have told a British journalist, "We would go to the Devil, if necessary, in order to get a bomb." See Flapan, "Nuclear Power in the Middle East," 39.

58. Feldman, *Nuclear Weapons and Arms Control*, 130. A high-level Egyptian official also referenced the sabotage incident in relation to German assistance, saying, "Our cooperation with German scientists was botched by foreign intelligence." Interview with senior Egyptian nuclear expert, Cairo, March 2004.

59. Barnaby, *The Invisible Bomb*, 86.

60. Gregory, "Egypt's Nuclear Program," 21. It is rumored that the Soviets also offered either to provide a nuclear guarantee or to transfer nuclear weapons to Egyptian soil (under Soviet control) should Israel threaten Egypt with nuclear weapons.

However, this rumor cannot be confirmed, and my sources denied knowledge of it. In addition, it is questionable whether Nasser would ask the Chinese for a nuclear device after already receiving such a pledge from the Soviets. If so, then he likely did not place much trust in the Soviet pledge.

61. Interview with former senior Egyptian science official, Cairo, March 2004. On the Egyptian visit to China after their atomic detonation, see Selim, "Egypt," 138–39.

62. Interview with senior Egyptian nuclear expert, Cairo, March 2004.

63. Heikal, *The Cairo Documents*, 313.

64. Bhatia, *Nuclear Rivals*, 57.

65. "All the Revolution's Men," *Al-Ahram Weekly*, no. 595 (July 18, 2002), 1.

66. Beattie, *Egypt during the Nasser Years*, 160–62. Beattie says, "From late 1962 on, Nasser and Amer maintained their own, independent bases of power. Then, from 1962 forward, Nasser — supreme commander of the armed forces — was forbidden oversight of military affairs, and Amer was able to ignore Nasser's orders." For a lengthy discussion of the Nasser-Amer conflict, see el-Sadat, *In Search of Identity*, 157–71. Beattie notes that the former Minister of War, Amin Huweidi, said that "Nasser wanted to get rid of Amer, but he couldn't; Amer was the strongest man in Egypt" (161). Hinnebusch reports that other Free Officers believed Amer was trying to "turn the army into a personal fiefdom and expand his influence into civilian domains." Hinnebusch, *Egyptian Politics under Sadat*, 16.

67. Walsh, *Bombs Unbuilt*, 143.

68. Interview with former senior Egyptian military officer, Cairo, March 2004.

69. For decades Egypt has had the best-trained personnel in nuclear technology in the Arab world. University programs were set up in the 1950s, with students traveling to both the Soviet Union and India for specialized training. In fact, after the shutdown of the nuclear program in 1967, Egyptian nuclear personnel began leaving the country to find work in other countries. Egyptians were instrumental in helping design Iraq's Osirak reactor. One report from the mid-1970s posited that Egypt had the technological capacity not only to build a bomb but also to develop a second-strike capability, albeit a primitive one. See Evron, "A Nuclear Balance of Deterrence." Barnaby notes: "Egypt has built up a cadre of highly competent nuclear scientists and technologists. Some 500 of them work at the nuclear research center in Inchas and at the atomic energy authorities headquarters in Cairo. Egyptian nuclear scientists are often appointed to senior international posts, such as with the IAEA. Egypt would have no difficultly in putting together a team to design and construct nuclear weapons, once it had acquired a stock of plutonium and had taken the political decision to acquire nuclear weapons." Barnaby, *The Invisible Bomb*, 83.

70. Interview with senior Egyptian nuclear expert, Cairo, March 2004. The lack of program expertise also likely contributed to infighting, according to this senior expert in Egyptian defense issues, who added, "If you have everything you need, but bad administration, people will fight with each other and you will fail."

71. Interview with senior Egyptian nuclear expert, Cairo, March 2004.

72. Interview with former senior Egyptian science official, Cairo, March 2004. Walsh's research also complements this finding; he notes that "the AEE and its programs did not have an explicit military objective" and "no official work of the AEE was bomb related"; Walsh, *Bombs Unbuilt*, 155.

73. Interview with senior Egyptian science official, Cairo, March 2004.

74. Interview with senior Egyptian nuclear expert, Cairo, March 2004.

75. Walsh, *Bombs Unbuilt*, 215.

76. Ibid., 217.

77. Hinnebusch, *Egyptian Politics under Sadat*, 28–29.

78. See, for example, Walsh, *Bombs Unbuilt*, 172.

79. Nasser froze the nuclear program after the 1967 war because he wanted to direct funds to conventional weaponry and rebuilding the army so that he could retake the Sinai. Building an indigenous nuclear program would have required more resources than he was willing to devote to it, especially because Egypt was a decade away from a functional nuclear weapon — not soon enough to help with the Sinai problem. However, if Nasser could have acquired a nuclear device from another source, it would have been available immediately to use as leverage to regain the Sinai. Nasser may also have hoped that the Soviets and/or Chinese would make a nuclear device available to him for less than the cost of building one indigenously. If so, he may have believed it would be worth the cost — even though it would take away from conventional weaponry — because it would be available soon enough to bring into play on the Sinai issue.

80. Barnett, *Confronting the Costs*, 94.

81. Walt, *Origins of Alliances*, 53.

82. Stein, "Proliferation, Non-Proliferation," 37.

83. See Evron, "A Nuclear Balance of Deterrence," 21–22; Flapan, "Nuclear Power in the Middle East," 39–40; Pajak, "Nuclear Status and Policies," 595.

84. Interview with U.S. Egyptian expert, Washington, D.C., February 2004.

85. For example, at the Arab Foreign Ministers meeting in Baghdad in February 1961, "Arab representatives at the United Nations were to urge the United Nations to entrust the International Atomic Agency to investigate the Israeli situation" (Evron, "A Nuclear Balance of Deterrence," 21). See also Flapan, "Nuclear Power in the Middle East," 39–40.

86. Pajak, "Nuclear Status and Policies," 591.

87. Egypt was a member of the Committee on Disarmament, created in 1961, which concluded the Partial Test Ban Treaty in 1963. Egypt also participated in the Committee on Disarmament from its establishment in 1965. See Saif, "Egypt: A Non-Nuclear Proactivist," 11–12.

88. Interview with U.S. government official, Washington, D.C., February 2004.

89. Interview with senior Egyptian diplomat, Cairo, March 2004.

90. For an extensive discussion of the Kennedy-Nasser correspondence, see Heikal, *The Cairo Documents*, 187–224. On Kennedy's requests that Egypt remain non-nuclear, see ibid., 208, and Evron, "A Nuclear Balance of Deterrence," 27.

91. Walsh, *Bombs Unbuilt*, 171.

92. Interview with former senior Egyptian science official, Cairo, March 2004.

93. Saif, "Egypt: A Non-Nuclear Proactivist," 40.

94. Saif, "Egypt: A Non-Nuclear Proactivist," 32.

95. Interview with former senior Egyptian science official, Cairo, March 2004. Another Egyptian expert noted, "Nasser gave up early, he didn't insist." Interview with senior Egyptian nuclear expert, Cairo, March 2004.

96. Ministry of Foreign Affairs of the Arab Republic of Egypt, *Egypt and the Treaty*, 7.

97. Interview with senior Egyptian nuclear expert, Cairo, March 2004.

98. For detailed analyses of Israel's policy of nuclear ambiguity, see Cohen, *Israel and the Bomb*, and Feldman, *Israeli Nuclear Deterrence*.

99. Interview with former senior Egyptian science official, Cairo, March 2004.

100. Interview with senior Egyptian nuclear expert, Cairo, March 2004.

101. Interview with senior Egyptian nuclear expert, Cairo, March 2004.

102. Interview with former senior Egyptian military officer, Cairo, March 2004.

103. Interview with former senior Egyptian military officer, Cairo, March 2004.

104. Bar-Joseph, "The Hidden Debate," 207.

105. Interview with former senior Egyptian military officer, Cairo, March 2004.

106. Interview with former senior Egyptian military officer, Cairo, March 2004. On Sadat's assurances to the United States that Egypt had closed its nuclear option, see "Nuclear Power for Cairo," *New York Times*, 17 June 1974, 30.

107. Interview with former senior Egyptian science official, Cairo, March 2004.

108. Karawan, "Identity and Foreign Policy," 162. Karawan analyzed Sadat's political statements and speeches and concluded that Sadat had viewed Israel "in demonic terms" and that it is "difficult to explain Egypt's foreign-policy shift since the mid-1970s in light of the weight of [Sadat's] sheer personal characteristics and political beliefs." See Karawan, "Sadat and the Egyptian-Israeli Peace Revisited."

109. Pace, "Anwar el-Sadat."

110. Karawan, "Identity and Foreign Policy," 162.

111. Barnett, *Confronting the Costs*, 107. Also see Hinnebusch, *Egyptian Politics under Sadat*, 65–66.

112. Barnett notes: "The importance of these resources for Egypt's fiscal well-being is underscored by the fact that revenue estimates from the Suez Canal alone covered nearly two-thirds of the balance of payments deficit for 1966." Barnett, *Confronting the Costs*, 111.

113. Hinnebusch, *Egyptian Politics under Sadat*, 42.

114. Both the West and oil-producing Arab states did give Egypt foreign assistance in the aftermath of the 1973 war. See Burrell and Kelidar, *Egypt: The Dilemmas*, 22.

115. Waterbury, *The Egypt of Nasser and Sadat*, 127.

116. Barnett, *Confronting the Costs*, 128. Less favorable interpretations of Sadat's historical change of heart have been offered. For example, one Egyptian author argued that after the 1973 war, "President Sadat saw fit to reverse course and decided to abandon the political, economic and military front he helped forge in 1973; he also began to unilaterally disarm Egypt, advancing the naïve argument that he was ushering in a new era in international relations. He believed that his mastery of what he called the 'science of diplomacy,' which he claimed his foreign policy professionals could not even understand, would resolve all outstanding problems with Washington and Tel Aviv" (Safty, "Proliferation," 25–26).

117. Hinnebusch notes: "The Soviets, though unable to deliver a diplomatic solution, seemed unprepared to give Egypt the offensive military equipment which might give her a chance for a wholly military one." Hinnebusch, *Egyptian Politics under Sadat*, 47.

118. Ibid.

119. Barnett notes that both the Soviet Union and the United States were "shocked" when Egypt turned from the Soviets to the Americans. Barnett, *Confronting the Costs*, 129.

120. Ibid., quote on 251; on military spending, see 130.

121. "Mideast Nuclear Deals," *New York Times*, 19 June 1974, 44.

122. According to Weisman and Krosney, "The Israelis rejected the offer, which for reasons of American politics ended the offer for Egypt as well. In part, the Israelis were not willing to accept Washington's requirement that they open their entire nuclear program, and not just the reactor to be acquired, to inspection. They preferred to sacrifice their own hopes for civilian nuclear power in order to keep their freedom to exploit the 'nuclear option.' Above all, they did not want the Egyptians, potentially their deadliest Arab rival, to get even the possibility of producing weapons-usable plutonium." Weissman and Krosney, *The Islamic Bomb*, 322.

123. Selim, "Egypt," 141.

124. Nashif, *Nuclear Warfare in the Middle East*, 29.

125. Selim, "Egypt," 142. The Egyptian government openly noted this fact. In a statement before the People's Assembly in February 1981, Kamal Hassan Aly, deputy prime minister and minister of foreign affairs, said, "In view of this new climate [with strict application of nuclear safeguards], Egypt found itself unable to develop its electric power through access to nuclear energy unless it ratified the Non-Proliferation Treaty and accepted the application of the safeguards system of the International Atomic Energy Agency on its peaceful uses of nuclear energy. Egypt faced this problem when it contacted a number of supplier countries, including the United States, Canada, the

Federal Republic of Germany, and France." Ministry of Foreign Affairs of the Arab Republic of Egypt, *Egypt and the Treaty*, 89.

126. Interview with senior Egyptian science official, Cairo, March 2004.

127. Interview with former senior Egyptian diplomat, Cairo, March 2004.

128. Ministry of Foreign Affairs of the Arab Republic of Egypt, *Egypt and the Treaty*, 76–77. Egypt's concerns about its energy needs are evident in the statement made by Deputy Prime Minister and Minister of Foreign Affairs Kamal Hassan Aly to the Shura Assembly in February 1981. He said that if Egypt did not ratify the NPT, "we allow others to veto the development and promotion of our peaceful programmes needed to achieve prosperity and well-being of our people, whereas a large number of developing countries have covered great strides in the development of their nuclear technology. Egypt's need to develop its electric power by the end of this century is undisputed. To this end, the use of nuclear energy has become imperative for several reasons and considerations" (76).

129. Kats, "Egypt," 187. See also "Nuclear Developments," *Al-Majallah* (London), 3 July 1989, 35, quoted in "Nuclear Program Path Strewn with Obstacles."

130. Interview with senior Egyptian science official, Cairo, March 2004.

131. Bhatia, *Nuclear Rivals*, 60.

132. Interview with former senior Egyptian science official, Cairo, March 2004.

133. Ibid.

134. "Egyptian Minister of Egypt's Nuclear Program," *Al-Majallah* (London), 2 January 2000, 15. One interviewee noted that natural gas is an uncontroversial source, as opposed to nuclear power, which raises concerns both internationally and domestically. Interview with senior Egyptian nuclear expert, Cairo, March 2004.

135. Interview with former senior Egyptian diplomat, Cairo, March 2004.

136. "Menem Inaugurates a Nuclear Reactor in Egypt."

137. For an overview of Egyptian diplomatic initiatives on disarmament, see Abdel-Aal, "Egyptian Diplomacy and Issues."

138. Cohen, "Patterns of Nuclear Opacity," 30.

139. Leonard and Prawitz, "The Middle East as a NWFZ or WMDFZ Application," 263.

140. Shortly after Mubarak's proposal, Egypt submitted it to the United Nations. One of Egypt's senior diplomats, Nabil Fahmy, said Mubarak "proposed making the Middle East a zone free from all types of weapons of mass destruction. He emphasized that all weapons of mass destruction, without exception, should be prohibited in the region — nuclear, chemical, biological, and so forth; that all states of the region should make equal and reciprocal commitments in this regard; and that the ban should be enforced with verification measures." Fahmy noted that by delivering the proposal to the UN, Egypt "served notice that it intended to pursue the idea with dispatch." Fahmy, "Egypt's Disarmament Initiative," 9.

141. Jentleson and Kaye, "Explaining Regional Security Cooperation," 205. Jentleson and Kaye note that the other four working groups dealt with other issues of "common regional concern: regional economic development and cooperation (REDWG), water, the environment, and refugees" (fn. 2, 204).

142. Ibid., 205.

143. Interview with U.S. government official, Washington, D.C., February 2004.

144. Interview with senior Arab League arms control official, Cairo, March 2004.

145. Interview with senior Arab League arms control official, Cairo, March 2004.

146. The African NWFZ established by the Pelindaba Treaty is considered one of the most comprehensive: "It prohibits the development, production, storage, and possession of nuclear weapons. The countries of Africa are also forbidden to conduct nuclear explosions or bury nuclear waste anywhere in the continent or surrounding sea." See Hammad and Ahmed, "A Comparative Study of Nuclear-Weapon-Free Zones."

147. See "Toward a Nuclear-Weapon-Free World." The other members of the NAC include Brazil, Ireland, Mexico, New Zealand, South Africa, Sweden, and Slovenia, although Slovenia later withdrew its membership. Japan was approached to join the NAC, but MOFA felt it would create too much strain in their relationship with the United States.

148. Egypt tends to use whatever diplomatic channels provide an opportunity to raise the Israeli nuclear issue, from IAEA conferences to environmental fora. See Al-Qanawati, "Nuclear Developments," 8. For a discussion of Egyptian use of environmental fora to highlight Israeli nuclear waste, see Feldman, *Nuclear Weapons and Arms Control*, 216.

149. Interview with senior Egyptian diplomat, Cairo, March 2004.

150. Interview with former senior Egyptian diplomat, Cairo, March 2004.

151. Interview with senior Arab League arms control official, Cairo, March 2004.

152. Ibid.

153. "Egyptian President's Son Proposes Developing Nuclear Energy."

154. Salama and Gabrera-Farraj, "Renewed Egyptian Ambitions."

155. Ibid.

156. Sands, "Egypt Looks East."

157. "Egypt to Start Building Nuclear Power Plants."

158. See, for example, Salama, "Arab Attitudes toward Iran's Nuclear Program."

159. Interview, former senior Egyptian diplomat, Cairo, March 2004.

160. Hurst, "Is Mideast on Brink of an Arms Race?"

161. Salama and Hilal, "Egyptian Muslim Brotherhood."

162. Hurst, "Is Mideast on Brink of an Arms Race?"

163. For example, Egypt's energy minister said about the nuclear program: "The people are searching for a dream, a national project that proves to us that we are strong

and capable of doing something fitting of the grandeur of a country that some have begun to doubt." Salama and Gabrera-Farraj, "Renewed Egyptian Ambitions."

164. Salam, "The Arab Position."

165. Salama and Hilal, "Egyptian Muslim Brotherhood."

166. "Egypt and Nuclear Power."

167. Salam, "Questions on the Egyptian Nuclear Programme."

168. Salama and Gabrera-Farraj, "Renewed Egyptian Ambitions."

169. El-Hennawy, "Power to the People."

170. Danielson, "Egypt's Nuclear Program," 9.

171. "Egypt Unveils Nuclear Power Plan," BBC News.

172. Einhorn, "Egypt: Frustrated," 57–58.

173. Landau, "Egypt's Nuclear Dilemma," 5.

174. Einhorn, "Egypt: Frustrated," 66.

175. Interview with senior Egyptian nuclear expert, Cairo, March 2004.

176. Interview with former senior U.S. diplomat, Washington, D.C., February 2003.

177. Einhorn, "Egypt: Frustrated," 52–53.

178. Interview with former senior Egyptian military officer, Cairo, March 2004.

179. Einhorn, "Egypt: Frustrated," 56.

180. Interview with former senior Egyptian diplomat, Cairo, March 2004.

181. Walsh, *Bombs Unbuilt*, 187.

182. Interview with senior Egyptian nuclear expert, Cairo, March 2004.

183. Landau, "Egypt's Nuclear Dilemma," 4.

184. Interview with U.S. government official, Washington, D.C., February 2004.

185. Interview with U.S. government official, Washington, D.C., February 2004.

186. Interview with former senior Egyptian military officer, Cairo, March 2004.

187. Einhorn, "Egypt: Frustrated," 54.

188. For example, Khan argues that since there is a tacit agreement among Arab states not to use nuclear weapons against each other, and Egypt supported to some extent the Iraqi drive for nuclear weapons (*Nuclear Proliferation Dynamics*, 254). He says, "Though the Egyptian aim may not be to see an aggressive Arab country like Iraq possessing nuclear capability, it is nonetheless acceptable under circumstances where the major Arab enemy, Israel, has the capacity" (255).

189. Einhorn, "Egypt: Frustrated," 64. Interview with senior Egyptian diplomat, Cairo, March 2004; interview with senior Egyptian diplomat, Washington, D.C., February 2004.

190. Interview with senior Egyptian nuclear expert, Cairo, March 2004.

191. For a discussion of the supposed Soviet security guarantee and why it is unlikely that such a guarantee was ever given, see Evron, "The Arab Position," 28. In 1981, the Egyptian press reported that the Soviet Union had declined to give Egypt either nuclear weapons or a nuclear guarantee. See Shikaki, "The Nuclearization Debates."

192. Einhorn, "Egypt: Frustrated," 49.

193. Ibid., 81.

194. According to the Nuclear Threat Initiative (NTI), "Most assessments by security experts indicate that while Egypt has a strong technical base in applied microbiology, it lacks the necessary infrastructure for developing or producing BW. Furthermore, there is no corroborated open-source evidence of any organized BW-related research activity." "Biological Weapons," *Egypt Country Overview.*

195. See "Chemical Weapons," *Egypt Country Overview*, 2.

196. Panofsky, "Dismantling the Concept."

197. Ibid., 1. Should an effective national missile defense be created, this would change. However, such countermeasures would be far outside the technical and economic scope of Egypt, whereas chemical weapons countermeasures are much cheaper and easier to obtain.

198. Khan, *Nuclear Proliferation Dynamics*, 253.

199. Siler, *Explaining Variation in Nuclear Outcomes*, 76.

200. Interview with former senior Egyptian military officer, Cairo, March 2004.

201. Interview with former senior Egyptian diplomat, Cairo, March 2004.

202. Interview with former senior Egyptian military officer, Cairo, March 2004.

203. Interview with senior Israeli nuclear expert, Washington, D.C., February 2004.

204. Interview with senior Egyptian diplomat, Cairo, March 2004.

205. Interview with former senior Egyptian military officer, Cairo, March 2004.

206. Barnett, *Confronting the Costs*, 129.

207. For example, see Safty, "Proliferation."

208. Einhorn, "Egypt: Frustrated," 58.

209. Interview with former senior U.S. government official, Washington, D.C., February 2004.

210. Interview with U.S. government official, Washington, D.C., February 2004.

211. "Mubarak Says He Turned Down Offer to Buy Nuclear Bomb," *Associated Press*, June 19, 1998. This offer was confirmed by an interview with senior Egyptian diplomat, Washington, D.C., February 2004, and an interview with senior Egyptian nuclear expert, Cairo, March 2004.

212. For example, in 1995 writer Salah al-Din Hafez argued, "Israel insists on retaining its nuclear weapons, not only as a military deterrent but also as a psychological deterrent. I believe the perception that Israel is the sole possessor of nuclear weapons in the region is psychologically humiliating to us as Arabs, even more so than its military and political hegemony." Ta 'imah, "National Conference To Discuss Nuclear Dangers."

213. Landau, "Egypt's Nuclear Dilemma," 5.

214. Ministry of Foreign Affairs of the Arab Republic of Egypt, *Egypt and the Treaty*, 100.

215. Feldman, *Nuclear Weapons and Arms Control*, 69; Einhorn, "Egypt: Frustrated," 59.

216. Interview with former senior Egyptian military official, Cairo, March 2004.

217. Interview with senior Egyptian diplomat, Cairo, March 2004.

218. Sadat's reframing of acceptable ways to deal with enemies eventually spilled over to other Arab nations. Michael Weir notes: "It may be that Sadat's most enduring legacy is to have established almost unanimous acceptance among both Arabs and Israelis of the principle that a settlement of the Palestine problem should be sought through negotiation" (Wier, "External Relations," 86).

CHAPTER FIVE. **Nuclear Decision-Making in Libya, Sweden, and Germany**

1. Alterman, "Libya and the U.S."

2. Cirincione et al., *Deadly Arsenals*, 307.

3. "Rumors of Libyan Atomic Bomb Quest Raise Fears."

4. "Libya's Nuclear Update: 2004."

5. "Libya Nuclear Chronology: 1968–1979."

6. Weiss, "Pakistan," 52. See also "Libya Nuclear Chronology: 1968–1979."

7. Bradsher, "India Official Says Qaddafi Sought Atom-Arms Technology in '70s." The article noted: "[The offer] had been made when Morarji Desai was Prime Minister of India. Mr. Desai held office from 1977 to 1979, and India's foreign debt rose from $15.50 billion to $17.89 billion during that period."

8. Cooley, "Qadhafi's Great Aim."

9. Gelb, "Nuclear Nations Agree."

10. "Libya Nuclear Chronology: 1980–1989."

11. "Saudi Nuclear Pact."

12. R. Jeffrey Smith, "Facing a 'Messy' Nuclear Scenario."

13. "Libya Nuclear Chronology: 1990–1999."

14. "Libya Set to Allow Nuclear Inspections."

15. "Libya Nuclear Chronology: 1990–1999."

16. "Orchestrating Libya's Metamorphosis."

17. "Implementation of the NPT Safeguards Agreement of the Socialist People's Libyan Arab Jamahiriya," International Atomic Energy Agency, GOV/2004/12, February 20, 2004, 5.

18. Alterman, "Libya and the U.S.," 4.

19. Indyk, "Iraq War Did Not Force."

20. "Implementation of the NPT Safeguards Agreement." See also "Libya Nuclear Chronology: 2000–2003."

21. "The New Qadhafi,"CBS News.

22. Miller, "How Qadhafi Lost His Groove."

23. Hochman, "Rehabilitating a Rogue," 66.
24. Miller, "How Qadhafi Lost His Groove."
25. Indyk, "Iraq War Did Not Force," 1.
26. "What Does Libya's Disarmament Teach about Rogue States?"
27. Salama, "Was Libyan WMD Disarmament a Significant Success?"
28. Joffe, "Why Gaddafi Gave Up WMD," BBC News.
29. Salama, "Was Libyan WMD Disarmament a Significant Success?" 3.
30. See, for example, Salama, "Was Libyan WMD Disarmament a Significant Success?" 3, and Indyk, "Iraq War Did Not Force," 1.
31. Indyk, "Iraq War Did Not Force," 1.
32. "U.S. Opposes Lifting of Sanctions on Libya." CNN.com.;
33. "U.S. Opposes Lifting of Sanctions on Libya," 1.
34. Garwood, "End of Sanctions Opens Doors."
35. Ibid., 2.
36. Ibid.
37. Hesseldahl, "Time to Go Back to Libya."
38. Ibid., 1.
39. For example, one of the most optimistic assessments of sanctions as a means of achieving policy goals found that in 34 percent of cases, sanctions were at least somewhat successful. See Hufbauer et al., *Economic Sanctions Reconsidered.* However, some argue that even this assessment is overly optimistic and that proper coding of cases would have led the authors to conclude that sanctions were effective only 7 percent of the time. See, for example, Pape, "Why Economic Sanctions Still Do Not Work."
40. Kaempfer and Lowenberg, "International Sanctions," 233.
41. Interview with Egyptian diplomat, Cairo, March 2003.
42. Takeyh, "The Rogue," 63.
43. Ibid., 65.
44. "Orchestrating Libya's Metamorphosis," 1.
45. Ibid.
46. "The New Qadhafi," CBS News.
47. Ronen, "Libya's Rising Star," 140. See also "The New Qadhafi," 2.
48. "Qadhafi's Son Tells Al-Hayat."
49. Takeyh, "The Rogue," 66.
50. Galadari, "Which Way Reforms in Libya?"
51. For example, the Libyan command economy is based on Qadhafi's revolutionary writings, the *Green Book.* Yet today Qadhafi calls for a free market economy.
52. See, for example, "Qadhafi: Arab Nationalism Is Dead," Aljazeera.net.
53. Ibid., 1.
54. See Butt, "Colonel Gaddafi's Libya," BBC News. See also, "Saif Gaddafi's Vision for Libya," BBC News.

55. Hochman, "Rehabilitating a Rogue," 68.

56. See, for example, Dunne, *Libya: Security Is Not Enough*, and Gwertzman, "Lisa Anderson: Qaddafi, Desperate."

57. Sheikh, "Al-Qadhafi Son: Israel Is Not a Threat," Aljazeera.net.

58. "Libyan Leader Invites Bush Visit," Aljazeera.net.

59. "Qadhafi Calls for Self-Reliance," Aljazeera.net.

60. "Qaddafi's Son Tells Al-Hayat," 2.

61. The nine processes identified in chapter 2 are descriptive norms, injunctive norms, and subjective norms (the three types of norms); activation, linking, and consistency (the ways that norms are processed); and uncertainty, similarity, and conflict (the conditions that affect norm potency).

62. Gwertzman, "Lisa Anderson: Qaddafi, Desperate," 1.

63. "Qadhafi Calls for Self-Reliance."

64. "Qadhafi Calls for Self-Reliance," 1.

65. Dunne, *Libya: Security Is Not Enough*, 6.

66. Galadari, "Which Way Reforms in Libya?" 1.

67. "IAEA Chief El Baradei Cites Libya's Cooperation," IAEA *Staff Report*, February 24, 2004, accessed September 6, 2006, available from http://www.iaea.org/NewsCenter/News/2004/libya-coop2402.html.

68. "Libya Purchased Nuclear Weapons Plans from Pakistan, Qadhafi's Son Says."

69. "What Does Libya's Disarmament Teach about Rogue States?" 2.

70. Alterman, "Libya and the U.S.," 2.

71. Kelman, "Compliance, Identification, and Internalization," 53.

72. Takeyh, "The Rogue," 66.

73. Ibid., 67.

74. Gwertzman, "Lisa Anderson: Qaddafi, Desperate," 2.

75. Crampton, "Qaddafi Son Sets Out Economic Reforms."

76. Jawad, "Libyan Entrepreneurs Enjoy Boom," BBC News.

77. Takeyh, "The Rogue," 66.

78. Ibid., 67.

79. "Libyan Leader Invites Bush Visit"; Sheikh, "Al-Qadhafi Son: Israel Is Not a Threat."

80. Gwertzman, "Lisa Anderson: Qaddafi, Desperate," 1.

81. The U.S. government believed that Sweden would eventually acquire nuclear weapons. See U.S. Embassy, Sweden, "Untitled Reactions to National Intelligence Estimate No. 100-2-58," *Development of Nuclear Capabilities by Fourth Countries*, September 2, 1958.

82. Prawitz, *From Nuclear Option to Non-Nuclear Promotion*, iv.

83. Cole, *Atomic Bombast*, 9.

84. Reiss, *Without the Bomb*, 43.

85. Cole, *Atomic Bombast*, 14.

86. Reiss, *Without the Bomb*, 47.

87. Ibid., 50.

88. The Conservative Party supported outright nuclear weapons acquisition and/or production, while the Liberal and Centre parties supported funding nuclear weapons research. The ruling party, the Social Democratic Party, was split on the issue. See Reiss, *Without the Bomb*, 48, and Paul, *Power versus Prudence*, 87.

89. Arnett, "Norms and Nuclear Proliferation," 35.

90. "ÖB 57," p. 294, quoted in Reiss, *Without the Bomb*, 51.

91. Reiss, *Without the Bomb*, 54.

92. Paul, *Power versus Prudence*, 88.

93. Cole, *Atomic Bombast*, 15.

94. Ibid., 23.

95. Paul, *Power versus Prudence*, 86.

96. Ibid., 7.

97. Quester, *Politics of Nuclear Proliferation*, 124.

98. Cole, *Atomic Bombast*, 8.

99. Ibid., 8.

100. Kennedy, "Lucky Dragon," *CNN Interactive*.

101. Bunn, *Arms Control by Committee*, 18.

102. Müller et al., *Nuclear Non-Proliferation*, 18.

103. Reiss, *Without the Bomb*, 49.

104. Van Dassen, "Sweden and the Making," 13.

105. Ibid., 14.

106. Ibid.

107. Arnett, "Norms and Nuclear Proliferation," 33.

108. Quoted in Reiss, *Without the Bomb*, 65.

109. Van Dassen, "Sweden and the Making," 18.

110. Cole, *Atomic Bombast*, 23.

111. Van Dassen, "Sweden and the Making," 20; Fischer, *History of the International Atomic Energy Agency*, 85.

112. Reiss, *Without the Bomb*, 55.

113. Pande, "Scope for Nuclear Weapon Free Zone."

114. Reiss, *Without the Bomb*, 67.

115. Quester, *Politics of Nuclear Proliferation*, 128.

116. Arnett, "Norms and Nuclear Proliferation," 33.

117. "Alva Myrdal: A Biography." Her work on nuclear disarmament led to a Nobel Peace Prize in 1982, further confirming that the proper Swedish role in the world was leadership in nuclear nonproliferation.

118. Cole, *Atomic Bombast*, 8–9.

119. Arnett, "Norms and Nuclear Proliferation," 37.

120. Ibid., 34. Reiss notes that in the late 1950s, the Swedish defense budget increased almost 5.5 percent per year, increases larger than in most other Western European countries (*Without the Bomb*, 60).

121. Cole, *Atomic Bombast*, 18–19. Cole details the problems in the U.S.-Swedish relationship, including some colorful anecdotes that help explain why the Swedish should not have relied on a nuclear umbrella that had never been extended in the first place. For example, after a Swedish cabinet member "compared the American bombings of Vietnam to Nazi extermination camps, Secretary of State Kissinger, who said the United States did not have to establish its anti-fascist credentials, reminded Palme of who had fought against Nazi Germany (America) and who had sold the Nazis ball bearings during World War II (Sweden)" (Cole, *Atomic Bombast*, 19).

122. Arnett, "Norms and Nuclear Proliferation," 34.

123. Reiss, *Without the Bomb*, 61–62.

124. "ÖB 57," p 294, quoted in Reiss, *Without the Bomb*, 51.

125. Arnett, "Norms and Nuclear Proliferation,"38.

126. Ibid.

127. Reiss, *Without the Bomb*, 69.

128. Ibid., 61.

129. Reiss notes that the Social Democrats were sensitive to the criticism that they were weak on security and, in response, submitted record increases in defense budgets in the early 1960s to counter this criticism (*Without the Bomb*, 59).

130. See, for example, Quester, *Politics of Nuclear Proliferation*, 126, and Van Dassen, "Sweden and the Making," 15.

131. Arnett, "Norms and Nuclear Proliferation," 35.

132. Cole, *Atomic Bombast*, 27.

133. Ibid.

134. Ibid., 16.

135. Arnett, "Norms and Nuclear Proliferation," 36.

136. Cole, *Atomic Bombast*, 23.

137. Cathleen S. Fisher, "Preface," in Cole, *Atomic Bombast*, iv.

138. In the Swedish case, similarity did not seem to make the norms more potent. This is in part because Sweden saw itself as unique — a neutral state poised between East and West, with the unique potential role of bridge builder.

139. Kennedy, "Lucky Dragon," 1.

140. Reiss, *Without the Bomb*, 49.

141. Müller et al., *Nuclear Non-Proliferation*, 18.

142. Van Dassen, "Sweden and the Making," 28.

143. Quester, *Politics of Nuclear Proliferation*, 126.

144. Some point to newspaper reports of Swedish nuclear "tests" in the 1970s to show that Sweden had not truly given up its nuclear program. A number of analysts have examined the charges and found them based on poor reporting. Reiss says: "In fact, Stockholm carried out three different activities during the 1960s and 1970s: implosion experiments, compressibility tests on plutonium, and neutron pulse generator experiments. These activities were theoretically within the 'protective research' program which had been recommended by the Committee for the Study of the Atomic Weapons Question in November 1959. This research was not designed to give Sweden nuclear weapons, these tests were not nuclear weapons tests, and Sweden did not violate its obligations under the NPT or corresponding safeguards agreements with the IAEA" (Reiss, *Without the Bomb*, 74). A 1994 *Washington Post* report implied that because Sweden's heavy-water nuclear reactor Agesta had been shut down but not decommissioned, Sweden might attempt to use the reactor for weapons-grade nuclear material at some point in the future. Arnett debunks the report: "In fact, Agesta is being maintained to prevent its becoming an environmental risk, pending a decision on Sweden's strategy for high-level waste disposal, and could not be used to produce weapons quickly. If it were to be used for making plutonium, it would require new fuel and heavy water, which is not available in Sweden" ("Norms and Nuclear Proliferation," 37). See Prawitz, *From Nuclear Option to Non-Nuclear Promotion*, 46–47 for additional rebuttal.

145. Van Dassen, "Sweden and the Making," 2.

146. Ibid., 4.

147. Reiss, *Without the Bomb*, 66–67, 71.

148. For a brief overview of Sweden's extensive nonproliferation activities, see Prawitz, *From Nuclear Option to Non-Nuclear Promotion*, 28–34.

149. Swedish Ambassador Henrik Salander, "Statement at the Third Session of the Preparatory Committee for the 2000 Review Conference."

150. Van Dassen notes that the Swedish see neutrality as the "the desire to be equally antagonistic towards everyone else — this in contrast to Finland, where the policy of neutrality was to be equally friendly with all other states" ("Sweden and the Making," 26).

151. De Young, "Swedish Officials Defend A-Research."

152. Henrik Salander, a Swedish rock star turned diplomat, was a key figure in creating the NAC. See Arita, "Swedish Diplomat Salander."

153. In May 2006, over 70 percent of Germans polled expressed support for a nuclear-free Europe. Currently only one party in the German parliament — the Christian Democrats — supports U.S. nuclear weapons located on German soil. See Meier, "An End to U.S. Tactical Nuclear Weapons in Europe?"

154. Müller, "German National Identity," 2. Carson relates how as early as 1954, German defense officials questioned nuclear scientists about military applications (*Going Nuclear*, 22).

155. Cioc, *Pax Atomica*, 43.

156. In fact, early on German leadership did not want to make any commitments to the Soviet Union about their non-nuclear status. In 1962 Leonard Beaton and John Maddox wrote of Germany: "The federal government has equally refused to countenance any extension of its non-nuclear commitment to a treaty involving the Soviet Union because it says that this would give its potential enemy an unacceptable say in its long-term defense policy. The restrictions on sovereignty now in effect were not made to the concert of powers or to the international community as a whole: they were given to Western European Union and are, so to speak, the private affair of Western Europe." Beaton and Maddox, *Spread of Nuclear Weapons*, 111.

157. Coffey, "Threat, Reassurance, and Nuclear Proliferation." See also Coffey, "Strategy, Alliance Policy, and Nuclear Proliferation."

158. Müller, "German National Identity," 2.

159. Kelleher, *Germany and the Politics of Nuclear Weapons*, 44–46.

160. Cioc, *Pax Atomica*, 33.

161. Ibid., 26.

162. Beaton and Maddox, *Spread of Nuclear Weapons*, 114.

163. Carson, *Going Nuclear*, 23.

164. Müller, "German National Identity," 2.

165. Kotch, "NATO Nuclear Arrangements."

166. Ibid., 2.

167. Müller, "German National Identity," 3.

168. Cioc, *Pax Atomica*, 25.

169. For a detailed examination of public and party reaction to Carte Blanche, see Speier, *German Rearmament and Atomic War*, 182–93.

170. Kelleher, *Germany and the Politics of Nuclear Weapons*, 36.

171. Ibid., 38.

172. Mackby and Slocombe, "Germany: The Model Case," 184.

173. Carson, *Going Nuclear*, 15.

174. Schrafstetter, "Long Shadow," 123; Carson, *Going Nuclear*, 23.

175. Gose, "The New Germany," 2.

176. Berger, *Cultures of Antimilitarism*, 49.

177. Boutwell, *German Nuclear Dilemma*, 3.

178. Ibid., 148–49.

179. Worsley, "On the Brink," 27.

180. Enders et al., "The New Germany and Nuclear Weapons," 128.

181. Boutwell, *German Nuclear Dilemma*, 3.

182. Müller et al., "The German Debate," 115.

183. Boese, "Germany Raises No-First-Use Issue."

184. Fisher, *Reformation and Resistance*, 55.

185. The German government has also made "urgent appeals to the United States to ratify the CTBT." Makhijani and Smith, "NATO's Nuclear Conflict," 3.

186. Mackby and Slocombe, "Germany: The Model Case," 204.

187. Paul, *Power versus Prudence*, 43.

188. Kelleher, *Germany and the Politics of Nuclear Weapons*, 74.

189. Carson, *Going Nuclear*, 23.

190. Kotch, "NATO Nuclear Arrangements," 3.

191. Wittner, *Resisting the Bomb*, 62.

192. Paul, *Power versus Prudence*, 45.

193. Enders et al., "The New Germany and Nuclear Weapons," 140.

194. Müller, "German National Identity," 3.

195. Paul, *Power versus Prudence*, 45.

196. Gose, "The New Germany," 3.

197. Wittner, *Resisting the Bomb*, 63.

198. Schrafstetter, "Long Shadow," 123.

199. Wittner, *Resisting the Bomb*, 19.

200. For example, the scientists who produced the Göttingen Manifesto founded the Federation of German Scientists (using the model of the Federation of American Scientists). See Cioc, *Pax Atomica*, 87. In addition, one of the eighteen scientists, Carl-Friedrich von Weizsacker, published a follow-up to the manifesto, advocating for disarmament—after meeting with international leaders in the nonproliferation and disarmament movement. His follow-up publication made a strong impact on SPD leaders, including Helmut Schmidt (Cioc, *Pax Atomica*, 88–91).

201. Wittner, *Resisting the Bomb*, 31.

202. Ibid., 32.

203. Even German churches publicly activated the emerging norm by advocating for a test ban treaty. See Cioc, *Pax Atomica*, 94–95.

204. Herf, "War, Peace and the Intellectuals," 191–93.

205. See Müller, "German National Identity," for an excellent interpretation of West Germany's evolving role and identity as a non-nuclear state.

206. For a thorough review of German antimilitarism after World War II, see Berger, *Cultures of Antimilitarism*.

207. Beaton and Maddox, *Spread of Nuclear Weapons*, 120.

208. Enders et al., "The New Germany and Nuclear Weapons," 140.

209. Others in Europe noticed that the German trade-off worked well. Swede Alva Myrdal noted, "Both [Germany and Japan] have piled up much prestige and economic

benefits by having forsworn nuclear armaments; it seems unlikely that they would divert their assets to an independent nuclear arsenal even if they believed in the French position of not being convinced of protection by the U.S. nuclear arsenal." Myrdal, *Game of Disarmament*, 181–82.

210. Berger, *Cultures of Antimilitarism*, 4.

211. Van Ourdenaren, "Nuclear Weapons in the 1990s and Beyond," 46.

212. Ibid., 47.

213. Gose, "The New Germany," 1.

214. For example, see Mearsheimer, "Back to the Future,"

215. Müller, "German National Identity," 5.

216. Abolition Europe 2000, *Meeting Report*.

217. Müller, "German National Identity," 5.

CHAPTER SIX. **Reflections on Theory and Policy**

1. Interview with former senior Egyptian diplomat, March 2004, Cairo.

2. Interview with Japanese nuclear policy expert, July 2003, Tokyo.

3. Walsh, *Bombs Unbuilt*, 215.

4. Ibid., 217.

5. A 1973 report notes: "The size of the defense budgets of Egypt since 1967 suggest that had Egypt decided to develop a nuclear option, she could manage — financially — to do it within a span of five to ten years." Evron, "The Arab Position," 30.

6. Solingen, "Domestic Sources of Regional Regimes," 327.

7. Interview with Japanese nuclear policy expert, May 2003, Washington, D.C.

8. Interview with former senior Egyptian military official, March 2004, Cairo.

9. Berger, "From Sword to Chrysanthemum," 135–36.

10. Interview with senior American expert on Japanese nuclear policy, May 2003, Washington, D.C.

11. Interview with former senior Egyptian military official, March 2004, Cairo.

12. Interview with senior Egyptian academic, March 2004, Cairo.

13. Müller, "German National Identity," 5.

14. For example, some constructivists — such as pioneer Alexander Wendt — are state-centric. For a discussion of why constructivists should investigate "the interaction between international structures and local agents," see Finnemore, *National Interests*, 136–38, 144.

15. Arnett, "Norms and Nuclear Proliferation," 32.

16. Interview with Arab League disarmament expert, March 2004, Cairo.

17. Wurst, "NPT Parties Criticized on Disarmament."

18. Wurst, "U.S. Says Nonproliferation Treaty Faces Crisis."

19. Interview with former senior American diplomat, September 2003, Washington, D.C.

20. Applegarth, "Brazil Permits Greater IAEA Inspection."

21. "Bush Hails Partnership with India," BBC News.

22. Campbell et al., *Nuclear Tipping Point*, 345.

23. Ibid., 324.

24. Bunn and du Preez, "More Than Words."

25. Cirincione, "Bush Unleashes the Nuclear Beast."

26. Campbell et al., *Nuclear Tipping Point*, 344.

27. Robbins, "Libya 'Let Down' by West," BBC News.

BIBLIOGRAPHY

Government Documents

"Attempts to Purchase 150 Megawatt Nuclear Reactor by the United Arab Republic." Secret Cable, 17 January 1965, From United States Embassy in Egypt, Office of Air Attaché, to United States Air Force Chief of Staff. Digital National Security Archive, Item Number NP01098.

"Implementation of the NPT Safeguards Agreement of the Socialist People's Libyan Arab Jamahiriya." International Atomic Energy Agency, GOV/2004/12, 20 February 2004.

"Japan Rethinking Security Policy." SC No. 00767/66B, Central Intelligence Agency. 29 April 1965.

"Main Trends in Japan's External Relations." National Intelligence Estimate No. 41–68. Central Intelligence Agency. 11 January 1968.

"Need to Reassure President Nasser on the Peaceful Nature of the Dimona Reactor." Memorandum from the U.S. Department of State's Executive Secretary (Read) to the President's Special Assistant for National Security Affairs (Bundy). 11 February 1964.

"Prospects for Further Proliferation of Nuclear Weapons." CIA Memorandum 55-1, DCI NIO 1945/74. 4 September 1974.United Nations and Disarmament: 1945–85, The. New York: United Nations, 1985.

U.S. Embassy, Sweden. "Untitled Reactions to National Intelligence Estimate No. 100-2-58." Development of Nuclear Capabilities by Fourth Countries, 2 September 1958. Accessed July 9, 2006, available from http://www.gwu.edu/~nsarchiv/NSAEBB/NSAEBB155/index.htm.

Interviews

In accordance with rules governing human subjects research, all interview subjects must remain confidential. Interviews were conducted with knowledgeable academics and policymakers in Egypt, Japan, and the United States from July 2003 to June 2004. Additional interviews took place in Japan in August 2006 and March 2007.

Books, Articles, Dissertations, Theses, Papers Presented
at Meetings, and Lectures

Abdel-Aal, Abdel-Rahman. "Egyptian Diplomacy and Issues of Disarmament in the United Nations, 1981–1998." *Al-Siyassa Al-Dawliya (The International Politics Journal)*, no. 144 (April 2001). Accessed on April 16, 2004, available from http://www.siyassa.org.eg/esiyassa/ahram/2001/4/1/STUD3.HTM.

Abolition Europe 2000. *Meeting Report: General Meeting New York* (May 6, 2005). Accessed September 16, 2006, available at http://abolition2000europe.org/index.php?op=ViewArticle&articleId=25&blogId=1.

Ajami, Fouad. *The Arab Predicament*. Cambridge: Cambridge University Press, 1992.

Akiyama, Nobumasa. "The Socio-Political Roots of Japan's Non-Nuclear Posture." In Benjamin Self and Jeffrey Thompson, eds., *Japan's Nuclear Option: Security, Politics and Policy in the 21st Century*, 64–91. Washington, D.C.: Henry L. Stimson Center, 2003.

Albright, David, and Kevin O'Neill. "The North Korean Nuclear Program: Unresolved Issues." Institute for Science and International Security, June 6, 1994. Accessed August 17, 2007, available from http://www.isis-online.org/publications/dprk/fs060694.html.

"All the Revolution's Men." *Al-Ahram Weekly*, no. 595, 18 July 2002, 1.

Alterman, Jon B. "Libya and the U.S.: The Unique Libyan Case." *Middle East Quarterly* (January 2006). Accessed July 15, 2006, available from http://www.meforum.org/pf.php?id=886.

"Alva Myrdal: A Biography." *Les Prix Nobel, The Nobel Prizes 1982*, ed. Wilhelm Odelberg. Stockholm: Nobel Foundation, 1982. Accessed July 8, 2006, available from http://nobelprize.org/nobel_prizes/peace/laureates/1982/myrdal-bio.html.

"A-Pact Ratification Deferred." *Facts on File World News Digest*, 28 June 1975, 462 A1.

Applegarth, Claire. "Brazil Permits Greater IAEA Inspection." *Arms Control Today* (November 2004). Accessed September 16, 2006, available at http://www.armscontrol.org/act/2004_11/Brazil.asp.

Arita, Tsukasa. "Swedish Diplomat Salander Has Unique Background." *Kyodo World Service*, 10 November 2004.

Arnett, Eric. "Norms and Nuclear Proliferation: Sweden's Lessons for Assessing Iran." *Nonproliferation Review* (Winter 1998): 32–43.

Avant, Deborah. *Political Institutions and Military Change: Lessons from Peripheral Wars*. Ithaca: Cornell University Press, 1994.

Bar-Joseph, Uri. "The Hidden Debate: The Formation of Nuclear Doctrines in the Middle East." *Journal of Strategic Studies* 5, no. 2 (June 1982).

Barnaby, Frank. *The Invisible Bomb: The Nuclear Arms Race in the Middle East*. London: I. B. Tauris and Company, 1989.

Barnett, Michael N. *Confronting the Costs of War: Military Power, State and Society in Egypt and Israel*. Princeton: Princeton University Press, 1992.

Barnett, Michael N., and Shibley Telhami, eds. *Identity and Foreign Policy in the Middle East*. Ithaca: Cornell University Press, 2002.

Beaton, Leonard, and John Maddox. *The Spread of Nuclear Weapons*. London: Institute for Strategic Studies, 1962.

Beattie, Kirk. *Egypt during the Nasser Years: Ideology, Politics, and Civil Society*. Boulder: Westview Press, 1994.

Berger, Thomas U. *Cultures of Antimilitarism: National Security in Germany and Japan*. Baltimore: Johns Hopkins University Press, 1998.

———. "From Sword to Chrysanthemum: Japan's Culture of Anti-militarism." *International Security* 17, no. 4 (Spring 1993).

Bhatia, Shyam. *Nuclear Rivals in the Middle East*. New York: Routledge, 1988.

"Biological Weapons." *Egypt Country Overview*. Washington, D.C.: Nuclear Threat Initiative, 2004. Accessed April 15, 2004, available from http://www.nti.org/e_research/profiles/Egypt/index.html.

Boese, Wade. "Germany Raises No-First-Use Issue at NATO Meeting." *Arms Control Today* (November–December 1988).

"Bomb: From Hiroshima to . . . , The." *Newsweek*, 9 August 1965, 53.

Bordens, Kenneth S., and Irwin A. Horowitz. *Social Psychology*, 2d ed. Mahwah, N.J.: Lawrence Erlbaum, 2002.

Boutwell, Jeffrey. *The German Nuclear Dilemma*. Ithaca: Cornell University Press, 1990.

Boyer, Paul. "From Activism to Apathy: The American People and Nuclear Weapons, 1963–1980." *Journal of American History* 70, no. 4 (March 1984): 821–44.

Bradsher, Keith. "India Official Says Qaddafi Sought Atom-Arms Technology in '70s." *New York Times*, 10 October 1991, A11.

Braut-Hegghammer, Malfrid. "Libya's Nuclear Turnaround: Perspectives from Tripoli." *Middle East Journal* 62, no. 1 (2008).

Brewer, M. B., and R. J. Brown. "Intergroup Relations." In D. T. Gilbert and S. T. Fiske, eds., *The Handbook of Social Psychology*, Vol. 2, 4th ed. New York: McGraw Hill, 1998.

Buckley, Brian. *Canada's Early Nuclear Policy: Fate, Chance and Character*. Montreal: McGill-Queen's University Press, 2000.

Bunn, George. *Arms Control by Committee: Managing Negotiations with the Russians*. Stanford: Stanford University Press, 1992.

———. "The Status of Norms against Nuclear Testing." *Nonproliferation Review* (Winter 1999): 20–32.

Bunn, George, and Jean du Preez. "More Than Words: The Value of U.S. Non-Nuclear-Use Promises." *Arms Control Today* (July–August 2007).

Burrell, R. Michael, and Abbas R. Kelidar. *Egypt: The Dilemmas of a Nation, 1970–1977*. Beverly Hills: Sage, 1977.

"Bush Hails Partnership with India." BBC News, 3 March 2006. Accessed September 20, 2007, available at http://news.bbc.co.uk/2/hi/south_asia/4770946.stm.

Butt, Gerald. "Colonel Gaddafi's Libya." BBC News, 15 May 2006. Accessed July 15, 2006, available from http://news.bbc.co.uk/2/hi/middle_east/3336059.stm.

Campbell, Kurt M. "Nuclear Proliferation Beyond Rogues." Washington Quarterly 26, no. 1 (Winter 2002–3): 7–15.

Campbell, Kurt, Robert Einhorn, and Mitchell Reiss, eds. The Nuclear Tipping Point: Why States Reconsider Their Nuclear Choices. Washington, D.C.: Brookings, 2004.

Campbell, Kurt, and Tsuyoshi Sunohara. "Japan: Thinking the Unthinkable." In Kurt Campbell, Robert Einhorn, and Mitchell Reiss, eds., The Nuclear Tipping Point: Why States Reconsider Their Nuclear Choices. Washington, D.C.: Brookings, 2004.

Carson, Cathryn. Going Nuclear: Science, Politics, and Risk in the Federal Republic of Germany in the 1950s. BMW Center for German and European Studies Working Paper N.8-04. March 2004.

Chafez, Glenn. "The End of the Cold War and the Future of Nuclear Proliferation: An Alternative to the Neorealist Perspective." In Zachary Davis and Benjamin Frankel, eds., The Proliferation Puzzle: Why Nuclear Weapons Spread, 129–58. London: Frank Cass, 1993.

———. "The Political Psychology of the Nuclear Nonproliferation Regime." Journal of Politics 57, no. 3 (August 1995): 743–75.

Checkel, Jeffrey T. "The Constructivist Turn in International Relations Theory." World Politics 50 (January 1998): 324–48.

"Chemical and Biological Weapons Programs: Possession and Programs Past and Present." Monterey, Calif.: Center for Nonproliferation Studies, 2004. Accessed May 26, 2004, available from http://cns.miis.edu/research/cbw/possess.htm#14.

"Chemical Weapons." Egypt Country Overview. Washington, D.C.: Nuclear Threat Initiative, 2004. Accessed April 15, 2004, available from http://www.nti.org/e_research/profiles/Egypt/index.html.

Chinworth, Michael W. Inside Japan's Defense. London: Brassey's, 1992.

Cialdini, Robert B. Influence: Science and Practice, 4th ed. Boston: Allyn and Bacon, 2001.

Cialdini, R. B., and M. R. Trost. "Social Influence: Social Norms, Conformity, and Compliance." In D. T. Gilbert and S. T. Fiske, eds., The Handbook of Social Psychology, Vol. 2, 4th ed., 151–92. New York: McGraw Hill, 1998.

Cioc, Mark. Pax Atomica: The Nuclear Defense Debate in West Germany During the Adenauer Era. New York: Columbia University Press, 1988.

Cirincione, Joseph. "Bush Unleashes the Nuclear Beast." Los Angeles Times, 15 October 2006.

Cirincione, Joseph, Jon Wolfsthal, and Miriam Rajkumar. *Deadly Arsenals: Nuclear, Biological, and Chemical Threats*. 2nd ed. Washington, D.C.: Carnegie Endowment for International Peace, 2005.

Clarke, Richard. *Against All Enemies: Inside America's War on Terror*. New York: Free Press, 2004.

Clearwater, John. *Canadian Nuclear Weapons*. Toronto: Dundurn Press, 1998.

Clemons, Steven. "Paralysis in U.S.-Japan Policy." *Daily Yomiuri*, 4 February 1999.

Coffey, J. I. "Strategy, Alliance Policy, and Nuclear Proliferation." *Orbis* 11, no. 4 (Winter 1968).

———. "Threat, Reassurance, and Nuclear Proliferation." Paper prepared for the American Society of International Law, Panel on Nuclear Energy and World Order, February 1970.

Cohen, Avner. "Patterns of Nuclear Opacity in the Middle East: Understanding the Past, Implications for the Future." In Tariq Rauf, ed., *Regional Approaches to Curbing Nuclear Proliferation in the Middle East and South Asia*, Aurora Papers No. 16. Ottawa: Canadian Centre for Global Security, 1992.

———. *Israel and the Bomb*. New York: Columbia University Press, 1998.

Cole, Paul M. *Atomic Bombast: Nuclear Weapon Decisionmaking in Sweden, 1945–1972*, Occasional Paper no. 26. Washington, D.C.: Henry L. Stimson Center, 1996.

Cooley, John K. "Qadhafi's Great Aim for Libya Is a Nuclear Capability of Its Own." *Christian Science Monitor*, 12 November 1980, 14.

Crampton, Thomas. "Qaddafi Son Sets Out Economic Reforms: Libya Plans to Shed Old and Begin a New Era." *International Herald Tribune*, 28 January 2005.

Crawford, Neta. "The Passion of World Politics: Propositions on Emotion and Emotional Relationships." *International Security* 24, no. 4 (Spring 2000): 116–56.

Danielson, Rob. "Egypt's Nuclear Program." Unpublished graduate thesis, Naval Postgraduate School, Monterey, Calif., 2007.

Davis, Zachary, and Benjamin Frankel, eds. *The Proliferation Puzzle: Why Nuclear Weapons Spread*. London: Frank Cass, 1993.

"Defense Agency Sees 'No Merit' in Japan Going Nuclear." *Kyodo News Service*, 20 February 2003.

de Klerk, Piet. "Notes on History and Meaning of the NPT." In Huub Jaspers, ed., *Beyond the Bomb: The Extension of the Nonproliferation Treaty and the Future of Nuclear Weapons*. Amsterdam: Colophon Publishers, 1996.

De Young, Karen. "Swedish Officials Defend A-Research." *Washington Post*, 5 May 1985, A1.

"Diet to Get Nuclear Nonproliferation Pact." *Facts on File World New Digest*, 24 January 1976, 51 C2.

Di Filippo, Anthony. "Can Japan Craft an International Disarmament Policy?" Paper presented at the 1999 International Studies Association Convention, Washington, D.C.

"Discretion Needed in Extension of NPT." *Asahi News Service,* 1 September 1993.

Dower, John. *Embracing Defeat: Japan in the Wake of World War II.* New York: W. W. Norton, 1999.

Dunne, Michele. *Libya: Security Is Not Enough.* Carnegie Endowment for International Peace Policy Brief 32 (October 2004).

"Egypt and Nuclear Power: Nuclear Succession." *Economist,* 28 September 2006.

"Egypt to Start Building Nuclear Power Plants Soon, Minister Says." *Associated Press,* 24 September 2006.

"Egypt Unveils Nuclear Power Plan." BBC News, 25 September 2006.

"Egyptian Minister of Egypt's Nuclear Program." *Al-Majallah* (London), 2 January 2000, 15.

"Egyptian President's Son Proposes Developing Nuclear Energy." *Associated Press,* 19 September 2006.

Einhorn, Robert. "Egypt: Frustrated but Still on a Non-Nuclear Course." Washington, D.C.: Center for Strategic and International Studies, 2004.

El-Hennawy, Noha. "Power to the People." *Egypt Today* (November 2006). Accessed September 7, 2007, available at http://www.egypttoday.com/article.aspx?ArticleID =7036.

Enders, Thomas, Holger H. Mey, and Michael Ruhle. "The New Germany and Nuclear Weapons." In Patrick J. Garrity and Steven A. Maaranen, eds. *Nuclear Weapons in the Changing World: Perspectives from Europe, Asia, and North America.* New York: Plenum, 1992.

Erickson, Stanley A. "Economic and Technological Trends Affecting Nuclear Nonproliferation." *Nonproliferation Review* (Summer 2001): 40–54.

Evron, Yair. "The Arab Position in the Nuclear Field: A Study of Policies up to 1967." *Cooperation and Conflict* 8 (1973).

———. "A Nuclear Balance of Deterrence in the Middle East." *New Outlook* 18 (July–August 1975): 15–19.

Fahmy, Nabil. "Egypt's Disarmament Initiative." *Bulletin of Atomic Scientists* 26, no. 9 (November 1990): 9–10.

Feldman, Shai. *Israeli Nuclear Deterrence.* New York: Columbia University Press, 1983.

———. *Nuclear Weapons and Arms Control in the Middle East.* Cambridge, Mass.: MITPress, 1997.

Finnemore, Martha. *National Interests in International Society.* Ithaca: Cornell University Press, 1996.

———. "Norms, Culture and World Politics: Insights from Sociology's Institutional-ism." *International Organization* 50, no. 2 (Spring 1996): 325–47.

Finnemore, Martha, and Kathryn Sikkink. "International Norm Dynamics and Politi-cal Change." *International Organization* 52, no. 4 (August 1998): 887–917.

Fischer, David. *History of the International Atomic Energy Agency: The First Forty Years.* Vienna: IAEA, 1997.

Fishbein, M., and I. Ajzen. *Belief, Attitude, Intention and Behavior: An Introduction to Theory and Research.* Reading, Mass.: Addison-Wesley, 1975.

Fisher, Cathleen S. "Preface." In Paul M. Cole, *Atomic Bombast: Nuclear Weapon Decisionmaking in Sweden, 1945–1972,* Occasional Paper no. 26. Washington, D.C.: Henry L. Stimson Center, 1996.

———. *Reformation and Resistance: Nongovernmental Organizations and the Future of Nuclear Weapons,* Report no. 29. Washington, D.C.: Henry L. Stimson Center, May 1999.

Flapan, Simha. "Nuclear Power in the Middle East: The Critical Years." *New Outlook* (October 1974).

Flank, Steven. "Exploding the Black Box: The Historical Sociology of Nuclear Prolif-eration." *Security Studies* 3, no. 2 (Winter 1993/94): 259–94.

Forgas, Joseph P., and Kipling D. Williams, eds. *Social Influence: Direct and Indirect Processes.* Philadelphia: Psychology Press, 2001.

Frankel, Benjamin. "The Brooding Shadow: Systemic Incentives and Nuclear Weap-ons Proliferation." In Zachary Davis and Benjamin Frankel, eds., *The Proliferation Puzzle: Why Nuclear Weapons Spread.* London: Frank Cass, 1993.

Frankel, Joseph. "Domestic Politics of Japan's Foreign Policy: A Case Study of the Ratification of the Non-Proliferation Treaty." *British Journal of International Stud-ies,* no. 3 (1977).

French, Howard W. "Taboo against Nuclear Arms Is Being Challenged in Japan." *New York Times,* 9 June 2002, 1.

Fukumoto, Yoko. "G-7 Failed to Declare Indefinite Extension of NPT." *Mainchi Daily News,* 9 July 1993.

Furukawa, Katsuhisa. "Nuclear Option, Arms Control, and Extended Deterrence." In Benjamin Self and Jeffrey Thompson, eds., *Japan's Nuclear Option: Security, Politics and Policy in the 21st Century.* Washington, D.C.: Henry L. Stimson Center, 2003.

Galadari, Mohammed A. R. "Which Way Reforms in Libya?" *Khaleej Times,* 11 March 2006.

Garrity, Patrick J., and Steven A. Maaranen, eds. *Nuclear Weapons in the Changing World: Perspectives from Europe, Asia, and North America.* New York: Plenum, 1992.

Garwood, Paul. "End of Sanctions Opens Doors for Libya." *Associated Press*, 13 September 2003.

Gelb, Leslie H. "Nuclear Nations Agree to Tighten Export Controls." *New York Times*, 16 July 1984, A1.

Gilbert, D. T., and S. T. Fiske, eds. *The Handbook of Social Psychology, Vol. 2*, 4th ed. New York: McGraw Hill, 1998.

Glosserman, Brad, and Yumiko Nakagawa. "Nuclear Taboo Remains Strong." *Japan Times*, 25 June 2002, 2.

Goldblat, Jozef, ed. *Non-Proliferation: The Why and The Wherefore*. Philadelphia: Taylor and Francis, 1985.

Goldgeier, James, and Michael McFaul. "A Tale of Two Worlds: Core and Periphery in the Post–Cold War Era." *International Organization* 46, no. 2 (Spring 1992): 467–91.

Gose, Mark N. "The New Germany and Nuclear Weapons: Options for the Future." *Airpower Journal* (Special Edition 1996).

Green, Michael J., and Katsuhisa Furukawa. "New Ambitions, Old Obstacles: Japan and Its Search for an Arms Control Strategy." *Arms Control Today* (July/August 2000).

Gregory, Barbara M. "Egypt's Nuclear Program: Assessing Supplier-Based and Other Developmental Constraints." *Nonproliferation Review* (Fall 1995): 20–27.

Gwertzman, Bernard. "Lisa Anderson: Qaddafi, Desperate to End Libya's Isolation, Sends a 'Gift' to President Bush." Council on Foreign Relations Interview, 22 December 2003. Accessed September 4, 2006, available from http://www.cfr.org/publication/6617/.

Haggard, Stephen, and Beth A. Simmons. "Theories of International Regimes." *International Organization* 41, no. 3 (Summer 1987): 491–517.

Hammad, Fawzi, and Adel Mohammed Ahmed. "A Comparative Study of Nuclear-Weapon-Free Zones." *Al-Siyassa Al-Dawliya (The International Politics Journal)*, no. 144 (April 2001). Accessed on April 14, 2004, available at http://www.siyassa.org.eg/esiyassa/ahram/2001/4/1/STUD2.HTM.

Hanley, Charles J. "Japan and the Bomb: 'Never Say Never.'" *Chicago Sun-Times*, 7 May 1995, 34.

Harris, Lillian Craig, ed. *Egypt: Internal Challenges and Regional Stability*. London: Routledge, 1988.

Harrison, Selig S. "Japan and Nuclear Weapons." In Selig S. Harrison, ed., *Japan's Nuclear Future: The Plutonium Debate and East Asian Security*. New York: Carnegie Endowment for International Peace, 1996.

———, ed. *Japan's Nuclear Future: The Plutonium Debate and East Asian Security*. New York: Carnegie Endowment for International Peace, 1996.

Heikal, Mohammed Hassanein. *The Cairo Documents*. Garden City: Doubleday, 1973.

Herf, Jeffrey. "War, Peace and the Intellectuals: The West German Peace Movement." *International Security* 10, no. 4 (Spring 1986): 172–200.

Hesseldahl, Arik. "Time to Go Back to Libya." *Forbes*, 3 July 2002. Accessed September 4, 2006, available from http://www.forbes.com/2002/03/07/0307libya.html.

Hibbs, Mark. "Fukushima Links Its Critique of MOX to Latest Japanese Weapons Debate." *Nuclear Fuel* 27, no. 12 (June 10, 2002): 5.

Hinnebusch, Raymond A. *Egyptian Politics under Sadat: The Post-Populist Development of an Authoritarian-Modernizing State*. Cambridge: Cambridge University Press, 1985.

Hochman, Dafna. "Rehabilitating a Rogue: Libya's WMD Reversal and Lessons for US Policy." *Parameters* (Spring 2006).

Hufbauer, Gary Clyde, Jeffrey Schott, and Kimberly Ann Elliott. *Economic Sanctions Reconsidered*, 2nd ed. Washington, D.C.: Institute for International Economics, 1990.

Hughes, Llewelyn. "Why Japan Will Not Go Nuclear (Yet)." *International Security* 31, no. 4 (Spring 2007): 67–96.

Hurst, Lynda. "Is Mideast on Brink of an Arms Race?" *Toronto Star*, 27 January 2007.

Hymans, Jacques E. C. "Isotopes and Identity: Australia and the Nuclear Weapons Option, 1949–1999." *Nonproliferation Review* 7, no. 1 (Spring 2000): 1–23.

———. "Theories of Nuclear Proliferation: The State of the Field." *Nonproliferation Review* 13, no. 3 (November 2006).

"IAEA Chief El Baradei Cites Libya's Cooperation." *IAEA Staff Report*, 24 February 2004. Accessed September 6, 2006, available from http://www.iaea.org/NewsCenter/News/2004/libya-coop2402.html.

Indyk, Martin S. "The Iraq War Did Not Force Qadhafi's Hand." *Financial Times*, 9 March 2004.

"Iran Threatens to Resume Uranium Enrichment." *Global Security Newswire*, National Journal Group, 27 May 2004.

Ito, Masami. "Abe Says No to Nukes but Allows Discussion." *Japan Times*, 9 November 2006.

Izumi, Hajime, and Katsuhisa Furukawa. "Not Going Nuclear: Japan's Response to North Korea's Nuclear Test." *Arms Control Today* (June 2007).

Jabber, Paul. *A Nuclear Middle East: Infrastructure, Likely Military Postures and Prospects for Strategic Stability*, Center for Arms Control and International Security Working Paper No. 6. Los Angeles: University of California, 1977.

"Japan: Bombs Away." *Economist*, 29 May 1976, 62.

"Japan Debated Nuke Arsenal." CNN.com, 21 February 2003. Accessed January 12, 2004, available from http://taiwansecurity.org/CNN/2003/CNN-022103.htm.

"Japanese Papers Rap NPT Issues in G-7 Declaration." *Kyodo News Service*, 9 July 1993.

"Japan's DPJ Leader Hatoyama Raps Remarks against Non-Nuclear Policy." *Agence France-Press*, 1 June 2002, 1.

Japan's Proactive Peace and Security Strategies — Including the Question of "Nuclear Umbrella." National Institute for Research Advancement (NIRA) Research Report No. 20000005. Tokyo: NIRA, March 2001.

Jaspers, Huub, ed. *Beyond the Bomb: The Extension of the Nonproliferation Treaty and the Future of Nuclear Weapons*. Amsterdam: Colophon Publishers, 1996.

Jawad, Rana. "Libyan Entrepreneurs Enjoy Boom." BBC News, 18 November 2005. Accessed July 15, 2006, available from http://news.bbc.co.uk/1/hi/world/africa/4443610.stm.

Jentleson, Bruce W., and Dalia Dassa Kaye. "Explaining Regional Security Cooperation and Its Limits in the Middle East." *Security Studies* 8, no. 1 (Autumn 1998).

Jervis, Robert. "Political Psychology: Some Challenges and Opportunities." *Political Psychology* 10, no. 3 (1989): 481–93.

Joffe, George. "Why Gaddafi Gave Up WMD," BBC News, 21 December 2003. Accessed July 7, 2006, available from http://news.bbc.co.uk/1/hi/world/africa/3338713.stm.

Johnston, Alastair Iain. "Treating International Institutions as Social Environments." *International Studies Quarterly* 45 (2001): 487–515.

Jones, Rodney W., and Mark G. McDonough. *Tracking Nuclear Proliferation*. Washington, D.C.: Brookings Institution Press, 1998.

Kaempfer, William, and Anton Lowenberg. "International Sanctions." *Journal of Economic Perspectives* 17, no. 4 (Autumn 2003).

Kamiya, Matake. "A Disillusioned Japan Confronts North Korea." *Arms Control Today* (May 2003).

——. "Nuclear Japan: Oxymoron or Coming Soon?" *Washington Quarterly* 26, no. 1 (Winter 2003).

Karawan, Ibrahim A. "Identity and Foreign Policy: The Case of Egypt." In Michael Barnett and Shibley Telhami, eds., *Identity and Foreign Policy in the Middle East*. Ithaca: Cornell University Press, 2002.

——. "Sadat and the Egyptian-Israeli Peace Revisited." *International Journal of Middle East Studies* 26 (1994): 187–95.

Kase, Yuri. "The Costs and Benefits of Japan's Nuclearization: An Insight into the 1968/70 Internal Report." *Nonproliferation Review* (Summer 2001): 55–68.

——. *The Evolution of Japan's Security Policy towards Nuclear Weapons: 1945–1998*. Ph.D. dissertation, University of Southampton, 1999.

Kats, Gregory. "Egypt." In Jozef Goldblat, ed. *Non-Proliferation: The Why and The Wherefore*. Philadelphia: Taylor and Francis, 1985.

Katz, James Everett, and Onkar S. Marwah, eds. *Nuclear Power in Developing Countries*. Lexington, Mass.: D. C. Heath and Company, 1982.

Katzenstein, Peter J. *Cultural Norms and National Security: Police and Military in Postwar Japan*. Ithaca: Cornell University Press, 1996.

——, ed. *The Culture of National Security: Norms and Identity in World Politics*. New York: Columbia University Press, 1996.

Katzenstein, Peter J., and Nobuo Okawara. "Japan's National Security: Structures, Norms and Policies." *International Security* 17, no. 4 (Spring 1993).

Kaye, Dalia Dassa. *Beyond the Handshake: Multilateral Cooperation in the Arab-Israeli Peace Process, 1991–1996*. New York: Columbia University Press, 2001.

——. *Europe, Syria and Weapons of Mass Destruction*. Policywatch no. 824. Washington, D.C.: Washington Institute, 2004.

Kelleher, Catherine. *Germany and the Politics of Nuclear Weapons*. New York: Columbia University Press, 1975.

Kelman, Herbert C. "Compliance, Identification, and Internalization: Three Processes of Attitude Change." *Journal of Conflict Resolution* 2, no. 1 (1958).

Kemp, Geoffrey. *The Control of the Middle East Arms Race*. Washington, D.C.: Carnegie Endowment for International Peace, 1991.

Kennedy, Bruce. "The Lucky Dragon." *CNN Interactive*. Accessed January 10, 2004, available from http://edition.cnn.com/SPECIALS/cold.war/episodes/08/spotlight/.

Keohane, Robert, and Lisa Martin. "The Promise of Institutionalist Theory." *International Security* 20, no. 1 (Summer 1995): 39–51.

Khan, Saira. *Nuclear Proliferation Dynamics in Protracted Conflict Regions: A Comparative Study of South Asia and the Middle East*. Burlington, Vt.: Ashgate, 2002.

Kier, Elizabeth, and Jonathan Mercer. "Setting Precedents in Anarchy: Military Intervention and Weapons of Mass Destruction." *International Security* 20, no. 4 (1996): 77–107.

Knopf, Jeffrey W. *Domestic Society and International Cooperation: The Impact of Protest on US Arms Control Policy*. Cambridge: Cambridge University Press, 1998.

Kotch, John B. "NATO Nuclear Arrangements in the Aftermath of MLF: Perspectives on a Continuing Dilemma." *Air University Review* (March–April 1967). Accessed September 18, 2006, available at http://www.airpower.maxwell.af.mil/airchronicles/aureview/1967/mar-apr/kotch.html.

Krasner, Stephen. "Structural Causes and Regime Consequences: Regimes as Intervening Variables." In Stephen Krasner, ed., *International Regimes*. Ithaca: Cornell University Press, 1983.

——, ed. *International Regimes*. Ithaca: Cornell University Press, 1983.

Kurosawa, Mitsuru. "Japan's View of Nuclear Weapons." Paper presented at U.S.-Japan Second Track Meeting on Arms Control, Disarmament, Nonproliferation, and Verification, Washington D.C., March 2006.

Kyodo News. "Abe's Pledge to Afghan Mission Raises Opposition's Ire." *Japan Times*, September 10, 2007. Accessed September 11, 2007, available at http://search.japantimes .co.jp/cgi-bin/nn20070910a2.html.

Lakin, Jessica, and Tanya Chartrand. "Using Nonconscious Behavioral Mimicry to Create Affiliation and Rapport." *Psychological Science* 14, no. 4 (July 2003): 334–40.

Landau, Emily B. "Egypt's Nuclear Dilemma." *Strategic Assessment* 5, no. 3 (November 2002).

Legro, Jeffrey, and Andrew Moravcsik. "Is Anybody Still a Realist?" *International Security* 24, no. 2 (Fall 1999): 5–55.

Leonard, James F., and Jan Prawitz. "The Middle East as a NWFZ or WMDFZ Application." *Pacifica Review* 11, no. 3 (October 1999).

Levine, John M., and E. Tory Higgins. "Shared Reality and Social Influence in Groups and Organizations." In Gabriel Mugny and Fabrizio Butera, eds., *Social Influence in Social Reality: Promoting Individual and Social Change*. Toronto: Hogrefe and Huber, 2001.

Levite, Ariel E. "Never Say Never Again: Nuclear Reversal Revisited." *International Security* 27, no. 3 (Winter 2002–3): 59–88.

"Libyan Leader Invites Bush Visit." Aljazeera.net, 20 August 2005. Accessed July 16, 2006, available from http://english.aljazeera.net/NR/exeres/7F4265FF-4070-43E5-B171-CF1C11933CF5.htm.

"Libya Nuclear Chronology: 1968–1979." National Threat Initiative. Accessed July 12, 2006, available from http://www.nti.org/e_research/profiles/Libya/4132_4135.html.

"Libya Nuclear Chronology: 1980–1989." National Threat Initiative. Accessed July 12, 2006, available from http://www.nti.org/e_research/profiles/Libya/4132_5203.html.

"Libya Nuclear Chronology: 1990–1999." National Threat Initiative. Accessed July 12, 2006, available from http://www.nti.org/e_research/profiles/Libya/4132_5204.html.

"Libya Nuclear Chronology: 2000–2003." National Threat Initiative. Accessed July 12, 2006, available from http://www.nti.org/e_research/profiles/Libya/4132_5205.html.

"Libya Purchased Nuclear Weapons Plans from Pakistan, Qadhafi's Son Says." *Global Security Newswire*, National Journal Group, 5 January 2004.

"Libya Set to Allow Nuclear Inspections." *Toronto Star*, 3 February 1992, A12.

"Libya's Nuclear Update: 2004." *Risk Report* 10, no. 2 (March–April 2004). Accessed July 16, 2006, available from http://www.wisconsinproject.org/countries/libya/libya-nuc.htm.

Lim, Robyn. "Nuclear Temptation in Japan." *International Herald Tribune*, 15 April 2002, 1.

Long, William J., and Suzette R. Grillot. "Ideas, Beliefs, and Nuclear Policies: The Cases of South Africa and Ukraine." *Nonproliferation Review* 7, no. 1 (Spring 2000): 24–40.

Mackby, Jenifer, and Walter Slocombe. "Germany: The Model Case, A Historical Imperative." In Kurt Campbell et al., eds., *The Nuclear Tipping Point: Why States Reconsider Their Nuclear Choices*. Washington, D.C.: Brookings, 2004.

Maeda, Naohito. "Shinzo Abe." *Asahi Shimbun*, 12 June 2002, 1.

Makhijani, Arjun, and Brice Smith. "NATO's Nuclear Conflict." *Science for Democratic Action* 12, no. 1 (December 2003).

Maki, John, ed. *Japan's Commission on the Constitution: The Final Report*. Seattle: University of Washington Press, 1980.

Mearsheimer, John. "Back to the Future: Instability in Europe after the Cold War." *International Security* 15, no. 1 (Summer 1990): 5–56.

———. "The False Promise of International Institutions." *International Security* 19, no. 3 (Winter 1994–95): 5–49.

———. Lecture at the George Washington University Political Science Department, October 31, 2002.

Meier, Oliver. "An End to U.S. Tactical Nuclear Weapons in Europe?" *Arms Control Today* (July–August 2006). Accessed September 12, 2006, available from http://www .armscontrol.org/act/2006_07-08/NewsAnalysis.asp.

"Menem Inaugurates a Nuclear Reactor in Egypt." *Nuclear Developments* (Monterey: Center for Nonproliferation Studies), 4 February 1998, 1.

Mercer, Jonathan. "Anarchy and Identity." *International Organization* 49 (Spring 1995): 229–52.

Meyer, Stephen M. *The Dynamics of Nuclear Nonproliferation*. Chicago: University of Chicago Press, 1984.

"Mideast Nuclear Deals." *New York Times*, 19 June 1974, 44.

Miller, Judith. "How Qadhafi Lost His Groove." *Wall Street Journal*, 16 May 2006, A14.

Ministry of Foreign Affairs of the Arab Republic of Egypt. *Egypt and the Treaty on the Non-Proliferation of Nuclear Weapons*. Cairo: State Information Service, 1981.

Mitchell, Ronald B. "International Control of Nuclear Proliferation: Beyond Carrots and Sticks." *Nonproliferation Review* (Fall 1997): 40–52.

Mizumoto, Kazumi. "Non-Nuclear and Nuclear Disarmament Policies of Japan." Unpublished paper, Hiroshima Peace Institute, 2003.

"More Than 40 Countries Could Have Nuclear Weapons Know-How." *Global Security Newswire*, National Journal Group, 22 September 2004.

"Mubarak Says He Turned Down Offer to Buy Nuclear Bomb," *Associated Press*, June 19, 1998.

Mugny, Gabriel, and Fabrizio Butera, eds. *Social Influence in Social Reality: Promoting Individual and Social Change*. Toronto: Hogrefe and Huber, 2001.

Müller, Harald. "German National Identity and WMD Proliferation." *Nonproliferation Review* (Summer 2003): 1–20.

Müller, Harald, David Fischer, and Wolfgang Kötter. *Nuclear Non-Proliferation and Global Order*. Oxford: Oxford University Press, 1994.

Müller, Harald, Alexander Kelle, Katja Frank, Sylvia Meier, and Annette Schaper. "The German Debate on Nuclear Weapons and Disarmament." *Washington Quarterly* 20, no. 3 (Summer 1997).

Myrdal, Alva. *The Game of Disarmament*. New York: Pantheon, 1982.

Nabeshima, Keizo. "Even Nuclear Talk Distracts." *Japan Times*, October 30, 2006. Accessed August 23, 2007, available at http://search.japantimes.co.jp/cgi-bin/eo20061030kn.html.

Nashif, Taysir N. *Nuclear Warfare in the Middle East: Dimensions and Responsibilities*. Princeton: Kingston Press, 1984.

"Nasser Threatens Israel on A-Bomb." *New York Times*, 24 December 1960, 1.

Nasu, Masamota. *Hiroshima: A Tragedy Never to Be Repeated*. Tokyo: Fukuinkan Shoten, 1998.

"New Qadhafi, The" (transcript). 60 Minutes II, CBS News, 10 March 2004. Accessed July 15, 2006, available at http://www.cbsnews.com/stories/2004/03/09/60II/printable604971.shtml.

Nishihara, Masashi. "North Korea's Trojan Horse." *Washington Post*, 14 August 2003, A19.

"No More Hiroshimas, No More Nagasakis: History of the Movement against A- and H-Bomb." *What Is Gensuikin?* Accessed January 22, 2004, available from http://www.gensuikin.org/english/whatis.html.

"North Korea Says 'Arms, Not Words' Appropriate for Dealing with Japan." *Agence France Presse*, 11 October 2003.

"November Opinion Polls." *Yomiuri Shimbun*, November 2007, *Mansfield Asian Opinion Poll Database*. Accessed June 7, 2007, available at http://www.mansfieldfdn.org/polls/poll-06-18.htm.

"Nuclear Activities." *Arms Control Today* (March 1995): 33–36.

"Nuclear Power for Cairo." *New York Times*, 17 June 1974, 30.

"Nuclear Program Path Strewn with Obstacles." *Nuclear Developments* (Monterey: Center for Nonproliferation Studies), 4 February 1998, 12.

Ogilvie-White, Tanya. "Is There a Theory of Nuclear Proliferation? An Analysis of the Contemporary Debate." *Nonproliferation Review* (Fall 1996).

"Orchestrating Libya's Metamorphosis." *Tufts E-news*, 10 January 10, 2005. Accessed July 15, 2006, available from http://chalcedony.tccs.tufts.edu/scripts/phpprint/phpprint.php.

Oros, Andrew. "Godzilla's Return: The New Nuclear Politics in an Insecure Japan." In Benjamin Self and Jeffrey Thompson, eds., *Japan's Nuclear Option: Security, Politics and Policy in the 21st Century*. Washington, D.C.: Henry L. Stimson Center, 2003.

Ota, Masakatsu. *Will Japan Keep Renouncing Nuclear Weapons in the Coming Century? Lessons from the 1960s to Deter the Decision to 'Go Nuclear.'* Program on Global Security Disarmament, Issue Brief 2, August 2000. Accessed January 5, 2004), available from http://www.bsos.umd.edu/pgsd/publications/issbrief2PGSD.htm.

Ottaway, David B. "South Africa Agrees to Treaty Curbing Nuclear Weapons." *Washington Post*, 28 June 1991, A25.

Pace, Eric. "Anwar el-Sadat, the Daring Arab Pioneer of Peace With Israel." *New York Times*, 7 October 1981, A10.

Pajak, Roger F. "Nuclear Status and Policies of the Middle East Countries." *International Affairs* 59, no. 4 (Autumn 1983).

"Pakistan's Nuclear Weapons." Globalsecurity.org. Accessed August 17, 2007, available from http://www.globalsecurity.org/wmd/world/pakistan/nuke.htm.

Pande, Savita. "Scope for Nuclear Weapon Free Zone in Central and Eastern Europe." *Strategic Analysis* 22, no. 7 (October 1998). Accessed July 7, 2006, available from http://www.ciaonet.org/olj/sa/sa_98pns01.html.

Panofsky, Wolfgang K. H. "Dismantling the Concept of 'Weapons of Mass Destruction.'" *Arms Control Today* (April 1998). Accessed April 15, 2004, available from http://www.armscontrol.org/act/1998_04/wkhp98.asp.

Pape, Robert A. "Why Economic Sanctions Still Do Not Work." *International Security* 23, no. 1 (Summer 1998): 66–77.

Paul, Anthony. "Explosive Talk." *Courier Mail* (Queensland, Australia), 13 April 2002, 30.

Paul, T. V. *Power versus Prudence: Why Nations Forgo Nuclear Weapons.* Quebec City: McGill-Queen's University Press, 2000.

Payne, Rodger A. "Persuasion, Frames, and Norm Construction." *European Journal of International Relations* 7, no. 1 (March 2001): 37–62.

Perkovich, George. *India's Nuclear Bomb: The Impact on Global Proliferation.* Berkeley: University of California Press, 1999.

Perloff, Richard. *Dynamics of Persuasion.* Hillsdale, N.J.: Lawrence Erlbaum, 1993.

Petty, Richard E., and Duane T. Wegener. "Attitude Change: Multiple Roles for Persuasion Variables." In D. T. Gilbert and S. T. Fiske, eds., *The Handbook of Social Psychology, Vol. 2,* 4th ed., 323–90. New York: McGraw Hill, 1998.

Pranger, Robert J., and Dale R. Tahtinen. *Nuclear Threat in the Middle East,* Foreign Affairs Study no. 23. Washington, D.C.: American Enterprise Institute, 1975.

Prawitz, Jan. *From Nuclear Option to Non-Nuclear Promotion: The Sweden Case,* Research Report 20. Stockholm: Swedish Institute of International Affairs, 1995.

Price, Richard, and Nina Tannenwald. "Norms and Deterrence: The Nuclear and Chemical Weapons Taboos." In Peter J. Katzenstein, ed., *The Culture of National Security: Norms and Identity in World Politics.* New York: Columbia University Press, 1996.

"Qadhafi: Arab Nationalism Is Dead." Aljazeera.net, 5 October 2003. Accessed September 4, 2006, available from http://english.aljazeera.net/NR/exeres/ D46CAoDo-E3C3-40D2-B719-E91B442982A1.htm.

"Qadhafi Calls for Self-Reliance." Aljazeera.net, 28 August 2006. Accessed September 8, 2006, available from http://english.aljazeera.net/NR/exeres/ 940D71D9-31B8-4CB3-AE87-B11178A701BE.htm.

"Qadhafi's Son Tells Al-Hayat: 'Libya Must Be a Democratic and Open Country.'" MEMRI Special Dispatch Series, no. 685 (March 24, 2004). Accessed July 15, 2006, available at http://memri.org/bin/opener.cgi?Page=archives&ID=SP68504.

Qanawati, Mahmud Al-. "Nuclear Developments." Al-Ahram (Cairo), 13 October 1989, 8.

Quester, George. The Politics of Nuclear Proliferation. Baltimore: Johns Hopkins University Press, 1973.

Rauf, Tariq, ed. Regional Approaches to Curbing Nuclear Proliferation in the Middle East and South Asia, Aurora Papers no. 16. Ottawa: Canadian Centre for Global Security, 1992.

Reiss, Mitchell. Bridled Ambition: Why Countries Constrain Their Nuclear Capabilities. Washington, D.C.: Woodrow Wilson Center Press, 1995.

———. Without the Bomb: The Politics of Nuclear Nonproliferation. New York: Columbia University Press, 1988.

"Report: Japan Looked into Developing Nuclear Warhead." AP News, 26 December 2006.

Robbins, James. "Libya 'Let Down' by West." BBC News, 2 March 2007. Accessed September 26, 2007, available at http://news.bbc.co.uk/2/hi/africa/6413813.stm.

Ronen, Yehudit. "Libya's Rising Star: Saif Al-Islam and Succession." Middle East Policy 12, no. 3 (Fall 2005).

Rublee, Maria Rost. "Egypt's Nuclear Weapons Program: Lessons Learned." Nonproliferation Review 13, no. 3 (2006): 555–67.

———. "Taking Stock of the Nuclear Nonproliferation Regime: Using Social Psychology to Understand Regime Effectiveness." International Studies Review 10, no. 3 (2008): 420–50.

"Rumors of Libyan Atomic Bomb Quest Raise Fears." Washington Post, 30 July 1979, A9.

Ryukichi Imai. "Post–Cold War Nuclear Non-Proliferation and Japan." In The United States, Japan, and the Future of Nuclear Weapons. Washington, D.C.: Carnegie Endowment for International Peace, 1995.

el-Sadat, Anwar. In Search of Identity. New York: Harper and Row, 1977.

Safty, Adel. "Proliferation, Balance of Power, and Nuclear Deterrence: Should Egypt Pursue a Nuclear Option?" International Studies 33, no. 1 (1996): 21–34.

Sagan, Scott D. "Why Do States Build Nuclear Weapons?" International Security 21, no. 3 (Winter 1996–97): 54–86.

Saif, Mostafa Elwi. "Egypt: A Non-Nuclear Proactivist in a Volatile Region." Paper presented at the Peace Research Institute's Conference, "The Domestic Roots of Proactivist Non-Nuclear Policy: A New Approach to Non-Proliferation," Bellagio, Italy, September 29–October 3, 1997.

"Saif Gaddafi's Vision for Libya." BBC News, 14 November 2004. Accessed July 15, 2006, available from http://news.bbc.co.uk/2/hi/africa/4014147.stm.

Salam, Mohammad Abdel. "The Arab Position on Iranian Nuclear Issues." Al-Ahram Center Egyptian Commentary, no. 21, 9 September 2004.

———. "Questions on the Egyptian Nuclear Programme." Al-Ahram Center Egyptian Commentary, no. 64, (29 September 2006). Available at http://www.ahram.org.eg/acpss/eng/ahram/2004/7/5/EGYP25.HTM.

Salama, Sammy. "Arab Attitudes toward Iran's Nuclear Program: Government Views vs. Public Opinion." WMD Insights (March 2006).

———. "Was Libyan WMD Disarmament a Significant Success for Nonproliferation?" Issue Brief, Monterey Institute of International Studies (September 2004). Accessed July 12, 2006, available at http://www.nti.or/e_research/e3_561.html.

Salama, Sammy, and Gina Gabrera-Farraj. "Renewed Egyptian Ambitions for a Peaceful Nuclear Program." WMD Insights (November 2006).

Salama, Sammy, and Khalid Hilal. "Egyptian Muslim Brotherhood Presses Government for Nuclear Weapons." WMD Insights (November 2006).

Salander, Henrik. "Statement at the Third Session of the Preparatory Committee for the 2000 Review Conference of the Parties to the Treaty on the Nonproliferation of Nuclear Weapons, Cluster 2 Safeguards." 12 May 1999. Accessed on July 15, 2006, available at http://www.basicint.org/nuclear/NPT/1999prepcom/99Cluster2_Sweden.htm.

Samaddar, Sujeet. "Thinking Proliferation Theoretically." Nonproliferation Review 12, no. 3 (November 2005): 435–71.

Sands, Derek. "Egypt Looks East for Nuke Power." United Press International, 13 November 2006.

"Saudi Nuclear Pact." Washington Post, 18 January 1981, A22.

Scheffran, Jürgen. "Nuclear Disarmament after the NPT Extension and the Role of NGOs." In Huub Jaspers, ed., Beyond the Bomb: The Extension of the Nonproliferation Treaty and the Future of Nuclear Weapons. Amsterdam: Colophon Publishers, 1996.

Schoenberger, Karl. "Citing North Korea, National Pride, Japan Reconsiders Nuclear Bombs." San Jose Mercury News, 19 June 2003, 2.

Schrafstetter, Susanna. "The Long Shadow of the Past: History, Memory and the Debate over West Germany and Nuclear Weapons." History and Memory 16, no. 1 (2004): 118–45.

"Secretary-General Calls for Renewed Vow Never to Repeat Hiroshima/Nagasaki Tragedies." United Nations Press Release SG/SM/7907 (June 8, 2001). Accessed July 28, 2004, available from http://www.un.org/News/Press/docs/2001/sgsm7907.doc.htm.

Selim, Mohammed El-Sayed. "Egypt." In James Everett Katz and Onkar S. Marwah, eds., *Nuclear Power in Developing Countries.* Lexington, Mass.: D. C. Heath and Company, 1982.

Self, Benjamin, and Jeffrey Thompson, eds. *Japan's Nuclear Option: Security, Politics and Policy in the 21st Century.* Washington, D.C.: Henry L. Stimson Center, 2003.

Sell, Susan. *Power and Ideas: North-South Politics of Intellectual Property and Antitrust.* Albany: State University of New York Press, 1998.

Sheikh, Ahmed. "Al-Qadhafi Son: Israel Is Not a Threat." Aljazeera.net, 8 January 2004. Accessed July 16, 2006, available from http://english.aljazeera.net/NR/exeres/ 19CA9DA6-59BD-4A13-9EAD-1F5DACECoB41.htm.

Shikaki, Khalil. "The Nuclearization Debates: The Cases of Israel and Egypt." *Journal of Palestine Studies* 14, no. 4 (Summer 1985): 77–91.

Siler, Michael. *Explaining Variation in Nuclear Outcomes among Southern States: Bargaining Analysis of U.S. Non-Proliferation Policies towards Brazil, Egypt, India and South Korea.* Ph.D. Dissertation, University of Southern California, 1992.

Smith, R. Jeffrey. "Facing a 'Messy' Nuclear Scenario: U.S. Seeks to Avert Sale or Theft of Soviet Arms, Technology." *Washington Post,* 26 November 1991, A17.

Smith, Roger K. "Explaining the Nonproliferation Regime: Anomalies for Contemporary International Relations." *International Organization* 41, no. 2 (Spring 1987): 253–81.

Solingen, Etel. "The Domestic Sources of Regional Regimes: The Evolution of Nuclear Ambiguity." *International Studies Quarterly* 38 (1994).

———. "The New Multilateralism and Nonproliferation: Bringing in Domestic Politics." *Global Governance* 1, no. 2 (May–August 1995).

———. *Nuclear Postures: Influencing 'Fence-Sitters' in the Post–Cold War Era,* Institute on Global Conflict and Cooperation Policy Paper no. 8. Berkeley: University of California Multi-Campus Research Unit, 1994.

———. "The Political Economy of Nuclear Restraint." *International Security* 19, no. 2 (Fall 1994).

"South Korean Ambassador Asks Japan to Explain Its Nuclear Treaty Stance." *Kyodo News Service,* 14 July 1993.

Speier, Hans. *German Rearmament and Atomic War.* Evanston: Row, Peterson, and Company, 1957.

Spiegel, Steven, Jennifer Kibbe, and Elizabeth Matthews, eds. *The Dynamics of Middle East Nuclear Proliferation.* Lewiston, N.Y.: Edwin Mellen Press, 2001.

"Spokesman Says Japan Not 'Preserving Nuclear Option.'" *Kyodo News Service,* 13 July 1993.

Stein, Janice Gross. "Proliferation, Non-Proliferation, and Anti-Proliferation: Egypt and Israel in the Middle East." In Steven Spiegel, Jennifer Kibbe, and Elizabeth Matthews, eds., *The Dynamics of Middle East Nuclear Proliferation.* Lewiston, N.Y.: Edwin Mellen Press, 2001.

Stevens, Rebecca, and Amin Tarzi. *Egypt and the Middle East Resolution at the NPT 2000 Review Conference.* Monterey, Calif.: Center for Nonproliferation Studies, 2000.

Stoessinger, John G. *Why Nations Go to War.* Belmont, Calif.: Thomson/Wadsworth, 2004.

Suskind, Ron. *The Price of Loyalty: George W. Bush, the White House, and the Education of Paul O'Neill.* New York: Simon and Schuster, 2004.

Ta 'imah, Muhammad. "National Conference to Discuss Nuclear Dangers and the Future of the Nonproliferation Treaty." *Al-Ahram,* 13 February 1995, FBIS-NES-95-092.

Takeyh, Ray. "The Rogue Who Came In from the Cold." *Foreign Affairs* 80, no. 3 (May–June 2001): 62–72.

Tannenwald, Nina. "The Nuclear Taboo: The United States and the Normative Basis of Nuclear Non-Use." *International Organization* 53, no. 3 (Summer 1999): 433–68.

———. "U.S. Arms Control Policy in a Time Warp." *Ethics and International Affairs* 15, no. 1 (2001): 51–72.

Taylor, Paul, and Louis Charbonneau. "EU Big Three Offered Iran Carrot for Nuclear Deal." *Reuters News Service,* 19 September 2003.

Terry, Deborah J., and Michael A. Hogg. "Attitudes, Behavior and Social Context: The Role of Norms and Group Membership in Social Influence Processes." In Joseph P. Forgas and Kipling D. Williams, eds., *Social Influence: Direct and Indirect Processes,* 253–70. Philadelphia: Psychology Press, 2001.

Tetlock, Philip, and James Goldgeier, "Human Nature and World Politics: Cognition, Identity, and Influence." *International Journal of Psychology* 35, no. 2 (2000): 87–96.

———. "Psychology and International Relations Theory." *Annual Review of Political Science* 4 (2001).

Tianri, Tang. "Maintain Sharp Vigilance against Shingo Nishimura's 'Nuclear Armament' Theory." *Liaowang International Review,* no. 44 (November 1999), translated by Xinhua Hong Kong Service.

"Tokyo Politician Warns Beijing It Can Go Nuke 'Overnight.'" *Agence France Presse,* 8 April 2002, 1.

"Toward a Nuclear-Weapon-Free World: The Need for a New Agenda." 9 June 1998. Accessed on April 14, 2004, available from http://www.basicint.org/nuclear/NPT/NAC/8nations.htm.

"Treaty on the Non-Proliferation of Nuclear Weapons: History." Monterey, Calif.: Center for Nonproliferation Studies, 2004. Accessed on July 28, 2004, available from http://cnsdl.miis.edu/npt/npt_3/history.htm.

2006 World Fact Book. Washington, D.C.: U.S. Central Intelligence Agency, 2006. Accessed September 23, 2006, available from https://www.cia.gov/cia/publications/factbook/rankorder/2178rank.html.

United States, Japan, and the Future of Nuclear Weapons, The. Washington, D.C.: Carnegie Endowment for International Peace, 1995.

"U.S. Opposes Lifting of Sanctions on Libya." CNN.com, 1 July 1999. Accessed September 3, 2006, available from http://www.cnn.com/US/9907/01/us.libya.

Van Dassen, Lars. "Sweden and the Making of Nuclear Nonproliferation: From Indecision to Assertiveness." SKI Report 98:16. Stockholm: SKI, 1998.

Van de Velde, James R. "Japan's Nuclear Umbrella: US Extended Nuclear Deterrence for Japan." *Journal of Northeast Asian Studies* 7, no. 1 (Winter 1988).

Van Ourdenaren, John. "Nuclear Weapons in the 1990s and Beyond." In Patrick J. Garrity and Steven A. Maaranen, eds. *Nuclear Weapons in the Changing World: Perspectives from Europe, Asia, and North America.* New York: Plenum, 1992.

Walsh, James. *Bombs Unbuilt: Power, Ideas and Institutions in International Politics.* Ph.D. dissertation, Massachusetts Institute of Technology, 2001.

Walt, Stephen M. *Origins of Alliances.* Ithaca: Cornell University Press, 1987.

Waltz, Kenneth. *The Spread of Nuclear Weapons: Why More May Be Better.* Adelphi Papers 171. London: International Institute for Strategic Studies 1981.

———. *Theory of International Politics.* New York: Random House, 1979.

Waterbury, John. *The Egypt of Nasser and Sadat.* Princeton: Princeton University Press, 1983.

Weart, Spencer. *Nuclear Fear: A History of Images.* Cambridge, Mass.: Harvard University Press, 1988.

Weiss, Leonard. "Pakistan: It's Déjà Vu All Over Again." *Bulletin of the Atomic Scientists* 60, no. 3 (May–June 2004).

Weissman, Steve, and Herbert Krosney. *The Islamic Bomb: The Nuclear Threat to Israel and the Middle East.* New York: Times Books, 1981.

Wendt, Alexander. "Anarchy Is What States Make of It." *International Organization* 46, no. 2 (Spring, 1992): 391–425.

———. *Social Theory of International Politics.* New York: Cambridge University Press, 1999.

"What Does Libya's Disarmament Teach about Rogue States?" *Middle East Institute Policy Brief* with Ambassador Martin S. Indyk and Ambassador Edward S. Walker, 7 April 2004. Accessed July 15, 2006, available at http://www.mideasti.org/articles/doc192.html.

Wier, Michael. "External Relations." In Lillian Craig Harris, ed., *Egypt: Internal Challenges and Regional Stability,* 79–99. London: Routledge, 1988.

Willenson, Kim. "Japan: Paradise Lost?" *Newsweek,* 23 June 1975, 36.

Wittner, Lawrence S. *One World or None: A History of the World Nuclear Disarmament Movement.* Stanford: Stanford University Press, 1993.

———. *Resisting the Bomb: A History of the World Nuclear Disarmament Movement, 1954–1970* (vol. 2 of *The Struggle against the Bomb*). Stanford: Stanford University Press, 1997.

Worsley, Peter. "On the Brink." In Peter Worsley and Kofi Buenor Hadjor, eds. *On the Brink: Nuclear Proliferation and the Third World.* London: Third World Communications, 1987.

Worsley, Peter, and Kofi Buenor Hadjor, eds. *On the Brink: Nuclear Proliferation and the Third World.* London: Third World Communications, 1987.

Wurst, Jim. "NPT Parties Criticized on Disarmament, Nonproliferation Compliance." *Global Security Newswire,* 26 April 2004.

———. "U.S. Says Nonproliferation Treaty Faces Crisis." *Global Security Newswire,* 27 April 2004.

Young, Michael, and Mark Schafer. "Is There Method in Our Madness? Ways of Assessing Cognition in International Relations." *International Studies Review* 42 (May 1998): 63–96.

INDEX

Abdel Rahman, Ibrahim Hilmy, 106, 108

Abe, Shinzo, 59, 75–76, 88, 239n123

ACRS (Working Group on Arms Control & Regional Security), 123–24, 135

Adenauer, Konrad, 185–87, 193, 196

African NWFZ, 125, 153

Albright, Madeline, 72

Al-Jamahiriya (newspaper), 160

Aly, Kamal Hassan, 248n125, 249n128

Amer, Abdel Hakim, 108, 111, 245n66

Anderson, Lisa, 168

antinuclear norm: activation of, 48; development, promotion, and support of, 35–37, 202–3, 215–16; and domestic policies, 212; in Egypt, 120–28; in Germany, 185, 188–89, 192, 195, 198–99; in Japan, 54–57, 59–61, 71–76, 79, 84–85, 92; in Sweden, 181, 184

Arab League, 102–3, 124–26, 129, 213

Arab Republic of Egypt. *See* Egypt

Arafat, Yasir, 159

Argentina, 7, 162, 221

Arnett, Eric, 174, 176, 212

Article 9, of Japanese Peace Constitution, 54–55, 62, 74, 86

Asahi Shimbun (newspaper), 63, 76

Aso, Taro, 60

attitude change: and constructivism, 17, 143; and similarity, 219–20; as social psychology concept, 3, 16; and subjective norms, 41

Atoms for Peace, 106

Australia, 14, 123, 221

Badri, Salim al-, 159

Baradei, Mohamed El, 165

Barnett, Michael, 113, 119–20

Beaton, Leonard, 197

Begin, Menachem, 101

behavioral change: mechanisms of, 17–19, 46–47; and normative influences, 40–42, 46–47, 49–50, 163–69, 221; as social psychology concept, 2–3, 216–17

Belarus, 7, 163

Belgium, nuclear cooperation of, with Egypt, 121

Berger, Thomas, 55, 199, 209

Berlusconi, Silvio, 154

Blix, Hans, 153

Boese, Wade, 189

Bolton, John, 213

Boyer, Paul, 35

Brazil, 7, 162, 214–15

Brewer, M. B., 18

Britain: and Libya, 153–55, 163–64; nuclear cooperation of, with Egypt, 121

Brown, R. J., 18

Bungei Shunju (periodical), 67

Bunn, George, 218

Bush, George W., 73, 77–78, 168, 215, 218, 220

Camp David summit/accords, 102–3
Campbell, Kurt, 88, 216–18
Canada, 30–31t, 121
Carson, Cathryn, 191
case studies criteria/methodology, 12, 28–33, 87–88, 136–37, 202
chemical-biological weapons, 24–25, 137–38, 146, 204, 252n194
Cheney, Dick, 214
China: and Egypt, 110, 113, 115; and Japan, 62–66, 74, 84; and North Korea, 219
Christian Democrat Party (Germany), 258n153
Cialdini, R. B., 45–46, 132
Cirincione, Joseph, 218
Clinton, Bill, 95, 155
coalitions: NAC, 125, 142–43, 145t, 213; and neoliberalism, 12–13, 39; Zangger, 39
Coffey, J. I., 185
Cohen, Avner, 123
Cold War, and nuclear forbearance, 7, 9, 73–74, 171
Cole, Paul, 171–72, 174, 176, 179
compliance monitoring, 3, 10, 25–27
Comprehensive Test Ban Treaty. See CTBT
conflict: lessons from, 220; as normative influence, 50–52, 84–85, 135, 164–65, 182, 196–97; as polarizing, 220
conformity, and international social environment, 165
constructivism: expectations of, for nuclear restraint, 27–28; and Japan's nuclear forbearance, 53; and national identity, 14–16, 85, 209, 227n39; and NPT, 208–11; on preference-driven change, 17; and security, 208; and social environment, 16, 148, 221–22;

theoretical analysis of, 92–95, 97t, 140–49, 208–9; theorists of, 3, 14. See also neoliberal institutionalism; realism
conventional weapons, as nuclear incentive, 177–79, 226n18
cost-benefit calculations: and behavioral change, 17, 197, 202; and constructivist expectations, 28, 93–94, 142–43; and security concerns, 14, 25, 87, 217; and social environment, 50–51, 82–83, 85–86, 134
CTBT (Comprehensive Test Ban Treaty), 39, 77, 93, 189, 199, 240n147
Cuban missile crisis, 36

de Gaulle, Charles, 186
decision-making. See nuclear decision-making
defense: in Japan, 59, 67, 69–70, 76, 240n157; in Sweden, 171–72, 177–78, 181
Democratic Party of Japan (DPJ), 59
democratic regimes: and behavioral consistency, 46–47, 216; Libya's view of, 159–60; and neoliberal institutionalism, 12; and nuclear decision-making, 31; and postwar Japan, 83–84
descriptive norms: and antinuclear norm, 202, 212–13; consistency of, 214; defined/described, 40, 128, 255n61; transmission of, 42–43, 77, 128–29, 162, 180–81, 193–94; United States propagates new version of, 213–14; weakening of, 213
diplomacy, 120–28; of Egypt, 104–5, 114–16, 119–28, 141–42, 210; of Germany, 192; of Japan, 68, 74, 89–90, 93, 98; Kissinger and Middle East,

101; of Libya, 167; of Palestine, 210; of Sweden, 172

disarmament: as goal of Egypt, 143–44, 213; as international norm, 39, 213; NAC, 125, 142–43, 145t; NPT, 36–37, 66, 213

Diwan, Roger, 157

domestic politics, and international social environment, 211–12

Dower, John, 55–56, 83

DPJ (Democratic Party of Japan), 59

du Preez, Jean, 218

Dunne, Michele, 165

economic development and nuclear decision-making: case studies, 156–57, 160, 167, 206–8, 254n51; in Egypt, 159; in Germany, 193, 198–99, 260n209; in Japan, 65–66, 73–74, 87–88, 91–93, 98, 207–8; and trade sanctions, 153, 156–57, 254n39

Egypt: and AEE, 106, 109–12, 117, 120–21; ambitions of, 125–28, 203, 261n5; and Arab League, 102, 104, 125–26; and Australia, 123; and Camp David summit/accords, 102–3; as case study, 203; chemical weapons program of, 99–100, 137–38, 144t, 146, 148; and China, 110, 113, 115; and diplomacy, 103–5, 114–16, 119, 125–26, 132–33; and disarmament initiatives, 123–24, 213, 217; economic deterioration in, 118; energy shortage in, 121, 128, 248–49n125; and IAEA, 115, 120; Inchas Nuclear Research Center, 110; and India, 121; and Indonesia, 121; and Iran, 126, 204–5; and Iraq, 102; and Israel, 100–103, 107–9, 117–18, 129, 133, 137, 204–5, 242n4; leadership

in UN, 103–5, 114–15; and Libya, 136; and Muslim Brotherhood, 127–28; and national identity, 102–3, 209–10; natural gas in, 122, 127, 249n134; and New Agenda Coalition, 184; as non-nuclear state, 31–32, 115–20, 249n140; norm linking by, 130–31; and NPT, 120–21, 128–35, 213, 242n14, 248n125; and nuclear forbearance, 168; and NWFZ resolution, 46, 125, 133, 207; refuses to sign Chemical Weapons Convention, 137; science/technology of, 111–12, 245n9; security dilemma of, 120, 145, 148; social environment of, 7, 14, 100–105, 242nn4; and Soviet Union, 107–10, 112, 115, 119–20, 145, 148, 251n191; theoretical analysis of decision-making of, 136–48, 144t, 204, 208–9; and UAR, 102; and UN Committee on Disarmament, 103; weapons of, 137, 204. See also United States: and Egypt
—nuclear decision-making of, 105–6, 120–28, 206; in 1950s, 106–8; in 1960s, 109–15, 130–33, 138, 143, 209; 1968–1973, 115–20, 139–40, 221; in 2000s, 126–35, 142–43, 145t, 146

Egyptian Council on Foreign Relations, 125

Egyptian Foreign Ministry, 132

Eighteen Nation Disarmament Committee (ENDC), 65, 103, 175–76

Einhorn, Robert, 110, 132, 136, 146

Eisenhower, Dwight D., 36, 59, 106, 173, 181

Eklund, Sigvard, 175

El Baradei, Mohamed, 165

ENDC (Eighteen Nation Disarmament Committee), 65, 103, 175–76

Eriksson, Bo, 183
Etsuro, Kato, 83–84
Euratom (European Atomic Energy Community), 68
European Union (EU), 39

Fahmy, Nabil, 249n140
Federation of German Scientists, 260n200
Feldman, Shai, 110, 146
Finnemore, Martha, 3
Four Pillars, and 3NNP (Japan), 58
France: as antinuclear, 186; Japan's view of, 64; and MLF, 187; nuclear cooperation of, with Egypt, 121; nuclear cooperation of, with Germany, 186, 188, 191; nuclear development by, 36, 241n159
Frankel, Benjamin, 7
Fukuda, Yasuo, 58, 75–76, 239n123
Furukawa, Katsuhisa, 78

Germany: and domestic politics, 188–89, 192–95, 211–12; and Egypt, 244n58; and fear of American abandonment, 185–86, 190–91; and Göttingen Manifesto, 188, 192, 196, 260n200; lessons learned from, 193–200, 204; and Libya, 151, 157–58; and MLF, 186–87; nuclear cooperation of, with Egypt, 121; nuclear cooperation of, with Italy and France, 186, 188, 191; nuclear decision-making of, 185–90, 192–200, 206, 221, 259n156; nuclear forbearance of, 190–91; as nuclear-capable, 33, 151; Ostpolitik policy of, 192; and SPD, 187, 211; Ten-Point Initiative proposed by, 189. See also United States: and Germany
Ghanem, Shukri, 159

Goldgeier, James, 46
Gose, Mark, 198
Green Party (Germany), 189
Greenpeace, 45
Grieco, Joseph, 3, 22
Grillot, Suzette, 15

Hafez, Salah al-Din, 252n212
Hatakeyama, Shigeru, 70
Hedayat, Salah, 108, 111
Higgins, E. Tory, 51
Hiroshima/Nagasaki bombing, as nuclear deterrent, 56–57, 79–80, 87, 181
Hitler, Adolf, 195
Hughes, Llewelyn, 61, 80, 88
Hussain, Abid, 152
Hymans, Jacques, 9, 14–15, 240n159

IAEA (International Atomic Energy Agency): as component of NPT, 38; and Egypt, 106, 115, 120, 123, 127; inspections by, in Libya, 152, 154, 161; and Japan, 68, 82, 85; and North Korean crisis, 69–70; protocols of, 50–51, 70, 183; refused by Brazil, 214
Ichiro, Ozawa, 75
idea-centered analysis, on proliferation/nonproliferation, 13–16
identification: as behavioral change mechanism, 18–19, 166, 183; as constructivist expectation, 28–29, 94–95, 97–98, 143, 145t; defined/described, 18–19, 228n51; as diplomatic outcome, 2, 4–5, 199; and in-group behavior, 18–19, 229n54; and norm linking, 79–80
Ikeda, Hayato, 88
Inchas Nuclear Research Center (Egypt), 110

India: and Egypt, 121; as nuclear state, 20, 29, 31, 37, 42, 164; and United States, 20, 215; weakens descriptive norm, 77, 129, 163, 215
Indonesia, 121
Indyk, Martin, 155–56
INF (intermediate-range nuclear forces), 189
injunctive norms: and antinuclear norm, 202; and Arab concern over Israel and United States, 213; consistency of, 214; defined/described, 40–41, 255n61; of NPT, 42, 77–78, 129–30; strengthened (1998), 163; transmission of, 44, 77–78, 129–30, 162, 181, 194
intermediate-range nuclear forces (INF), 189
International Atomic Energy Agency. See IAEA
international relations: methodology for examination of, 21; and nonproliferation, 87–88, 94–95, 174–75; as socially constructed, 17–18; theories of, 1–3. See also constructivism; neoliberal institutionalism; realism
international social environment: and antinuclear norm, 202, 221–22; and constructivism, 16, 146; and cost-benefit calculations, 50–51; and domestic politics, 211–12; and norm potency, 50–51, 82–85; and norm transmission, 42–44, 52, 65–66, 77–78, 128–30, 193–94; and norms and ideas, 4, 16, 42–44, 47–49; and NPT regime, 202, 221–22; and nuclear decision-making, 76–77, 82, 100, 148–49, 173–77, 180–84; as pivotal consideration, 208, 221
Iran: and calls for NWFZ, 123; and inducements to stop nuclear de-

velopment, 48; as leadership threat to Egypt, 126, 204–5; and Muslim Brotherhood, 126; and neoliberalism, 10; and nuclear development, 129; as policy challenge, 4–5; withdrawal of, from NPT, 51
Iraq: invasion of, 226n20; leads drive to expel Egypt, 102; as Libyan focal point, 163; nuclear weapons of, 251n188; as outside NPT, 51
Iraq War, Japanese attitude toward, 73
Ireland, 36
Ishihara, Shintaro, 64
Islamic fundamentalism, as threat to Libya, 161
Israel: bombs Iraq, 213; and Camp David summit/accords, 102–3; Dimona Reactor of, 108–9, 204, 244n46; and Egypt, 100–102, 129, 133, 137, 204–5, 242n4; and Libya, 162; and NPT, 123–26; nuclear weapons of, 108, 226n19, 252n212
Italy: and Germany, 186, 191; and Libya, 157

Jalloud, Abdelssalem, 159
Jamahiriya, Al- (newspaper), 160
Japan: and antiterrorism operations, 59; diplomacy preference, 89–90, 93; domestic politics, 211; hibakusha, 56; identification of, with United States, 95, 97; and KEDO, 72; MOFA peace activities, 68, 82, 93; and national identity, 54–55, 73–74, 85–86, 92–93; 1968–70 Report (Japan), 63–66, 87–88; and North Korea, 70–76; as nuclear capable, 29, 31–32, 63–66, 74–75; reconnaissance satellites of, 72–73; and SDF, 59, 240n157; secret nuclear studies of, 63, 76; theoretical

Japan (*continued*)
   analysis of decision-making of, 86–95,
     96–97t, 204. *See also* United States:
     and Japan
  —nuclear decision-making of: in 1960s,
     59–61, 63–66, 206, 209, 235n38,
     260n209; in 1970s, 66–68, 221; in
     1980s and 1990s, 69–71; in 2000s,
     71–76, 79–85, 87–90, 215–16
  —Peace Constitution of, 54–55, 75,
     233nn7–8; Article 9, 54–55, 62,
     74, 86
Japanese Coast Guard (JCG), 71
Japanese Communist Party (JCP), 59, 66
Japanese Defense Agency (JDA), 69–
     70, 76
Japanese Socialist Party (JSP), 59, 66–68
Japan–North Korea summit, 71
JCG (Japanese Coast Guard), 71
JCP (Japanese Communist Party), 59, 66
JDA (Japanese Defense Agency), 69–
     70, 76
Jentleson, Bruce, 124
Johnson-Sato Joint Communiqué, 65
Johnston, Alastair Iain, 17
Jordan, 103
JSP (Japanese Socialist Party), 59, 66–68

Karawan, Ibrahim, 117
Kase, Yuri, 64, 67
Kataoka, Tetsuya, 54
Kaye, Dalia Dassa, 124
Kazakhstan, 7, 162
KEDO (Korean Peninsular Energy Devel-
     opment Organization), 71
Kelman, Herbert, 18, 166
Kennedy, John F., 114, 135
Keohane, Robert, 3, 10, 25
Khan, A. Q., 51, 154, 165, 205, 212

Khan, Saira, 138, 251n188
Kim Jong Il, 216, 220
Kinkel, Klaud, 190
Kishi, Nobuske, 59, 233n7, 239n123
Kissinger, Henry, 67, 101, 177
Kono, Taro, 72
Korean Peninsular Energy Development
     Organization (KEDO), 71
Kusa, Musa, 167

Landau, Emily, 129, 133
LDP (Liberal Democratic Party; Japan),
     59, 66–68, 76, 84, 88, 91
Levine, John M., 51
Levite, Ariel, 18
Liberal Democratic Party (Japan) *See*
   LDP
Libya: and Britain, 153–55, 163–64; as
     case study, 32, 203; on democratic
     regimes, 159–60; and disarmament
     initiatives, 217; domestic reforms
     of, 168; economic development of,
     156–57, 160, 167, 207–8, 254n51; and
     Egypt, 136; foreign policy of, 167–68;
     and Germany, 151, 157–58; and
     IAEA, 152, 154, 161; and Iraq, 163; and
     Israel, 162; and Italy, 157; as model
     for future, 151; and national identity,
     163; and Niger, 152; and North Korea,
     219–20; nuclear forbearance lessons
     learned from, 162–69, 180–84, 218–19;
     as outside NPT, 51; and Pakistan, 152;
     and Pan Am–Lockerbie bombing,
     153, 155–56, 158, 160; seeks Western
     technology, 152–55; self-identified
     as African, 161; and Soviet Union,
     152, 155, 158–59; theoretical anal-
     ysis of decision-making of, 162–69,
     202; and UN sanctions, 153, 156–57,

164, 207, 254n39; and United States, 159–60, 167. *See also* United States: and Libya
—nuclear decision-making of: in 1980s, 152–53, 206–7, 209, 221; in 1990s, 7, 150, 153–54, 156, 163, 166; in 2000s, 154–57, 166, 218–19
linking: and activation/consistency, 215–17; and nonproliferation policy development, 214; and North Korea, 216. *See also under* norms: processing of
Long, William, 15
Lucky Dragon incident, 35, 55–57, 79

Maddox, John, 197
Madrid Peace Process, 123
Mandela, Nelson, 159
Martin, Lisa, 3, 10, 25
McCain, John, 214
Mearsheimer, John, 6–7, 10
media, as fostering antinuclear sentiment (Japan), 57, 81, 234n24, 239n123
Meyer, Stephen M., 22
Miki, Takeo, 67
military power: Japan's attitude toward, 55–57, 71–76; as realist argument, 6
Miller, Judith, 155
Miyazawa, Kiichi, 67
Mizumoto, Kazumi, 60
MLF (multilateral nuclear force), U.S.-German, 186–87
Mubarak, Gamal, 126–28
Mubarak, Hosni, 102, 105, 122–23, 130, 132–33
multilateral institutions, 3, 10, 17–18, 25–26, 227–28n46
multilateral nuclear force (MLF), U.S.-German, 186–87
multipolarity, and proliferation, 7

Muntasir, Umar al-, 159
Muslim Brotherhood, 126–27
Muto, Kabun, 69
Myrdal, Alva, 176, 256n117

NAC (New Agenda Coalition), 125, 142–43, 145t, 184, 213
Nakagawa, Shoichi, 60
Nakasone, Yasuhiro, 95, 238n107
Nasser, Gamal Abdel: attitude of, towards technology, 106, 110–13; as constructivist, 145t, 208; Free Officers of, 108; and Israel, 109, 128, 207; nationalizes Suez Canal, 100–101, 242n7; and nuclear weapons, 110–14, 168–69, 203, 246n79; Pan-Arabism of, 102, 113–14; pledge of, to Kennedy, 114, 135; popularity of, 210; power struggle of, with Amer, 113, 245n66; signs NPT, 130, 139, 143; and social conformity, 146–48
national identity. *See under individual countries*
national security. *See* security
NATO (North Atlantic Treaty Organization): and Germany, 186–87; and INF, 189; and nuclear no-first-use policy, 189, 199; and Sweden, 177, 179, 187
Nehru, Jawaharlal, 35–36
neoliberal institutionalism: and coalition types, 12–13, 39; and economics, 205–8; expectations of, for nuclear restraint, 25–27, 96t, 144t, 201; and factual record, 16; on proliferation/nonproliferation, 2, 10–13; and security dilemma, 205; and theoretical analysis of nuclear restraint, 90–91, 96, 139–40, 144t; theorists of, 3. *See also* constructivism; realism

neorealism. *See* realism

neutrality ethos, of Sweden, 172, 184

New Agenda Coalition. *See* NAC

New York Times (newspaper), 212

NGOs (nongovernmental organizations): Egyptian Council on Foreign Relations, 125; and norm linking in Japan, 79, 85; and peace endeavors, 215–16. *See also* peace endeavors

Niger, supplies Libya yellowcake, 152

1968–70 Report (Japan), 63–66, 87–88

Nishimura, Shingo, 74–75

Nixon, Richard, 120

Nobel Peace Prize: for Alva Myrdal, 156n117; for Eisaku Sato, 58

nongovernmental organizations. *See* NGOs

non-nuclear weapons states, 30t, 54–58

Nonproliferation Treaty. *See* NPT

norms: categorization of, 231n30; conditions influencing, 49–50, 202–3, 211–12; disarmament as, 39, 174–76; internalization of, 46, 79, 163–69, 173–74, 232nn45–47; and nuclear issues, 34–38, 212–14; potency of, conditions affecting, 49–52, 82–85, 163–64, 217, 255n61 (*see also* conflict; similarity; uncertainty); social psychological understanding of, 3, 16–21, 32. *See also* descriptive norms; injunctive norms; subjective norms

—processing of: and activation, 45–46, 48–49, 80–81, 231n42; and consistency, 46–49, 81–82, 131–33, 163, 196, 216; and linking, 44–45, 48, 79–80, 98, 130–31, 163–64, 194–95; mechanisms for, 44–47, 255n61; and nuclear decision-making, 80–81, 131, 162–64, 195, 215; and social environment, 47–52, 79–82, 130–33

—transmission of: and norm entrepreneurs, 49–50, 231n42; and social environment, 42–44, 51, 65–66, 77–79, 128–30, 193–94. *See also* similarity

North Atlantic Treaty Organization. *See* NATO

North Korea: and China, 219; and Japan, 70–76; and Libya, 219–20; and neoliberalism, 10; and NPT, 42, 51, 69, 77, 129, 202; and similarity, 219–20; spy ships of, 71; and UN, 70; and United States, 70, 215–16, 219–20

—nuclear weapons of: in 1990s, 20, 32, 37, 69–70, 226n19; in 2000s, 71–76, 129

NPT (Nonproliferation Treaty): acceptance of normative message of, 222–23; and ACRS group, 123–24, 135; Additional Protocol, 183, 217; Article 6 (disarmament), 36–37, 66, 70, 213; and constructivism, 208–11; and cost-benefit equations, 25–26, 90–91, 134; countries outside of, 42, 51, 69, 77, 123–26, 129, 202; and Egypt, 120–21, 128–35, 213, 242n14, 248n125; erosion of normative weight of, 213; extension of, 69–71, 124; and IAEA, 38; injunctive norms of, 42, 77–78, 129–30; and international social environment, 162, 202, 221–22; and linking violations, 214; and martial benefits argument, 206–8; Middle East Resolution, 213; Proliferation Security Initiative, 217; as universal disarmament norm, 13–14, 38–39, 66, 79, 173, 182–83, 194

—signed/ratified: by Arab League, 124–25; by Egypt, 121, 132, 139–41, 203; by Germany, 187–88, 193, 196; by Japan, 59, 66–68; by Libya, 151–52, 164; in

1990s (numerous states), 162–63; by Sweden, 169, 175, 183

NPT Review Conferences: and antinuclear NGOs, 37, 211, 215; and Egypt, 125; and Japan, 70–71, 81, 211, 215; and U.S. actions, 125, 213; year 1995, 37, 70–71; year 2000, 81, 125; year 2005, 213

NTI (Nuclear Threat Initiative), on Egypt's biological weapons, 252n194

nuclear activities: distinguished from nuclear weapons, 90, 229n61; international opinion against, 35–36

nuclear decision-making: definition of, 232n2; influenced by ideas/beliefs, 15, 79; and international social environment, 76–77, 82, 100, 148–49, 173–77, 180–84; and regime type, 31–32; social psychology of, 2, 16–21, 74. *See also individual countries*

nuclear energy: Atoms for Peace, 106; Egyptian interest in, 106–8, 120–22; for Sweden, 169–70; and weapons forbearance, 25–26, 53, 68, 90–91. *See also individual countries*

nuclear forbearance/restraint: explanations for, 5, 221; idea-centered view of, 11–16; and IR theory measurement, 17; neoliberal view of, 10–13; policy significance of, 4–5, 222; promotion of, 215–19; realist view of, 9–10; theoretical significance of, 3. *See also* security guarantees and forbearance; *and individual countries*

nuclear hedging, 18, 228n47

nuclear nonproliferation norm. *See* antinuclear norm

nuclear potential states, defined, 29–31t

Nuclear Suppliers Group, 39

Nuclear Threat Initiative (NTI), on Egypt's biological weapons, 252n194

nuclear weapons: as deterrent, 7–8, 74–75, 173–74, 204; Libya's divestment of, 168; and national prestige, 172; as realist response, 6; and U.S. Nuclear Posture Review, 73, 77; as weakening security, 14, 24, 88–90, 133–34, 177–78, 202–3; WMDs as related to, and nuclear restraint, 24–25. *See also* antinuclear norm

oil industry, and Libyan economic development, 155–57, 160

Organization of African Unity, 167

Pakistan: and Libya, 152; as nuclear state, 20, 37, 164, 226n19; and Saudi Arabia, 153; weakens descriptive norm, 77, 129, 163

Pan Am–Lockerbie incident, 153, 155–56, 158, 160

Pan-Arabism, 102–3, 113–14, 119, 158–59, 161

Paris Agreements/Accords, 185, 193

Partial Test Ban Treaty. *See* PTBT

Paul, T. V., 6, 13–14, 23, 98, 190

Payne, Rodger, 17, 47

peace endeavors: Conference on Peaceful Uses of the Atom, 175; Egyptian embrace of, 103–5; Frameworks for Peace, 102; Geneva peace conference, 101, 175; Hiroshima Peace Cultural Foundation, 79, 173; Madrid Peace Process, 123; MOFA peace activities, 68, 82, 93; Nuclear Abolition Caucus, 37; Peace Constitution of Japan, 54–55, 75, 233nn7–8; Peace Depot (Japan), 81, 215. *See also* NGOs

Pelindaba Treaty, 125

People for the Ethical Treatment of Animals (PETA), 44

persuasion: and behavioral change, 17, 46, 147, 168–69, 183–84, 198–200; as constructivist expectation, 27, 92, 97t, 98, 141–42, 145t; as diplomatic outcome, 2, 4–5; and social conformity, 18, 51, 54, 213–14, 229n56; and uncertainty, 49

PETA (People for the Ethical Treatment of Animals), 44

policy strategy: development of, 4–5, 15; and idea-centered analysis, 13–16; neoliberal view of, 10–13; and norm potency, 82–83; realist view of, 6; and social influence mechanisms, 212, 215; and use of social psychology, 16–21

power: Japanese redefinition of, 92; realist view of, 8–9

Prawitz, Jan, 169, 178

PTBT (Partial Test Ban Treaty): Germany signs, 185, 188, 193–94; Sweden signs, 175, 183

public opinion, as deterrent, 64, 79–81, 88–89, 92, 94

public relations, as norm activation, 45

Pugwash movement, 195

Qadhafi, Muammar: effect of normative messages on, 163–65; on free market, 167; on nuclear weapons, 154–64, 203; vision of, for Libya, 167–69, 207–8, 210; on Western promises, 218

Qadhafi, Saif Aleslam al-, 153, 159–62, 165, 168–69, 203

Quester, George, 172, 175, 181–82

Rahman, Ibrahim Hilmy Adbel, 106, 108

Reagan, Ronald, 95, 153

realism: expectations of, for nuclear restraint, 22–25, 113, 201, 222–23; versus factual record, 16; and nuclear forbearance, 6–10, 53, 87–90, 136, 168–69, 190–93; rejection of, 162, 189–90, 208; and security, 204–5; theoretical analysis of, 86–90, 96, 136–38, 144t, 204–5; theorists of, 2, 15. *See also* constructivism; neoliberal institutionalism

Reiss, Mitchell, 169–71

rejection, as potential outcome, 229n1

Rice, Condoleezza, 61

Sabri, Ali, 118

Sadat, Anwar: assassinated, 122, 210; as constructivist, 140–41, 143, 145t, 146, 208–9; Corrective Movement purge by, 118; goals of, for Egyptian development, 116–20, 134–35, 139, 207, 209; on Israel, 101–3, 117–19, 135, 203, 247n108, 253n218; and social conformity, 147–48

Saif, Mostafa Elwi, 115

Salama, Salama Ahmed, 104, 156

Salama, Sammy, 156

Samaddar, Sujeet, 6

Sanusi, Idris al-, 151

Sato, Eisaku: on Japanese public opinion, 94; on Japanese security, 64, 79, 87, 236n58; and Johnson-Sato Joint Communiqué, 65; as Nobel Peace Prize recipient, 58; secret nuclear study of, 63; 3NNP pledge of, 58, 234n29

Saudi Arabia, 29, 103, 153

Schmidt, Helmut, 189, 260n200

Schweitzer, Albert, 195

security: attitudes about, 201–3, 221; and constructivism, 97t; as criterion for case study, 29, 87–88, 136–37,

202–3; and neoliberalism, 26–27, 96t, 144t; NPT and cost-benefit analyses of, 14, 87, 134, 221; nuclear weapons weakening of, 14, 88–90, 133–34, 177–78; and realism, 8–10, 23–24, 96t, 144t, 204–5
—views on: in Egypt, 100–105, 168–69, 213; in Germany, 185–86; in Japan, 59–61, 92–93, 98, 206; in Libya, 154, 162; in Sweden, 177–78; in United States, 72, 213
security dilemma: and Egypt's decision-making, 120, 145, 148; escape from, 26–27; neoliberal view of, 10–11, 91, 139–40, 205; realist view of, 7
security guarantees and forbearance: for Germany, 184–85, 190, 198, 203; for Japan, 31–32, 70–72, 203; as realist expectation, 9, 23–24, 87–90, 198; for Sweden, 184, 203
self-help. See realism
Siemens Company, and Egypt, 109
Siler, Michael, 138
similarity: as normative influence, 49–52, 83–84, 134–35, 164, 196; policy opportunities for, 219–20; versus self-perceived uniqueness, 257n138
social conformity: as constructivist expectation, 27–28, 97t, 145t, 146–47, 228n46; of Germany, 197; and group norms, 51, 178–80, 213–14; and persuasion, 18, 229n56
social influence: as cost-benefit calculation, 18; policy significance of, 2, 4–5
social psychology: and international relations, 3, 16–21; as tool to explain nonproliferation, 2, 201–3, 221–23
Solingen, Etel, 11–13, 207, 211

South Africa, 7, 13, 15, 44–45, 163, 221
South Korea, 69–70
Soviet Union: collapse of, and Libyan decision-making, 155, 158–59; on early NPT, 36; and Egypt, 107–10, 112, 115, 119, 244n49, 251n191; and Germany, 185; objects to MLF, 187; provides reactor to Libya, 152; and Sweden, 170–71, 182
Stein, Janice, 113
Stevenson, Adlai E., 36, 173
Strauss, Franz Josef, 196
Stuart, Jan, 157
subjective norms: defined/described, 41–42, 130, 163, 255n61; shaped by injunctive/descriptive norms, 214; transmission of, 44, 78–79, 130, 162, 181, 194
Suez Canal, nationalized, 100–101, 242n7, 247n112
suicide rate, in Japan, 74
Sunohara, Tsuyoshi, 88, 94
Sweden: as case study, 32, 151; and domestic politics, 173–76, 211; and military support for nuclear weapons, 177–79; and NAC, 184; neutrality policy of, 171–72, 178–81, 210; nuclear decision-making of, 169–80, 182–83, 206, 221, 258n144; nuclear forbearance of, 171–80, 204, 256n88; pride of, in technological prowess, 169, 172; ratifies NPT, 169; Social Democrats of, 170–71, 173–76, 178–81, 210–11; and United States, 184, 255n81
Swedish Parliamentary Commission on Defense, 171
Switzerland, 121, 221
Syria, 111, 163
Szilard, Leo, 34

Takeyh, Ray, 158–59, 160
Tannenwald, Nina, 35, 37
TCA (Trade and Cooperation Agreements), 39
terrorism, and Pan Am–Lockerbie bombings, 153, 155–56, 158, 160
Tetlock, Philip, 46
threat: as criterion for case study, 29; Hyman's view of, 14–15; realist view of, 7–8, 22–23, 136
3NNP (Three Non-Nuclear Principles): and Four Pillars, 57–58; Japan's commitment to, 66, 68, 76, 82, 87; as subject to amendment, 75
Trade and Cooperation Agreements (TCA), 39
Trost, M. R., 45
Truman. Harry S., 35
trust: realist view of, 8, 23, 226n21; U.S.-German, 190–91; U.S.-Japanese, 67–68, 70–73, 76, 238n107.

UAR (United Arab Republic), 102, 111
Ukraine, 7, 15, 162
uncertainty: and norm potency, 16, 82–84, 133–35, 182–83; as normative influence, 49–52, 82–84, 133–35, 164, 182–83, 196; policy opportunities for, 217–18; and soft tactics, 217–18
Undén, Östen, 175
United Arab Republic (UAR), 102, 111
United Kingdom. See Britain
United Nations: Atomic Energy Conference, 106; Chemical Weapons Convention, 137; Egypt's leadership in, 103–5, 114–15; ENDC, 36, 175; General Assembly on Disarmament, 37; Japanese attitude toward, 73; and North Korean crisis (1990s), 70; NWFZ of, 46, 48, 123, 125, 249n140; Partial

Test Ban Treaty, 36; sanctions against Libya, 153, 156–57, 164, 207, 254n39; on Suez War, 100–101; test-ban petition, 173, 181; UNSCOM, 213
United States, 45; antinuclear movements within, 36–37; and antinuclear norm, 217–18; and CTBT, 77, 240n147; drops MLF, 186; military view of NPT, 229n55; Nuclear Posture Review/Strategy, 37, 73, 77, 213, 218; as nuclear weapons producer, 217–18
—and Egypt: Kennedy-Nasser communication, 135; no formalized security guarantee, 136–37; nuclear cooperation agreement, 120–21, 123; Sadat's goals for, 116–20, 140–41, 207; strain over Israeli weapons, 124–25, 129
—and Germany: MLF, 185, 191, 258n153; security crisis of credibility, 186–87; strategic policy, 185–86, 190–91, 204
—and India, 20, 215
—and Japan: and bombing, 34, 56–57, 79–80, 87; during Cold War, 238n107; Defense Cooperation Committee, 67; postwar negotiations, 61–68, 83–84; security guarantees, 88–90, 93, 204, 214; Security Treaty, 61–62, 65–66, 68, 72–73, 85
—and Libya, 154–55, 160, 164–67, 207
—and North Korea, 70, 216–17, 219–20
—and Sweden, 184, 255n81

Van Dassen, Lars, 181–82

Walker, Elliot, 92–93
Walsh, James, 22, 112
Walt, Stephen, 113
Waltz, Kenneth, 3, 6, 22, 26
wars: Arab-Israeli, 100–103, 110–11, 117–18, 209–10; Germany's view of, 211;

Japan renounces, 54, 208; Libya's view of, 10; Yemen civil war, 137
Washington Post, 76, 183, 212
Wells, H. G., 34
Wendt, Alexander, 3
West Germany. *See* Germany
Western European Union, 185
Westinghouse, and Egypt, 109–11

Working Group on Arms Control & Regional Security (ACRS), 123–24, 135

Yoshida, Shigeru, 88, 209
Yoshida doctrine, 65, 86, 97, 207–9

Zangger Coalition, 39